Complete Java™ 2 Certification Study Guide, Fourth Edition

Exam # CX-310-035: Part I Sun Certified Programmer for Java 2 Platform 1.4

OBJECTIVE	CHAPTER
SECTION 1: DECLARATIONS AND ACCESS CONTROL	**1, 3, 6**
1.1 Write code that declares, constructs and initializes arrays of any base type using any of the permitted forms both for declaration and for initialization.	1
1.2 Declare classes, nested classes, methods, instance variables, static variables and automatic (method local) variables making appropriate use of all permitted modifiers (such as public, final, static, abstract, etc.). State the significance of each of these modifiers both singly and in combination and state the effect of package relationships on declared items qualified by these modifiers.	3
1.3 For a given class, determine if a default constructor will be created and if so state the prototype of that constructor.	1
1.4 Identify legal return types for any method given the declarations of all related methods in this or parent classes.	6
SECTION 2: FLOW CONTROL, ASSERTIONS, AND EXCEPTION HANDLING	**5**
2.1 Write code using if and switch statements and identify legal argument types for these statements.	5
2.2 Write code using all forms of loops including labeled and unlabeled, use of break and continue, and state the values taken by loop counter variables during and after loop execution.	5
2.3 Write code that makes proper use of exceptions and exception handling clauses (try, catch, finally) and declares methods and overriding methods that throw exceptions.	5
2.4 Recognize the effect of an exception arising at a specified point in a code fragment. Note: The exception may be a runtime exception, a checked exception, or an error (the code may include try, catch, or finally clauses in any legitimate combination).	5
2.5 Write code that makes proper use of assertions, and distinguish appropriate from inappropriate uses of assertions.	5
2.6 Identify correct statements about the assertion mechanism.	5

OBJECTIVE	CHAPTER
SECTION 3: GARBAGE COLLECTION	1
3.1 State the behavior that is guaranteed by the garbage collection system.	1
3.2 Write code that explicitly makes objects eligible for garbage collection.	1
3.3 Recognize the point in a piece of source code at which an object becomes eligible for garbage collection.	1
SECTION 4: LANGUAGE FUNDAMENTALS	1, 3, 7
4.1 Identify correctly constructed package declarations, import statements, class declarations (of all forms including inner classes), interface declarations, method declarations (including the main method that is used to start execution of a class), variable declarations, and identifiers.	1, 3
4.2 Identify classes that correctly implement an interface where that interface is either java.lang.Runnable or a fully specified interface in the question.	7
4.3 State the correspondence between index values in the argument array passed to a main method and command line arguments.	1
4.4 Identify all Java programming language keywords. Note: There will not be any questions regarding esoteric distinctions between keywords and manifest constants.	1
4.5 State the effect of using a variable or array element of any kind when no explicit assignment has been made to it.	1
4.6 State the range of all primitive formats, data types and declare literal values for String and all primitive types using all permitted formats bases and representations.	1
SECTION 5: OPERATORS AND ASSIGNMENTS	1, 2, 4
5.1 Determine the result of applying any operator (including assignment operators and instance of) to operands of any type class scope or accessibility or any combination of these.	2, 4
5.2 Determine the result of applying the boolean equals (Object) method to objects of any combination of the classes java.lang.String, java.lang.Boolean and java.lang.Object.	2
5.3 In an expression involving the operators &, |, &&, || and variables of known values state which operands are evaluated and the value of the expression.	2
5.4 Determine the effect upon objects and primitive values of passing variables into methods and performing assignments or other modifying operations in that method.	1

Exam objectives and content are subject to change at any time without prior notice at Sun's sole discretion. Please visit Sun's Certification website at www.training.sun.com/US/certification/java for the most current information of their exam content.

OBJECTIVE	CHAPTER
SECTION 6: OVERLOADING, OVERRIDING, RUNTIME TYPE AND OBJECT ORIENTATION	**6**
6.1 State the benefits of encapsulation in object oriented design and write code that implements tightly encapsulated classes and the relationships "is a" and "has a".	6
6.2 Write code to invoke overridden or overloaded methods and parental or overloaded constructors; and describe the effect of invoking these methods.	6
6.3 Write code to construct instances of any concrete class including normal top level classes and nested classes.	6
SECTION 7: THREADS	**7**
7.1 Write code to define, instantiate and start new threads using both java.lang.Thread and java.lang.Runnable.	7
7.2 Recognize conditions that might prevent a thread from executing.	7
7.3 Write code using synchronized wait, notify and notifyAll to protect against concurrent access problems and to communicate between threads.	7
7.4 Define the interaction among threads and object locks when executing synchronized wait, notify or notifyAll.	7
SECTION 8: FUNDAMENTAL CLASSES IN THE JAVA.LANG PACKAGE	**8**
8.1 Write code using the following methods of the java.lang.Math class: abs, ceil, floor, max, min, random, round, sin, cos, tan, sqrt.	8
8.2 Describe the significance of the immutability of String objects.	8
8.3 Describe the significance of wrapper classes, including making appropriate selections in the wrapper classes to suit specified behavior requirements, stating the result of executing a fragment of code that includes an instance of one of the wrapper classes, and writing code using the following methods of the wrapper classes (e.g., Integer, Double, etc.): doubleValue; floatValue; intValue; longValue; parseXxx; getXxx; toString; toHexString.	8
SECTION 9: THE COLLECTIONS FRAMEWORK	**8**
9.1 Make appropriate selection of collection classes/interfaces to suit specified behavior requirements.	8
9.2 Distinguish between correct and incorrect implementations of hashcode methods.	8

Complete Java™ 2 Certification Study Guide, Fourth Edition

CX-310-252A and CX-310-027: Part II SUN Certified Developer for JAVA 2 Platform, Steps 1 and 2

STEPS	CHAPTER
STEP 1: SUN CERTIFIED DEVELOPER FOR JAVA 2 PLATFORM, PROGRAMMING ASSIGNMENT (CX-310-252A)	**PART II**
Write an application program using Java technology. The application requires the following:	9
A graphical user interface demonstrating good principles of design.	10, 11
A network connection, using a specified protocol, to connect to an information server.	12, 13
A network server, which connects to a previously specified Java technology database.	12, 13
A database, created by extending the functionality of a previously written piece of code, for which only limited documentation is available.	14, 15
STEP 2: SUN CERTIFIED DEVELOPER FOR JAVA 2 PLATFORM, ESSAY EXAM (CX-310-027)	**PART II**
List some of the major choices you must make during the implementation of the above.	
List some of the main advantages and disadvantages of each of your choices.	
Briefly justify your choices in terms of the comparison of design and implementation objectives with the advantages and disadvantages of each.	

Exam objectives and content are subject to change at any time without prior notice at Sun's sole discretion. Please visit Sun's Certification website at www.training.sun.com/US/certification/java for the most current information of their exam content.

Complete Java™ 2 Certification Study Guide
Study Guide
4th Edition

Philip Heller

Simon Roberts

BPB PUBLICATIONS
B-14, CONNAUGHT PLACE, NEW DELHI-110001

FIRST INDIAN EDITION 2004

Distributors:

MICRO BOOK CENTRE
2, City Centre, CG Road,
Near Swastic Char Rasta,
AHMEDABAD-380009 Phone: 26421611

COMPUTER BOOK CENTRE
12, Shrungar Shopping Centre, M.G. Road,
BANGALORE-560001 Phone: 5587923, 5584641

MICRO BOOKS
Shanti Niketan Building, 8, Camac Street,
KOLKATTA-700017 Phone: 2826518, 2826519

BUSINESS PROMOTION BUREAU
8/1, Ritchie Street, Mount Road,
CHENNAI-600002 Phone: 28534796, 28550491

DECCAN AGENCIES
4-3-329, Bank Street,
HYDERABAD-500195 Phone: 24756400, 24756967

MICRO MEDIA
Shop No. 5, Mahendra Chambers, 150 D.N. Road,
Next to Capital Cinema V.T. (C.S.T.) Station,
MUMBAI-400001
Ph.: 22078296, 22078297, 22002732

BPB PUBLICATIONS
B-14, Connaught Place, **NEW DELHI-110001**
Phone: 23325760, 23723393, 23737742

INFOTECH
G-2, Sidhartha Building, 96 Nehru Place,
NEW DELHI-110019
Phone: 26438245, 26415092, 26234208

INFOTECH
Shop No. 2, F-38, South Extension Part-1
NEW DELHI-110049
Phone: 24691288, 24641941

BPB BOOK CENTRE
376, Old Lajpat Rai Market,
DELHI-110006 PHONE: 23861747

NOTE: THE CD-ROM INCLUDED WITH THE BOOK HAS NO COMMERCIAL VALUE AND CANNOT BE SOLD SEPARATELY.

Original ISBN 0-7821-4276-1

SYBEX and the SYBEX logo are registered trademarks of SYBEX Inc.

TRADEMARKS: SYBEX has attempted throughout this book to distinguish propreitary trademarks from descriptive terms by following the capitalization style used by the manufacturer.

SYBEX is not affiliated with any manufacturer.

Every effort has been made to supply complete and accurate information. However, SYBEX assumes no responsibility for its use, nor for any infringement of the intellectual property rights of third parties which would result from such use.

Copyright © SYBEX Inc., USA. World Right Reserved. No part of this publications may be stored in a retrieval system, transmitted, or reproduced in any way, including but not limited to photocopy, photograph, magnetic or other record without the prior agreement and written permission of the publisher.

This edition is Authorized for sale only in the following countries : INDIA, BANGLADESH, NEPAL, PAKISTAN SRI LANKA AND MALDIVES.

Printed in India by arrangement with
SYBEX Inc., USA.

Price : Rs. 399/-

ISBN 81-7656-881-3

Published by Manish Jain for BPB Publications, B-14, Connaught Place,
New Delhi-110001 and Printed by Kwality Offset Printing Press

To Our Valued Readers:

Thank you for looking to Sybex for your Java 2 certification exam prep needs. We at Sybex are proud of the reputation we've established for providing certification candidates with the practical knowledge and skills needed to succeed in the highly competitive IT marketplace. Sybex has helped thousands of Java certification candidates prepare for their exams over the years, and we are excited about having the continued opportunity to provide IT professionals with the most essential programming and development skills.

With its latest 1.4 release of the Java 2 program, Sun has raised the bar for programmers yet again. Certification in this program demonstrates proficiency in the fundamentals of the Java programming language using the Java 2 Platform—indeed an invaluable skill and necessary to advance your career in today's ever changing programming market.

The authors and editors have worked hard to ensure that the Study Guide you hold in your hand is comprehensive, in-depth, and pedagogically sound. We're confident that this book will exceed the demanding standards of the certification marketplace and help you, the Java 2 certification candidate, succeed in your endeavors.

As always, your feedback is important to us. Please send comments, questions, or suggestions to support@sybex.com. At Sybex we're continually striving to meet the needs of individuals preparing for IT certification exams.

Good luck in pursuit of your Java 2 certification!

Neil Edde

Software License Agreement: Terms and Conditions

The media and/or any online materials accompanying this book that are available now or in the future contain programs and/or text files (the "Software") to be used in connection with the book. SYBEX hereby grants to you a license to use the Software, subject to the terms that follow. Your purchase, acceptance, or use of the Software will constitute your acceptance of such terms.

The Software compilation is the property of SYBEX unless otherwise indicated and is protected by copyright to SYBEX or other copyright owner(s) as indicated in the media files (the "Owner(s)"). You are hereby granted a single-user license to use the Software for your personal, noncommercial use only. You may not reproduce, sell, distribute, publish, circulate, or commercially exploit the Software, or any portion thereof, without the written consent of SYBEX and the specific copyright owner(s) of any component software included on this media.

In the event that the Software or components include specific license requirements or end-user agreements, statements of condition, disclaimers, limitations or warranties ("End-User License"), those End-User Licenses supersede the terms and conditions herein as to that particular Software component. Your purchase, acceptance, or use of the Software will constitute your acceptance of such End-User Licenses.

By purchase, use or acceptance of the Software you further agree to comply with all export laws and regulations of the United States as such laws and regulations may exist from time to time.

Software Support

Components of the supplemental Software and any offers associated with them may be supported by the specific Owner(s) of that material, but they are not supported by SYBEX. Information regarding any available support may be obtained from the Owner(s) using the information provided in the appropriate read.me files or listed elsewhere on the media.

Should the manufacturer(s) or other Owner(s) cease to offer support or decline to honor any offer, SYBEX bears no responsibility. This notice concerning support for the Software is provided for your information only. SYBEX is not the agent or principal of the Owner(s), and SYBEX is in no way responsible for providing any support for the Software, nor is it liable or responsible for any support provided, or not provided, by the Owner(s).

Warranty

SYBEX warrants the enclosed media to be free of physical defects for a period of ninety (90) days after purchase. The Software is not available from SYBEX in any other form or media than that enclosed herein or posted to www.sybex.com. If you discover a defect in the media during this warranty period, you may obtain a replacement of identical format at no charge by sending the defective media, postage prepaid, with proof of purchase to:

BPB PUBLICATIONS

B-14, Connaught Place, New Delhi - 110 001
Phone : 3281723, 3272329, 3267741
             3254990, 3254991, 3255271
Fax   : 3266427 / 3351856 / 3262008
E-mail : bpb@vsnl.com

After the 90 days period, you can obtain replacement media of identical format by sending us the defective disk, proof of purchase, and a check or money order.for Rs. 100/-, payable to BPB Publications.

Disclaimer

SYBEX makes no warranty or representation, either expressed or implied, with respect to the Software or its contents, quality, performance, merchantability, or fitness for a particular purpose. In no event will SYBEX, its distributors, or dealers be liable to you or any other party for direct, indirect, special, incidental, consequential, or other damages arising out of the use of or inability to use the Software or its contents even if advised of the possibility of such damage. In the event that the Software includes an online update feature, SYBEX further disclaims any obligation to provide this feature for any specific duration other than the initial posting.

The exclusion of implied warranties is not permitted by some states. Therefore, the above exclusion may not apply to you. This warranty provides you with specific legal rights; there may be other rights that you may have that vary from state to state. The pricing of the book with the Software by SYBEX reflects the allocation of risk and limitations on liability contained in this agreement of Terms and Conditions.

Shareware Distribution

This Software may contain various programs that are distributed as shareware. Copyright laws apply to both shareware and ordinary commercial software, and the copyright Owner(s) retains all rights. If you try a shareware program and continue using it, you are expected to register it. Individual programs differ on details of trial periods, registration, and payment. Please observe the requirements stated in appropriate files.

Copy Protection

The Software in whole or in part may or may not be copy-protected or encrypted. However, in all cases, reselling or redistributing these files without authorization is expressly forbidden except as specifically provided for by the Owner(s) therein.

To Richard Philip Gross, 1903–2002: a man of his century, and so much more

—Philip

For my children, Emily and Bethan

—Simon

To my brother Tom, for introducing me to Java

—James

Acknowledgments

The authors would like to acknowledge the dedicated and talented people at Sybex who worked on this edition: Elizabeth Hurley Peterson, Sally Engelfried, James Nuzzi, and Leslie Light.

The authors would also like to acknowledge their students and readers of previous editions who have provided the invaluable comments and suggestions that motivated the changes in this edition.

Finally, the authors thank you—the consumer of this edition—for choosing this book to prepare you for your Java certifications.

Contents at a Glance

Introduction   *xix*

Assessment Test   *xxv*

Part I	**The Programmer's Exam**	**1**
Chapter 1	Language Fundamentals	3
Chapter 2	Operators and Assignments	29
Chapter 3	Modifiers	71
Chapter 4	Converting and Casting	97
Chapter 5	Flow Control, Assertions, and Exception Handling	123
Chapter 6	Objects and Classes	159
Chapter 7	Threads	193
Chapter 8	The *java.lang* and *java.util* Packages	227
Part II	**The Developer's Exam**	**261**
Chapter 9	Taking the Developer's Exam	263
Chapter 10	Creating the User Interface with Swing	295
Chapter 11	Layout Managers	337
Chapter 12	Writing the Network Protocol	379
Chapter 13	Connecting Client and Server	415
Chapter 14	Enhancing and Extending the Database	439
Chapter 15	Building the Database Server	465
Appendix A	Practice Exam	485
Glossary		505

Index   *519*

Contents

Introduction *xix*

Assessment Test *xxv*

Part I The Programmer's Exam 1

Chapter 1 Language Fundamentals 3

Source Files 4
Keywords and Identifiers 5
Primitive Data Types 6
Literals 9
    boolean Literals 9
    char Literals 9
    Integral Literals 10
    Floating-Point Literals 10
    String Literals 10
Arrays 11
Class Fundamentals 13
    The *main()* Method 14
    Variables and Initialization 14
Argument Passing: By Reference or By Value 16
Garbage Collection 19
Summary 21
Exam Essentials 22
Key Terms 23
Review Questions 24
Answers to Review Questions 27

Chapter 2 Operators and Assignments 29

Evaluation Order 31
The Unary Operators 31
    The Increment and Decrement Operators: ++ and -- 32
    The Unary Plus and Minus Operators: + and - 32
    The Bitwise Inversion Operator: ~ 33
    The *Boolean* Complement Operator: ! 33
    The Cast Operator: *(type)* 34
The Arithmetic Operators 35
    The Multiplication and Division Operators: * and / 35
    The Modulo Operator: % 36
    The Addition and Subtraction Operators: + and - 37
    Arithmetic Error Conditions 40

	The Shift Operators: <<, >>, and >>>	41
	Fundamentals of Shifting	41
	Shifting Negative Numbers	42
	Reduction of the Right Operand	45
	Arithmetic Promotion of Operands	46
	The Comparison Operators	47
	Ordinal Comparisons with <, <=, >, and >=	47
	The *instanceof* Operator	48
	The Equality Comparison Operators: == and !=	50
	The Bitwise Operators: &, ^, and |	51
	Boolean Operations	54
	The Short-Circuit Logical Operators	56
	The Conditional Operator: ?:	58
	The Assignment Operators	59
	An Assignment Has Value	60
	Summary	61
	Exam Essentials	63
	Key Terms	64
	Review Questions	65
	Answers to Review Questions	68
Chapter 3	**Modifiers**	**71**
	Modifier Overview	72
	The Access Modifiers	72
	public	73
	private	73
	Default	75
	protected	76
	Subclasses and Method Privacy	78
	Summary of Access Modes	79
	Other Modifiers	79
	final	79
	abstract	80
	static	82
	Static Initializers	85
	native	85
	transient	86
	synchronized	87
	volatile	87
	Modifiers and Features	87
	Summary	88
	Exam Essentials	89
	Key Terms	89
	Review Questions	90
	Answers to Review Questions	95

Chapter	4	**Converting and Casting**	**97**
		Explicit and Implicit Type Changes	98
		Primitives and Conversion	99
		Primitive Conversion: Assignment	99
		Assignment Conversion, Narrower Primitives, and	
		Literal Values	102
		Primitive Conversion: Method Call	103
		Primitive Conversion: Arithmetic Promotion	103
		Primitives and Casting	105
		Object Reference Conversion	107
		Object Reference Assignment Conversion	108
		Object Method-Call Conversion	110
		Object Reference Casting	111
		Summary	115
		Exam Essentials	115
		Key Terms	116
		Review Questions	117
		Answers to Review Questions	121
Chapter	5	**Flow Control, Assertions, and Exception Handling**	**123**
		The Loop Constructs	124
		The *while()* Loop	124
		The *do* Loop	126
		The *for()* Loop	126
		The *break* and *continue* Statements in Loops	129
		The Selection Statements	131
		The *if()/else* Construct	131
		The *switch()* Construct	132
		Exceptions	133
		Flow of Control in Exception Conditions	133
		Throwing Exceptions	137
		Assertions	143
		Assertions and Compilation	144
		Runtime Enabling of Assertions	144
		Using Assertions	144
		Summary	146
		Exam Essentials	147
		Key Terms	148
		Review Questions	149
		Answers to Review Questions	156
Chapter	6	**Objects and Classes**	**159**
		Benefits of Object-Oriented Implementation	160

Encapsulation	160
Re-use	162
Implementing Object-Oriented Relationships	162
Overloading and Overriding	163
Overloading Method Names	164
Method Overriding	166
Constructors and Subclassing	170
Overloading Constructors	172
Inner Classes	173
The Enclosing *this* Reference and Construction of Inner Classes	175
Member Classes	176
Classes Defined Inside Methods	177
Summary	183
Exam Essentials	183
Key Terms	184
Review Questions	185
Answers to Review Questions	190

Chapter 7 Threads 193

Thread Fundamentals	194
What a Thread Executes	195
When Execution Ends	197
Thread States	197
Thread Priorities	198
Controlling Threads	199
Yielding	199
Suspending	201
Sleeping	201
Blocking	202
Monitor States	204
Scheduling Implementations	204
Monitors, *wait()*, and *notify()*	205
The Object Lock and Synchronization	207
wait() and *notify()*	208
The Class Lock	213
Beyond the Pure Model	213
Deadlock	215
Another Way to Synchronize	217
Summary	218
Exam Essentials	219

Contents

Key Terms	220
Review Questions	221
Answers to Review Questions	225

Chapter 8 The *java.lang* and *java.util* Packages — 227

The *Object* Class	228
The *Math* Class	229
The Wrapper Classes	231
Strings	234
The *String* Class	235
The *StringBuffer* Class	238
String Concatenation the Easy Way	240
The Collections API	241
Collection Types	242
Collections, Equality, and Sorting	244
The *hashCode()* Method	245
Collection Implementations in the API	246
Collections and Code Maintenance	247
Summary	253
Summary of Collections	254
Exam Essentials	254
Key Terms	255
Review Questions	256
Answers to Review Questions	259

Part II The Developer's Exam — 261

Chapter 9 Taking the Developer's Exam — 263

Are You Ready for the Exam?	264
Formalities of the Exam	266
Downloading the Assignment	266
Taking the Follow-up Exam	267
What the Assignment Covers	267
How the Assignment and Exam Are Graded	268
Structure of the Assignment	268
Code and APIs Provided	269
Example Assignment: Build a	
Trouble-Ticket System	270
GUI Development	272
Database/Server Development	273
Client-Server Logic	274
Coding Tips	275
Adhere to Supplied Naming	275

Stress Readability	275
Use Standard Design Patterns	276
Submission Requirements	276
Using *javadoc*	278
File Structure	279
Writing the README file	281
Using the JAR Tool	282
Preparation for the Follow-up Exam	284
What Are the Choices for Data Structures?	284
Is Implementing *Runnable* Better Than Extending *Thread*?	284
How Elaborate Should an Exception Class Structure Get?	285
How Many Ways Can You Set Up "Listener" Relationships? Which One Is Best?	285
How Do I Know Which Layout Manager to Use?	286
Which Design Patterns Are Most Useful in This Kind of Project?	287
When Does It Make Sense to Use *protected* and *default* Scope?	287
Doesn't an Abstract Class Let the Developer Specify More Behavior Than an Interface?	289
Summary	290
Exam Essentials	291
Key Terms	291
Review Questions	292
Answers to Review Questions	293

Chapter 10 Creating the User Interface with Swing — 295

Defining the GUI's Requirements	297
Identifying Needed Components	297
Sketching the GUI	298
Isolating Regions of Behavior	299
Choosing Layout Managers	300
Common Swing Methods	300
getSize() and *setSize()*	301
getLocation() and *setLocation()*	301
setForeground() and *setBackground()*	301
setFont()	301
setEnabled()	301
Basic Swing Components	302
Container Components	302
Ordinary Components	303
Menu Components	314
Building a *JTable*	316
Using *AbstractTableModel*	319

	Building a *JTree*	323
	JMenus and Actions	327
	Panes	329
	JSplitPane	*330*
	JOptionPane	*331*
	Summary	332
	Exam Essentials	333
	Key Terms	333
	Review Questions	334
	Answers to Review Questions	335
Chapter 11	**Layout Managers**	**337**
	Layout Manager Theory	338
	Component Size and Position	341
	Layout Policies	343
	The Flow Layout Manager	343
	The Grid Layout Manager	345
	The Border Layout Manager	347
	The Card Layout Manager	354
	The GridBag Layout Manager	359
	Other Layout Options	374
	Summary	375
	Exam Essentials	375
	Key Terms	376
	Review Questions	377
	Answers to Review Questions	378
Chapter 12	**Writing the Network Protocol**	**379**
	Client-Server from Scratch	381
	Server Operation	381
	Connecting Clients to the Server	384
	Communication Protocol	384
	The Client Request Structure	387
	Limitations of the Model	394
	Remote Method Invocation (RMI)	395
	A Model RMI Transaction	396
	Implementing RMI	397
	Limitations of RMI	401
	More on Threads	402
	Sharing Threads	403
	Summary	410
	Exam Essentials	410
	Key Terms	411

		Review Questions	412
		Answers to Review Questions	413
Chapter	13	**Connecting Client and Server**	**415**
		Events Basics	416
		Event Naming Conventions	417
		Event Notification	417
		Using Java Bean Conventions	420
		Java Beans and the MVC Design Pattern	423
		Listeners	425
		Remote Notification	432
		Using Distributed Notification	434
		Summary	435
		Exam Essentials	435
		Key Terms	436
		Review Questions	437
		Answers to Review Questions	438
Chapter	14	**Enhancing and Extending the Database**	**439**
		Two-Tier Databases	440
		Designing a Basic Scheme	441
		Using Interfaces	442
		Using Abstract Classes	447
		Issues in Implementation	451
		Exception Handling	451
		Design Impediments	454
		Thread Safety	456
		Supporting New Features	459
		Summary	460
		Exam Essentials	460
		Key Terms	461
		Review Questions	462
		Answers to Review Questions	463
Chapter	15	**Building the Database Server**	**465**
		Database Requirements	466
		Implementing RMI	467
		Exporting with *UnicastRemoteObject*	471
		Exporting an *Activatable* Object	475
		Record Locking	479
		Summary	481
		Exam Essentials	482
		Key Terms	482

	Review Questions	483
	Answers to Review Questions	484
Appendix A	**Practice Exam**	**485**
	Answers to Practice Exam	500
Glossary		**505**
Index		*519*

Introduction

Welcome to the fourth edition of this book!

Inside you'll find detailed explanations for many of the questions and problems you'll encounter in the CX-310-035, CX-310-252A, and CS-310-027 Java certifications, otherwise known as the Programmer's Exam, Developer's Programming Assignment, and Developer's Essay Exam, respectively.

The first part of the book contains eight chapters that discuss the content of every objective of the Programmer's Exam. The second part of the book contains seven chapters that prepare you to write the programming assignment and take the essay exam for the Developer's certification.

There are several ways to prepare for the Java certification exams, including attending seminars and study groups, visiting websites and newsgroups, programming at home and at work, and of course, reading study guides such as this. We're glad you chose our book as one of your preparation tools, and we encourage you to exploit as many other resources as you can to ensure your success.

We believe you'll find this book particularly helpful because it was written by Java instructors and practitioners who have also taken part in the writing of the Java certification exams.

Why Become Java 2 Certified?

There are a number of reasons for becoming Java 2 certified:

- It provides proof of professional achievement.
- It increases your marketability.
- It provides greater opportunity for advancement in your field.
- It is increasingly found as a requirement for some types of advanced training.
- It raises customer confidence in you and your company's services.

Let's explore each reason in detail.

Provides Proof of Professional Achievement

Specialized certifications are the best way to stand out from the crowd. In this age of technology certifications, you will find hundreds of thousands of administrators who have successfully completed the Microsoft and Novell certification tracks. To set yourself apart from the crowd, you need a little bit more. The Java 2 Certification is the starting point for the Java Certification Track and will give you the recognition you deserve.

Increases Your Marketability

Almost anyone can bluff their way through an interview. Once you have been certified in Java, you will have the credentials to prove your competency. And certifications are not something that can be taken from you when you change jobs. Once certified, you can take that certification with you to any of the positions you accept.

Provides Opportunity for Advancement

Those individuals who prove themselves as competent and dedicated are the ones who will most likely be promoted. Becoming certified is a great way to prove your skill level, and it shows your employers that you are committed to improving your skill set. Look around you at those who are certified. They are probably the ones who receive good pay raises and promotions when they come up.

Fulfills Training Requirements

Many companies have set training requirements for their staff so that they stay up-to-date on the latest technologies. Having a certification program for the Sun's Java family of products provides administrators another certification path to follow when they have exhausted some of the other industry-standard certifications.

Raises Customer Confidence

As companies continue to write their production software using Java, they will undoubtedly require qualified staff to embrace this ever-changing technology. Many companies outsource the work to consulting firms with experience working with Java. Those firms that have certified staff have a definite advantage over other firms that do not.

Who Should Buy This Book?

If you want to acquire a solid foundation in Java and your goal is to prepare for the exam by learning how to program and develop in Java, this book is for you. You'll find clear explanations of the concepts you need to grasp and plenty of help to achieve the high level of professional competency you need in order to succeed in your chosen field.

If you want to become certified as a Java programmer and developer, this book is definitely for you. However, if you just want to attempt to pass the exam without really understanding Java, this study guide is not for you. It is written for people who want to acquire hands-on skills and in-depth knowledge of programming Java.

How to Become a Sun Certified Programmer for the Java 2 Platform 1.4

You can take the Java Certification Exam whenever you like by making an appointment with Sun Educational Services. Sun contracts with third-party test centers throughout the world, so you probably won't have to travel far. The cost of taking the exam is $150.

Introduction   xxi

 The U.S. telephone number for Sun Educational Services is (800) 422-8020; their URL is http://suned.sun.com. From there it will be easy to find the links you need. We hesitate to give more detailed instructions, because the site layout may change.

You can make an appointment for any time during regular business hours. When you make the appointment, ask how much time you will have. This is subject to change; on average, you'll be given two minutes per question. You will not be allowed to bring food or personal belongings into the test area. One piece of scratch paper is permitted; you will not be allowed to keep it after you have finished the exam. Most sites have security cameras.

You will be escorted to a cubicle containing a PC. The exam program will present you with randomly selected questions. Navigation buttons take you to the next or previous question for review and checking. When you have finished the test, the program will immediately present you with your score and a pass/fail indication. You will also be given feedback that indicates how well you performed in each of the dozen or so categories of the objectives. You will not be told which particular questions you got right or wrong.

Formalities of the Programmer's Exam

There are no trick questions on the exam, but every question requires careful thought. The wording of the questions is highly precise; the exam has been reviewed not just by Java experts, but also by language experts whose task was to eliminate any possible ambiguity. All you have to worry about is knowing Java; your score will not depend on your ability to second-guess the examiners.

It is not a good idea to try to second-guess the question layout. For example, do not be biased toward answer C simply because C has not come up recently. The questions are taken from a pool and presented to you in a random order, so it is entirely possible to get a run of a particular option; it is also possible to get the answers neatly spread out.

Most of the questions are multiple-choice. Of these, some have a single answer and others require you to select all the appropriate responses. The graphical user interface of the test system indicates which kind of answer you should supply. If a question only has one correct answer, you will be presented with radio buttons, so that selecting a second answer cancels the selection of a previous answer. With this kind of question, you have to select the most appropriate answer. If, on the other hand, you are presented with check boxes, then you may need to make more than one selection, so every possible answer must be considered on its own merits, not weighed against the others.

You should be aware that where multiple answers are possible, you are being asked to make a decision about each answer, almost as though the question were five individual true/false questions. This requires more effort and understanding from you, because you have to get all the pieces correct. Think carefully, and always base your answer on your knowledge of Java.

The short-answer, type-in questions often cause undue concern. How are they marked? What happens if you omit a semicolon? These worries can stem from the knowledge that the questions are marked electronically and the belief that an answer might be marked wrong simply because the machine didn't have the sense to recognize a good variation of what it was programmed to accept.

As with all exam questions, you should be careful to answer precisely what is asked. However, you should also be aware that the system does accept a variety of different answers; it has been set up with all the variations the examination panel considered to be reasonable.

Some of the type-in questions *do*, however, provide specific instructions concerning the format of the answer. Take this guidance seriously. If, for example, a question says, "Answer in the form methodname()", then your answer should be

method()

and not any of the following:

object.method()
method();
method(a, b)
method

Some of the other answers might well be accepted, but programming is a precision job, and you should be accustomed to following precise directions.

The test is taken using a windowed interface that can be driven almost entirely with the mouse. Many of the screens require scrolling; the scroll bar is on the right side of the screen. Always check the scroll bar so you can be sure you have read a question in its entirety. It would be a shame to get a question wrong because you didn't realize you needed to scroll down a few lines.

The exam contains 61 questions. Some of the questions are easier than others, and undoubtedly you will be able to answer some more quickly than others. However, you really do need to answer all the questions if you possibly can. The test system allows you to review your work after you reach the end. The system will explicitly direct your attention toward any multiple-choice questions that have no items selected. So, if you find a particular question difficult, consider moving on and coming back to it later. You must score at least 52 percent (32 out of 61 questions answered correctly) to pass the Progammer's Exam.

Conventions Used in This Book

This book uses a number of conventions to present information in as readable a manner as possible. Tips, Notes, and Warnings, shown here, appear from time to time in the text in order to call attention to specific highlights.

This is a Tip. Tips contain specific programming information.

 This is a Note. Notes contain important side discussions.

 This is a Warning. Warnings call attention to bugs, design omissions, and other trouble spots.

This book takes advantage of several font styles. **Bold font** in text indicates something that the user types. A monospaced font is used for code, output, URLs, and file and directory names. A *monospaced italic font* is used for code variables mentioned in text.

These style conventions are intended to facilitate your learning experience with this book—in other words, to increase your chances of passing the exam.

If you type, compile, and run the sample code in this book, you may observe slightly different results than what you see in the book. This is particularly true with code that has a GUI. Each platform has it's own windowing system that displays buttons, checkboxes, and so on differently.

How to Use This Book and the CD

We've included several testing features in both the book and on the CD bound at the back of the book. These tools will help you retain vital exam content as well as prepare to sit for the actual exam. Using our custom test engine, you can identify weak areas up front and then develop a solid studying strategy using each of these robust testing features. Our thorough readme will walk you through the quick and easy installation process.

Before You Begin At the beginning of the book (right after this introduction, in fact) is an assessment test that you can use to check your readiness for the actual exam. Take this test before you start reading the book. It will help you determine the areas you may need to brush up on. The answers to each assessment test appear on a separate page after the last question of the test. Each answer also includes an explanation and a note telling you in which chapter this material appears.

Chapter Review Questions To test your knowledge as you progress through the book, there are review questions at the end of each chapter. As you finish each chapter, answer the review questions and then check to see if your answers are right—the correct answers appear on the page following the last review question. You can go back to reread the section that deals with each question you got wrong to ensure that you get the answer correctly the next time you are tested on the material.

Test Engine In addition to the assessment test and the chapter review tests, you'll find four sample exams, three that are only on the CD and one that is both printed and electronic. Take these practice exams just as if you were taking the actual exam (that is, without any reference material). When you have finished the first exam, move onto the next one to solidify your test-taking skills. If you get more than 90 percent of the answers correct, you're ready to go ahead and take the certification exam.

Full Text of the Book in PDF If you have to travel but still need to study for the Java 2 programming exam and you have a laptop with a CD drive, you can carry this entire book with you just by taking along the CD. The CD contains this book in PDF (Adobe Acrobat) format so it can be easily read on any computer.

About the Authors and Technical Editor

Philip Heller is a technical author, novelist, public speaker, and consultant. He has been instrumental in the creation and maintenance of the Java Programmer and Developer exams. His popular seminars on certification have been delivered internationally. He is the co-author of several books on Java, all available from Sybex.

Simon Roberts is a Sun Microsystems programmer, an instructor, an authority on the Java language, and the key player in the development of the entire Java certification program.

James Casaletto has been writing Java code since he was a computer science graduate student back in 1996. His Java projects include writing educational software for the Department of Computer Science at SFSU, developing websites for a Bay Area startup company, and leading study groups of EECS students at UC Berkeley. James has been teaching Java programming for Sun Educational Services since 1998 and has authored several of their course books. James enjoys living in San Jose, playing music, and appreciating the splendor of being an instance of the human race.

James Nuzzi, the technical editor, is a Sun Certified Web Component Developer, a Sun Certified Java Developer, and a Sun Certified Java Programmer (1.2 and 1.4). He has a B.S. in Computer Science from SUNY-Stony Brook. James has over six years of development experience, with the last three and a half years focusing on Java programming. He also has experience with servlets, JSP, EJB, JNDI, JDBC (Oracle), Weblogic, and WebSphere.

Assessment Test

1. Given the following code, which of the results that follow would you expect?
   ```
   1. package mail;
   2.
   3. interface Box {
   4.     protected void open();
   5.     void close();
   6.     public void empty();
   7. }
   ```
   A. The code will not compile because of line 4.
   B. The code will not compile because of line 5.
   C. The code will not compile because of line 6.
   D. The code will compile.

2. You can determine all the keys in a Map
   A. By getting a Set object from the Map and iterating through it.
   B. By iterating through the Iterator of the Map.
   C. By enumerating through the Enumeration of the Map.
   D. By getting a List from the Map and enumerating through the List.
   E. You cannot determine the keys in a Map.

3. What keyword is used to prevent an object from being serialized?
   A. private
   B. volatile
   C. protected
   D. transient
   E. None of the above

4. An abstract class can contain methods with declared bodies.
   A. True
   B. False

5. Select the order of access modifiers from least restrictive to most restrictive.
   A. public, private, protected, default
   B. default, protected, private, public
   C. public, default, protected, private
   D. default, public, protected, private
   E. public, protected, default, private

6. Which access modifier allows you to access method calls in libraries not created in Java?
   A. public
   B. static
   C. native
   D. transient
   E. volatile

7. Which of the following statements are true? (Select all that apply.)
   A. A final object's data cannot be changed.
   B. A final class can be subclassed.
   C. A final method cannot be overloaded.
   D. A final object cannot be reassigned a new address in memory.
   E. E. None of the above.

8. The keyword extends refers to what type of relationship?
   A. "is a"
   B. "has a"w Ro0810
   C. "was a"w Ro0810
   D. "will be a"0810
   E. None of the above

9. Which of the following keywords is used to invoke a method in the parent class?
   A. this
   B. super
   C. final
   D. static

10. Given the following code, what will be the outcome?
    ```
    public class Funcs extends java.lang.Math {
        public int add(int x, int y) {
    ```

```
        return x + y;
    }
    public int sub(int x, int y) {
        return x - y;
    }
    public static void main(String [] a) {
        Funcs f = new Funcs();
        System.out.println("" + f.add(1, 2));
    }
}
```

A. The code compiles but does not output anything.
B. "3" is printed out to the console.
C. The code does not compile.
D. None of the above.

11. Given the following code, what is the expected outcome?

```
public class Test {
    public static void main(String [] a) {
        int [] b = [1,2,3,4,5,6,7,8,9,0];
        System.out.println("a[2]=" + a[2]);
    }
}
```

A. The code compiles but does not output anything.
B. "a[2]=3" is printed out to the console.
C. "a[2]=2" is printed out to the console.
D. The code does not compile.
E. None of the above.

12. What is the value of x after the following operation is performed?

x = 23 % 4;

A. 23
B. 4
C. 5.3
D. 3
E. 5

13. Given the following code, what keyword must be used at line 4 in order to stop execution of the for loop?

```
1. boolean b = true;
2. for (;;) {
3.     if (b) {
4.         <insert code>
5.     }
6.     // do something
7. }
```

   A. stop
   B. continue
   C. break
   D. None of the above

14. What method call is used to tell a thread that it has the opportunity to run?
   A. wait()
   B. notify()
   C. start()
   D. run()

15. Which of the following types of Collections does not permit duplicate keys and is optimized for searching?
   A. Map
   B. Set
   C. List
   D. Collection
   E. None of the above

16. Assertions are used to enforce all but which of the following?
   A. Preconditions
   B. Postconditions
   C. Exceptions
   D. Class invariants

17. The developer can force garbage collection by calling System.gc().
   A. True
   B. False

18. Select the valid primitive data types. (Select all that apply.)
   A. boolean
   B. bit
   C. char
   D. float
   E. All of the above

19. How many bits does a float contain?
   A. 1
   B. 8
   C. 16
   D. 32
   E. 64

20. What is the value of x after the following line is executed?
   x = 32 * (31 - 10 * 3);
   A. 32
   B. 31
   C. 3
   D. 704
   E. None of the above

21. A StringBuffer reallocates memory for each modification to its String representation.
   A. True
   B. False

22. Select the list of primitives ordered in smallest to largest bit size representation.
   A. boolean, char, byte, double
   B. byte, int, float, char
   C. char, short, long, float
   D. char, int, float, long
   E. None of the above

23. Given the binary value 00101100, what is the value after a bitwise inversion is applied?
   A. 00101100
   B. 11010111
   C. 11010011
   D. None of the above

24. The following line of code is valid.

    ```
    int x = 9; byte b = x;
    ```

    A. True
    B. False

25. Select all the valid Java keywords.

    A. NULL
    B. if
    C. goto
    D. gosub
    E. None of the above

26. What will be the output of the following code?

    ```
    public class StringTest {
        public static void main(String [] a) {
            String s1 = "test string";
            String s2 = "test string";
            if (s1 == s2) {
                System.out.println("same");
            } else {
                System.out.println("different");
            }
        }
    }
    ```

    A. The code will compile but not run.
    B. The code will not compile.
    C. "different" will be printed out to the console.
    D. "same" will be printed out to the console.
    E. None of the above.

27. Java arrays always start at index 1.

    A. True
    B. False

28. Which of the following statements accurately describes how variables are passed to methods?
    A. Arguments are always passed by value.
    B. Arguments are always passed by reference.
    C. Arguments that are primitive type are passed by value.
    D. Arguments that are passed with the & operator are passed by reference.

29. How do you change the value that is encapsulated by a wrapper class after you have instantiated it?
    A. Use the setXXX() method defined for the wrapper class.
    B. Use the parseXXX() method defined for the wrapper class.
    C. Use the equals() method defined for the wrapper class.
    D. None of the above.

30. Which of the following methods from the java.lang.Math class returns an integer that may be greater than its single argument?
    A. abs() and random()
    B. ceil() and round()
    C. ceil() and sqrt()
    D. floor() and max()

Answers to Assessment Test

1. **A.** All methods in an interface must be `public`. The default access modifier automatically assumes the method or constant to be `public`. See Chapter 1 for more information.

2. **A.** A `Map` contains a `Set`, which is a list that does not allow duplicates. Once you acquire the `Set` you can iterate through the keys. See Chapter 8 for more information.

3. **D.** By placing the keyword `transient` before an object's declaration, that value will not be included with the serialized data of the parent object. See Chapter 3 for more information.

4. **A.** Abstract classes can contain methods that are defined and methods that are not defined. See Chapter 3 for more information.

5. **E.** The `public` access modifier means the element is available to all; `protected` lets those within the class, package, or subclass gain access to the element. The lack of a modifier, that is, "default", means that it is accessible only within the package. Finally, `private` is the most restrictive and provides access within the class only. See Chapter 3 for more information.

6. **C.** The `native` modifier is an indicator to the Java Virtual Machine that the method actually lives in a library outside of Java. The `System.loadLibrary()` method is required to indicate which library contains the method. See Chapter 3 for more information.

7. **D.** An object denoted as `final` can have its data changed; however, the address location is what is determined as unchangeable. The third statement is false because a `final` method means it cannot be overridden, and the second statement is false because a `final` class means it *cannot* be subclassed. See Chapter 3 for more information.

8. **A.** The keyword `extends` is used when referring to another class. The extending class will have all access to all the available methods in the extended class, and the methods may be called as though they are defined in the extending class. If the extending class defines a method that exists in the extended class, that method is said to be overridden in the extending class. Because the extending class does not have to define any of the methods available in the extended class, it is said that the subclass X "is a" Y. See Chapter 6 for more information.

9. **B.** The `super` keyword is used to invoke a method or constructor in a parent class. See Chapter 6 for more information.

10. **C.** The code does not compile because it extends the `Math` class, which has been declared as `final`. A class cannot extend a class which has been declared `final`. See Chapter 3 for more information.

11. **D.** The declaration of the integer array is incorrect. An array is declared by using curly braces (`{}`) instead of square brackets (`[]`). See Chapter 1 for more information.

12. **D.** The modulo (%) operator returns the leftover value after a division operation. In the given example, 23 / 4 = 5, with 3 remaining after the division. Therefore, the answer is 3. See Chapter 2 for more information.

13. **C.** The `break` keyword is used to stop execution of a loop. See Chapter 5 for more information.

14. **B.** The `notify()` method is used to tell a pool of waiting threads that one of them can run. There is no guarantee as to which thread will run, though. See Chapter 7 for more information.

15. **A.** A `Map` supports searching on a key field, which must contain unique values. See Chapter 8 for more information.

16. **C.** Assertions do not enforce exceptions in any way. Assertions do, however, augment the use of exceptions to ensure that code is used correctly. See Chapter 5 for more information.

17. **B.** Garbage collection cannot be forced by the developer. The call to `System.gc()` schedules garbage collection in the thread queue, but it is up to the Java Virtual Machine to allow the garbage collection to run. See Chapter 1 for more information.

18. **A, C, D.** The second option is incorrect because there is no primitive named "bit"; there is a primitive named byte, however. See Chapter 1 for more information.

19. **D.** A float is represented using 32 bits for data storage. See Chapter 1 for more information.

20. **A.** Using the order of precedence, the equation contained within the parentheses is evaluated first. Again, using the order of precedence within the parentheses, the multiplication is executed first (10 * 3 = 30), than the subtraction (31 - 30 = 1). Once this is completed, the final equation is executed as 32 * 1, which equals 32. See Chapter 2 for more information.

21. **B.** The `StringBuffer` object allocates a predetermined amount of memory when it is created and only reallocates memory when the amount of its internal storage has been filled up. See Chapter 8 for more information.

22. **D.** The size of the primitives are as follows: `byte`, 8 bits; `char`, 16 bits; `short`, 16 bits; `int`, 32 bits; `float`, 32 bits; `long`, 64 bits; `double`, 64 bits. The Java specification does not state the size of a `boolean`, so it is not accurate to call it the smallest primitive. See Chapter 1 for more information.

23. **C.** The bitwise inversion operator (~), when applied to a binary value, changes all ones to zeros and all zeros to ones. Given this, the correct answer is 11010011. See Chapter 2 for more information.

24. **B.** Due to the rules of widening conversions, the integer value of x cannot be automatically converted to a byte. The assignment of the variable x to the variable b would require an explicit cast. This cast could result in a loss of data, though. See Chapter 4 for more information.

25. **B, C.** The first option is incorrect because NULL (with all capital letters) is not a keyword, although `null` (with all lowercase letters) is a keyword. The fourth option is incorrect because there is no "gosub" keyword in the Java language. See Chapter 1 for more information.

26. **D.** Both `String` variables are assigned the same string, "test string". Because these strings are not created using the `new String()` method, the strings are placed in the string pool, and a reference to those strings is stored in the `String` variables. Because the reference to the string pool is the same, the `==` comparison will return true. If the strings were created using the `new String()` method, the references would be different and the `==` comparison would return false. See Chapter 8 for more information.

27. B. Java arrays always start at index 0. See Chapter 1 for more information.

28. C. Arguments are not always passed only by reference or only by value. It depends on the argument itself, and primitives are always passed by value. Java does not use the & operator to denote "pass by reference" as is done in the C programming language. See Chapter 1 for more information.

29. D. The value encapsulated by a wrapper class is immutable. See Chapter 8 for more information.

30. B. The `random()` method does not take any arguments. The `sqrt()` method returns the square root of a number which is always less than (or equal to) its single argument. The `max()` method takes more than one argument. See Chapter 8 for more information.

PART 1

The Programmer's Exam

Chapter 1

Language Fundamentals

JAVA CERTIFICATION EXAM OBJECTIVES COVERED IN THIS CHAPTER:

- ✓ 1.1 Write code that declares, constructs, and initializes arrays of any base type using any of the permitted forms both for declaration and for initialization.

- ✓ 1.3 For a given class, determine if a default constructor will be created and if so, state the prototype of that constructor.

- ✓ 3.1 State the behavior that is guaranteed by the garbage collection system.

- ✓ 3.2 Write code that explicitly makes objects eligible for garbage collection.

- ✓ 3.3 Recognize the point in a piece of source code at which an object becomes eligible for garbage collection.

- ✓ 4.1 Identify correctly constructed source files, package declarations, import statements, class declarations (of all forms including inner classes), interface declarations and implementations (for `java.lang.Runnable` or other interfaces described in the test), method declarations (including the main method that is used to start execution of a class), variable declarations, and identifiers.

- ✓ 4.3 State the correspondence between index values in the argument array passed to a main method and command-line arguments.

- ✓ 4.4 Identify all Java programming language keywords and correctly constructed identifiers.

- ✓ 4.5 State the effect of using a variable or array element of any kind when no explicit assignment has been made to it.

- ✓ 4.6 State the range of all primitive formats, data types, and declare literal values for String and all primitive types using all permitted formats bases and representations.

- ✓ 5.4 Determine the effect upon objects and primitive values of passing variables into methods and performing assignments or other modifying operations in that method.

This book is not an introduction to Java. Because you are preparing for certification, you are obviously already familiar with the fundamentals. The purpose of this chapter is to review those fundamentals covered by the Certification Exam objectives.

Source Files

All Java source files must end with the `.java` extension. A source file should generally contain, at most, one top-level public class definition; if a public class is present, the class name should match the unextended filename. For example, if a source file contains a public class called `RayTraceApplet`, then the file must be called `RayTraceApplet.java`. A source file may contain an unlimited number of non-public class definitions.

> **NOTE** This is not actually a language requirement, but it is an implementation requirement of many compilers, including the reference compilers from Sun. It is therefore unwise to ignore this convention, because doing so limits the portability of your source files (but not, of course, your compiled files).

Three top-level elements known as *compilation units* may appear in a file. None of these elements is required. If they are present, then they must appear in the following order:

1. Package declaration
2. Import statements
3. Class definitions

The format of the package declaration is quite simple. The keyword `package` occurs first and is followed by the package name. The package name is a series of elements separated by periods. When class files are created, they must be placed in a directory hierarchy that reflects their package names. You must be careful that each component of your package name hierarchy is a legitimate directory name on all platforms. Therefore, you must not use characters such as the space, forward slash, backslash, or other symbols. Use only alphanumeric characters in package names.

Import statements have a similar form, but you may import either an individual class from a package or the entire package. To import an individual class, simply place the fully qualified class name after the `import` keyword and finish the statement with a semicolon (;); to import an entire package, simply add an asterisk (*) to the end of the package name.

White space and comments may appear before or after any of these elements. For example, a file called `Test.java` might look like this:

```
1. // Package declaration
2. package exam.prepguide;
3.
4. // Imports
5. import java.awt.Button;  // imports a specific class
6. import java.util.*;      // imports an entire package
7.
8. // Class definition
9. public class Test {...}
```

> **NOTE** Sometimes you might use classes with the same name in two different packages, such as the Date classes in the packages `java.util` and `java.sql`. If you use the asterisk form of import to import both entire packages and then attempt to use a class simply called Date, you will get a compiler error reporting that this usage is ambiguous. You must either make an additional import, naming one or the other Date class explicitly, or you must refer to the class using its fully qualified name.

Keywords and Identifiers

The Java language specifies 52 keywords and other reserved words, which are listed in Table 1.1.

TABLE 1.1 Java Keywords and Reserved Words

abstract	class	false	import	package	super	try
assert	const	final	instanceof	private	switch	void
boolean	continue	finally	int	protected	synchronized	volatile
break	default	float	interface	public	this	while
byte	do	for	long	return	throw	
case	double	goto	native	short	throws	
catch	else	if	new	static	transient	
char	extends	implements	null	strictfp	true	

The words `goto` and `const` are reserved words. However, they have no meaning in Java and programmers may not use them as identifiers.

An *identifier* is a word used by a programmer to name a variable, method, class, or label. Keywords and reserved words may not be used as identifiers. An identifier must begin with a letter, a dollar sign ($), or an underscore (_); subsequent characters may be letters, dollar signs, underscores, or digits. Some examples are

```
1. foobar              // legal
2. BIGinterface        // legal: embedded keywords
3.                     // are OK.
4. $incomeAfterExpenses // legal
5. 3_node5             // illegal: starts with a digit
6. !theCase            // illegal: must start with
7.                     // letter, $, or _
```

Identifiers are case sensitive—for example, `radius` and `Radius` are distinct identifiers.

> **NOTE** The exam is careful to avoid potentially ambiguous questions that require you to make purely academic distinctions between reserved words and keywords.

Primitive Data Types

Java's primitive data types are

- boolean
- char
- byte
- short
- int
- long
- float
- double

The apparent bit patterns of these types are defined in the Java language specification, and their effective sizes are listed in Table 1.2.

TABLE 1.2 Primitive Data Types and Their Effective Sizes

Type	Effective Representation Size (bits)	Type	Effective Representation Size (bits)
boolean	1	char	16
byte	8	short	16
int	32	long	64
float	32	double	64

Variables of type `boolean` may take only the values `true` or `false`.

The actual storage size and memory layout for these data items are not, in fact, required by the language specification. The specification does dictate the *apparent* behavior; so, for example, the effect of bit mask operations, shifts, and so on are entirely predictable at the Java level. If you write native code, you might find things are different from these tables. This means that you cannot reliably calculate the amount of memory consumed by adding up data sizes.

> **NOTE** The exam is careful to avoid potentially ambiguous questions and asks about variables only from the Java language perspective, not the underlying implementation.

The four signed integral data types are

- byte
- short
- int
- long

Variables of these types are two's-complement numbers; their ranges are given in Table 1.3. Notice that for each type, the exponent of 2 in the minimum and maximum is one less than the size of the type.

> **NOTE** Two's-complement is a way of representing signed integers that was originally developed for microprocessors in such a way as to have a single binary representation for the number 0. The most significant bit is used as the sign bit, where 0 is positive and 1 is negative.

TABLE 1.3 Ranges of the Integral Primitive Types

Type	Size	Minimum	Maximum
byte	8 bits	-2^7	$2^7 - 1$
short	16 bits	-2^{15}	$2^{15} - 1$
int	32 bits	-2^{31}	$2^{31} - 1$
long	64 bits	-2^{63}	$2^{63} - 1$

The char type is integral but unsigned. The range of a variable of type char is from 0 through $2^{16} - 1$. Java characters are in Unicode, which is a 16-bit encoding capable of representing a wide range of international characters. If the most significant 9 bits of a char are all 0, then the encoding is the same as 7-bit ASCII.

The two floating-point types are

- float
- double

The ranges of the floating-point primitive types are given in Table 1.4.

TABLE 1.4 Ranges of the Floating-Point Primitive Types

Type	Size	Minimum	Maximum
float	32 bits	$+/-1.40239846^{-45}$	$+/-3.40282347^{+38}$
double	16 bits	$+/-4.94065645841246544^{-324}$	$+/-1.79769313486231570^{+308}$

These types conform to the IEEE 754 specification. Many mathematical operations can yield results that have no expression in numbers (infinity, for example). To describe such non-numeric situations, both doubles and floats can take on values that are bit patterns that do not represent numbers. Rather, these patterns represent non-numeric values. The patterns are defined in the Float and Double classes and may be referenced as follows (NaN stands for Not a Number):

- Float.NaN
- Float.NEGATIVE_INFINITY
- Float.POSITIVE_INFINITY
- Double.NaN
- Double.NEGATIVE_INFINITY
- Double.POSITIVE_INFINITY

The following code fragment shows the use of these constants:

```
1. double d = -10.0 / 0.0;
2. if (d == Double.NEGATIVE_INFINITY) {
3.   System.out.println("d just exploded: " + d);
4. }
```

In this code fragment, the test on line 2 passes, so line 3 is executed.

> **NOTE** All numeric primitive types are signed.

Literals

A *literal* is a value specified in the program source, as opposed to one determined at runtime. Literals can represent primitive or string variables, and may appear on the right side of assignments or in method calls. You cannot assign values into literals, so they cannot appear on the left side of assignments.

boolean Literals

The only valid literals of boolean type are true and false. For example:

```
1. boolean isBig = true;
2. boolean isLittle = false;
```

char Literals

A char literal can be expressed by enclosing the desired character in single quotes, as shown here:

```
char c = 'w';
```

Of course, this technique only works if the desired character is available on the keyboard at hand. Another way to express a character literal is as a Unicode value specified using four hexadecimal digits, preceded by \u, with the entire expression in single quotes. For example:

```
char c1 = '\u4567';
```

Java supports a few escape sequences for denoting special characters:

- '\n' for new line
- '\r' for return

- `'\t'` for tab
- `'\b'` for backspace
- `'\f'` for formfeed
- `'\''` for single quote
- `'\"'` for double quote
- `'\\'` for backslash

Integral Literals

Integral literals may be expressed in decimal, octal, or hexadecimal. The default is decimal. To indicate octal, prefix the literal with 0 (zero). To indicate hexadecimal, prefix the literal with 0x or 0X; the hex digits may be upper- or lowercase. The value 28 may thus be expressed six ways:

- 28
- 034
- 0x1c
- 0x1C
- 0X1c
- 0X1C

By default, an integral literal is a 32-bit value. To indicate a long (64-bit) literal, append the suffix L to the literal expression. (The suffix can be lowercase, but then it looks so much like a one that your readers are bound to be confused.)

Floating-Point Literals

A *floating-point* literal expresses a floating-point number. In order to be interpreted as a floating-point literal, a numerical expression must contain one of the following:

- A decimal point: 1.414
- The letter E or e, indicating scientific notation: 4.23E+21
- The suffix F or f, indicating a float literal: 1.828f
- The suffix D or d, indicating a double literal: 1234d

A floating-point literal with no F or D suffix defaults to double type.

String Literals

A *string literal* is a sequence of characters enclosed in double quotes. For example:

```
String s = "Characters in strings are 16-bit Unicode.";
```

Java provides many advanced facilities for specifying non-literal string values, including a concatenation operator and some sophisticated constructors for the `String` class. These facilities are discussed in detail in Chapter 8, "The `java.lang` and `java.util` Packages."

Arrays

A Java *array* is an ordered collection of primitives, object references, or other arrays. Java arrays are homogeneous: except as allowed by polymorphism, all elements of an array must be of the same type. That is, when you create an array, you specify the element type, and the resulting array can contain only elements that are instances of that class or subclasses of that class.

To create and use an array, you must follow three steps:

1. Declaration
2. Construction
3. Initialization

Declaration tells the compiler the array's name and what type its elements will be. For example:

```
1. int[] ints;
2. Dimension[] dims;
3. float[][] twoDee;
```

Line 1 declares an array of a primitive type. Line 2 declares an array of object references (`Dimension` is a class in the `java.awt` package). Line 3 declares a two-dimensional array—that is, an array of arrays of `float`s.

The square brackets can come before or after the array variable name. This is also true, and perhaps most useful, in method declarations. A method that takes an array of `double`s could be declared as `myMethod(double dubs[])` or as `myMethod(double[] dubs)`; a method that returns an array of doubles may be declared as either `double[] anotherMethod()` or as `double anotherMethod()[]`. In this last case, the first form is probably more readable.

> **TIP** Generally, placing the square brackets adjacent to the type, rather than following the variable or method, allows the type declaration part to be read as a single unit: "int array" or "float array", which might make more sense. However, C/C++ programmers will be more familiar with the form where the brackets are placed to the right of the variable or method declaration. Given the number of magazine articles that have been dedicated to ways to correctly interpret complex C/C++ declarations (perhaps you recall the "spiral rule"), it's probably not a bad thing that Java has modified the syntax for these declarations. Either way, you need to recognize both forms.

Notice that the declaration does not specify the size of an array. Size is specified at runtime, when the array is allocated via the `new` keyword. For example:

1. `int[] ints;`   `// Declaration to the compiler`
2. `ints = new int[25];`   `// Runtime construction`

Since array size is not used until runtime, it is legal to specify size with a variable rather than a literal:

1. `int size = 1152 * 900;`
2. `int[] raster;`
3. `raster = new int[size];`

Declaration and construction may be performed in a single line:

1. `int[] ints = new int[25];`

When an array is constructed, its elements are automatically initialized to their default values. These defaults are the same as for object member variables. Numerical elements are initialized to 0; non-numeric elements are initialized to 0-like values, as shown in Table 1.5.

TABLE 1.5 Array Element Initialization Values

Element Type	Initial Value	Element Type	Initial Value
byte	0	short	0
int	0	long	0L
float	0.0f	double	0.0d
char	'\u0000'	boolean	false
object reference	null		

NOTE Arrays are actually objects, even to the extent that you can execute methods on them (mostly the methods of the Object class), although you cannot subclass the array class. Therefore, this initialization is exactly the same as for other objects, and as a consequence you will see this table again in the next section.

If you want to initialize an array to values other than those shown in Table 1.5, you can combine declaration, construction, and initialization into a single step. The following line of code creates a custom-initialized array of five floats:

1. `float[] diameters = {1.1f, 2.2f, 3.3f, 4.4f, 5.5f};`

The array size is inferred from the number of elements within the curly braces.

Of course, an array can also be initialized by explicitly assigning a value to each element, starting at array index 0:

```
1. long[] squares;
2. squares = new long[6000];
3. for (int i = 0; i < 6000; i++) {
4.    squares[i] = i * i;
5. }
```

When the array is created at line 2, it is full of default values (0L) which are replaced in lines 3–4. The code in the example works but can be improved. If you later need to change the array size (in line 2), the loop counter will have to change (in line 3), and the program could be damaged if line 3 is not taken care of. The safest way to refer to the size of an array is to append the `.length` member variable to the array name. Thus, our example becomes:

```
1. long[] squares;
2. squares = new long[6000];
3. for (int i = 0; i < squares.length; i++) {
4.    squares[i] = i * i;
5. }
```

> **TIP** Java allows you to create non-rectangular arrays. Because multi-dimensional arrays are simply arrays of arrays, each subarray is a separate object, and there is no requirement that the dimension of each subarray be the same. Of course, this type of array requires more care in handling because you cannot simply iterate each subarray using the same limits.

Class Fundamentals

Java is all about classes, and a review of the Certification Exam objectives will show that you need to be intimately familiar with them. Classes are discussed in detail in Chapter 6, "Objects and Classes"; for now, let's examine a few fundamentals.

The *main()* Method

The `main()` method is the entry point for standalone Java applications. To create an application, you write a class definition that includes a `main()` method. To execute an application, type java at the command line, followed by the name of the class containing the main() method to be executed.

The signature for main() is

```
public static void main(String[] args)
```

The main() method is declared public by convention. However, it is a requirement that it be static so that it can be executed without the necessity of constructing an instance of the corresponding class.

The args array contains any arguments that the user might have entered on the command line. For example, consider the following command line:

```
% java Mapper France Belgium
```

With this command line, the args[] array has two elements: France in args[0], and Belgium in args[1]. Note that neither the class name (Mapper) nor the command name (java) appears in the array. Of course, the name args is purely arbitrary: any legal identifier may be used, provided the array is a single-dimensional array of String objects.

Variables and Initialization

Java supports variables of three different lifetimes:

Member variable   A *member variable* of a class is created when an instance is created, and it is destroyed when the object is destroyed. Subject to accessibility rules and the need for a reference to the object, member variables are accessible as long as the enclosing object exists.

Automatic variable   An *automatic variable* of a method (also known as a *method local*) is created on entry to the method and exists only during execution of the method, and therefore is accessible only during the execution of that method. (You'll see an exception to this rule when you look at inner classes, but don't worry about that for now.)

Class variable   A *class variable* (also known as a *static variable*) is created when the class is loaded and is destroyed when the class is unloaded. There is only one copy of a class variable, and it exists regardless of the number of instances of the class, even if the class is never instantiated.

All member variables that are not explicitly assigned a value upon declaration are automatically assigned an initial value. The initialization value for member variables depends on the member variable's type. Values are listed in Table 1.6.

TABLE 1.6 Initialization Values for Member Variables

Element Type	Initial Value	Element Type	Initial Value
byte	0	short	0
int	0	long	0L
float	0.0f	double	0.0d
char	'\u0000'	boolean	false
object reference	null		

The values in Table 1.6 are the same as those in Table 1.5; member variable initialization values are the same as array element initialization values.

A member value may be initialized in its own declaration line:

```
1. class HasVariables {
2.    int x = 20;
3.    static int y = 30;
```

When this technique is used, nonstatic instance variables are initialized just before the class constructor is executed; here x would be set to 20 just before invocation of any `HasVariables` constructor. Static variables are initialized at class load time; here y would be set to 30 when the `HasVariables` class is loaded.

Automatic variables (also known as *local variables*) are not initialized by the system; every automatic variable must be explicitly initialized before being used. For example, this method will not compile:

```
1. public int wrong() {
2.    int i;
3.    return i+5;
4. }
```

The compiler error at line 3 is, "Variable i may not have been initialized." This error often appears when initialization of an automatic variable occurs at a lower level of curly braces than the use of that variable. For example, the following method below returns the fourth root of a positive number:

```
1. public double fourthRoot(double d) {
2.    double result;
3.    if (d >= 0) {
4.       result = Math.sqrt(Math.sqrt(d));
5.    }
```

```
6.    return result;
7. }
```

Here the result is initialized on line 4, but the initialization takes place within the curly braces of lines 3 and 5. The compiler will flag line 6, complaining that "Variable `result` may not have been initialized." A common solution is to initialize `result` to some reasonable default as soon as it is declared:

```
1. public double fourthRoot(double d) {
2.    double result = 0.0;   // Initialize
3.    if (d >= 0) {
4.       result = Math.sqrt(Math.sqrt(d));
5.    }
6.    return result;
7. }
```

Now `result` is satisfactorily initialized. Line 2 demonstrates that an automatic variable may be initialized in its declaration line. Initialization on a separate line is also possible.

Class variables are initialized in the same manner as for member variables.

Argument Passing: By Reference or By Value

When Java passes an argument into a method call, a *copy* of the argument is actually passed. Consider the following code fragment:

```
1. double radians = 1.2345;
2. System.out.println("Sine of " + radians +
3.                    " = " + Math.sin(radians));
```

The variable `radians` contains a pattern of bits that represents the number 1.2345. On line 2, a copy of this bit pattern is passed into the method-calling apparatus of the Java Virtual Machine (JVM).

When an argument is passed into a method, changes to the argument value by the method do not affect the original data. Consider the following method:

```
1. public void bumper(int bumpMe) {
2.    bumpMe += 15;
3. }
```

Line 2 modifies a copy of the parameter passed by the caller. For example:

```
1. int xx = 12345;
2. bumper(xx);
```

Argument Passing: By Reference or By Value   17

3. `System.out.println("Now xx is " + xx);`

On line 2, the caller's `xx` variable is copied; the copy is passed into the `bumper()` method and incremented by 15. Because the original `xx` is untouched, line 3 will report that `xx` is still 12345.

This is also true when the argument to be passed is an object rather than a primitive. However, it is crucial for you to understand that the effect is very different. In order to understand the process, you have to understand the concept of the *object reference*.

Java programs do not deal directly with objects. When an object is constructed, the constructor returns a value—a bit pattern—that uniquely identifies the object. This value is known as a *reference* to the object. For example, consider the following code:

1. `Button btn;`
2. `btn = new Button("Ok");`

In line 2, the `Button` constructor returns a reference to the just-constructed button—not the actual button object or a copy of the button object. This reference is stored in the variable `btn`. In some implementations of the JVM, a reference is simply the address of the object; however, the JVM specification gives wide latitude as to how references can be implemented. You can think of a reference as simply a pattern of bits that uniquely identifies an individual object.

> **NOTE** In most JVMs, the reference value is actually the address of an address. This second address refers to the real data. This approach, called *double indirection*, allows the garbage collector to relocate objects to reduce memory fragmentation.

When Java code appears to store objects in variables or pass objects into method calls, the object references are stored or passed.

Consider this code fragment:

1. `Button btn;`
2. `btn = new Button("Pink");`
3. `replacer(btn);`
4. `System.out.println(btn.getLabel());`
5.
6. `public void replacer(Button replaceMe) {`
7. `    replaceMe = new Button("Blue");`
8. `}`

Line 2 constructs a button and stores a reference to that button in `btn`. In line 3, a copy of the reference is passed into the `replacer()` method. Before execution of line 7, the value in `replaceMe` is a reference to the Pink button. Then line 7 constructs a second button and stores a reference to the second button in `replaceMe`, thus overwriting the reference to the Pink button. However, the caller's copy of the reference is not affected, so on line 4 the call to `btn.getLabel()` calls the original button; the string printed out is "Pink".

You have seen that called methods cannot affect the original value of their arguments—that is, the values stored by the caller. However, when the called method operates on an object via the reference value that is passed to it, there are important consequences. If the method modifies the object via the reference, as distinguished from modifying the method argument—the reference—then the changes will be visible to the caller. For example:

```
1. Button btn;
2. btn = new Button("Pink");
3. changer(btn);
4. System.out.println(btn.getLabel());
5.
6. public void changer(Button changeMe) {
7.    changeMe.setLabel("Blue");
8. }
```

In this example, the variable changeMe is a copy of the reference btn, just as before. However, this time the code uses the copy of the reference to change the actual original object rather than trying to change the reference. Because the caller's object is changed rather than the callee's reference, the change is visible and the value printed out by line 4 is "Blue".

Arrays are objects, meaning that programs deal with references to arrays, not with arrays themselves. What gets passed into a method is a copy of a reference to an array. It is therefore possible for a called method to modify the contents of a caller's array.

How to Create a Reference to a Primitive

This is a useful technique if you need to create the effect of passing primitive values by reference. Simply pass an array of one primitive element over the method call, and the called method can now change the value seen by the caller. To do so, use code like this:

```
1. public class PrimitiveReference {
2.    public static void main(String args[]) {
3.       int [] myValue = { 1 };
4.       modifyIt(myValue);
5.       System.out.println("myValue contains " +
6.                          myValue[0]);
7.    }
8.    public static void modifyIt(int [] value) {
9.       value[0]++;
10.   }
11. }
```

Garbage Collection

Most modern languages permit you to allocate data storage during a program run. In Java, this is done directly when you create an object with the new operation and indirectly when you call a method that has local variables or arguments. Method locals and arguments are allocated space on the stack and are discarded when the method exits, but objects are allocated space on the heap and have a longer lifetime.

> **NOTE** Each process has its own stack and heap, and they are located on opposite sides of the process address space. The sizes of the stack and heap are limited by the amount of memory that is available on the host running the program. They may be further limited by the operating system or user-specific limits.

It is important to recognize that objects are always allocated on the heap. Even if they are created in a method using code like

```
public void aMethod() {
    MyClass mc = new MyClass();
}
```

the local variable mc is a reference, allocated on the stack, whereas the object to which that variable refers, an instance of MyClass, is allocated on the heap.

This section is concerned with recovery of space allocated on the heap. The increased lifetime raises the question of when storage allocation on the heap can be released. Some languages require that you, the programmer, explicitly release the storage when you have finished with it. This approach has proven seriously error-prone, because you might release the storage too soon (causing corrupted data if any other reference to the data is still in use) or forget to release it altogether (causing a memory shortage). Java's garbage collection solves the first of these problems and greatly simplifies the second.

In Java, you never explicitly free memory that you have allocated; instead, Java provides automatic garbage collection. The runtime system keeps track of the memory that is allocated and is able to determine whether that memory is still useable. This work is usually done in the background by a low-priority thread that is referred to as the *garbage collector*. When the garbage collector finds memory that is no longer accessible from any live thread (the object is out of scope), it takes steps to release it back into the heap for re-use. Specifically, the garbage collector calls the class destructor method called finalize() (if it is defined) and then frees the memory.

Garbage collection can be done in a number of different ways; each has advantages and disadvantages, depending on the type of program that is running. A real time control system, for example, needs to know that nothing will prevent it from responding quickly to interrupts; this application requires a garbage collector that can work in small chunks or that can be interrupted easily. On the other hand, a memory-intensive program might work better with a garbage collector that stops the program from time to time but recovers memory more urgently as a result. At present, garbage collection is hardwired into the Java runtime system; most garbage collection algorithms use an approach that gives a reasonable compromise between speed of memory recovery and responsiveness. In the future, you will probably be able to plug in different garbage-collection algorithms or buy different JVMs with appropriate collection algorithms, according to your particular needs.

This discussion leaves one crucial question unanswered: When is storage recovered? The best answer is that storage is not recovered unless it is definitely no longer in use. That's it. Even though you are not using an object any longer, you cannot say if it will be collected in 1 millisecond, in 100 milliseconds, or even if it will be collected at all. The methods `System.gc()` and `Runtime.gc()` look as if they run the garbage collector, but even these cannot be relied upon in general, because some other thread might prevent the garbage collection thread from running. In fact, the documentation for the `gc()` methods states:

> Calling this method suggests that the Java Virtual Machine expends effort toward recycling unused objects

How to Cause Leaks in a Garbage Collection System

The nature of automatic garbage collection has an important consequence: you can still get memory leaks. If you allow live, accessible references to unneeded objects to persist in your programs, then those objects cannot be garbage collected. Therefore, it may be a good idea to explicitly assign `null` into a variable when you have finished with it. This issue is particularly noticeable if you are implementing a collection of some kind.

In this example, assume the array `storage` is being used to maintain the storage of a stack. This `pop()` method is inappropriate:

```
1. public Object pop() {
2.    return storage[index--];
3. }
```

If the caller of this `pop()` method abandons the popped value, it will not be eligible for garbage collection until the array element containing a reference to it is overwritten. This might take a long time. You can speed up the process like this:

```
1. public Object pop() {
2.    Object returnValue = storage[index];
3.    storage[index--] = null;
4.    return returnValue;
5. }
```

Summary

This chapter has covered quite a bit of ground and a large variety of topics. You learned that a source file's elements must appear in this order:

1. Package declaration
2. Import statements
3. Class definitions

There should be, at most, one public class definition per source file; the filename must match the name of the public class.

You also learned that an identifier must begin with a letter, a dollar sign, or an underscore; subsequent characters may be letters, dollar signs, underscores, or digits. Java has four signed integral primitive data types: `byte`, `short`, `int`, and `long`; all four types display the behavior of two's-complement representation. Java's two floating-point primitive data types are `float` and `double`, the `char` type is unsigned and represents a Unicode character, and the `boolean` type may only take on the values `true` and `false`.

In addition, you learned that arrays must be (in order):

1. Declared
2. Constructed
3. Initialized

Default initialization is applied to member variables, class variables, and array elements, but not automatic variables. The default values are 0 for numeric types, the `null` value for object references, the null character for `char`, and `false` for `boolean`. The `length` member of an array gives the number of elements in the array. A class with a `main()` method can be invoked from the command line as a Java application. The signature for `main()` is `public static void main(String[] args)`. The `args[]` array contains all command-line arguments that appeared after the name of the application class.

You should also understand that method arguments are copies, not originals. For arguments of primitive data type, this means that modifications to an argument within a method are not visible to the caller of the method. For arguments of object type (including arrays), modifications to an argument value within a method are still not visible to the caller of the method; however, modifications in the object or array to which the argument refers *do* appear to the caller.

Finally, Java's garbage collection mechanism may only recover memory that is definitely unused. It is not possible to force garbage collection reliably. It is not possible to predict when a piece of unused memory will be collected, only to say when it becomes *eligible* for collection. Garbage collection does not prevent memory leaks; they can still occur if unused references are not cleared to `null` or destroyed.

Exam Essentials

Recognize and create correctly constructed source files. You should know the various kinds of compilation units and their required order of appearance.

Recognize and create correctly constructed declarations. You should be familiar with declarations of packages, classes, interfaces, methods, and variables.

Recognize Java keywords. You should recognize the keywords and reserved words listed in Table 1.1.

Distinguish between legal and illegal identifiers. You should know the rules that restrict the first character and the subsequent characters of an identifier.

Know all the primitive data types and the ranges of the integral data types. These are summarized in Tables 1.2 and 1.3.

Recognize correctly formatted literals. You should be familiar with all formats for literal characters, strings, and numbers.

Know how to declare and construct arrays. The declaration includes one empty pair of square brackets for each dimension of the array. The square brackets can appear before or after the array name. Arrays are constructed with the keyword `new`.

Know the default initialization values for all possible types of class variables and array elements. Know when data is initialized. Initialization takes place when a class or array is constructed. The initialization values are 0 for numeric type arrays, `false` for `boolean` arrays, and `null` for object reference type arrays.

Know the contents of the argument list of an application's `main()` method, given the command line that invoked the application. Be aware that the list is an array of `String`s containing everything on the command line except the `java` command, command-line options, and the name of the class.

Know that Java passes method arguments by value. Changes made to a method argument are not visible to the caller, because the method argument changes a copy of the argument. Objects are not passed to methods; only references to objects are passed.

Understand memory reclamation and the circumstances under which memory will be reclaimed. If an object is still accessible to any live thread, that object will certainly not be collected. This is true even if the program will never access the object again—the logic is simple and cannot make inferences about the semantics of the code. No guarantees are made about reclaiming available memory or the timing of reclamation if it does occur. A standard JVM has no entirely reliable, platform-independent way to force garbage collection. The `System` and `Runtime` classes each have a `gc()` method, and these methods make it more likely that garbage collection will run, but they provide no guarantee.

Key Terms

Before you take the exam, be certain you are familiar with the following terms:

array	local variable
automatic variable	member variable
class variable	method local
compilation units	object reference
floating-point	reference
garbage collector	static variable
identifier	string literal
literal	

Review Questions

1. A signed data type has an equal number of non-zero positive and negative values available.
   A. True
   B. False

2. Choose the valid identifiers from those listed here. (Choose all that apply.)
   A. `BigOlLongStringWithMeaninglessName`
   B. `$int`
   C. `bytes`
   D. `$1`
   E. `finalist`

3. Which of the following signatures are valid for the `main()` method entry point of an application? (Choose all that apply.)
   A. `public static void main()`
   B. `public static void main(String arg[])`
   C. `public void main(String [] arg)`
   D. `public static void main(String[] args)`
   E. `public static int main(String [] arg)`

4. If all three top-level elements occur in a source file, they must appear in which order?
   A. Imports, package declarations, classes
   B. Classes, imports, package declarations
   C. Package declarations must come first; order for imports and class definitions is not significant
   D. Package declarations, imports, classes
   E. Imports must come first; order for package declarations and class definitions is not significant

5. Consider the following line of code:
   `int[] x = new int[25];`

After execution, which statements are true? (Choose all that apply.)

A. x[24] is 0.
B. x[24] is undefined.
C. x[25] is 0.
D. x[0] is null.
E. x.length is 25.

6. Consider the following application:

```
1.  class Q6 {
2.    public static void main(String args[]) {
3.      Holder h = new Holder();
4.      h.held = 100;
5.      h.bump(h);
6.      System.out.println(h.held);
7.    }
8.  }
9.
10. class Holder {
11.   public int held;
12.   public void bump(Holder theHolder) {
13.     theHolder.held++; }
14. }
15. }
```

What value is printed out at line 6?

A. 0
B. 1
C. 100
D. 101

7. Consider the following application:

```
1.  class Q7 {
2.    public static void main(String args[]) {
3.      double d = 12.3;
```

```
4.      Decrementer dec = new Decrementer();
5.      dec.decrement(d);
6.      System.out.println(d);
7.    }
8.  }
9.
10. class Decrementer {
11.   public void decrement(double decMe) {
12.     decMe = decMe - 1.0;
13.   }
14. }
```

What value is printed out at line 6?

A. 0.0

B. 1.0

C. 12.3

D. 11.3

8. How can you force garbage collection of an object?

   A. Garbage collection cannot be forced.

   B. Call System.gc().

   C. Call System.gc(), passing in a reference to the object to be garbage-collected.

   D. Call Runtime.gc().

   E. Set all references to the object to new values (null, for example).

9. What is the range of values that can be assigned to a variable of type short?

   A. Depends on the underlying hardware

   B. 0 through $2^{16} - 1$

   C. 0 through $2^{32} - 1$

   D. -2^{15} through $2^{15} - 1$

   E. -2^{31} through $2^{31} - 1$

10. What is the range of values that can be assigned to a variable of type byte?

    A. Depends on the underlying hardware

    B. 0 through $2^8 - 1$

    C. 0 through $2^{16} - 1$

    D. -2^7 through $2^7 - 1$

    E. -2^{15} through $2^{15} - 1$

Answers to Review Questions

1. B. The range of negative numbers is greater by one than the range of positive numbers.
2. A, B, C, D, E. All of the identifiers are valid.
3. B, D. All the choices are valid method signatures. However, in order to be the entry point of an application, a main() method must be public, static, and void; it must take a single argument of type String[].
4. D. This order must be strictly observed.
5. A, E. The array has 25 elements, indexed from 0 through 24. All elements are initialized to 0.
6. D. A holder is constructed on line 3. A reference to that holder is passed into method bump() on line 5. Within the method call, the holder's held variable is bumped from 100 to 101.
7. C. The decrement() method is passed a copy of the argument d, the copy gets decremented, but the original is untouched.
8. A. Garbage collection cannot be forced. Calling System.gc() or Runtime.gc() is not 100 percent reliable, because the garbage-collection thread might defer to a thread of higher priority; thus B and D are incorrect. C is incorrect because the two gc() methods do not take arguments; in fact, if you still have a reference to pass into any method, the object is not yet eligible to be collected. E will make the object eligible for collection the next time the garbage collector runs.
9. D. The range for a 16-bit short is -2^{15} through $2^{15} - 1$. This range is part of the Java specification, regardless of the underlying hardware.
10. D. The range for an 8-bit byte is -2^7 through 2^7-1. Table 1.3 lists the ranges for Java's integral primitive data types.

Chapter 2

Operators and Assignments

JAVA CERTIFICATION EXAM OBJECTIVES COVERED IN THIS CHAPTER:

✓ 5.1 Determine the result of applying any operator, including assignment operators, `instanceof`, and casts to operands of any type, class, scope, or accessibility, or any combination of these.

✓ 5.2 Determine the result of applying the boolean equals (object) method to objects of any combination of the classes `java.lang.String`, `java.lang.Boolean`, and `java.lang.Object`.

✓ 5.3 In an expression involving the operators &, |, &&, ||, and variables of known values, state which operands are evaluated and the value of the expression.

Java provides a full set of operators, most of which are taken from C and C++. However, Java's operators differ in some important aspects from their counterparts in these other languages, and you need to understand clearly how Java's operators behave. This chapter describes all the operators. Some are described briefly, whereas operators that sometimes cause confusion are described in more detail. You will also learn about the behavior of expressions under conditions of arithmetic overflow.

Java's operators are shown in Table 2.1. They are listed in precedence order, with the highest precedence at the top of the table. Each group has been given a name for reference purposes; that name is shown in the left column of the table. Arithmetic and comparison operators are each split further into two subgroupings because they have different levels of precedence. We'll discuss these groupings later.

TABLE 2.1 Operators in Java, in Descending Order of Precedence

Category	Operators
Unary	++ -- + - ! ~ (type)
Arithmetic	* / %
	+ -
Shift	<< >> >>>
Comparison	< <= > >= instanceof
	== !=
Bitwise	& ^ |
Short-circuit	&& ||
Conditional	?:
Assignment	= op=

The rest of this chapter examines each of these operators. But before we start, let's consider the general issue of evaluation order.

Evaluation Order

In Java, the order of evaluation of operands in an expression is fixed. Consider this code fragment:

```
1. int [] a = { 4, 4 };
2. int b = 1;
3. a[b] = b = 0;
```

In this case, it might be unclear which element of the array is modified: which value of b is used to select the array element, 0 or 1? An evaluation from left to right requires that the leftmost expression, a[b], be evaluated first, so it is a reference to the element a[1]. Next, b is evaluated, which is simply a reference to the variable called b. The constant expression 0 is evaluated next, which clearly does not involve any work. Now that the operands have been evaluated, the operations take place. This is done in the order specified by precedence and associativity. For assignments, associativity is right-to-left, so the value 0 is first assigned to the variable called b; then the value 0 is assigned into the last element of the array a.

The following sections examine each of these operators in turn.

> **TIP** Although Table 2.1 shows the precedence order, the degree of detail in this precedence ordering is rather high. It is generally better style to keep expressions simple and to use redundant bracketing to make it clear how any particular expression should be evaluated. This approach reduces the chance that less experienced programmers will have difficulty trying to read or maintain your code. Bear in mind that the code generated by the compiler will be the same despite redundant brackets.

The Unary Operators

The first group of operators in Table 2.1 consists of the *unary operators*. Most operators take two operands. When you multiply, for example, you work with two numbers. Unary operators, on the other hand, take only a single operand and work just on that. Java provides seven unary operators:

- The increment and decrement operators: ++ and --
- The unary plus and minus operators: + and -
- The bitwise inversion operator: ~
- The boolean complement operator: !
- The cast: ()

> **NOTE:** Strictly speaking, the cast is not an operator. However, we discuss it as if it were for simplicity, because it fits well with the rest of our discussion.

The Increment and Decrement Operators: ++ and --

These operators modify the value of an expression by adding or subtracting 1. So, for example, if an int variable x contains 10, then ++x results in 11. Similarly, --x, again applied when x contains 10, gives a value of 9. In this case, the expression --x itself describes storage (the value of the variable x), so the resulting value is stored in x.

The preceding examples show the operators positioned before the expression (known as *pre-increment* or *pre-decrement*). They can, however, be placed after the expression instead (known as *post-increment* or *post-decrement*). To understand how the position of these operators affects their operation, you must appreciate the difference between the value stored by these operators and the result value they give. Both x++ and ++x cause the same result in x. However, the value of the expression itself is different. For example, if you say y = x++;, then the value assigned to y is the original value of x. If you say y = ++x;, then the value assigned to y is 1 more than the original value of x. In both cases, the value of x is incremented by 1.

Table 2.2 shows the values of x and y before and after particular assignments using these operators.

TABLE 2.2 Examples of Pre-and Post- Increment and Decrement Operations

Initial Value of x	Expression	Final Value of y	Final Value of x
5	y = x++	5	6
5	y = ++x	6	6
5	y = x--	5	4
5	y = --x	4	4

The Unary Plus and Minus Operators: + and -

The unary operators + and - are distinct from the more common binary + and - operators, which are usually just referred to as + and - (add and subtract). Both the programmer and the compiler are able to determine which meaning these symbols should have in a given context.

Unary + has no effect beyond emphasizing the positive nature of a numeric literal. Unary - negates an expression. So, you might make a block of assignments like this:

1. x = -3;
2. y = +3;
3. z = -(y + 6);

In such an example, the only reasons for using the unary + operator are to make it explicit that y is assigned a positive value and perhaps to keep the code aligned more pleasingly. At line 3, notice that these operators are not restricted to literal values but can be applied to expressions equally well, so the value of z is initialized to −9.

The Bitwise Inversion Operator: ~

The ~ operator performs *bitwise inversion* on integral types.

For each primitive type, Java uses a virtual machine representation that is platform independent. This means that the bit pattern used to represent a particular value in a particular variable type is always the same. This feature makes bit-manipulation operators even more useful, because they do not introduce platform dependencies. The ~ operator works by inverting all the 1 bits in a binary value to 0s and all the 0 bits to 1s.

For example, applying this operator to a byte containing 00001111 would result in the value 11110000. The same simple logic applies, no matter how many bits there are in the value being operated on. This operator is often used in conjunction with shift operators (<<, >>, and >>>) to perform bit manipulation, for example when driving I/O ports.

The *Boolean* Complement Operator: !

The ! operator inverts the value of a boolean expression. So !true gives false and !false gives true.

This operator is often used in the test part of an if() statement. The effect is to change the value of the Boolean expression. In this way, for example, the body of the if() and else parts can be swapped. Consider these two equivalent code fragments:

1. public Object myMethod(Object x) {
2.   if (x instanceof String) {
3.   // do nothing
4.   }
5.   else {
6.   x = x.toString();
7.   }
8.   return x;
9. }

and

```
1. public Object myMethod(Object x) {
2.    if (!(x instanceof String)) {
3.       x = x.toString();
4.    }
5.    return x;
6. }
```

In the first fragment, a test is made at line 2, but the conversion and assignment, at line 6, occurs only if the test failed. This is achieved by the somewhat cumbersome technique of using only the else part of an if/else construction. The second fragment uses the complement operator so that the overall test performed at line 2 is reversed; it may be read as, "If it is false that x is an instance of a string" or more likely, "If x is not a string." Because of this change to the test, the conversion can be performed at line 3 in the situation that the test has succeeded; no else part is required, and the resulting code is cleaner and shorter.

This is a simple example, but such usage is common. This level of understanding will leave you well-armed for the Certification Exam.

The Cast Operator: (type)

Casting is used for explicit conversion of the type of an expression. This is possible only for plausible target types. The compiler and the runtime system check for conformance with typing rules, which are described later.

Casting Primitives

Casts can be applied to change the type of primitive values—for example, forcing a double value into an int variable like this:

```
int circum = (int)(Math.PI * diameter);
```

If the cast, which is represented by the (int) part, were not present, the compiler would reject the assignment; a double value, such as is returned by the arithmetic here, cannot be represented accurately by an int variable. The cast is the programmer's way to say to the compiler, "I know you think this is risky, but trust me—I'm an engineer." Of course, if the result loses value or precision to the extent that the program does not work properly, then you are on your own.

Casting Object References

Casts can also be applied to object references. This often happens when you use containers, such as the Vector object. If you put, for example, String objects into a Vector, then when you extract them, the return type of the `elementAt()` method is simply `Object`. To use the recovered value as a `String` reference, a cast is needed, like this:

1. `Vector v = new Vector();`
2. `v.add ("Hello");`
3. `String s = (String)v.get(0);`

The cast here occurs at line 3, in the form (`String`). Although the compiler allows this cast, checks occur at runtime to determine if the object extracted from the `Vector` really is a `String`. Chapter 4, "Converting and Casting," covers casting, the rules governing which casts are legal and which are not, and the nature of the runtime checks that are performed on cast operations.

Now that we have considered the unary operators, which have the highest precedence, we will discuss the five arithmetic operators.

The Arithmetic Operators

Next highest in precedence, after the unary operators, are the *arithmetic operators*. This group includes, but is not limited to, the four most familiar operators, which perform addition, subtraction, multiplication, and division. Arithmetic operators are split into two further subgroupings, as shown in Table 2.1. In the first group are *, /, and %; in the second group, at a lower precedence, are + and -. The following sections discuss these operators and also what happens when arithmetic goes wrong.

The Multiplication and Division Operators: * and /

The operators * and / perform multiplication and division on all primitive numeric types and `char`. Integer division will generate an `ArithmeticException` when attempting to divide by zero.

You probably understand multiplication and division quite well from years of rote learning at school. In programming, of course, some limitations are imposed by the representation of numbers in a computer. These limitations apply to all number formats, from `byte` to `double`, but are perhaps most noticeable in integer arithmetic.

If you multiply or divide two integers, the result will be calculated using integer arithmetic in either `int` or `long` representation. If the numbers are large enough, the result will be bigger than the maximum number that can be represented, and the final value will be meaningless. This condition is referred to as *overflow*. For example, `byte` values can represent a range of −128 to +127, so if two particular bytes have the values 64 and 4, then multiplying them should, arithmetically, give a value of 256 (100000000 in binary—note that this value has nine digits). Actually, when you store the result in a `byte` variable, you will get a value of 0, because only the low-order eight bits of the result can be represented.

On the other hand, when you divide with integer arithmetic, the result is forced into an integer and, typically, a lot of information that would have formed a fractional part of the answer is lost. This condition is referred to as *underflow*. For example, 7 / 4 should give 1.75, but integer arithmetic will result in a value of 1. You therefore have a choice in many expressions: multiply first and then divide, which risks overflow, or divide first and then multiply, which risks underflow. Conventional wisdom says that you should multiply first and then divide, because this at least might work perfectly, whereas dividing first almost definitely loses precision. Consider this example:

```
1.  int a = 12345, b = 234567, c, d;
2.  long e, f;
3.
4.  c = a * b / b; // this should equal a, that is, 12345
5.  d = a / b * b; // this should also equal a
6.  System.out.println("a is " + a +
7.     "\nb is " + b +
8.     "\nc is " + c +
9.     "\nd is " + d);
10.
11. e = (long)a * b / b;
12. f = (long)a / b * b;
13. System.out.println(
14.    "\ne is " + e +
15.    "\nf is " + f);
```

The output from this code is

```
a is 12345
b is 234567
c is -5965
d is 0
e is 12345
f is 0
```

Do not worry about the exact numbers in this example. The important feature is that in the case where multiplication is performed first, the calculation overflows when performed with `int` values, resulting in a nonsense answer. However, the result is correct if the representation is wide enough—as when using the `long` variables. In both cases, dividing first has a catastrophic effect on the result, regardless of the width of the representation.

The Modulo Operator: %

Although multiplication and division are generally familiar operations, the *modulo operator* is perhaps less well known. The modulo operator gives a value that is related to the remainder of a division. It is generally applied to two integers, although it can be applied to floating-point numbers, too. In school, we learned that 7 divided by 4 gives 1, remainder 3. In Java, we say x = 7 % 4; and expect that x will have the value 3.

The previous paragraph describes the essential behavior of the modulo operator, but additional concerns appear if you use negative or floating-point operands. In such cases, follow this procedure:

1. Reduce the magnitude of the left operand by the magnitude of the right one.
2. Repeat until the magnitude of the result is less than the magnitude of the right operand.

This result is the result of the modulo operator. Figure 2.1 shows some examples of this process.

FIGURE 2.1 Calculating the result of the modulo operator for a variety of conditions

```
17 % 5                          -5 % 2
  17 - 5 → 12                   Here, to reduce absolute value by 2, we must add
  12 - 5 → 7                      -5 + 2 = -3
   7 - 5 → 2                      -3 + 2 = -1
  2 < 5 so 17 % 5 = 2           Absolute value of -1 is 1 and 1 < 2
                                so  -5 % 2 = -1
21 % 7
  21 - 7 = 14                   -5 % -2
  14 - 7 = 7                    Again, we must reduce absolute value of -5
   7 - 7 = 0                    by the absolute value of -2 which is 2
  0 < 7 so 21 % 7 = 0             -5 - (-2) = -3
                                  -3 - (-2) = -1
7.6 % 2.9                       so again, -5 % -2 = -1
  7.6 - 2.9 = 4.7
  4.7 - 2.9 = 1.8
  1.8 < 2.9 so 7.6 % 2.9 = 1.8
```

Note that the sign of the result is entirely determined by the sign of the left operand. When the modulo operator is applied to floating-point types, the effect is to perform an integral number of subtractions, leaving a floating-point result that might well have a fractional part.

A useful rule of thumb for dealing with modulo calculations that involve negative numbers is this: Simply drop any negative signs from either operand and calculate the result. Then, if the original left operand was negative, negate the result. The sign of the right operand is irrelevant.

The modulo operation involves division during execution. As a result, it can throw an ArithmeticException if it's applied to integral types and the second operand is 0.

You might not have learned about the modulo operator in school, but you will certainly recognize the + and - operators. Although basically familiar, the + operator has some capabilities beyond simple addition.

The Addition and Subtraction Operators: + and -

The operators + and - perform addition and subtraction. They apply to operands of any numeric type but, uniquely, + is also permitted where either operand is a String object.

How the + Operator Is Overloaded

Java does not allow the programmer to perform operator overloading, but the + operator is overloaded by the language. This is not surprising, because in most languages that support multiple arithmetic types, the arithmetic operators (+, -, *, /, and so forth) are overloaded to handle these different types. Java, however, further overloads the + operator to support *concatenation*—that is, joining together—of String objects. The use of + with String arguments also performs conversions, and these can be succinct and expressive if you understand them. First, we will consider the use of the + operator in its conventional role of numeric addition.

> **NOTE** *Overloading* is the term given when the same name is used for more than one piece of code, and the code that is to be used is selected by the argument or operand types provided. For example, the println() method can be given a String argument or an int. These two uses actually refer to entirely different methods; only the name is reused. Similarly, the + symbol is used to indicate addition of int values, but the exact same symbol is also used to indicate the addition of float values. These two forms of addition require entirely different code to execute; again, the operand types are used to decide which code is to be run. Where an operator can take different operand types, we refer to *operator overloading*. Some languages, but not Java, allow you to use operator overloading to define multiple uses of operators for your own types. Overloading is described in detail in Chapter 6, "Objects and Classes."

Where the + operator is applied to purely numeric operands, its meaning is simple and familiar. The operands are added together to produce a result. Of course, some promotions might take place, according to the normal rules, and the result might overflow. Generally, however, numeric addition behaves as you would expect. Promotions are discussed in a later section, "Arithmetic Promotion of Operands."

If overflow or underflow occurs during numeric addition or subtraction, then data is lost but no exception occurs. A more detailed description of behavior in arithmetic error conditions appears in a later section, "Arithmetic Error Conditions." Most of the new understanding to be gained about the + operator relates to its role in concatenating text.

Where either of the operands of a + expression is a String object, the meaning of the operator is changed from numeric addition to string concatenation. In order to achieve this result, both operands must be handled as text. If both operands are in fact String objects, this is simple. If, however, one of the operands is not a String object, then the non-String operand is converted to a String object before the concatenation takes place.

How Operands Are Converted to String Objects

Although a review of the certification objectives will show that the Certification Exam does not require it, it is useful in practice to know a little about how + converts operands to String objects. For object types, conversion to a String object is performed simply by invoking the toString() method of that object. The toString() method is defined in java.lang.Object, which is the root of the class hierarchy, and therefore all objects have a toString() method.

Sometimes, the effect of the `toString()` method is to produce rather cryptic text that is suitable only for debugging output, but it definitely exists and may legally be called.

Conversion of an operand of primitive type to a `String` is typically achieved by using, indirectly, the conversion utility methods in the wrapper classes. So, for example, an `int` value is converted by the static method `Integer.toString()`.

The `toString()` method in the `java.lang.Object` class produces a `String` that contains the name of the object's class and some identifying value—typically its reference value, separated by the at symbol (@). For example, this `String` might look like `java.lang.Object@1cc6dd`. This behavior is inherited by subclasses unless they deliberately override it.

> **TIP** It is a good idea to define a helpful `toString()` method in all your classes, even if you do not require it as part of the class behavior. Code the `toString()` method so that it represents the state of the object in a fashion that can assist in debugging; for example, output the names and values of the main instance variables.

To prepare for the Certification Exam questions, and to use the + operator effectively in your own programs, you should understand the following points:

- For a + expression with two operands of primitive numeric type, the result
  - Is of a primitive numeric type.
  - Is at least `int`, because of normal promotions.
  - Is of a type at least as wide as the wider of the two operands.
  - Has a value calculated by promoting the operands to the result type, and then performing the addition using that type. This might result in overflow or loss of precision.
- For a + expression with any operand that is not of primitive numeric type,
  - At least one operand must be a `String` object or literal; otherwise, the expression is illegal.
  - Any remaining non-`String` operands are converted to `String`, and the result of the expression is the concatenation of all operands.
- To convert an operand of some object type to a `String`, the conversion is performed by invoking the `toString()` method of that object.
- To convert an operand of a primitive type to a `String`, the conversion is performed by a static method in a container class, such as `Integer.toString()`.

> **NOTE** If you want to control the formatting of the converted result, you should use the facilities in the `java.text` package.

Now that you understand arithmetic operators and the concatenation of text using the + operator, you should realize that sometimes arithmetic does not work as intended—it could result in an error of some kind. The next section discusses what happens under such error conditions.

Arithmetic Error Conditions

We expect arithmetic to produce "sensible" results that reflect the mathematical meaning of the expression being evaluated. However, because the computation is performed on a machine with specific limits on its ability to represent numbers, calculations can sometimes result in errors. You saw, in the section on the multiplication and division operators, that overflow and underflow can occur if the operands are too large or too small. In exceptional conditions, the following rules apply:

- Integer division by zero, including modulo (%) operation, results in an `ArithmeticException`.
- No other arithmetic causes any exception. Instead, the operation proceeds to a result, even though that result might be arithmetically incorrect.
- Floating-point calculations represent out-of-range values using the IEEE 754 infinity, minus infinity, and Not a Number (NaN) values. Named constants representing these are declared in both the `Float` and `Double` classes.
- Integer calculations, other than division by zero, that cause overflow or a similar error simply leave the final, typically truncated bit pattern in the result. This bit pattern is derived from the operation and the number representation and might even be of the wrong sign. Because the operations and number representations do not depend upon the platform, neither do the result values under error conditions.

These rules describe the effect of error conditions, but some additional significance is associated with the NaN values. NaN values are used to indicate that a calculation has no result in ordinary arithmetic, such as some calculations involving infinity or the square root of a negative number.

Comparisons with Not a Number

Some floating-point calculations can return a NaN. This occurs, for example, as a result of calculating the square root of a negative number. Two NaN values are defined in the `java.lang` package (`Float.NaN` and `Double.NaN`) and are considered non-ordinal for comparisons. This means that for *any* value of x, including NaN itself, all of the following comparisons will return false:

```
x < Float.NaN
x <= Float.NaN
x == Float.NaN
x > Float.NaN
x >= Float.NaN
```

In fact, the test

```
Float.NaN != Float.NaN
```

and the equivalent with `Double.NaN` return true, as you might deduce from the item indicating that x == `Float.NaN` gives false even if x contains `Float.NaN`.

The most appropriate way to test for a NaN result from a calculation is to use the Float.isNaN(float) or Double.isNaN(double) static method provided in the java.lang package.

The next section discusses a concept often used for manipulating bit patterns read from I/O ports: the shift operators <<, >>, and >>>.

The Shift Operators: <<, >>, and >>>

Java provides three *shift operators*. Two of these, << and >>, are taken directly from C/C++, but the third, >>>, is new in Java.

Shifting is common in control systems, where it can align bits that are read from or that are to be written to I/O ports. It can also provide efficient integer multiplication or division by powers of two. In Java, because the bit-level representation of all types is well defined and platform independent, you can use shifting with confidence.

Fundamentals of Shifting

Shifting is, on the face of it, a simple operation: it involves taking the binary representation of a number and moving the bit pattern left or right. However, the unsigned right-shift operator >>> is a common source of confusion.

The shift operators may be applied to arguments of integral types only. In fact, they should generally be applied only to operands of either int or long type. This is a consequence of the effects of promotion in expressions (see "Arithmetic Promotion of Operands" later in this chapter). Figure 2.2 illustrates the basic mechanism of shifting.

FIGURE 2.2 The basic mechanisms of shifting

Original data	192
in binary	00000000 00000000 00000000 11000000
Shifted left 1 bit	0 00000000 00000000 00000001 1000000?
Shifted right 1 bit	?0000000 00000000 00000000 01100000 0
Shifted left 4 bits	0000 00000000 00000000 00001100 0000????

Original data	−192
in binary	11111111 11111111 11111111 01000000
Shifted left 1 bit	1 11111111 11111111 11111110 1000000?
Shifted right 1 bit	?1111111 11111111 11111111 10100000 0

The diagram in Figure 2.2 shows the fundamental idea of shifting, which involves moving the bits that represent a number to positions either to the left or right of their starting points. This raises two questions:

- What happens to the bits that "fall off" the end? The type of the result will have the same number of bits as the original value, but the result of a shift looks as if it might have more bits than that original.
- What defines the value of the bits that are shifted in? These bits are marked by question marks in Figure 2.2.

The first question has a simple answer. Bits that move off the end of a representation are discarded.

> **Note:** In some languages, mostly assembly languages, an additional operation called *rotate* uses these bits to define the value of the bits at the other end of the result. Java, like most high-level languages, does not provide a rotate operation.

Shifting Negative Numbers

The second question, regarding the value of the bits that are shifted in, requires more attention. In the case of the left-shift << and the unsigned right-shift >>> operators, the new bits are set to 0. However, in the case of the signed right-shift >> operator, the new bits take the value of the most significant bit before the shift. Figure 2.3 shows this. Notice that where a 1 bit is in the most significant position before the shift (indicating a negative number), 1 bits are introduced to fill the spaces introduced by shifting. Conversely, when a 0 bit is in the most significant position before the shift, 0 bits are introduced during the shift.

FIGURE 2.3 Signed right shift of positive and negative numbers

Original data	192
in binary	00000000 00000000 00000000 11000000
Shifted right 1 bit	00000000 00000000 00000000 01100000
Shifted right 7 bits	00000000 00000000 00000000 00000001
Original data	−192
in binary	11111111 11111111 11111111 01000000
Shifted right 1 bit	11111111 11111111 11111111 10100000
Shifted right 7 bits	11111111 11111111 11111111 11111110

This might seem like an arbitrary and unduly complex rule governing the bits that are shifted in during a signed right-shift operation, but there is a good reason for the rule. If a binary number is shifted left one position (and provided none of the bits that move off the ends of a left-shift operation are lost), the effect of the shift is to double the original number. Shifts by more than one bit effectively double and double again, so the result is as if the number had been multiplied by 2, 4, 8, 16, and so on.

Real World Scenario

A Closer Look at Shifting

Write an application that illustrates the functionality of Java's shift operators: <<, >>, and >>>. The application should take two command-line int arguments, x and y, and should output the results of the following shifts:

x << y

x >> y

x >>> y

The values of x and the shift result should be displayed in both decimal and 32-bit binary. Sample output from the solution looks like this:

```
>java ShowShift -64 5

-64 << 5 = -2048
11111111111111111111111111000000 << 5 =
11111111111111111111100000000000

-64 >> 5 = -2
11111111111111111111111111000000 >> 5 =
11111111111111111111111111111110

-64 >>> 5 = 134217726
11111111111111111111111111000000 >>> 5 =
00000111111111111111111111111110
```

A static method called toBinaryString() in the Integer wrapper class outputs a binary string. Unfortunately, it truncates leading 0s, so it doesn't always give a 32-bit result. Try creating your own integer-to-binary-string method, using a shift operator. Play with the command-line input values x and y. Can you find values such that x is positive and x >>> y is negative? Can you find values such that x is negative and x >>> y is positive?

If shifting the bit pattern of a number left by one position doubles that number, then you might reasonably expect that shifting the pattern right, which apparently puts the bits back where they came from, would halve the number, returning it to its original value. If the right shift results in 0 bits being added at the most significant bit positions, then for positive numbers, this division does result. However, if the original number was negative, then the assumption is false.

Notice that with the negative number in two's-complement representation, the most significant bit is 1. In order to preserve the significance of a right shift as a division by two when dealing with negative numbers, you must bring in bits set to 1, rather than 0. This is how the behavior of the arithmetic right shift is determined. If a number is positive, its most significant bit is 0 and when shifting right, more 0 bits are brought in. However, if the number is negative, its most significant bit is 1, and more 1 bits must be propagated in when the shift occurs. This is illustrated in the examples in Figure 2.4.

FIGURE 2.4 Shifting positive and negative numbers right

		192		
Original data in binary	00000000	00000000	00000000	11000000
Shifted right 1 bit = 96 = 192 / 2	00000000	00000000	00000000	01100000
Shifted right 4 bits = 12 = 192 / 16 = 192 / 2^4	00000000	00000000	00000000	00001100

		−192		
Original data in binary	11111111	11111111	11111111	01000000
Shifted right 1 bit = −96 = −192 / 2	11111111	11111111	11111111	10100000
Shifted right 4 bits = −12 = −192 / 16 = −192 / 2^4	11111111	11111111	11111111	11110100

The Shift Operators: <<, >>, and >>>

> **NOTE** There is a feature of the arithmetic right shift that differs from simple division by 2. If you divide -1 by 2, the result will be 0. However, the result of the arithmetic shift right of -1 right is -1. You can think of this as the shift operation rounding down, whereas the division rounds toward 0.

You now have two right-shift operators: one that treats the left integer argument as a bit pattern with no special arithmetic significance and another that attempts to ensure that the arithmetic equivalence of shifting right with division by powers of two is maintained.

> **NOTE** Why does Java need a special operator for unsigned shift right, when neither C nor C++ required it? The answer is simple: both C and C++ provide for unsigned numeric types, but Java does not. If you shift an unsigned value right in either C or C++, you get the behavior associated with the >>> operator in Java. However, this does not work in Java simply because the numeric types (other than char) are signed.

Reduction of the Right Operand

The right argument of the shift operators is taken to be the number of bits by which the shift should move. However, for shifting to behave properly, this value should be smaller than the number of bits in the result. That is, if the shift is being done as an int type, then the right operand should be less than 32. If the shift is being done as long, then the right operand should be less than 64.

In fact, the shift operators do not reject values that exceed these limits. Instead, they calculate a new value by reducing the supplied value modulo the number of bits. This means that if you attempt to shift an int value by 33 bits, you will actually shift by 33 % 32—that is, by only one bit. This shift produces an anomalous result. You would expect that shifting a 32-bit number by 33 bits would produce 0 as a result (or possibly -1 in the signed right-shift case). However, because of the reduction of the right operand, this is not the case.

> **Why Java Reduces the Right Operand of Shift Operators, or "The Sad Story of the Sleepy Processor"**
>
> The first reason for reducing the number of bits to shift modulo the number of bits in the left operand is that many CPUs implement the shift operations in this way. Why should CPUs do this?
>
> Some years ago, a powerful and imaginatively designed CPU provided both shift and rotate operations and could shift by any number of bits specified by any of its registers. Because the registers were wide, this was a very large number, and as each bit position shifted took a finite time to complete, the effect was that you could code an instruction that would take minutes to complete.
>
> One of the intended target applications of this particular CPU was in control systems, and one of the most important features of real-time control systems is the worst-case time to respond to an external event, known as the *interrupt latency*. Unfortunately, because a single instruction on this CPU was indivisible—so that interrupts could not be serviced until it was complete—execution of a large shift instruction effectively crippled the CPU. The next version of that CPU changed the implementations of shift and rotate so that the number of bits by which to shift or rotate was treated as being limited to the size of the target data item. This change restored a sensible interrupt latency. Since then, many other CPUs have adopted reduction of the right operand.

Arithmetic Promotion of Operands

Arithmetic promotion of operands takes place before any binary operator is applied so that all numeric operands are at least `int` type. This promotion has an important consequence for the unsigned right-shift operator when applied to values that are narrower than `int`.

The diagram in Figure 2.5 shows the process by which a `byte` is shifted right. First the byte is promoted to an `int`, which is done treating the `byte` as a signed quantity. Next, the shift occurs, and 0 bits are indeed propagated into the top bits of the result—but these bits are not part of the original `byte`. When the result is cast down to a `byte` again, the high-order bits of that `byte` appear to have been created by a signed shift right, rather than an unsigned one. This is why you should generally not use the logical right-shift operator with operands smaller than an `int`: It is unlikely to produce the result you expected.

FIGURE 2.5 Unsigned right shift of a byte

Calculation for –64 >>> 4.

Original data (–64 decimal)				11000000
Promote to int gives:	11111111	11111111	11111111	11000000
Shift right unsigned 4 bits gives:	00001111	11111111	11111111	11111100
Truncate to byte gives:				11111100
Expected result was:				00001100

The Comparison Operators

Comparison operators—<, <=, >, >=, ==, and !=—return a `boolean` result; the relation as written is either true or it is false. Additionally, the `instanceof` operator determines whether or not a given object is an instance of a particular class. These operators are commonly used to form conditions, such as in `if()` statements or in loop control. There are three types of comparison: *ordinal* comparisons test the relative value of numeric operands. *Object-type comparisons* determine whether the runtime type of an object is of a particular type or a subclass of that particular type. *Equality comparisons* test whether two values are the same and may be applied to values of non-numeric types.

Ordinal Comparisons with <, <=, >, and >=

The ordinal comparison operators are
- Less than: <
- Less than or equal to: <=
- Greater than: >
- Greater than or equal to: >=

These are applicable to all numeric types and to char and produce a boolean result.

So, for example, given the following declarations,

```
int p = 9;
int q = 65;
int r = -12;
float f = 9.0F;
char c = 'A';
```

the following tests all return true:

```
p < q
f < q
f <= c
c > r
c >= q
```

Notice that arithmetic promotions are applied when these operators are used. This is entirely according to the normal rules discussed in Chapter 4. For example, although it would be an error to attempt to assign, say, the float value 9.0F to the char variable c, it is perfectly acceptable to compare the two. To achieve the result, Java promotes the smaller type to the larger type; hence the char value 'A' (represented by the Unicode value 65) is promoted to a float 65.0F. The comparison is then performed on the resulting float values.

Although the ordinal comparisons operate satisfactorily on dissimilar numeric types, including char, they are not applicable to any non-numeric types. They cannot take boolean or any class-type operands.

The *instanceof* Operator

The instanceof operator tests the class of an object at runtime. The left argument can be any object reference expression, usually a variable or an array element, whereas the right operand must be a class, interface, or array type. You cannot use a java.lang.Class object reference or a String representing the name of the class as the right operand. A compiler error results if the left operand cannot be cast to the right operand. (Casting is discussed in Chapter 4.)

This code fragment shows an example of how instanceof may be used. Assume that a class hierarchy exists with Person as a base class and Parent as a subclass:

```
1. public class Classroom {
2.    private Hashtable inTheRoom = new Hashtable();
3.    public void enterRoom(Person p) {
```

```
4.       inTheRoom.put(p.getName(), p);
5.     }
6.     public Person getParent(String name) {
7.       Object p = inTheRoom.get(name);
8.       if (p instanceof Parent) {
9.         return (Parent)p;
10.      }
11.      else {
12.        return null;
13.      }
14.    }
15. }
```

The method getParent() at lines 6–14 checks to see if the Hashtable contains a parent with the specified name. This is done by first searching the Hashtable for an entry with the given name and then testing to see if the entry that is returned is actually a Parent. The instanceof operator returns true if the class of the left argument is the same as, or is some subclass of, the class specified by the right operand.

The right operand may equally well be an interface. In such a case, the test determines if the object at the left argument implements the specified interface.

You can also use the instanceof operator to test whether a reference refers to an array. Because arrays are themselves objects in Java, this is natural enough, but the test that is performed actually checks two things: First, it checks if the object is an array, and then it checks if the element type of that array is some subclass of the element type of the right argument. This is a logical extension of the behavior that is shown for simple types and reflects the idea that an array of, say, Button objects is an array of Component objects, because a Button is a Component. A test for an array type looks like this:

```
if (x instanceof Component[])
```

Note, however, that you cannot simply test for "any array of any element type," as the syntax. This line is not legal:

```
if (x instanceof [])
```

Neither is it sufficient to test for arrays of Object element type like this:

```
if (x instanceof Object [])
```

because the array might be of a primitive base type, in which case the test will fail.

> Although it is not required by the Certification Exam, you might find it useful to know that you can determine if an object is in fact an array without regard to the base type. You can do this using the `isArray()` method of the `Class` class. For example, this test returns true if the variable myObject refers to an array: `myObject.getClass().isArray()`.

If the left argument of the `instanceof` operator is a `null` value, the `instanceof` test simply returns false; it does not cause an exception.

The Equality Comparison Operators: == and !=

The operators `==` and `!=` test for equality and inequality, respectively, returning a `boolean` value. For primitive types, the concept of equality is quite straightforward and is subject to promotion rules so that, for example, a `float` value of 10.0 is considered equal to a `byte` value of 10. For variables of object type, the "value" is taken as the reference to the object—typically, the memory address. You should not use these operators to compare the contents of objects, such as strings, because they will return true if two references refer to the same object, rather than if the two objects have equivalent value. *Object comparisons* compare the data of two objects, whereas *reference comparisons* compare the memory locations of two objects.

To achieve a content or semantic comparison, for example, so that two different `Double` objects containing the value 1234 are considered equal, you must use the `equals()` method rather than the `==` or `!=` operator.

To operate appropriately, the `equals()` method must have been defined for the class of the objects you are comparing. To determine whether it has, check the documentation supplied with the JDK or, for third-party classes, produced by javadoc. The documentation should report that an `equals()` method is defined for the class and overrides `equals()` in some superclass. If this is not indicated, then you should assume that the `equals()` method will not produce a useful content comparison. You also need to know that `equals()` is defined as accepting an `Object` argument, but the actual argument must be of the same type as the object upon which the method is invoked—that is, for `x.equals(y)`, the test `y instanceof the-type-of-x` must be true. If this is not the case, then `equals()` must return false.

Defining an *equals()* Method

The information in this warning is not required for the Certification Exam but is generally of value when writing real programs. If you define an `equals()` method in your own classes, you should be careful to observe three rules, or else your classes might behave incorrectly in some specific circumstances.

First, the argument to the `equals()` method is an `Object`; you must avoid the temptation to make the argument to `equals()` specific to the class you are defining. If you do this, you have overloaded the `equals()` method, not overridden it, and functionality in other parts of the Java APIs that depends on the `equals()` method will fail. Perhaps most significantly, lookup methods in containers, such as `containsKey()` and `get()` in the `HashMap`, will fail.

The second rule is that the `equals()` method should be commutative: the result of `x.equals(y)` should always be the same as the result of `y.equals(x)`.

The final rule is that if you define an `equals()` method, you should also define a `hashCode()` method. This method should return the same value for objects that compare equal using the `equals()` method. Again, this behavior is needed to support the containers and other classes. A minimal but acceptable behavior for the `hashCode()` method is simply to return 1. Doing so removes any efficiency gains that hashing would give, forcing a `HashMap` to behave like a linked list when storing such objects, but at least the behavior is correct.

The Bitwise Operators: &, ^, and |

The *bitwise operators* &, ^, and | provide bitwise AND, eXclusive-OR (XOR), and OR operations, respectively. They are applicable to integral types. Collections of bits are sometimes used to save storage space where several `boolean` values are needed or to represent the states of a collection of binary inputs from physical devices.

The bitwise operations calculate each bit of their results by comparing the corresponding bits of the two operands on the basis of these three rules:

- For AND operations, 1 AND 1 produces 1. Any other combination produces 0.
- For XOR operations, 1 XOR 0 produces 1, as does 0 XOR 1. (All these operations are commutative.) Any other combination produces 0.
- For OR operations, 0 OR 0 produces 0. Any other combination produces 1.

The names AND, XOR, and OR are intended to be mnemonic for these operations. You get a 1 result from an AND operation if both the first operand *and* the second operand are 1. An XOR gives a 1 result if one *or* the other operand, but not both (this is the *exclusiveness*), is 1. In the OR operation, you get a 1 result if either the first operand *or* the second operand (*or* both) is 1. These rules are represented in Tables 2.3 through 2.5.

TABLE 2.3 The AND Operation

Op1	Op2	Op1 AND Op2
0	0	0
0	1	0
1	0	0
1	1	1

TABLE 2.4 The XOR Operation

Op1	Op2	Op1 XOR Op2
0	0	0
0	1	1
1	0	1
1	1	0

TABLE 2.5 The OR Operation

Op1	Op2	Op1 OR Op2
0	0	0
0	1	1
1	0	1
1	1	1

Compare the rows of each table with the corresponding rule for the operations listed in the previous bullets. You will see that for the AND operation, the only situation that leads to a 1 bit as the result is when both operands are 1 bits. For XOR, a 1 bit results when one or the other (but not both) of the operands is a 1 bit. Finally, for the OR operation, the result is a 1 bit, except when both operands are 0 bits. Now let's see how this concept works when applied to whole binary numbers, rather than just single bits. The approach can be applied to any size of integer, but we will look at bytes because they serve to illustrate the idea without putting so many digits on the page as to cause confusion. Consider this example:

```
          00110011
          11110000
   AND    --------
          00110000
```

Observe that each bit in the result is calculated solely on the basis of the two bits appearing directly above it in the calculation. The next calculation looks at the least significant bit:

```
          00110011
          11110000
   AND    --------
          00110000
```

This result bit is calculated as 1 and 0, which gives 0.

For the fourth bit from the left, see the following calculation:

```
          00110011
          11110000
   AND    --------
          00110000
```

This result bit is calculated as 1 AND 1, which gives 1. All the other bits in the result are calculated in the same fashion, using the two corresponding bits and the rules stated earlier.

Exclusive-OR operations are done by a comparable approach, using the appropriate rules for calculating the individual bits, as the following calculations show:

```
          00110011                    00110011
          11110000                    11110000
   XOR    --------           XOR      --------
          11000011                    11000011
```

All the highlighted bits are calculated as either 1 XOR 0 or as 0 XOR 1, producing 1 in either case.

```
          00110011
          11110000
   XOR    --------
          11000011
```

In the previous calculation, the result bit is 0 because both operand bits were 1.

```
        00110011
        11110000
   XOR  --------
        11000011
```

And here, the 0 operand bits also result in a 0 result bit.

The OR operation again takes a similar approach, but with its own rules for calculating the result bits. Consider this example:

```
        00110011
        11110000
    OR  --------
        11110011
```

Here, the two operand bits are 1 and 0, so the result is 1.

```
        00110011
        11110000
    OR  --------
        11110011
```

However, in this calculation, both operand bits are 0, which is the condition that produces a 0 result bit for the OR operation.

Although programmers usually apply these operators to the bits in integer variables, it is also permitted to apply them to `boolean` operands.

Boolean Operations

The &, ^, and | operators behave in fundamentally the same way when applied to arguments of `boolean`, rather than integral, types. However, instead of calculating the result on a bit-by-bit basis, the `boolean` values are treated as single bits, with true corresponding to a 1 bit and false to a 0 bit. The general rules discussed in the previous section may be modified like this when applied to `boolean` values:

- For AND operations, true AND true produces true. Any other combination produces false.
- For XOR operations, true XOR false produces true, and false XOR true produces true. Other combinations produce false.
- For OR operations, false OR false produces false. Any other combination produces true.

These rules are represented in Tables 2.6 through 2.8.

TABLE 2.6 The AND Operation on *boolean* Values

Op1	Op2	Op1 AND Op2
false	false	false
false	true	false
true	false	false
true	true	true

TABLE 2.7 The XOR Operation on *boolean* Values

Op1	Op2	Op1 XOR Op2
false	false	false
false	true	true
true	false	true
true	true	false

TABLE 2.8 The OR Operation on *boolean* Values

Op1	Op2	Op1 OR Op2
false	false	false
false	true	true
true	false	true
true	true	true

Again, compare these tables with the rules stated in the bulleted list. Also compare them with Tables 2.3 through 2.5, which describe the same operations on bits. You will see that 1 bits are replaced by true, and 0 bits are replaced by false.

> **NOTE** As with all operations, the two operands must be of compatible types. So, if either operand is of boolean type, both must be. Java does not permit you to cast any type to boolean; instead you must use comparisons or methods that return boolean values.

The next section covers the short-circuit logical operators. These operators perform logical AND and OR operations, but are slightly different in implementation from the operators just discussed.

The Short-Circuit Logical Operators

The short-circuit logical operators && and || provide logical AND and OR operations on boolean types. Note that no XOR operation is provided. Superficially, these operators are similar to the & and | operators, with the limitation of being applicable only to boolean values and not integral types. However, the && and || operations have a valuable additional feature: the ability to "short circuit" a calculation if the result is definitely known. This feature makes these operators central to a popular null-reference-handling idiom in Java programming. They can also improve efficiency.

The main difference between the & and && and between the | and || operators is that the right operand might not be evaluated in the latter cases. We will look at how this happens in the rest of this section. This behavior is based on two mathematical rules that define conditions under which the result of a boolean AND or OR operation is entirely determined by one operand without regard for the value of the other:

- For an AND operation, if one operand is false, the result is false, without regard to the other operand.
- For an OR operation, if one operand is true, the result is true, without regard to the other operand.

To put it another way, for any boolean value X:

- false AND X = false
- true OR X = true

Given these rules, if the left operand of a boolean AND operation is false, then the result is definitely false, whatever the right operand. It is therefore unnecessary to evaluate the right operand. Similarly, if the left operand of a boolean OR operation is true, the result is definitely true and the right operand need not be evaluated.

The Short-Circuit Logical Operators

Consider a fragment of code intended to print out a String if that String exists and is longer than 20 characters:

```
1. if (s != null) {
2.    if (s.length() > 20) {
3.       System.out.println(s);
4.    }
5. }
```

However, the same operation can be coded very succinctly like this:

```
1. if ((s != null) && (s.length() > 20)) {
2.    System.out.println(s);
3. }
```

If the String reference s is null, then calling the s.length() method would raise a NullPointerException. In both of these examples, however, the situation never arises. In the second example, avoiding execution of the s.length() method is a direct consequence of the short-circuit behavior of the && operator. If the test (s != null) returns false (if s is in fact null), then the whole test expression is guaranteed to be false. Where the first operand is false, the && operator does not evaluate the second operand; so, in this case, the expression (s.length() > 20) is not evaluated.

Although these shortcuts do not affect the result of the operation, side effects might well be changed. If the evaluation of the right operand involves a side effect, then omitting the evaluation will change the overall meaning of the expression in some way. This behavior distinguishes these operators from the bitwise operators applied to boolean types. Consider these fragments:

```
//first example:
1. int val = (int)(2 * Math.random());
2. boolean test = (val == 0) || (++val == 2);
3. System.out.println("test = " + test + "\nval = " + val);
//second example:
1. int val = (int)(2 * Math.random());
2. boolean test = (val == 0) | (++val == 2);
3. System.out.println("test = " + test + "\nval = " + val);
```

The first example will sometimes print:

test = true
val = 0

and sometimes it will print:

test = true
val = 2

The second example will sometimes print:

```
test = true
val = 1
```

and sometimes it will print:

```
test = true
val = 2
```

The point is that in the case of the short circuit operator, if `val` starts out at 0, then the second part of the expression (++val) is never executed, and `val` remains at 0. Alternatively, `val` starts at 1 and is incremented to 2. In the second case, the non-short-circuit version, the increment always occurs, and `val` ends up as either 1 or 2, depending on the original value returned by the `random()` method. In all cases, the value of `test` is true, because either `val` starts out at 0, or it starts at 1 and the test (++val == 2) is true.

So, the essential points about the && and || operators are as follows:

- They accept `boolean` operands.
- They evaluate the right operand only if the outcome is not certain based solely on the left operand. This is determined using these identities:
  - false AND X = false
  - true OR X = true

The next section discusses the ternary, or conditional, operator. Like the short-circuit logical operators, this operator may be less familiar than others, especially to programmers without a background in C or C++.

The Conditional Operator: ?:

The *conditional operator* ?: (also known as a *ternary operator*, because it takes three operands) provides a way to code simple conditions (`if`/`else`) into a single expression. The (`boolean`) expression to the left of the ? is evaluated. If true, the result of the whole expression is the value of the expression to the left of the colon; otherwise it is the value of the expression to the right of the colon. The expressions on either side of the colon must be assignment-compatible with the result type.

For example, if a, b, and c are `int` variables, and x is a `boolean`, then the statement a = x ? b : c; is directly equivalent to the textually longer version:

```
1. if (x) {
2.     a = b;
3. }
```

```
4. else {
5.     a = c;
6. }
```

Of course x, a, b, and c can all be complex expressions if you desire.

> **TIP** Many people do not like the conditional operator, and in some companies its use is prohibited by the local style guide. This operator does keep source code more concise, but in many cases an optimizing compiler will generate equally compact and efficient code from the longer, and arguably more readable, `if/else` approach. One particularly effective way to abuse the conditional operator is to nest it, producing expressions of the form `a = b ? c ? d : e ? f : g : h ? i : j ? k : l;`. Whatever your feelings or corporate mandate, you should at least be able to read this operator, because you will find it used by other programmers.

Here are the points you should review for handling conditional operators in an exam question, or to use them properly in a program. In an expression of the form `a = x ? b : c;`:

- The types of the expressions b and c should be compatible and are made identical through conversion.
- The type of the expression x should be `boolean`.
- The types of the expressions b and c should be assignment-compatible with the type of a.
- The value assigned to a will be b if x is true or will be c if x is false.

Now that we have discussed the conditional (ternary) operator, only one group of operators remains: the assignment operators.

The Assignment Operators

Assignment operators set the value of a variable or expression to a new value. Assignments are supported by a battery of operators. Simple assignment uses =. Operators such as += and *= provide compound "calculate and assign" functions. These compound operators take a general form *op=*, where *op* can be any of the binary non-boolean operators already discussed. In general, for any compatible expressions x and y, the expression x *op=* y is a shorthand for x = x *op* y. However, there are two differences you must know. First, be aware that side effects in the expression x are evaluated exactly once, not twice, as the expanded view might suggest. The second issue is that the assignment operators include an implicit cast. Consider this situation:

```
1. byte x = 2;
2. x += 3;
```

If this had been written using the longhand approach

1. `byte x = 2;`
2. `x = (byte)(x + 3);`

the cast to `byte` would have been necessary because the result of an integer addition is at least an `int`. In the first case, using the assignment operator, this cast is implied. This is one of two situations where Java allows down-casting without explicit programmer intervention. (The other situation is in combined declaration and initialization.) Be sure to compare this with the general principles of assignment and casting laid out in Chapter 4.

> **TIP** The statement `x += 2;` involves typing two fewer characters, but is otherwise no more effective than the longer version `x = x + 2;` and is neither more nor less readable. However, if x is a complex expression, such as `target[temp.calculateOffset(1.9F) + depth++].item`, it is definitely more readable to express incrementing this value by 2 using the `+= 2` form. This is because these operators define that the exact same thing will be read on the right side as is written on the left side. So the maintainer does not have to struggle to decide whether the two complex expressions are actually the same, and the original programmer avoids some of the risk of mistyping a copy of the expression.

An Assignment Has Value

All the operators discussed up to this point have produced a value as a result of the operation. The expression 1 + 2, for example, results in a value 3, which can then be used in some further way—perhaps assignment to a variable. The assignment operators in Java are considered to be operators because they have a resulting value. So, given three `int` variables a, b, and c, the statement `a = b = c = 0;` is entirely legal. It is executed from right to left, so that first 0 is assigned into the variable c. After it has been executed, the expression `c = 0` takes the value that was assigned to the left side—that is, 0. Next, the assignment of b takes place, using the value of the expression to the right of the equals sign—again, 0. Similarly, that expression takes the value that was assigned, so finally the variable a is also set to 0.

Although *execution order* is determined by precedence and associativity, *evaluation order* of the arguments is not. Be sure you understand the points made in the section "Evaluation Order" at the start of this chapter.

> **TIP** As a general rule, avoid writing expressions that are complex enough for these issues to matter. A sequence of simply constructed expressions is easier to read and is less likely to cause confusion or other errors than complex ones. You are also likely to find that the compiler will optimize multiple simple expressions just as well as it would a single, very complex one.

Summary

We have covered a lot of material in this chapter, so let's recap some of the key points.

The unary operators were the first topics we covered. Recall that they take only a single operand. The seven unary operators are ++, --, +, -, !, ~, and (). Their key points are as follows:

- The ++ and -- operators increment and decrement expressions. The position of the operator (either prefix or suffix) is significant.
- The + operator has no effect on an expression other than to make it clear that a literal constant is positive. The - operator negates an expression's value.
- The ! operator inverts the value of a boolean expression.
- The ~ operator inverts the bit pattern of an integral expression.
- The (type) operator is used to persuade the compiler to permit certain assignments that the programmer believes are appropriate, but that break the normal, rigorous rules of the language. Its use is subject to extensive checks at compile time and runtime.

Next we covered arithmetic operators. We discussed in detail the four most familiar operators, which perform addition, subtraction, multiplication, and division. Recall that this group is further split into two subgroupings. There are five arithmetic operators:

- Multiplication: *
- Division: /
- Modulo: %
- Addition and String concatenation: +
- Subtraction: -

The arithmetic operators can be applied to any numeric type. Also, the + operator performs text concatenation if either of its operands is a String object. Under the conditions where one operand in a + expression is a String object, the other is forced to be a String object, too. Conversions are performed as necessary. They might result in cryptic text, but they are definitely legal.

Under conditions of arithmetic overflow or similar errors, accuracy is generally lost silently. Only integer division by zero can throw an exception. Floating-point calculations can produce NaN—indicating Not a Number (that is, the expression has no meaning in normal arithmetic)—or an infinity as their result under error conditions.

Java provides three shift operators. Two of them are derived directly from the C/C++ language, and a new one was added to Java.

These are the key points about the shift operators:

- The <<, >>, and >>> operators perform bit shifts of the binary representation of the left operand.
- The operands should be an integral type, generally either int or long.

- The right operand is reduced modulo x, where x depends on the type of the result of the operation. That type is either int or long, smaller operands being subjected to promotion. If the left operand is assignment-compatible with int, then x is 32. If the left operand is a long, then x is 64.
- The << operator shifts left. Zero bits are introduced at the least significant bit position.
- The >> operator performs a signed, or arithmetic, right shift. The result has 0 bits at the most significant positions if the original left operand was positive, and 1 bit at the most significant positions if the original left operand was negative. The result approximates dividing the left operand by two raised to the power of the right operand.
- The >>> operator performs an unsigned, or logical, right shift. The result has 0 bits at the most significant positions and might not represent a division of the original left operand.

We also discussed bitwise operators, which are sometimes used to save storage space, for instance. There are three bitwise operators: &, ^, and |. They are usually named AND, eXclusive-OR (XOR), and OR, respectively. For these operators, the following points apply:

- In bitwise operations, each result bit is calculated on the basis of the two bits from the same, corresponding position in the operands.
- For the AND operation, a 1 bit results if the first operand bit and the second operand bit are both 1.
- For the XOR operation, a 1 bit results only if exactly one operand bit is 1.
- For the OR operation, a 1 bit results if either the first operand bit or the second operand bit is 1.

For boolean operations, the arguments and results are treated as single-bit values with true represented by 1 and false by 0.

We described assignment operators, which set the value of a variable or expression to a new value. The key points about the assignment operators are as follows:

- Simple assignment, using =, assigns the value of the right operand to the left operand.
- The value of an object is its reference, not its contents.
- The right operand must be a type that is assignment-compatible with the left operand. Assignment compatibility and conversions are discussed in detail in Chapter 4.
- The assignment operators all return a value so that they can be used within larger expressions. The value returned is the value that was assigned to the left operand.
- The compound assignment operators, of the form *op*=, when applied in an expression like a *op*= b;, appear to behave like a = a *op* b;, except that the expression a and any of its side effects are evaluated only once.

Compound assignment operators exist for all binary, non-boolean operators: *=, /=, %=, +=, -=, <<=, >>=, >>>=, &=, ^=, and |=. We have now discussed all the operators provided by Java.

The ternary operator ?: (also referred to as the conditional operator) requires three operands and provides the programmer with a more compact way to write an if/else statement.

The short circuit Boolean operators && and || are binary operators that allow the programmer to circumvent evaluating one or more expressions, thereby making the code more efficient at runtime.

The remainder of the operators discussed in this chapter are the comparison operators <, <=, >, >=, and instanceof. These binary operators compare the left operand with the right operand and return a Boolean result of either true or false.

Exam Essentials

Understand the functionality of all the operators discussed in this section. These operators are

    Unary operators: ++ -- + - ! ~

    The cast operator: ()

    Binary arithmetic operators: * / % + -

    Shift operators: << >> >>>

    Comparison operators: < <= > >= == != instanceof

    Bitwise operators: & ^ |

    Short-circuit operators: && ||

    The ternary operator: ?:

    Assignment operators: = op=

Understand when arithmetic promotion takes place. You should know the type of the result of unary and binary arithmetic operations performed on operands of any type.

Understand the difference between object equality and reference equality; know the functionality of the equals() method of the Object, Boolean, and String classes. Object equality checks the data of two possibly distinct objects. Reference equality checks whether two references point to the same object. The Object version uses to a reference equality check; the Boolean and String versions compare encapsulated data.

Key Terms

Before you take the exam, be certain you are familiar with the following terms:

arithmetic operators

assignment operators

bitwise inversion

bitwise operators

comparison operators

concatenation

conditional operators

equality comparisons

modulo operators

object comparisons

object-type comparisons

ordinal

post-decrement

post-increment

pre-decrement

pre-increment

reference comparisons

shift operators

ternary operators

unary operators

Review Questions

1. After execution of the following code fragment, what are the values of the variables x, a, and b?
   ```
   1. int x, a = 6, b = 7;
   2. x = a++ + b++;
   ```
   A. x = 15, a = 7, b = 8
   B. x = 15, a = 6, b = 7
   C. x = 13, a = 7, b = 8
   D. x = 13, a = 6, b = 7

2. Which of the following expressions are legal? (Choose all that apply.)
   A. int x = 6; x = !x;
   B. int x = 6; if (!(x > 3)) {}
   C. int x = 6; x = ~x;

3. Which of the following expressions results in a positive value in x?
   A. int x = -1; x = x >>> 5;
   B. int x = -1; x = x >>> 32;
   C. byte x = -1; x = x >>> 5;
   D. int x = -1; x = x >> 5;

4. Which of the following expressions are legal? (Choose all that apply.)
   A. String x = "Hello"; int y = 9; x += y;
   B. String x = "Hello"; int y = 9; if (x == y) {}
   C. String x = "Hello"; int y = 9; x = x + y;
   D. String x = "Hello"; int y = 9; y = y + x;
   E. String x = null; int y = (x != null) && (x.length() > 0) ? x.length() : 0;

5. Which of the following code fragments would compile successfully and print "Equal" when run? (Choose all that apply.)
   A. int x = 100; float y = 100.0F; if (x == y){System.out.println("Equal");}
   B. int x = 100; Integer y = new Integer(100); if (x == y) {
      System.out.println("Equal");}
   C. Integer x = new Integer(100); Integer y = new Integer(100); if (x == y) {
      System.out.println("Equal");}
   D. String x = new String("100"); String y = new String("100"); if (x == y) {
      System.out.println("Equal");}
   E. String x = "100"; String y = "100"; if (x == y) {
      System.out.println("Equal");}

6. What results from running the following code?

```
1. public class Short {
2.    public static void main(String args[]) {
3.       StringBuffer s = new StringBuffer("Hello");
4.       if ((s.length() > 5) &&
5.          (s.append(" there").equals("False")))
6.          ; // do nothing
7.       System.out.println("value is " + s);
8.    }
9. }
```

A. The output: value is Hello

B. The output: value is Hello there

C. A compiler error at line 4 or 5

D. No output

E. A NullPointerException

7. What results from running the following code?

```
1. public class Xor {
2.    public static void main(String args[]) {
3.       byte b = 10; // 00001010 binary
4.       byte c = 15; // 00001111 binary
5.       b = (byte)(b ^ c);
6.       System.out.println("b contains " + b);
7.    }
8. }
```

A. The output: b contains 10

B. The output: b contains 5

C. The output: b contains 250

D. The output: b contains 245

8. What results from attempting to compile and run the following code?

```
1. public class Conditional {
2.    public static void main(String args[]) {
3.       int x = 4;
```

```
4.    System.out.println("value is " +
5.        ((x > 4) ? 99.99 : 9));
6.  }
7. }
```

A. The output: value is 99.99
B. The output: value is 9
C. The output: value is 9.0
D. A compiler error at line 5

9. What is the output of this code fragment?
```
1. int x = 3; int y = 10;
2. System.out.println(y % x);
```

A. 0
B. 1
C. 2
D. 3

10. What results from the following fragment of code?
```
1. int x = 1;
2. String [] names = { "Fred", "Jim", "Sheila" };
3. names[--x] += ".";
4. for (int i = 0; i < names.length; i++) {
5.     System.out.println(names[i]);
6. }
```

A. The output includes Fred. with a trailing period.
B. The output includes Jim. with a trailing period.
C. The output includes Sheila. with a trailing period.
D. None of the outputs show a trailing period.
E. An ArrayIndexOutOfBoundsException is thrown.

Answers to Review Questions

1. **C.** The assignment statement is evaluated as if it were

   `x = a + b; a = a + 1; b = b + 1;`

   Therefore, the assignment to x is made using the sum of 6 + 7, giving 13. After the addition, the values of a and b are incremented; the new values, 7 and 8, are stored in the variables.

2. **B, C.** In A, the use of ! is inappropriate, because x is of int type, not boolean. This is a common mistake among C and C++ programmers, because the expression would be valid in those languages. In B, the comparison is inelegant (being a cumbersome equivalent of if (x <= 3)) but valid, because the expression (x > 3) is a boolean type and the ! operator can properly be applied to it. In C, the bitwise inversion operator is applied to an integral type. The bit pattern of 6 looks like 0 0110 where the ellipsis represents 27 0 bits. The resulting bit pattern looks like 1 1001, where the ellipsis represents 27 1 bits.

3. **A.** In every case, the bit pattern for –1 is "all ones." In A, this pattern is shifted five places to the right with the introduction of 0 bits at the most significant positions. The result is 27 1 bits in the less significant positions of the int value. Because the most significant bit is 0, this result represents a positive value (134217727). In B, the shift value is 32 bits. This shift will result in no change at all to x, because the shift is actually performed by (32 mod 32) bits, which is 0. So in B, the value of x is unchanged at –1. C is illegal, because the result of x >>> 5 is of type int and cannot be assigned into the byte variable x without explicit casting. Even if the cast were added, giving

   `byte x = -1; x = (byte)(x >>> 5);`

   the result of the expression x >>> 5 would be calculated like this:

   1. Promote x to an int. Doing so gives a sign-extended result—that is, an int –1 with 32 1 bits.
   2. Perform the shift; it behaves the same as in A above, giving 134217727, which is the value of 27 1 bits in the less significant positions.
   3. Casting the result of the expression simply retains the less significant 8 bits; because these are all 1s, the resulting byte represents –1.

   Finally, D performs a signed shift, which propagates 1 bits into the most significant position. So, in this case, the resulting value of x is unchanged at –1.

4. **A, C, E.** In A, the use of += is treated as a shorthand for the expression in C. This attempts to "add" an int to a String, which results in conversion of the int to a String—"9" in this case—and the concatenation of the two String objects. So in this case, the value of x after the code is executed is "Hello9".

   In B, the comparison (x == y) is not legal, because variable y is an int type and cannot be compared with a reference value. Don't forget that comparison using == tests the values and that for objects, the "value" is the reference value and not the contents.

   C is identical to A without the use of the shorthand assignment operator.

D calculates y + x, which is legal in itself, because it produces a `String` in the same way as did x + y. It then attempts to assign the result, which is "9Hello", into an `int` variable. Because the result of y + x is a `String`, this assignment is not permitted.

E is rather different from the others. The important points are the use of the short-circuit operator `&&` and the conditional operator `?:`. The left operand of the `&&` operator is always evaluated, and in this case the condition (x != null) is false. Because this is false, the right part of the expression (x.length() > 0) need not be evaluated, as the result of the `&&` operator is known to be false. This short-circuit effect neatly avoids executing the method call x.length(), which would fail with a `NullPointerException` at runtime. This false result is then used in the evaluation of the conditional expression. Because the `boolean` value is false, the result of the overall expression is the value to the right of the colon, which is 0.

5. A, E. Although `int` and `float` are not assignment-compatible, they can generally be mixed on either side of an operator. Because `==` is not an assignment but is a comparison operator, it simply causes normal promotion, so that the `int` value 100 is promoted to a `float` value 100.0 and compared successfully with the other `float` value 100.0F. For this reason, A is true.

The code in B fails to compile, because of the mismatch between the `int` and the `Integer` object. The value of an object is its reference, and no conversions are ever possible between references and numeric types. As a result, the arguments cannot be promoted to the same type, and they cannot be compared.

In C, the code compiles successfully because the comparison is between two object references. However, the test for equality compares the value of the references (the memory address typically) and, because the variables x and y refer to two different objects, the test returns false. The code in D behaves exactly the same way.

Comparing E with D might persuade you that E should probably not print "Equal". In fact, it does so because of a required optimization. Because `String` objects are immutable, literal strings are inevitably constant strings, so the compiler re-uses the same `String` object if it sees the same literal value occur more than once in the source. This means that the variables x and y actually do refer to the same object; so the test (x == y) is true and the "Equal" message is printed. It is particularly important that you do not allow this special behavior to persuade you that the `==` operator can be used to compare the contents of objects in any general way.

6. A. The effect of the `&&` operator is first to evaluate the left operand. That is the expression (s.length() > 5). Because the length of the `StringBuffer` object s is 5, this test returns false. Using the logical identity false AND X = false, the value of the overall conditional is fully determined, and the `&&` operator therefore skips evaluation of the right operand. As a result, the value in the `StringBuffer` object is still simply "Hello" when it is printed out.

If the test on the left side of `&&` had returned true, as would have occurred had the `StringBuffer` contained a longer text segment, then the right side would have been evaluated. Although it might look a little strange, that expression, (s.append("there").equals("False")), is valid and returns a `boolean`. In fact, the value of the expression is guaranteed to be false, because it is clearly impossible for any `StringBuffer` to contain exactly "False" when it has just had the String "there" appended to it. This is irrelevant, however; the essence of this expression is that, if it is evaluated, it has the side effect of changing the original StringBuffer by appending the text "there".

7. B. The eXclusive-OR operator ^ works on the pairs of bits in equivalent positions in the two operands. In this example, this produces:

```
      00001010
      00001111
XOR   --------
      00000101
```

Notice that the only 1 bits in the answer are in those columns where exactly one of the operands has a 1 bit. If neither or both of the operands has a 1, then a 0 bit results.

The value 00000101 binary corresponds to 5 decimal.

It is worth remembering that, although this example has been shown as a byte calculation, the actual work is done using int (32-bit) values. This is why the explicit cast is required before the result is assigned back into the variable b in line 5.

8. C. In this code, the optional result values for the conditional operator, 99.99 (a double) and 9 (an int), are of different types. The result type of a conditional operator must be fully determined at compile time, and in this case the type chosen, using the rules of promotion for binary operands, is double. Because the result is a double, the output value is printed in a floating-point format.

The choice of which of the two values to output is made on the basis of the boolean value that precedes the ?. Because x is 4, the test (x > 4) is false. This causes the overall expression to take the second of the possible values, which is 9 rather than 99.99. Because the result type is promoted to a double, the output value is written as 9.0, rather than the more obvious 9.

If the two possible argument types had been entirely incompatible—for example, (x > 4) ? "Hello" : 9—then the compiler would have issued an error at that line.

9. B. In this case, the calculation is relatively straightforward, because only positive integers are involved. Dividing 10 by 3 gives 3 remainder 1, and this 1 forms the result of the modulo expression. Another way to think of this calculation is 10 – 3 = 7, 7 – 3 = 4, 4 – 3 = 1, 1 is less than 3, therefore the result is 1. The second approach is more general, because it handles floating-point calculations, too. Don't forget that for negative numbers, you should ignore the signs during the calculation part, and simply attach the sign of the left operand to the result.

10. A. The assignment operators of the form *op=* evaluate the left expression only once. So, the effect of decrementing x, in --x, occurs only once, resulting in a value of 0 and not –1. Therefore, no out-of-bounds array accesses are attempted. The array element that is affected by this operation is "Fred", because the decrement occurs before the += operation is performed. Although String objects themselves are immutable, the references that are the array elements are not. It is entirely possible to cause the value name[0] to be modified to refer to a newly constructed String, which happens to be "Fred".

Chapter 3

Modifiers

JAVA CERTIFICATION EXAM OBJECTIVES COVERED IN THIS CHAPTER:

✓ 1.2 Declare classes, nested classes, methods, instance variables, static variables, and automatic (method local) variables making appropriate use of all permitted modifiers (such as public, final, static, abstract, etc.). State the significance of each of these modifiers both singly and in combination and state the effect of package relationships on declared items qualified by these modifiers.

✓ 4.1 Identify correctly constructed package declarations, import statements, class declarations (of all forms including inner classes) interface declarations, method declarations (including the main method that is used to start execution of a class), variable declarations, and identifiers.

Modifiers are Java keywords that give the compiler information about the nature of code, data, or classes. Modifiers specify, for example, that a particular feature is static, final, or transient. (A *feature* is a class, a method, or a variable.) A group of modifiers, called *access modifiers*, dictates which classes are allowed to use a feature. Other modifiers can be used in combination to describe the attributes of a feature.

In this chapter you will learn about all of Java's modifiers as they apply to top-level classes. Inner classes are not discussed here but are covered in Chapter 6, "Objects and Classes".

Modifier Overview

The most common modifiers are the access modifiers: `public`, `protected`, and `private`. Access modifiers are covered in the next section. The remaining modifiers do not fall into any clear categorization. They are

- `final`
- `abstract`
- `static`
- `native`
- `transient`
- `synchronized`
- `volatile`

Each of these modifiers is discussed in its own section.

The Access Modifiers

Access modifiers control which classes may use a feature. A class's features are

- The class itself
- Its member variables
- Its methods and constructors

Note that, with rare exceptions, the only variables that may be controlled by access modifiers are class-level variables. The variables that you declare and use within a class's methods may not have access modifiers. This makes sense; a method variable can only be used within its method.

The access modifiers are

- public
- protected
- private

The only access modifier permitted to noninner classes is `public`; there is no such thing as a protected or private top-level class.

A feature may have at most one access modifier. If a feature has no access modifier, its access defaults to a mode that, unfortunately, has no standardized name. The default access mode is known variously as *friendly*, *package*, or *default*. In this book, we use the term *default*. Be aware that Sun is encouraging us to avoid the use of *friendly*, due to confusion with a somewhat similar concept in C++.

The following declarations are all legal (provided they appear in an appropriate context):

```
class Parser { ... }
public class EightDimensionalComplex { ... }
private int i;
Graphics offScreenGC;
protected double getChiSquared() { ... }
private class Horse { ... }
```

The following declarations are illegal:

```
public protected int x;      // At most 1 access modifier
default Button getBtn() {...} // ìdefaultî isn't a keyword
```

public

The most generous access modifier is `public`. A *public* class, variable, or method may be used in any Java program without restriction. An applet (a subclass of class `java.applet.Applet`) is declared as a public class so that it may be instantiated by browsers. An application declares its `main()` method to be public so that `main()` can be invoked from any Java runtime environment.

private

The least generous access modifier is `private`. Top-level (that is, not inner) classes may not be declared private. A *private* variable or method may only be used by an instance of the class that declares the variable or method. For an example of the private access modifier, consider the following code:

```
1.  class Complex {
2.      private double real, imaginary;
3.
4.      public Complex(double r, double i) {
5.          real = r; imaginary = i;
6.      }
7.      public Complex add(Complex c) {
8.          return new Complex(real + c.real,
9.              imaginary + c.imaginary);
10.     }
11. }
12.
13. class Client {
14.     void useThem() {
15.         Complex c1 = new Complex(1, 2);
16.         Complex c2 = new Complex(3, 4);
17.         Complex c3 = c1.add(c2);
18.         double d = c3.real;    // Illegal!
19.     }
20. }
```

On line 17, a call is made to c1.add(c2). Object c1 will execute the method using object c2 as a parameter. In line 8, c1 accesses its own private variables as well as those of c2. There is nothing wrong with this. Declaring real and imaginary to be private means that they can only be accessed by instances of the Complex class, but they can be accessed by any instance of Complex. Thus c1 may access its own real and imaginary variables, as well as the real and imaginary of any other instance of Complex. Access modifiers dictate which *classes*, not which *instances*, may access features.

Line 18 is illegal and will cause a compiler error. The error message says, "Variable real in class Complex not accessible from class Client". The private variable real may be accessed only by an instance of Complex.

Private data can be hidden from the very object that owns the data. If class Complex has a subclass called SubComplex, then every instance of SubComplex will inherit its own real and imaginary variables. Nevertheless, no instance of SubComplex can ever access those variables. Once again, the private features of Complex can only be accessed within the Complex class; an instance of a subclass is denied access. Thus, for example, the following code will not compile:

```
1.  class Complex {
2.      private double real, imaginary;
3.  }
```

```
 4.
 5.
 6. class SubComplex extends Complex {
 7.     SubComplex(double r, double i) {
 8.         real = r;              // Trouble!
 9.     }
10. }
```

In the constructor for class `SubComplex` (on line 8), the variable `real` is accessed. This line causes a compiler error, with a message that is very similar to the message of the previous example: "Undefined variable: real". The private nature of variable `real` prevents an instance of `SubComplex` from accessing one of its own variables!

Default

Default is the name of the access of classes, variables, and methods if you don't specify an access modifier. A class's data and methods may be default, as well as the class itself. A class's default features are accessible to any class in the same package as the class in question.

Default is not a Java keyword; it is simply a name that is given to the access level that results from not specifying an access modifier.

It would seem that default access is of interest only to people who are in the business of making packages. This is technically true, but actually everybody is always making packages, even if they aren't aware of it. The result of this behind-the-scenes package making is a degree of convenience for programmers that deserves investigation.

When you write an application that involves developing several different classes, you probably keep all your .java sources and all your .class class files in a single working directory. When you execute your code, you do so from that directory. The Java runtime environment considers that all class files in its current working directory constitute a package.

Imagine what happens when you develop several classes in this way and don't bother to provide access modifiers for your classes, data, or methods. These features are neither public nor private nor protected. They result in default access, which means they are accessible to any other classes in the package. Because Java considers that all the classes in the directory actually make up a package, all your classes get to access one another's features. This makes it easy to develop code quickly without worrying too much about access.

Now imagine what happens if you are deliberately developing your own package. A little extra work is required: You have to put a package statement in your source code, and you have to compile with the -d option. Any features of the package's classes that you do not explicitly mark with an access modifier will be accessible to all the members of the package, which is probably what you want. Fellow package members have a special relationship, and it stands to reason that they should get access not granted to classes outside the package. Classes outside the package may not access the default features, because the features are default, not public. Classes outside the package may subclass the classes in the package (you do something like this, for example, when you write an applet); however, even the subclasses may not access the default features, because the features are default, not protected or public. Figure 3.1 illustrates default access both within and outside a package.

FIGURE 3.1 Default access

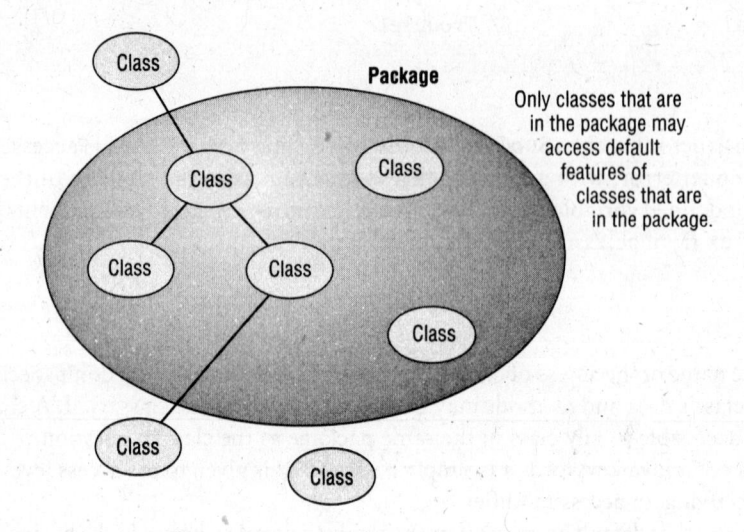

Only classes that are in the package may access default features of classes that are in the package.

protected

The name *protected* is a bit misleading. From the sound of it, you might guess that protected access is extremely restrictive—perhaps the next closest thing to private access. In fact, protected features are even more accessible than default features.

Only variables and methods may be declared protected. A protected feature of a class is available to all classes in the same package, just like a default feature. Moreover, a protected feature of a class is available to all subclasses of the class that owns the protected feature. This access is provided even to subclasses that reside in a different package from the class that owns the protected feature.

As an example of the protected access modifier, consider the following code:

```
1. package sportinggoods;
2. class Ski {
3.   void applyWax() { . . . }
4. }
```

The `applyWax()` method has default access. Now consider the following subclass:

```
1. package sportinggoods;
2. class DownhillSki extends Ski {
3.   void tuneup() {
```

```
4.      applyWax();
5.      // other tuneup functionality here
6.  }
7. }
```

The subclass calls the inherited method `applyWax()`. This is not a problem as long as both the Ski and DownhillSki classes reside in the same package. However, if either class were to be moved to a different package, DownhillSki would no longer have access to the inherited `applyWax()` method, and compilation would fail. The problem would be fixed by making `applyWax()` protected on line 3:

```
1. package adifferentpackage;     // Class Ski now in
                                  // a different package
2. class Ski {
3.    protected void applyWax() { . . . }
4. }
```

Real World Scenario

Protected Access in Depth

In this exercise, you will look at how protected data can be accessed from a subclass that belongs to a different package. Because access is enforced at compile time, you will not be writing any code that is intended to be executed. Rather, you will write several very simple classes and see which ones compile.

Begin by creating a public superclass called Bird, in a package called birdpack. This superclass should have a single data member: a protected int called nFeathers. Then, create four subclasses of Bird, all of which reside in a package called duckpack. Thus you will have subclasses whose package is different from their superclass's package; this is exactly the situation for which protected access is designed.

The first subclass, called Duck1, should have a method that accesses the nFeathers variable of the current instance of Duck1. Before compiling Duck1, ask yourself if the code should compile.

The second subclass, called Duck2, should have a method that constructs another instance of Duck2 and accesses the nFeathers variable of the other instance. Before compiling Duck2, ask yourself if the code should compile.

The third subclass, called Duck3, should have a method that constructs an instance of Bird (the superclass) and accesses the nFeathers variable of the Bird instance. Before compiling Duck3, ask yourself if the code should compile.

> The fourth subclass, called Swan, should have a method that constructs an instance of Duck1 and accesses the nFeathers variable of that object. Before compiling Swan, ask yourself if the code should compile.
>
> A note on compilation: When a source file contains a package declaration, it is generally most convenient to compile with the -d option. Doing so will ensure creation of an appropriate package directory hierarchy, with class files installed correctly. Thus, for example, the easiest way to compile Bird.java is with the following command line:
>
> ```
> javac -d . Bird.java
> ```

Subclasses and Method Privacy

Java specifies that methods may not be overridden to be more private. For example, most applets provide an init() method, which overrides the do-nothing version inherited from the java.applet.Applet superclass. The inherited version is declared public, so declaring the subclass version to be private, protected, or default would result in a compiler error. The error message says, "Methods can't be overridden to be more private."

Figure 3.2 shows the legal access types for subclasses. A method with some particular access type may be overridden by a method with a different access type, provided there is a path in the figure from the original type to the new type.

FIGURE 3.2 Legal overridden method access

Private → Default → Protected → Public

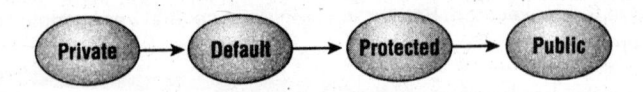

The rules for overriding can be summarized as follows:

- A private method may be overridden by a private, default, protected, or public method.
- A default method may be overridden by a default, protected, or public method.
- A protected method may be overridden by a protected or public method.
- A public method may only be overridden by a public method.

Figure 3.3 shows the illegal access types for subclasses. A method with some particular access type may not be shadowed by a method with a different access type, if there is a path in the figure from the original type to the new type.

FIGURE 3.3 Illegal overridden method access

Public → Protected → Default → Private

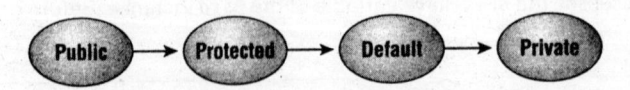

The illegal overriding combinations can be summarized as follows:
- A default method may not be overridden by a private method.
- A protected method may not be overridden by a default or private method.
- A public method may not be overridden by a protected, default, or private method.

Summary of Access Modes

To summarize, Java's access modes are

public A public feature may be accessed by any class.

protected A protected feature may only be accessed by a subclass of the class that owns the feature or by a member of the same package as the class that owns the feature.

default A default feature may only be accessed by a class from the same package as the class that owns the feature.

private A private feature may only be accessed by the class that owns the feature.

Other Modifiers

The rest of this chapter covers Java's other modifiers: `final`, `abstract`, `static`, `native`, `transient`, `synchronized`, and `volatile`. (Transient and volatile are not mentioned in the Certification Exam objectives, so they are just touched on briefly in this chapter.)

Java does not care about order of appearance of modifiers. Declaring a class to be `public final` is no different from declaring it `final public`. Declaring a method to be `protected static` has the same effect as declaring it `static protected`.

Not every modifier can be applied to every kind of feature. Table 3.1, at the end of this chapter, summarizes which modifiers apply to which features.

final

The *final* modifier applies to classes, methods, and variables. The meaning of `final` varies from context to context, but the essential idea is the same: final features may not be changed.

A final class cannot be subclassed. For example, the following code will not compile, because the `java.lang.Math` class is final:

```
class SubMath extends java.lang.Math { }
```

The compiler error says, "Can't subclass final classes".

A final variable cannot be modified once it has been assigned a value. In Java, final variables play the same role as `const`s in C++ and `#define` constants in C. For example, the `java.lang.Math` class has a final variable, of type `double`, called `PI`. Obviously, pi is not the sort of value that should be changed during the execution of a program.

If a final variable is a reference to an object, it is the reference that must stay the same, not the object. This is shown in the following code:

```
1.  class Walrus {
2.      int weight;
3.      Walrus(int w) { weight = w; }
4.  }
5.
6.  class Tester {
7.      final Walrus w1 = new Walrus(1500);
8.      void test() {
9.          w1 = new Walrus(1400);      // Illegal
10.         w1.weight = 1800;           // Legal
11.     }
12. }
```

Here the final variable is w1, declared on line 7. Because it is final, w1 cannot receive a new value; line 9 is illegal. However, the data inside w1 is not final, and line 10 is perfectly legal. In other words,

- You may *not* change a final object reference variable.
- You *may* change data owned by an object that is referred to by a final object reference variable.

A final method may not be overridden. For example, the following code will not compile:

```
1. class Mammal {
2.     final void getAround() { }
3. }
4.
5. class Dolphin extends Mammal {
6.     void getAround() { }
7. }
```

Dolphins get around in a very different way from most mammals, so it makes sense to try to override the inherited version of getAround(). However, getAround() is final, so the only result is a compiler error at line 6 that says, "Final methods can't be overridden."

abstract

The *abstract* modifier can be applied to classes and methods. A class that is abstract may not be instantiated (that is, you may not call its constructor).

Abstract classes provide a way to defer implementation to subclasses. Consider the class hierarchy shown in Figure 3.4.

FIGURE 3.4 A class hierarchy with abstraction

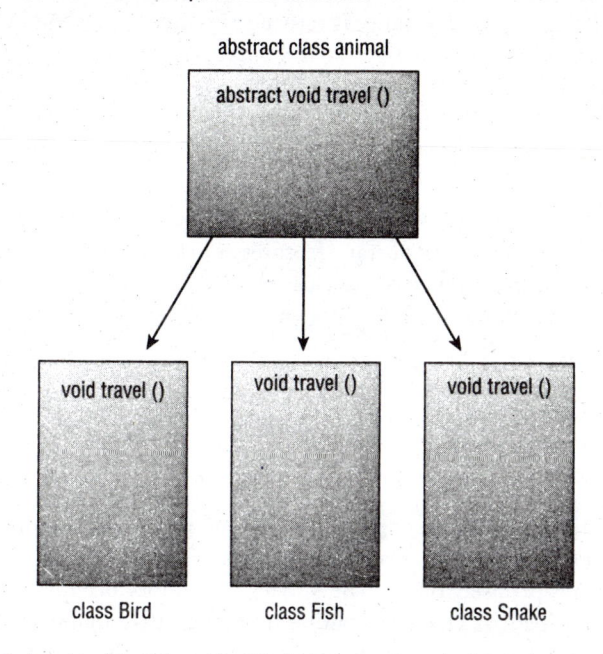

```
              abstract class animal
            ┌──────────────────────┐
            │ abstract void travel()│
            │                      │
            └──────────────────────┘
              ↙         ↓         ↘
    ┌──────────┐  ┌──────────┐  ┌──────────┐
    │void travel()│ │void travel()│ │void travel()│
    │          │  │          │  │          │
    │          │  │          │  │          │
    └──────────┘  └──────────┘  └──────────┘
     class Bird    class Fish    class Snake
```

The designer of class `Animal` has decided that every subclass should have a `travel()` method. Each subclass has its own unique way of traveling, so it is not possible to provide `travel()` in the superclass and have each subclass inherit the same parental version. Instead, the `Animal` superclass declares `travel()` to be abstract. The declaration looks like this:

`abstract void travel();`

At the end of the line is a semicolon where you would expect to find curly braces containing the body of the method. The method body—its implementation—is deferred to the subclasses. The superclass provides only the method name and signature. Any subclass of `Animal` must provide an implementation of `travel()` or declare itself to be abstract. In the latter case, implementation of `travel()` is deferred yet again, to a subclass of the subclass.

If a class contains one or more abstract methods, the compiler insists that the class must be declared abstract. This is a great convenience to people who will be using the class. they need to look in only one place (the class declaration) to find out if they are allowed to instantiate the class directly or if they have to build a subclass.

In fact, the compiler insists that a class must be declared abstract if any of the following conditions is true:

- The class has one or more abstract methods.
- The class inherits one or more abstract method (from an abstract parent) for which it does not provide implementations.
- The class declares that it implements an interface but does not provide implementations for every method of that interface.

These three conditions are very similar to one another. In each case, there is an incomplete class. Some part of the class's functionality is missing and must be provided by a subclass.

In a way, abstract is the opposite of final. A final class, for example, may not be subclassed; an abstract class *must* be subclassed.

static

The *static* modifier can be applied to variables, methods, and even a strange kind of code that is not part of a method. You can think of static features as belonging to a class, rather than being associated with an individual instance of the class.

The following example shows a simple class with a single static variable:

```
1. class Ecstatic{
2.     static int x = 0;
3.     Ecstatic() { x++; }
4. }
```

Variable x is static; this means that there is only one x, no matter how many instances of class Ecstatic might exist at any moment. There might be one Ecstatic instance, or many, or even none; yet there is always precisely one x. The 4 bytes of memory occupied by x are allocated when class Ecstatic is loaded. The initialization to 0 (line 2) also happens at class-load time. The static variable is incremented every time the constructor is called, so it is possible to know how many instances have been created.

You can reference a static variable two ways:

- Via a reference to any instance of the class
- Via the class name

The first method works, but it can result in confusing code and is considered bad form. The following example shows why:

```
1. Ecstatic e1 = new Ecstatic();
2. Ecstatic e2 = new Ecstatic();
3. e1.x = 100;
4. e2.x = 200;
5. reallyImportantVariable = e1.x;
```

If you didn't know that x is static, you might think that reallyImportantVariable gets set to 100 in line 5. In fact, it gets set to 200, because e1.x and e2.x refer to the same (static) variable.

A better way to refer to a static variable is via the class name. The following code is identical to the previous code:

```
1. Ecstatic e1 = new Ecstatic();
2. Ecstatic e2 = new Ecstatic();
```

3. Ecstatic.x = 100;   // Why did I do this?
4. Ecstatic.x = 200;
5. reallyImportantVariable = Ecstatic.x;

Now it is clear that line 3 is useless, and the value of reallyImportantVariable gets set to 200 in line 5. Referring to static features via the class name rather than an instance results in source code that more clearly describes what will happen at runtime.

Methods, as well as data, can be declared static. Static methods are not allowed to use the nonstatic features of their class (although they are free to access the class's static data and call its other static methods). Thus static methods are not concerned with individual instances of a class. They may be invoked before even a single instance of the class is constructed. Every Java application is an example, because every application has a main() method that is static:

```
1. class SomeClass {
2.    static int i = 48;
3.    int j = 1;
4.
5.    public static void main(String args[]) {
6.       i += 100;
7.       // j *= 5; Lucky for us this is commented out!
8.    }
9. }
```

When this application is started (that is, when somebody types **java SomeClass** on a command line), no instance of class SomeClass exists. At line 6, the i that gets incremented is static, so it exists even though there are no instances. Line 7 would result in a compiler error if it were not commented out, because j is nonstatic.

Instance methods have an implicit variable named this, which is a reference to the object executing the method. In nonstatic code, you can refer to a variable or method without specifying which object's variable or method you mean. The compiler assumes you mean this. For example, consider the following code:

```
1. class Xyzzy {
2.    int w;
3.
4.    void bumpW() {
5.       w++;
6.    }
7. }
```

On line 5, the programmer has not specified which object's w is to be incremented. The compiler assumes that line 5 is an abbreviation for this.w++;.

84   Chapter 3 · Modifiers

With static methods, there is no `this`. If you try to access an instance variable or call an instance method within a static method, you will get an error message that says, "Undefined variable: this." The concept of "the instance that is executing the current method" does not mean anything, because there is no such instance. Like static variables, static methods are not associated with any individual instance of their class.

If a static method needs to access a nonstatic variable or call a nonstatic method, it must specify which instance of its class owns the variable or executes the method. This situation is familiar to anyone who has ever written an application with a GUI:

```
1.  import java.awt.*;
2.
3.  public class MyFrame extends Frame {
4.    MyFrame() {
5.      setSize(300, 300);
6.    }
7.
8.    public static void main(String args[]) {
9.      MyFrame theFrame = new MyFrame();
10.     theFrame.setVisible(true);
11.   }
12. }
```

In line 9, the static method `main()` constructs an instance of class `MyFrame`. In the next line, that instance is told to execute the (nonstatic) method `setVisible()`. This technique bridges the gap from static to nonstatic, and it is frequently seen in applications.

The following code, for example, will not compile:

```
1. class Cattle {
2.   static void foo() {}
3. }
4.
5. class Sheep extends Cattle {
6.   void foo() {}
7. }
```

The compiler flags line 6 with the message, "Static methods can't be overridden." If line 6 were changed to `static void foo() { }`, then compilation would succeed. Static methods can appear to be overridden—a superclass and a subclass can have static methods with identical names, argument lists, and return types—but technically this is not considered overriding because the methods are static.

To summarize static methods:

- A static method may only access the static data of its class; it may not access nonstatic data.
- A static method may only call the static methods of its class; it may not call nonstatic methods.
- A static method has no `this`.
- A static method may not be overridden to be nonstatic.

Static Initializers

It is legal for a class to contain static code that does not exist within a method body. A class may have a block of initializer code that is simply surrounded by curly braces and labeled `static`. For example:

```
1.  public class StaticExample {
2.      static double d=1.23;
3.
4.      static {
5.          System.out.println("Static code: d=" + d++);
6.      }
7.
8.      public static void main(String args[]) {
9.          System.out.println("main: d = " + d++);
10.     }
11. }
```

Something seems to be missing from line 4. You might expect to see a complete method declaration there: `static void printAndBump()`, for example, instead of just `static`. In fact, line 4 is perfectly valid; it is known as *static initializer* code. The code inside the curlies is executed exactly once, at the time the class is loaded. At class-load time, all static initialization (such as line 2) and all free-floating static code (such as lines 4–6) are executed in order of appearance within the class definition.

> **TIP** Free-floating initializer code should be used with caution because it can easily be confusing and unclear. The compiler supports multiple initializer blocks within a class, but there is never a good reason for having more than one such block.

native

The *native* modifier can refer only to methods. Like the `abstract` keyword, native indicates that the body of a method is to be found elsewhere. In the case of abstract methods, the body is in a subclass; with native methods, the body lies entirely outside the Java Virtual Machine (JVM), in a library.

Native code is written in a non-Java language, typically C or C++, and compiled for a single target machine type. (Thus Java's platform independence is violated.) People who port Java to new platforms implement extensive native code to support GUI components, network communication, and a broad range of other platform-specific functionality. However, it is rare for application and applet programmers to need to write native code.

One technique, however, is of interest in light of the last section's discussion of static code. When a native method is invoked, the library that contains the native code ought to be loaded and available to the JVM; if it is not loaded, there will be a delay. The library is loaded by calling `System.loadLibrary ("library_name")` and, to avoid a delay, it is desirable to make this call as early as possible. Often programmers will use the technique shown in the following code sample, which assumes the library name is `MyNativeLib`:

```
1. class NativeExample {
2.    native void doSomethingLocal(int i);
3.
4.    static {
5.       System.loadLibrary("MyNativeLib");
6.    }
7. }
```

Notice the `native` declaration on line 2, which declares that the code that implements `doSomethingLocal()` resides in a local library. Lines 4–6 are static initializer code, so they are executed at the time that class `NativeExample` is loaded; this ensures that the library will be available by the time somebody needs it.

Callers of native methods do not have to know that the method is native. The call is made in exactly the same way as if it were nonnative:

```
1. NativeExample natex;
2. natex = new NativeExample();
3. natex.doSomethingLocal(5);
```

Many common methods are native, including the `clone()` and `notify()` methods of the `Object` class.

transient

The *transient* modifier applies only to variables. A transient variable is not stored as part of its object's persistent state.

Many objects (specifically, those that implement the `Serializable` or `Externalizable` interfaces) can have their state serialized and written to some destination outside the JVM. This is done by passing the object to the `writeObject()` method of the `ObjectOutputStream` class.

If the stream is chained to a `FileOutputStream`, then the object's state is written to a file. If the stream is chained to a socket's `OutputStream`, then the object's state is written to the network. In both cases, the object can be reconstituted by reading it from an `ObjectInputStream`.

Sometimes an object contains extremely sensitive information. Consider the following class:

```
1. class WealthyCustomer
2. extends Customer implements Serializable {
3.    private float $wealth;
4.    private String accessCode;
5. }
```

Once an object is written to a destination outside the JVM, none of Java's elaborate security mechanisms is in effect. If an instance of this class were to be written to a file or to the Internet, somebody could snoop the access code. Line 4 should be marked with the `transient` keyword:

```
1. class WealthyCustomer
2. extends Customer implements Serializable {
3.    private float $wealth;
4.    private transient String accessCode;
5. }
```

Now the value of `accessCode` will not be written out during serialization.

synchronized

The *synchronized* modifier is used to control access to critical code in multithreaded programs. Multithreading is an extensive topic in its own right and is covered in Chapter 7, "Threads."

volatile

The last modifier is *volatile*. It is mentioned here only to make our list complete; it is not mentioned in the exam objectives and is not yet in common use. Only variables may be volatile; declaring them so indicates that such variables might be modified asynchronously, so the compiler takes special precautions. Volatile variables are of interest in multiprocessor environments.

Modifiers and Features

Not all modifiers can be applied to all features. Top-level classes may not be protected. Methods may not be transient. Static is so general that you can apply it to free-floating blocks of code.

Table 3.1 shows all the possible combinations of features and modifiers. Note that classes here are strictly top-level (that is, not inner) classes. (Inner classes are covered in Chapter 6.)

TABLE 3.1 All Possible Combinations of Features and Modifiers

Modifier	Class	Variable	Method	Constructor	FreeFloating Block
public	yes	yes	yes	yes	no
protected	no	yes	yes	yes	no
(default)*	yes	yes	yes	yes	yes
private	no	yes	yes	yes	no
final	yes	yes	yes	no	no
abstract	yes	no	yes	no	no
static	no	yes	yes	no	yes
native	no	no	yes	no	no
transient	no	yes	no	no	no
volatile	no	yes	no	no	no
synchronized	no	no	yes	no	yes

* *Default* is not a modifier; it is just the name of the access if no modifier is specified.

Summary

The focus of this chapter was to understand how all of the modifiers work and how they *can* or *cannot* work together. Some modifiers can be used in combination. Java's access modifiers are

- public
- protected
- private

If a feature does not have an access modifier, its access is "default."
Java's other modifiers are

- final
- abstract
- static
- native

- transient
- synchronized
- volatile

Exam Essentials

Understand the four access modes and the corresponding keywords. You should know the significance of public, default, protected, and private access when applied to data and methods.

Know the effect of declaring a final class, variable, or method. A final class cannot be subclassed; a final variable cannot be modified after initialization; a final method cannot be overridden.

Know the effect of declaring an abstract class or method. An abstract class cannot be instantiated; an abstract method's definition is deferred to a subclass.

Understand the effect of declaring a static variable or method. Static variables belong to the class; static methods have no `this` pointer and may not access nonstatic variables and methods of their class.

Know how to reference a static variable or method. A static feature may be referenced through the class name—the preferred method—or through a reference to any instance of the class.

Be able to recognize static initializer code. Static initializer code appears in curly brackets with no method declaration. Such code is executed once, when the class is loaded.

Key Terms

Before you take the exam, be certain you are familiar with the following terms:

abstract	package
access modifiers	private
default	protected
feature	public
final	static
friendly	static initializer
instance method	synchronized
modifiers	transient
native	volatile

Review Questions

1. Which of the following declarations are illegal? (Choose all that apply.)
   A. `default String s;`
   B. `transient int i = 41;`
   C. `public final static native int w();`
   D. `abstract double d;`
   E. `abstract final double hyperbolicCosine();`

2. Which of the following statements is true?
   A. An abstract class may not have any final methods.
   B. A final class may not have any abstract methods.

3. What is the minimal modification that will make this code compile correctly?
   ```
   1.  final class Aaa
   2.  {
   3.      int xxx;
   4.      void yyy() { xxx = 1; }
   5.  }
   6.
   7.
   8.  class Bbb extends Aaa
   9.  {
   10.     final Aaa finalref = new Aaa();
   11.
   12.     final void yyy()
   13.     {
   14.         System.out.println("In method yyy()");
   15.         finalref.xxx = 12345;
   16.     }
   17. }
   ```

   A. On line 1, remove the `final` modifier.
   B. On line 10, remove the `final` modifier.
   C. Remove line 15.
   D. On lines 1 and 10, remove the `final` modifier.
   E. The code will compile as is. No modification is needed.

4. Which of the following statements is true?
   A. Transient methods may not be overridden.
   B. Transient methods must be overridden.
   C. Transient classes may not be serialized.
   D. Transient variables must be static.
   E. Transient variables are not serialized.

5. Which statement is true about this application?
```
1.  class StaticStuff
2.  {
3.      static int x = 10;
4.
5.      static { x += 5; }
6.
7.      public static void main(String args[])
8.      {
9.          System.out.println("x = " + x);
10.     }
11.
12.     static {x /= 5; }
13. }
```
   A. Lines 5 and 12 will not compile because the method names and return types are missing.
   B. Line 12 will not compile because you can only have one static initializer.
   C. The code compiles and execution produces the output x = 10.
   D. The code compiles and execution produces the output x = 15.
   E. The code compiles and execution produces the output x = 3.

6. Which statement is true about this code?
```
1.  class HasStatic
2.  {
3.      private static int x = 100;
4.
5.      public static void main(String args[])
6.      {
7.          HasStatic hs1 = new HasStatic();
8.          hs1.x++;
9.          HasStatic hs2 = new HasStatic();
10.         hs2.x++;
```

```
11.         hs1 = new HasStatic();
12.         hs1.x++;
13.         HasStatic.x++;
14.         System.out.println("x = " + x);
15.     }
16. }
```

    A. Line 8 will not compile because it is a static reference to a private variable.

    B. Line 13 will not compile because it is a static reference to a private variable.

    C. The program compiles and the output is x = 102.

    D. The program compiles and the output is x = 103.

    E. The program compiles and the output is x = 104.

7. Given the following code, and making no other changes, which combination of access modifiers (public, protected, or private) can legally be placed before aMethod() on line 3 and be placed before aMethod() on line 8?

```
1. class SuperDuper
2. {
3.     void aMethod() { }
4. }
5.
6. class Sub extends SuperDuper
7. {
8.     void aMethod() { }
9. }
```

    A. line 3: public; line 8: private

    B. line 3: protected; line 8: private

    C. line 3: default; line 8: private

    D. line 3: private; line 8: protected

    E. line 3: public; line 8: protected

8. Which modifier or modifiers should be used to denote a variable that should not be written out as part of its class's persistent state? (Choose the shortest possible answer.)

    A. private

    B. protected

    C. private protected

    D. transient

    E. private transient

9. This question concerns the following class definition:
   1. package abcde;
   2.
   3. public class Bird {
   4.   protected static int referenceCount = 0;
   5.   public Bird() { referenceCount++; }
   6.   protected void fly() { /* Flap wings, etc. */ }
   7.   static int getRefCount() { return referenceCount; }
   8. }

   Which statement is true about class Bird and the following class Parrot?
   1. package abcde;
   2.
   3. class Parrot extends abcde.Bird {
   4.   public void fly() {
   5.   /* Parrot-specific flight code. */
   6.   }
   7.   public int getRefCount() {
   8.   return referenceCount;
   9.   }
   10. }

   A. Compilation of Parrot.java fails at line 4 because method fly() is protected in the superclass, and classes Bird and Parrot are in the same package.
   B. Compilation of Parrot.java fails at line 4 because method fly() is protected in the superclass and public in the subclass, and methods may not be overridden to be more public.
   C. Compilation of Parrot.java fails at line 7 because method getRefCount() is static in the superclass, and static methods may not be overridden to be nonstatic.
   D. Compilation of Parrot.java succeeds, but a runtime exception is thrown if method fly() is ever called on an instance of class Parrot.
   E. Compilation of Parrot.java succeeds, but a runtime exception is thrown if method getRefCount() is ever called on an instance of class Parrot.

10. This question concerns the following class definition:
    1. package abcde;
    2.
    3. public class Bird {
    4.   protected static int referenceCount = 0;
    5.   public Bird() { referenceCount++; }
    6.   protected void fly() { /* Flap wings, etc. */ }

7.   `static int getRefCount() { return referenceCount; }`
8. `}`

Which statement is true about class `Bird` and the following class `Nightingale`?

1. `package singers;`
2.
3. `class Nightingale extends abcde.Bird {`
4.   `Nightingale() { referenceCount++; }`
5.
6.   `public static void main(String args[]) {`
7.   `System.out.print("Before: " + referenceCount);`
8.   `Nightingale florence = new Nightingale();`
9.   `System.out.println("  After: " + referenceCount);`
10.   `florence.fly();`
11.   `}`
12. `}`

- A. The program will compile and execute. The output will be Before: 0 After: 2.
- B. The program will compile and execute. The output will be Before: 0 After: 1.
- C. Compilation of `Nightingale` will fail at line 4 because static members cannot be overridden.
- D. Compilation of `Nightingale` will fail at line 10 because method `fly()` is protected in the superclass.
- E. Compilation of `Nightingale` will succeed, but an exception will be thrown at line 10, because method `fly()` is protected in the superclass.

Answers to Review Questions

1. **A, D, E.** A is illegal because "default" is not a keyword. B is a legal transient declaration. C is strange but legal. D is illegal because only methods and classes may be abstract. E is illegal because `abstract` and `final` are contradictory.

2. **B.** Any class with abstract methods must itself be abstract, and a class may not be both abstract and final. Statement A says that an abstract class may not have final methods, but there is nothing wrong with this. The abstract class will eventually be subclassed, and the subclass must avoid overriding the parent's final methods. Any other methods can be freely overridden.

3. **A.** The code will not compile because on line 1, class `Aaa` is declared final and may not be subclassed. Lines 10 and 15 are fine. The instance variable `finalref` is final, so it may not be modified; it can only reference the object created on line 10. However, the data within that object is not final, so nothing is wrong with line 15.

4. **E.** A, B, and C don't mean anything because only variables may be transient, not methods or classes. D is false because transient variables may never be static. E is a good one-sentence definition of transient.

5. **E.** Multiple static initializers (lines 5 and 12) are legal. All static initializer code is executed at class-load time, so before `main()` is ever run, the value of x is initialized to 10 (line 3), then bumped to 15 (line 5), and then divided by 5 (line 12).

6. **E.** The program compiles fine; the "static reference to a private variable" stuff in answers A and B is nonsense. The static variable x gets incremented four times, on lines 8, 10, 12, and 13.

7. **D.** The basic principle is that a method may not be overridden to be more private. (See Figure 3.2 in this chapter.) All choices except D make the access of the overriding method more private.

8. **D.** The other modifiers control access from other objects within the Java Virtual Machine. Answer E also works but is not minimal.

9. **C.** Static methods may not be overridden to be nonstatic. B is incorrect because it states the case backward: methods can be overridden to be more public, not more private. Answers A, D, and E make no sense.

10. **A.** There is nothing wrong with `Nightingale`. The static `referenceCount` is bumped twice: once on line 4 of `Nightingale` and once on line 5 of `Bird`. (The no-argument constructor of the superclass is always implicitly called at the beginning of a class's constructor, unless a different superclass constructor is requested. This has nothing to do with modifiers; see Chapter 6.) Because `referenceCount` is bumped twice and not just once, answer B is wrong. C says that statics cannot be overridden, but no static method is being overridden on line 4; all that is happening is an increment of an inherited static variable. D is wrong because `protected` is precisely the access modifier you want `Bird.fly()` to have: you are calling `Bird.fly()` from a subclass in a different package. Answer E is ridiculous, but it uses credible terminology.

Chapter 4

Converting and Casting

JAVA CERTIFICATION EXAM OBJECTIVE COVERED IN THIS CHAPTER:

- ✓ 5.1 Determine the result of applying any operator including assignment operators, instanceof, and casts to operands of any type, class, scope, or accessibility, or any combination of these.

Every Java variable has a type. Primitive data types include `int`, `long`, and `double`. Object reference data types may be classes (such as `Vector` or `Graphics`) or interfaces (such as `LayoutManager` or `Runnable`). There can also be arrays of primitives, objects, or arrays.

This chapter discusses the ways that a data value can change its type. Values can change type either explicitly or implicitly; that is, they change either at your request or at the system's initiative. Java places a lot of importance on type, and successful Java programming requires that you be aware of type changes.

Explicit and Implicit Type Changes

You can explicitly change the type of a value by *casting*. To cast an expression to a new type, just prefix the expression with the new type name in parentheses. For example, the following line of code retrieves an element from a vector, casts that element to type `Button`, and assigns the result to a variable called `btn`:

```
Button btn = (Button) (myVector.elementAt(5));
```

Of course, the sixth element of the vector must be capable of being treated as a `Button`. Compile-time rules and runtime rules must be observed. This chapter will familiarize you with those rules.

In some situations, the system implicitly changes the type of an expression without your explicitly performing a cast. For example, suppose you have a variable called `myColor` that refers to an instance of `Color`, and you want to store `myColor` in a vector. You would probably do the following:

```
myVector.add(myColor);
```

There is more to this code than meets the eye. The `add()` method of class `Vector` is declared with a parameter of type `Object`, not of type `Color`. As the argument is passed to the method, it undergoes an implicit type change. Such automatic, nonexplicit type changing is known as *conversion*. Conversion, like casting, is governed by rules. Unlike the casting rules, all conversion rules are enforced at compile time.

The number of casting and conversion rules is rather large, due to the large number of cases to be considered. (For example, can you cast a `char` to a `double`? Can you convert an interface to a final class? Yes to the first, no to the second.) The good news is that most of the rules accord with common sense, and most of the combinations can be generalized into rules of thumb. By the end of this chapter, you will know when you can explicitly cast and when the system will implicitly convert on your behalf.

Primitives and Conversion

The two broad categories of Java data types are primitives and objects. *Primitive* data types are ints, floats, booleans, and so on. (There are eight primitive data types in all; see Chapter 1, "Language Fundamentals," for a complete explanation of Java's primitives.) *Object* data types (or more properly, *object reference* data types) are the hundreds of classes and interfaces provided with the JDK, plus the infinitude of classes and interfaces to be invented by Java programmers.

Both primitive values and object references can be converted and cast, so you must consider four general cases:

- Conversion of primitives
- Casting of primitives
- Conversion of object references
- Casting of object references

The simplest topic is implicit conversion of primitives. All conversion of primitive data types takes place at compile time; this is the case because all the information needed to determine whether the conversion is legal is available at compile time.

Conversion of a primitive might occur in three contexts or situations:

- Assignment
- Method call
- Arithmetic promotion

The following sections deal with each of these contexts in turn.

Primitive Conversion: Assignment

Assignment conversion happens when you assign a value to a variable of a different type from the original value. For example:

```
1. int i;
2. double d;
3. i = 10;
4. d = i;  // Assign an int value to a double variable
```

Obviously, d cannot hold an integer value. At the moment that the fourth line of code is executed, the integer 10 that is stored in variable i gets converted to the double-precision value 10.0000000000000 (remaining zeros omitted for brevity).

Chapter 4 • Converting and Casting

The previous code is perfectly legal. Some assignments, on the other hand, are illegal. For example:

```
1. double d;
2. short s;
3. d = 1.2345;
4. s = d;    // Assign a double value to a short variable
```

This code will not compile. (The error message says, "Incompatible type for =.") The compiler recognizes that trying to cram a `double` value into a `short` variable is like trying to pour a quart of coffee into an eight-ounce teacup, as shown in Figure 4.1. It can be done (that is, the larger-to-smaller value assignment can be done; the coffee thing is impossible), but you must use an explicit cast, which will be explained in the following section.

FIGURE 4.1   Illegal conversion of a quart to a cup, with loss of data

The general rules for primitive assignment conversion can be stated as follows:

- A `boolean` cannot be converted to any other type.
- A non-`boolean` can be converted to another non-`boolean` type, provided the conversion is a *widening conversion*.
- A non-`boolean` cannot be converted to another non-`boolean` type if the conversion would be a *narrowing conversion*.

Widening conversions change a value to a type that accommodates a wider range of values than the original type can accommodate. In most cases, the new type has more bits than the original and can be visualized as being "wider" than the original, as shown in Figure 4.2.

FIGURE 4.2 Widening conversion of a positive value

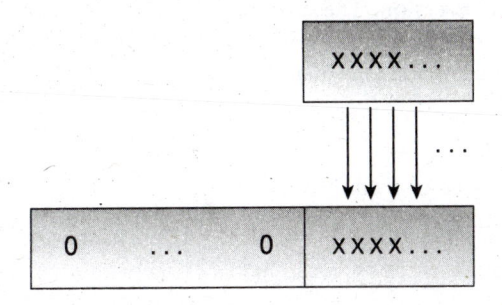

Widening conversions do not lose information about the magnitude of a value. In the first example in this section, an `int` value was assigned to a `double` variable. This conversion was legal because `double`s are wider (represented by more bits) than `int`s, so there is room in a `double` to accommodate the information in an `int`. Java's widening conversions are

- From a `byte` to a `short`, an `int`, a `long`, a `float`, or a `double`
- From a `short` to an `int`, a `long`, a `float`, or a `double`
- From a `char` to an `int`, a `long`, a `float`, or a `double`
- From an `int` to a `long`, a `float`, or a `double`
- From a `long` to a `float` or a `double`
- From a `float` to a `double`

Figure 4.3 illustrates all the widening conversions. The arrows can be taken to mean "can be widened to." To determine whether it is legal to convert from one type to another, find the first type in the figure and see if you can reach the second type by following the arrows.

FIGURE 4.3 Widening conversions

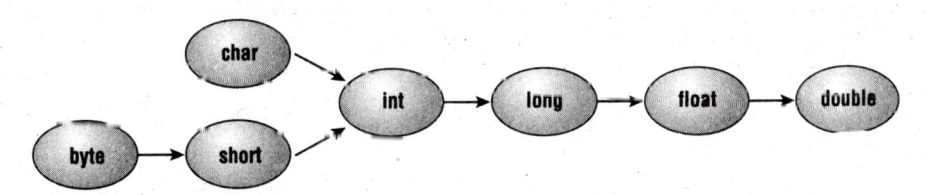

The figure shows, for example, that it is perfectly legal to assign a `byte` value to a `float` variable, because you can trace a path from `byte` to `float` by following the arrows (`byte` to `short` to `int` to `long` to `float`). You cannot, on the other hand, trace a path from `long` to `short`, so it is not legal to assign a `long` value to a `short` variable.

Figure 4.3 is easy to memorize. The figure consists mostly of the numeric data types in order of size. The only extra piece of information is `char`, but that goes in the only place it could go: a 16-bit `char` "fits inside" a 32-bit `int`. (Note that you can't convert a `byte` to a `char` or a `char` to a `short`, even though it seems reasonable to do so.)

Any conversion between primitive types that is not represented by a path of arrows in Figure 4.3 is a narrowing conversion. These conversions lose information about the magnitude of the value being converted and are not allowed in assignments. It is graphically impossible to portray the narrowing conversions in a figure like Figure 4.3, but they can be summarized as follows:

- From a `byte` to a `char`
- From a `short` to a `byte` or a `char`
- From a `char` to a `byte` or a `short`
- From an `int` to a `byte`, a `short`, or a `char`
- From a `long` to a `byte`, a `short`, a `char`, or an `int`
- From a `float` to a `byte`, a `short`, a `char`, an `int`, or a `long`
- From a `double` to a `byte`, a `short`, a `char`, an `int`, a `long`, or a `float`

You do not really need to memorize this list. It simply represents all the conversions not shown in Figure 4.3, which is easier to memorize.

Assignment Conversion, Narrower Primitives, and Literal Values

Java's assignment conversion rule is sometimes inconvenient when a literal value is assigned to a primitive. By default, a numeric literal is either a `double` or an `int`, so the following line of code generates a compiler error:

```
float f = 1.234;
```

The literal value 1.234 is a `double`, so it cannot be assigned to a `float` variable.

You might assume that assigning a literal `int` to some narrower integral type (`byte`, `short`, or `char`) would fail to compile in a similar way. For example, it would be reasonable to assume that all of the following lines generate compiler errors:

```
byte   b = 1;
short  s = 2;
char   c = 3;
```

In fact, all three of these lines compile without error. The reason is that Java relaxes its assignment conversion rule when a literal `int` value is assigned to a narrower primitive type (`byte`, `short`, or `char`), provided the literal value falls within the legal range of the primitive type.

This relaxation of the rule applies only when the assigned value is an integral literal. Thus the second line of the following code will *not* compile:

```
int i = 12;
byte b = I
```

Primitive Conversion: Method Call

Another kind of conversion is *method-call conversion*. A method-call conversion happens when you pass a value of one type as an argument to a method that expects a different type. For example, the cos() method of the Math class expects a single argument of type double. Consider the following code:

```
1. float frads;
2. double d;
3. frads = 2.34567f;
4. d = Math.cos(frads);   // Pass float to method
                          // that expects double
```

The float value in frads is automatically converted to a double value before it is handed to the cos() method. Just as with assignment conversions, strict rules govern which conversions are allowed and which conversions will be rejected by the compiler. The following code quite reasonably generates a compiler error (assuming there is a vector called myVector):

```
1. double d = 12.0;
2. Object ob = myVector.elementAt(d);
```

The compiler error message says, "Incompatible type for method. Explicit cast needed to convert double to int." This means the compiler can't convert the double argument to a type that is supported by a version of the elementAt() method. It turns out that the only version of elementAt() is the version that takes an integer argument. Thus a value can be passed to elementAt() only if that value is an int or can be converted to an int.

Fortunately, the rule that governs which method-call conversions are permitted is the same rule that governs assignment conversions. Widening conversions (as shown in Figure 4.3) are permitted; narrowing conversions are forbidden.

Primitive Conversion: Arithmetic Promotion

The last kind of primitive conversion to consider is *arithmetic promotion*. Arithmetic-promotion conversions happen within arithmetic statements while the compiler is trying to make sense out of many different possible kinds of operand.

Consider the following fragment:

```
1. short s = 9;
2. int i = 10;
3. float f = 11.1f;
4. double d = 12.2;
5. if (-s * i  >=  f / d)
6.    System.out.println(i
7. else
8.    System.out.println(i<<<<i);
```

The code on line 5 multiplies a negated `short` by an `int`; then it divides a `float` by a `double`; finally, it compares the two results. Behind the scenes, the system is doing extensive type conversion to ensure that the operands can be meaningfully incremented, multiplied, divided, and compared. These conversions are all widening conversions. Thus they are known as *arithmetic-promotion conversions* because values are *promoted* to wider types.

The rules that govern arithmetic promotion distinguish between unary and binary operators. Unary operators operate on a single value. Binary operators operate on two values. Figure 4.4 shows Java's unary and binary arithmetic operators.

FIGURE 4.4   Unary and binary arithmetic operators

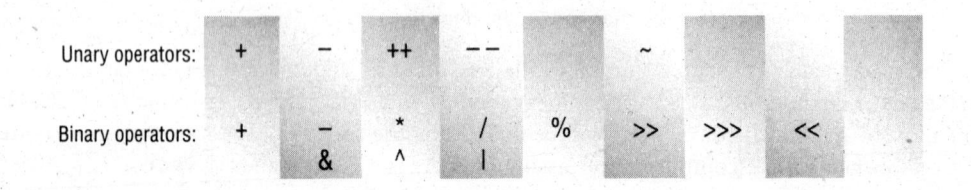

Unary operators: +   −   ++   −−   ~

Binary operators: +   −   *   /   %   >>   >>>   <<
                              &   ^ |

For unary operators, two rules apply, depending on the type of the single operand:

- If the operand is a `byte`, a `short`, or a `char`, it is converted to an `int` (unless the operator is ++ or --, in which case no conversion happens).
- Else there is no conversion.

For binary operators, there are four rules, depending on the types of the two operands:

- If one of the operands is a `double`, the other operand is converted to a `double`.
- Else if one of the operands is a `float`, the other operand is converted to a `float`.
- Else if one of the operands is a `long`, the other operand is converted to a `long`.
- Else both operands are converted to `int`s.

With these rules in mind, it is possible to determine what really happens in the code example given at the beginning of this section:

1. The `short` s is promoted to an `int` and then negated.
2. The result of step 1 (an `int`) is multiplied by the `int` i. Because both operands are of the same type, and that type is not narrower than an `int`, no conversion is necessary. The result of the multiplication is an `int`.
3. Before `float` f is divided by `double` d, f is widened to a `double`. The division generates a double-precision result.
4. The result of step 2 (an `int`) is to be compared to the result of step 3 (a `double`). The `int` is converted to a `double`, and the two operands are compared. The result of a comparison is always of type `boolean`.

Primitives and Casting

So far, this chapter has shown that Java is perfectly willing to perform widening conversions on primitives. These conversions are implicit and behind the scenes; you don't need to write any explicit code to make them happen.

Casting is explicitly telling Java to make a conversion. A casting operation may widen or narrow its argument. To cast, just precede a value with the parenthesized name of the desired type. For example, the following lines of code cast an `int` to a `double`:

```
1. int i = 5;
2. double d = (double)i;
```

Of course, the cast is not always necessary. The following code, in which the cast has been omitted, would do an assignment conversion on i, with the same result as the previous example:

```
1. int i = 5;
2. double d = i;
```

Casts are required when you want to perform a narrowing conversion. Such conversion will never be performed implicitly; you have to program an explicit cast to convince the compiler that what you really want is a narrowing conversion. Narrowing runs the risk of losing information; the cast tells the compiler that you accept the risk.

For example, the following code generates a compiler error:

```
1. short s = 259;
2. byte b = s;    // Compiler error
3. System.out.println("s = " + s + ", b = " + b);
```

The compiler error message for the second line will say (among other things), "Explicit cast needed to convert short to byte." Adding an explicit cast is easy:

```
1. short s = 259;
2. byte b = (byte)s;    // Explicit cast
3. System.out.println("b = " + i + b);
```

When this code is executed, the number 259 (binary 100000011) must be squeezed into a single byte. This is accomplished by preserving the low-order byte of the value and discarding the rest. The code prints out the (perhaps surprising) message:

b = 3

The 1 bit in bit position 8 is discarded, leaving only 3, as shown in Figure 4.5. Narrowing conversions can result in radical value changes; this is why the compiler requires you to cast explicitly. The cast tells the compiler, "Yes, I really want to do it."

FIGURE 4.5 Casting a short to a byte

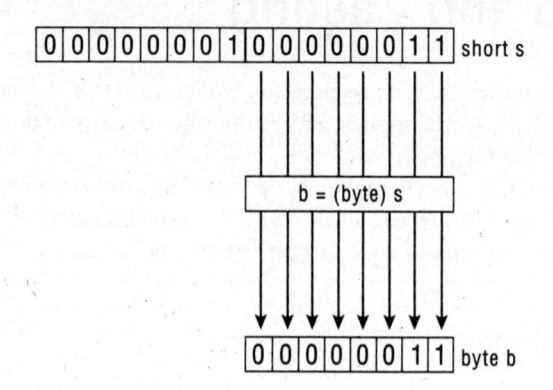

```
0 0 0 0 0 0 0 1 0 0 0 0 0 0 1 1  short s

            b = (byte) s

              0 0 0 0 0 0 1 1  byte b
```

Casting a value to a wider value (as shown in Figure 4.3) is always permitted but never required; if you omit the cast, an implicit conversion will be performed on your behalf. However, explicitly casting can make your code a bit more readable. For example:

1. int i = 2;
2. double radians;
   .   // Hundreds of
   .   // lines of
   .   // code
600. radians = (double)i;

The cast in the last line is not required, but it serves as a good reminder to any readers (including yourself) who might have forgotten the type of radians.

Two simple rules govern casting of primitive types:

- You can cast any non-boolean type to any other non-boolean type.
- You cannot cast a boolean to any other type; you cannot cast any other type to a boolean.

Note that although casting is ordinarily used when narrowing, it is perfectly legal to cast when widening. The cast is unnecessary, but provides a bit of clarity.

Real World Scenario

Legal and Illegal Casts

Write an application that illustrates legal and illegal casts. Work with the following class (and interface) hierarchy:

```
class Fruit class Apple extends Fruit interface Squeezable class Citrus extends
Fruit implements Squeezableclass Orange extends Citrus
```

> Your application should construct one instance of each of the following classes:
>
> - Object
> - Fruit
> - Apple
> - Citrus
> - Orange
>
> Try to cast each of these objects to each of the following types:
>
> - Fruit
> - Apple
> - Squeezable
> - Citrus
> - Orange
>
> For each attempted cast, print out a message stating whether the attempted cast succeeded. (A ClassCastException is thrown if the cast failed; if no exception is thrown, the cast succeeded.) A fragment of the output of the sample solution looks like this:
>
> ```
> Checking casts for Fruit      Fruit: OK
>       Apple: NO      Squeezable: NO      Citrus: NO      Orange: NO
> Checking casts for Apple      Fruit: OK      Apple: OK      Squeezable: NO
> Citrus: NO      Orange: NO
> ```

Object Reference Conversion

Object reference variables, like primitive values, participate in assignment conversion, method-call conversion, and casting. (There is no arithmetic promotion of object references, because references cannot be arithmetic operands.) Object reference conversion is more complicated than primitive conversion, because there are more possible combinations of old and new types—and more combinations mean more rules.

Reference conversion, like primitive conversion, takes place at compile time, because the compiler has all the information it needs to determine whether the conversion is legal. Later you will see that this is not the case for object casting.

The following sections examine object reference assignment, method-call, and casting conversions.

Object Reference Assignment Conversion

Object reference assignment conversion happens when you assign an object reference value to a variable of a different type. There are three general kinds of object reference type:

- A class type, such as `Button` or `FileWriter`
- An interface type, such as `Cloneable` or `LayoutManager`
- An array type, such as `int[][]` or `TextArea[]`

Generally speaking, assignment conversion of a reference looks like this:

1. `Oldtype x = new Oldtype();`
2. `Newtype y = x;    // reference assignment conversion`

This is the general format of an assignment conversion from an `Oldtype` to a `Newtype`. Unfortunately, `Oldtype` can be a class, an interface, or an array; `Newtype` can also be a class, an interface, or an array. Thus there are nine (= 3 ∴ 3) possible combinations to consider. Figure 4.6 shows the rules for all nine cases.

FIGURE 4.6 The rules for object reference assignment conversion

Converting `Oldtype` to `Newtype`:

	`Oldtype` is a class	`Oldtype` is an interface	`Oldtype` is an array
`Newtype` is a class	`Oldtype` must be a subclass of `Newtype`	`Newtype` must be `Object`	`Newtype` must be `Object`
`Newtype` is an interface	`Oldtype` must implement interface `Newtype`	`Oldtype` must be a subinterface of `Newtype`	`Newtype` must be `Cloneable` or `Serializable`
`Newtype` is an array	Compiler error	Compiler error	`Oldtype` must be an array of some object reference type that can be converted to whatever `Newtype` is an array of

It would be difficult to memorize the nine rules shown in Figure 4.6. Fortunately, there is a rule of thumb.

Recall that with primitives, conversions were permitted, provided they were widening conversions. The notion of widening does not really apply to references, but a similar principle is at work. In general, object reference conversion is permitted when the direction of the conversion is "up" the inheritance hierarchy; that is, the old type should inherit from the new type. This rule of thumb does not cover all nine cases, but it is a helpful way to look at things.

The rules for object reference conversion can be stated as follows:

- An interface type can be converted only to an interface type or to `Object`. If the new type is an interface, it must be a superinterface of the old type.
- A class type can be converted to a class type or to an interface type. If converting to a class type, the new type must be a superclass of the old type. If converting to an interface type, the old class must implement the interface.
- An array may be converted to the class `Object`, to the interface `Cloneable` or `Serializable`, or to an array. Only an array of object reference types can be converted to an array, and the old element type must be convertible to the new element type.

To illustrate these rules, consider the inheritance hierarchy shown in Figure 4.7 (assume there is an interface called `Squeezable`).

FIGURE 4.7 A simple class hierarchy

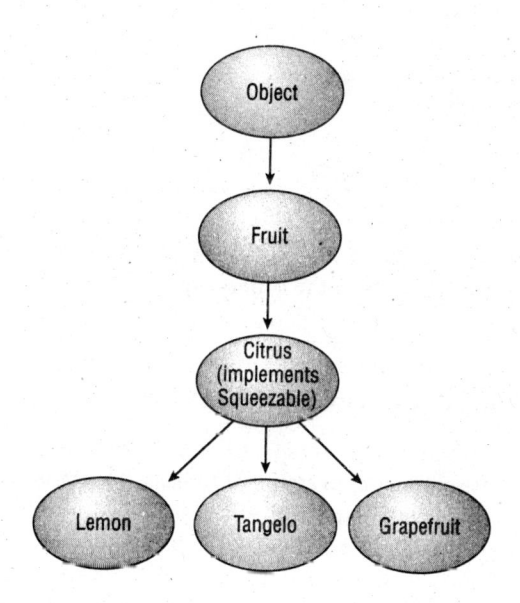

As a first example, consider the following code:

1. `Tangelo tange = new Tangelo();`
2. `Citrus cit = tange;`

This code is fine. A `Tangelo` is being converted to a `Citrus`. The new type is a superclass of the old type, so the conversion is allowed. Converting in the other direction ("down" the hierarchy tree) is not allowed:

1. `Citrus cit = new Citrus();`
2. `Tangelo tange = cit;`

This code will result in a compiler error.

What happens when one of the types is an interface?

1. Grapefruit g = new Grapefruit();
2. Squeezable squee = g;   // No problem
3. Grapefruit g2 = squee;   // Error

The second line ("No problem") changes a class type (Grapefruit) to an interface type. This is correct, provided Grapefruit really implements Squeezable. A glance at Figure 4.7 shows that this is indeed the case, because Grapefruit inherits from Citrus, which implements Squeezable. The third line is an error, because an interface can never be implicitly converted to any reference type other than Object.

Finally, consider an example with arrays:

1. Fruit fruits[];
2. Lemon lemons[];
3. Citrus citruses[] = new Citrus[10];
4. for (int i = 0; i < 10; i++) {
5.   citruses[i] = new Citrus();
6. }
7. fruits = citruses;   // No problem
8. lemons = citruses;   // Error

Line 7 converts an array of Citrus to an array of Fruit. This is fine, because Fruit is a superclass of Citrus. Line 8 converts in the other direction and fails, because Lemon is not a superclass of Citrus.

Object Method-Call Conversion

Fortunately, the rules for method-call conversion of object reference values are the same as the rules described earlier for assignment conversion of objects. The general rule of thumb is that converting to a superclass is permitted and converting to a subclass is not permitted.

To see how the rules make sense in the context of method calls, consider the extremely useful java.lang.Vector class. You can store anything you like in a vector (anything nonprimitive, that is) by calling the method add (Object ob). For example, the following code stores a Tangelo in a vector:

1. Vector myVec = new Vector();
2. Tangelo tange = new Tangelo();
3. myVec.add (tange);

The tange argument will automatically be converted to type Object. The automatic conversion means that the people who wrote the java.lang.Vector class didn't have to write a separate method for every possible type of object that anyone might conceivably want to store in a vector. This is fortunate: the `Tangelo` class was developed years after the invention of the vector, so the developer of the `Vector` class could not possibly have written specific `Tangelo`-handling code. An object of any class (and even an array of any type) can be passed into the single `add (Object ob)` method.

Object Reference Casting

Object reference casting is like primitive casting: by using a cast, you convince the compiler to let you do a conversion that otherwise might not be allowed.

Any kind of conversion that is allowed for assignments or method calls is allowed for explicit casting. For example, the following code is legal:

```
1. Lemon lem = new Lemon();
2. Citrus cit = (Citrus)lem;
```

The cast is legal but not needed; if you leave it out, the compiler will do an implicit assignment conversion. The power of casting appears when you explicitly cast to a type that is not allowed by the rules of implicit conversion.

To understand how object casting works, it is important to understand the difference between objects and object reference variables. Every object (well, nearly every object—there are some obscure cases) is constructed via the new operator. The class name following new determines for all time the true class of the object. For example, if an object is constructed by calling `new Color(222, 0, 255)`, then throughout that object's lifetime, its class will be `Color`.

Java programs do not deal directly with objects. They deal with references to objects. For example, consider the following code:

```
Color purple = new Color(222, 0, 255);
```

The variable `purple` is not an object; it is a reference to an object. The object itself lives in memory somewhere in the Java Virtual Machine (JVM). The variable `purple` contains something similar to the address of the object. This address is known as a *reference* to the object. The difference between a reference and an object is illustrated in Figure 4.8. References are stored in variables, and variables have types that are specified by the programmer at compile time. Object reference variable types can be classes (such as `Graphics` or `FileWriter`), interfaces (such as `Runnable` or `LayoutManager`), or arrays (such as `int[][]` or `Vector[]`).

Chapter 4 · Converting and Casting

FIGURE 4.8 Reference and object

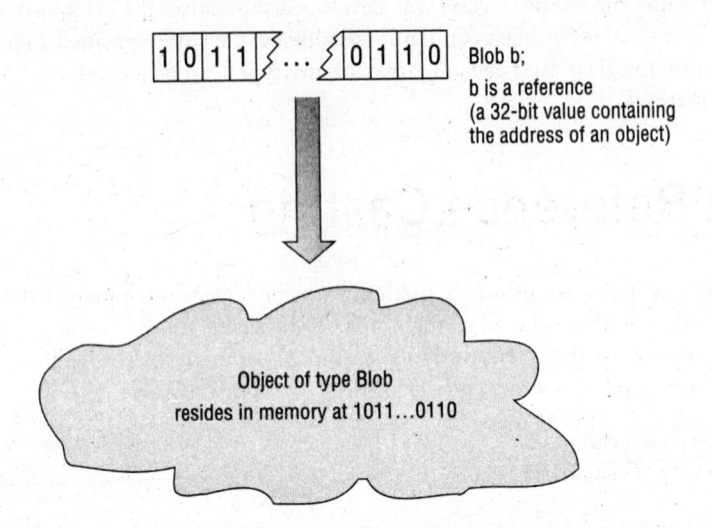

```
|1|0|1|1|...|0|1|1|0|   Blob b;
                         b is a reference
                         (a 32-bit value containing
                         the address of an object)
```

Object of type Blob resides in memory at 1011...0110

Although an object's class is unchanging, it may be referenced by variables of many different types. For example, consider a stack. It is constructed by calling new Stack(), so its class really is Stack. Yet at various moments during the lifetime of this object, it may be referenced by variables of type Stack (of course), or of type Vector (because Stack inherits from Vector), or of type Object (because everything inherits from Object). It may even be referenced by variables of type Serializable, which is an interface, because the Stack class implements the Serializable interface. This situation is shown in Figure 4.9.

FIGURE 4.9 Many variable types, one class

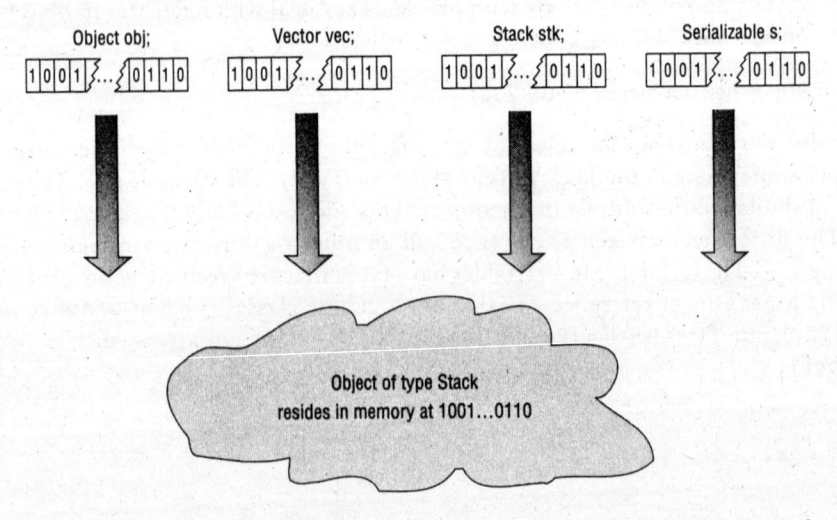

Object obj;   Vector vec;   Stack stk;   Serializable s;

Object of type Stack resides in memory at 1001...0110

The type of a reference variable is obvious at compile time. However, the class of an object referenced by such a variable cannot be known until runtime. This lack of knowledge is not a shortcoming of Java technology; it results from a fundamental principle of computer science. The distinction between compile-time knowledge and runtime knowledge was not relevant to our discussion of conversions; however, the difference becomes important with reference value casting. The rules for casting are a bit broader than those for conversion. Some of these rules concern reference type and can be enforced by the compiler at compile time; other rules concern object class and can be enforced only during execution.

Quite a few rules govern object casting because a large number of obscure cases must be covered. For the exam, the important rules to remember when casting from Oldtype to Newtype are as follows:

- When both Oldtype and Newtype are classes, one class must be a subclass of the other.
- When both Oldtype and Newtype are arrays, both arrays must contain reference types (not primitives), and it must be legal to cast an element of Oldtype to an element of Newtype.
- You can always cast between an interface and a nonfinal object.

Assuming that a desired cast survives compilation, a second check must occur at runtime. The second check determines whether the class of the object being cast is compatible with the new type. (This check could not be made at compile time, because the object being cast did not exist then.) Here, *compatible* means that the class can be converted according to the conversion rules discussed in the previous two sections. The following rules cover the most common runtime cases:

- If Newtype is a class, the class of the expression being converted must be Newtype or must inherit from Newtype.
- If Newtype is an interface, the class of the expression being converted must implement Newtype.

It is definitely time for some examples! Look once again at the Fruit/Citrus hierarchy that you saw earlier in this chapter, which is repeated in Figure 4.10.

FIGURE 4.10   Fruit hierarchy (reprise)

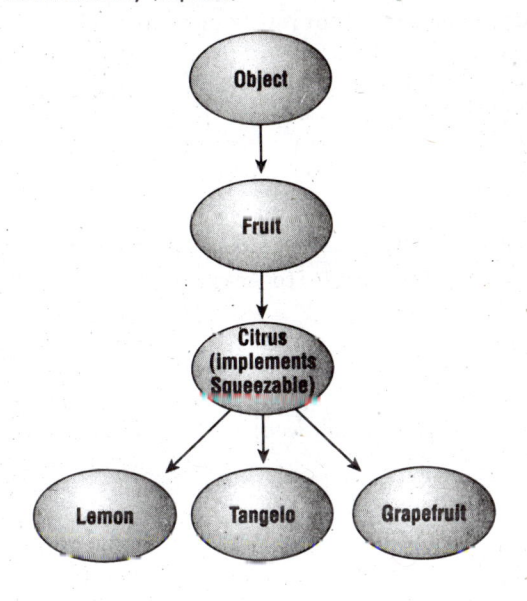

First, consider the following code:

```
1. Grapefruit g, g1;
2. Citrus c;
3. Tangelo t;
4. g = new Grapefruit();  // Class is Grapefruit
5. c = g;                  // Legal assignment conversion,
                           // no cast needed
6. g1 = (Grapefruit)c;     // Legal cast
7. t = (Tangelo)c;         // Illegal cast
                           // (throws an exception)
```

This code has four references but only one object. The object's class is Grapefruit, because Grapefruit's constructor is called on line 4. The assignment c = g on line 5 is a perfectly legal assignment conversion ("up" the inheritance hierarchy), so no explicit cast is required. In lines 6 and 7, the Citrus is cast to a Grapefruit and to a Tangelo. Recall that for casting between class types, one of the two classes (it doesn't matter which one) must be a subclass of the other. The first cast is from a Citrus to its subclass Grapefruit; the second cast is from a Citrus to its subclass Tangelo. Thus both casts are legal—at compile time. The compiler cannot determine the class of the object referenced by c, so it accepts both casts and lets fate determine the outcome at runtime.

When the code is executed, eventually the JVM attempts to execute line 6: g1 = (Grapefruit)c;. The class of c is determined to be Grapefruit, and there is no objection to converting a Grapefruit to a Grapefruit.

Line 7 attempts (at runtime) to cast c to type Tangelo. The class of c is still Grapefruit, and a Grapefruit cannot be cast to a Tangelo. In order for the cast to be legal, the class of c would have to be Tangelo itself or some subclass of Tangelo. Because this is not the case, a runtime exception (java.lang.ClassCastException) is thrown.

Now take an example where an object is cast to an interface type. Begin by considering the following code fragment:

```
1. Grapefruit g, g1;
2. Squeezable s;
3. g = new Grapefruit();
4. s = g;      // Convert Grapefruit to Squeezable (OK)
5. g1 = s;     // Convert Squeezable to Grapefruit
               // (Compile error)
```

This code will not compile. Line 5 attempts to convert an interface (Squeezable) to a class (Grapefruit). It doesn't matter that Grapefruit implements Squeezable. Implicitly converting an interface to a class is never allowed; it is one of those cases where you have to use an explicit cast to tell the compiler that you really know what you're doing. With the cast, line 5 becomes

```
5. g1 = (Grapefruit)s;
```

Adding the cast makes the compiler happy. At runtime, the JVM checks whether the class of s (which is Grapefruit) can be converted to Grapefruit. It certainly can, so the cast is allowed.

For a final example, involving arrays, look at the following code:

```
1. Grapefruit g[];
2. Squeezable s[];
3. Citrus c[];
4. g = new Grapefruit[500];
5. s = g;            // Convert Grapefruit array to
                     // Squeezable array (OK)
6. c = (Citrus[])s;  // Cast Squeezable array to Citrus
                     // array (OK)
```

Line 6 casts an array of Squeezables (s) to an array of Citruses (c). An array cast is legal if casting the array element types is legal (and if the element types are references, not primitives). In this example, the question is whether a Squeezable (the element type of array s) can be cast to a Citrus (the element type of the cast array). The previous example showed that this is a legal cast.

Summary

Primitive values and object references are very different kinds of data. Both can be converted (implicitly) or cast (explicitly). Primitive type changes are caused by assignment conversion, method-call conversion, arithmetic-promotion conversion, or explicit casting.

Primitives can be converted only if the conversion widens the data. Primitives can be narrowed by casting, as long as neither the old nor the new type is boolean.

Object references can be converted or cast; the rules that govern these activities are extensive because many combinations of cases must be covered. In general, going "up" the inheritance tree can be accomplished implicitly through conversion; going "down" the tree requires explicit casting. Object reference type changes are caused by assignment conversion, method-call conversion, or explicit casting.

Exam Essentials

Understand when primitive conversion takes place. Assignment and method-call conversion take place when the new data type is the same as or wider than the old type. Type widths are summarized in Figure 4.3.

Understand when arithmetic promotion takes place. You should know the type of result of unary and binary arithmetic operations performed on operands of any type.

Understand when primitive casting is required. Casting is required when the new data type is neither the same as nor wider than the old type.

Understand when object reference conversion takes place. The rules are summarized in Figure 4.6. The most common case is when the new type is a parent class of the old type.

Understand when object reference casting is required. The most common case is when the new type inherits from the old type.

Key Terms

Before you take the exam, be certain you are familiar with the following terms:

arithmetic promotion	method-call conversion
arithmetic-promotion conversion	narrowing conversion
assignment conversion	reference
casting	widening conversion
conversion	

Review Questions

1. Which of the following statements is correct? (Choose one.)
   A. Only primitives are converted automatically; to change the type of an object reference, you have to do a cast.
   B. Only object references are converted automatically; to change the type of a primitive, you have to do a cast.
   C. Arithmetic promotion of object references requires explicit casting.
   D. Both primitives and object references can be both converted and cast.
   E. Casting of numeric types may require a runtime check.

2. Which one line in the following code will not compile?
   A. `byte b = 5;`
   B. `char c = '5';`
   C. `short s = 55;`
   D. `int i = 555;`
   E. `float f = 555.5f;`
   F. `b = s;`
   G. `i = c;`
   H. `if (f > b)`
   I. `f = i;`

3. Will the following code compile?
   ```
   1. byte b = 2;
   2. byte b1 = 3;
   3. b = b * b1;
   ```
   A. Yes
   B. No

4. In the following code, what are the possible types for variable `result`? (Choose the most complete true answer.)
   ```
   1. byte b = 11;
   2. short s = 13;
   ```

3. `result = b * ++s;`

   A. byte, short, int, long, float, double
   B. boolean, byte, short, char, int, long, float, double
   C. byte, short, char, int, long, float, double
   D. byte, short, char
   E. int, long, float, double

5. Consider the following class:

```
1.  class Cruncher {
2.    void crunch(int i) {
3.      System.out.println(ìint versionî);
4.    }
5.    void crunch(String s) {
6.      System.out.println(ìString versionî);
7.    }
8.
9.    public static void main(String args[]) {
10.     Cruncher crun = new Cruncher();
11.     char ch = 'p';
12.     crun.crunch(ch);
13.   }
14. }
```

   Which of the following statements is true? (Choose one.)
   A. Line 5 will not compile, because void methods cannot be overridden.
   B. Line 12 will not compile, because no version of crunch() takes a char argument.
   C. The code will compile but will throw an exception at line 12.
   D. The code will compile and produce the following output: int version.
   E. The code will compile and produce the following output: String version.

6. Which of the following statements is true? (Choose one.)
   A. Object references can be converted in assignments but not in method calls.
   B. Object references can be converted in method calls but not in assignments.
   C. Object references can be converted in both method calls and assignments, but the rules governing these conversions are very different.
   D. Object references can be converted in both method calls and assignments, and the rules governing these conversions are identical.
   E. Object references can never be converted.

7. Consider the following code. Which line will not compile?
   A. `Object ob = new Object();`
   B. `String stringarr[] = new String[50];`
   C. `Float floater = new Float(3.14f);`
   D.
   E. `ob = stringarr;`
   F. `ob = stringarr[5];`
   G. `floater = ob;`
   H. `ob = floater;`

8. Questions 8–10 refer to the class hierarchy shown in Figure 4.11.

   FIGURE 4.11 Class hierarchy for questions 8, 9, and 10

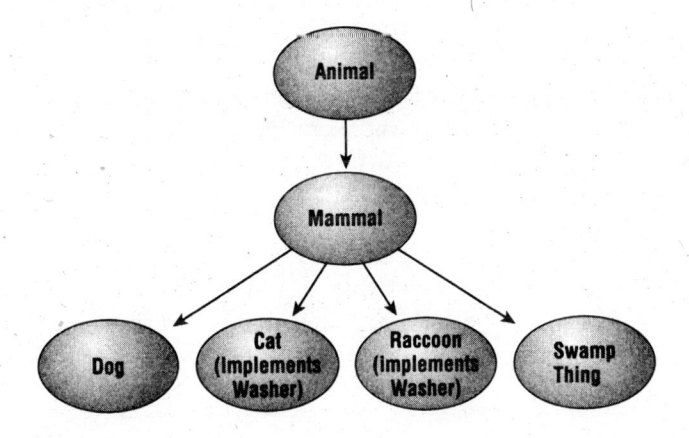

   Consider the following code:
   ```
   1. Dog       rover, fido;
   2. Animal    anim;
   3.
   4. rover = new Dog();
   5. anim = rover;
   6. fido = (Dog)anim;
   ```

   Which of the following statements is true? (Choose one.)
   A. Line 5 will not compile.
   B. Line 6 will not compile.
   C. The code will compile but will throw an exception at line 6.
   D. The code will compile and run.
   E. The code will compile and run, but the cast in line 6 is not required and can be eliminated.

9. Consider the following code:
   1. `Cat sunflower;`
   2. `Washer wawa;`
   3. `SwampThing pogo;`
   4.
   5. `sunflower = new Cat();`
   6. `wawa = sunflower;`
   7. `pogo = (SwampThing)wawa;`

   Which of the following statements is true? (Choose one.)
   A. Line 6 will not compile; an explicit cast is required to convert a `Cat` to a `Washer`.
   B. Line 7 will not compile, because you cannot cast an interface to a class.
   C. The code will compile and run, but the cast in line 7 is not required and can be eliminated.
   D. The code will compile but will throw an exception at line 7, because runtime conversion from an interface to a class is not permitted.
   E. The code will compile but will throw an exception at line 7, because the runtime class of `wawa` cannot be converted to type `SwampThing`.

10. Consider the following code:
    1. `Raccoon rocky;`
    2. `SwampThing pogo;`
    3. `Washer w;`
    4.
    5. `rocky = new Raccoon();`
    6. `w = rocky;`
    7. `pogo = w;`

    Which of the following statements is true? (Choose one.)
    A. Line 6 will not compile; an explicit cast is required to convert a `Raccoon` to a `Washer`.
    B. Line 7 will not compile; an explicit cast is required to convert a `Washer` to a `SwampThing`.
    C. The code will compile and run.
    D. The code will compile but will throw an exception at line 7, because runtime conversion from an interface to a class is not permitted.
    E. The code will compile but will throw an exception at line 7, because the runtime class of `w` cannot be converted to type `SwampThing`.

Answers to Review Questions

1. D. D is correct because in Java primitives and object references can be both converted and cast. A and B are wrong because they contradict D. C is wrong because objects do not take part in arithmetic operations. E is wrong because only casting of object references potentially requires a runtime check.

2. F. The code b = s will not compile, because converting a short to a byte is a narrowing conversion, which requires an explicit cast. The other assignments in the code are widening conversions.

3. B. Surprisingly, the code will fail to compile at line 3. The two operands, which are originally bytes, are converted to ints before the multiplication. The result of the multiplication is an int, which cannot be assigned to byte b.

4. E. The result of the calculation on line 2 is an int (because all arithmetic results are ints or wider). An int can be assigned to an int, long, float, or double.

5. D. At line 12, the char argument ch is widened to type int (a method-call conversion) and passed to the int version of method crunch().

6. D. Method-call and assignment conversions are governed by the same rules concerning the legal relationships between the old and new types.

7. G. Changing an Object to a Float is going "down" the inheritance hierarchy tree, so an explicit cast is required.

8. D. The code will compile and run. The cast in line 6 is required, because changing an Animal to a Dog is going "down" the tree.

9. E. The cast in line 7 is required. Answer D is a preposterous statement expressed in a tone of authority.

10. B. The conversion in line 6 is fine (class to interface), but the conversion in line 7 (interface to class) is not allowed. A cast in line 7 will make the code compile, but then at runtime a ClassCastException will be thrown, because Washer and SwampThing are incompatible.

Chapter 5

Flow Control, Assertions, and Exception Handling

JAVA CERTIFICATION EXAM OBJECTIVES COVERED IN THIS CHAPTER:

- ✓ 2.1 Write code using `if` and `switch` **statements, and identify legal argument types for these statements.**
- ✓ 2.2 Write code using all forms of loops including labeled and unlabeled use of `break` and `continue`, **and state the values taken by loop counter variables during and after loop execution.**
- ✓ 2.3 Write code that makes proper use of exceptions and exception handling clauses (`try`, `catch`, `finally`) **and declares methods and overriding methods that throw exceptions.**
- ✓ 2.4 Recognize the effect of an exception arising at a specified point in a code fragment. Note: The exception may be a runtime exception, a checked exception, or an error (the code may include `try`, `catch`, or `finally` **clauses in any legitimate combination).**
- ✓ 2.5 Write code that makes proper use of assertions, and distinguish appropriate from inappropriate uses of assertions.
- ✓ 2.6 Identify correct statements about the assertion mechanism.

Flow control is a fundamental facility of almost any programming language. Sequence, iteration, and selection are the major elements of flow control, and Java provides these in forms that are familiar to C and C++ programmers. Additionally, Java provides for exception handling.

Sequence control is provided simply by the specification that, within a single block of code, execution starts at the top and proceeds toward the bottom. Iteration is catered for by three styles of loop: the `for()`, `while()`, and `do` constructs. Selection occurs when either the `if()/else` or `switch()` construct is used.

Java omits one common element of flow control: the idea of a `goto` statement. When Java was being designed, the team responsible did some analysis of a large body of existing code and determined that the use of `goto` was appropriate in two situations in new code: when code breaks out of nested loops and during the handling of exception conditions or errors. The designers left out `goto` and, in its place, provided alternative constructions to handle these particular conditions. The `break` and `continue` statements that control the execution of loops were extended to handle nested loops, and formalized exception handling was introduced, using ideas similar to those of C++.

This chapter discusses the flow-control facilities of Java. We will look closely at the exception mechanism, because this area commonly causes some confusion. But first, we will discuss the loop mechanisms.

The Loop Constructs

Java provides three loop constructions. Taken from C and C++, these are the `while()`, `do`, and `for()` constructs. Each provides the facility for repeating the execution of a block of code until some condition occurs. We will discuss the `while()` loop, which is perhaps the simplest, first.

The *while()* Loop

The general form of the `while()` loop is

1. `while (boolean_condition)`
2.   `repeated_statement_or_block`

In such a construct, the element *boolean_condition* must be an expression that returns a `boolean` result. Notice that this differs from C and C++, where a variety of types may be used: In Java you can *only* use a `boolean` expression. Typically, you might use a comparison of some kind, such as `x > 5`.

The `repeated_statement_or_block` will be executed again and again as long as the `boolean_condition` is true. If the condition never becomes false, then the loop will repeat forever. In practice, this really means that the loop will repeat until the program is stopped or the machine is turned off.

Notice that we've described the loop body as a "repeated statement or block." We need to make two important points here. The first is one of coding style, and as such is not directly related to the Programmer's Exam (although it might be relevant to the Developer's Exam when you take that). The second is the strict interpretation of the language specification, and as such might be needed in the Programmer's Exam. The two issues are related, so we will discuss them over the next few paragraphs.

The first point is that you would be well advised always to write a block to contain the code for the body of a loop or an if() statement. That is, always use a pair of braces so your code will look like this:

```
1. while (boolean_condition) {
2.     statement(s);
3. }
```

You should do so even where the loop contains only a single statement. The reason is that in many situations, you will change from a single line to multiple lines, and if the braces are in position already, that is one less thing to forget. One typical situation where this arises is when you add debug output to the middle of a loop to see how many times the loop is executed. It's very frustrating to realize after 20 minutes of messing about that the loop was executed 10 times, although the message was printed only on exit from the loop. It's perhaps worse to see the message printed 10 times but to have moved the proper body of the loop outside of it entirely.

The second point is that, from the position of strict correctness, you need to know that a single statement without braces is allowed in loops and if statements. So, the following code is correct and prints "five times" five times, but "once" only once:

```
1. int i = 0;
2. while (i++ < 5)
3.     System.out.println("five times");
4. System.out.println("once");
```

It is highly unlikely that you will be presented with code that uses a single nonblocked statement as the body of a loop or the conditional part of an if statement, but if you do, you need to recognize how it will behave, and that it is not incorrect.

> **TIP** The exact position of the opening curly brace that marks a block of code is a matter of near-religious contention. Some programmers put it at the end of a line, as in most of the examples in this book. Others put it on a line by itself. Provided it is otherwise placed in the correct sequence, it does not matter how many space, tab, and newline characters are placed before or after the opening curly brace. In other words, this positioning is not relevant to syntactic correctness. You should be aware, however, that the style used in presenting the exam questions, as well as that used for the code in the developer-level exam, is the style shown here, where the opening brace is placed at the end of the line.

Observe that if the *boolean_condition* is already false when the loop is first encountered, then the body of the loop will never be executed. This fact relates to the main distinguishing feature of the do loop, which we will discuss next.

The *do* Loop

The general form of the do loop is

1. do
2.   *repeated_statement_or_block*
3. while (*boolean_condition*);

It is similar to the while() loop just discussed, and as before, it is best to have a loop body formed with a block:

1. do {
2.   do_something
3.   do_more
4. } while (*boolean_condition*);

Again, repetition of the loop is terminated when the *boolean_condition* becomes false. The significant difference is that this loop always executes the body of the loop at least once, because the test is performed at the end of the body.

Notice that the do loop (as opposed to the while loop) is guaranteed to run at least once, regardless of the value of the conditional expression. The do loop is probably used less frequently than the while() loop, but the third loop format is perhaps the most common. The third form is the for() loop, which we will discuss next.

The *for()* Loop

A common requirement in programming is to perform a loop so that a single variable is incremented over a range of values between two limits. This ability is frequently provided by a loop that uses the keyword for. Java's while() loop can achieve this effect, but it is most commonly achieved using the for() loop. However, as with C and C++, using the for() loop is more general than simply providing for iteration over a sequence of values.

The general form of the for() loop is

1. for (*statement* ; *condition* ; *expression*)
2.   *loop_body*

Again, a block should normally be used as the *loop_body* part, like this:

1. for (*statement* ; *condition* ; *expression*) {
2.   do_something
3.   do_more
4. }

The keys to this loop are in the three parts contained in the brackets following the for keyword:

- The *statement* is executed immediately before the loop itself is started. It is often used to set up starting conditions. You will see shortly that it can also contain variable declarations.
- The *condition* must be a boolean expression and is treated exactly the same as in the while() loop. The body of the loop will be executed repeatedly until the condition ceases to be true. As with the while() loop, it is possible that the body of a for() loop might never be executed. This occurs if the condition is already false at the start of the loop.
- The *expression* (short for "iteration expression") is executed immediately after the body of the loop, just before the test is performed again. Commonly, it is used to increment a loop counter.

If you have already declared an int variable x, you can code a simple sequence-counting loop like this:

```
1. for (x = 0; x < 10; x++) {
2.    System.out.println(ivalue is i + x);
3. }
```

This code would result in 10 lines of output, starting with

value is 0

and ending with

value is 9

In fact, because for() loops commonly need a counting variable, you are allowed to declare variables in the *statement* part. The scope of such a variable is restricted to the statement or block following the for() statement and the for() part itself. This limitation protects loop counter variables from interfering with each other and prevents leftover loop count values from accidental re-use. The result is code like this:

```
1. for (int x = 0; x < 10; x++) {
2.    System.out.println(ivalue is i + x);
3. }
```

It might be useful to look at the equivalent of this code implemented using a while() loop:

```
1. {
2.    int x = 0;
3.    while (x < 10) {
4.       System.out.println(ivalue is i + x);
5.       x++;
6.    }
7. }
```

This version reinforces a couple of points. First, the scope of the variable x, declared in the `statement` part of the `for()` loop, is restricted to the loop and its control parts (that is, the `statement`, `condition`, and `expression`). Second, the `expression` is executed after the rest of the loop body, effectively before control comes back to the test condition.

Empty *for()* Loops

Any part of a `for()` loop's control may be omitted if you wish. Omitting the test is equivalent to a perpetually true test, so the construct

```
for(;;) {}
```

creates a loop that repeats forever. Notice that both semicolons must still be included for correct syntax, even though the statement, condition, and expression are omitted.

The *for()* Loop and the Comma Separator

The `for()` loop allows the use of the comma separator in a special way. The `statement` and `expression` parts described previously can contain a sequence of expressions rather than just a single one. If you want such a sequence, you should separate those expressions, not with a semicolon (which would be mistaken as the separator between the three parts of the `for()` loop control structure), but with a comma. This behavior is borrowed from C and C++, where the comma is an operator; in Java the comma serves only as a special case separator for conditions where the semicolon would be unsuitable. This example demonstrates:

```
1. int j, k;
2. for (j = 3, k = 6; j + k < 20; j++, k +=2) {
3.     System.out.println("j is " + j + " k is " + k);
4. }
```

Note that although you can use the comma to separate several expressions, you cannot mix expressions with variable declarations, nor can you have multiple declarations of different types. So these would be illegal:

```
1. int i = 7;
2. for (i++, int j = 0; i < 10; j++) { } // illegal!
```

```
1. for (int i = 7, long j = 0; i < 10; j++) { } // illegal!
```

A final note on this issue is that the use of the comma to separate multiple declarations of a single type is allowed, like this:

```
1. for (int i = 7, j = 0; i < 10; j++) { }
```

This line declares two `int` variables, i and j, and initializes them to 7 and 0 respectively. This, however, is a standard feature of declarations and is not specific to the `for()` loop.

We have now discussed the three loop constructions in their basic forms. The next section looks at more advanced flow control in loops, specifically the use of the `break` and `continue` statements.

The *break* and *continue* Statements in Loops

Sometimes you need to abandon execution of the body of a loop—or perhaps a number of nested loops. The Java development team recognized this situation as a legitimate use for a goto statement. Java provides two statements, break and continue, which can be used instead of goto to achieve this effect.

Using *continue*

Suppose you have a loop that is processing an array of items that each contain two String references. The first String is always non-null, but the second might not be present. To process this, you might decide that you want, in pseudocode, something along these lines:

```
for each element of the array
   process the first String
   if the second String exists
      process the second String
   endif
endfor
```

You will recognize that this can be coded easily by using an if block to control processing of the second String. However, you can also use the continue statement like this:

```
1. for (int i = 0; i < array.length; i++) {
2.    // process first string
3.    if (array[i].secondString == null) {
4.       continue;
5.    }
6.    // process second string
7. }
```

In this case, the example is sufficiently simple that you probably do not see any advantage over using the if() condition to control the execution of the second part. If the second String processing was long, and perhaps heavily indented in its own right, you might find that the use of continue was slightly simpler visually.

The real strength of continue is that it is able to skip out of multiple levels of loop. Suppose the example, instead of being two String objects, is two-dimensional arrays of char values. Now you will need to nest your loops. Consider this sample:

```
1. mainLoop: for (int i = 0; i < array.length; i++) {
2.    for (int j = 0; j < array[i].length; j++) {
3.       if (array[i][j] == '\u0000') {
4.          continue mainLoop;
5.       }
6.    }
7. }
```

Notice particularly the label `mainLoop` that has been applied to the `for()` on line 1. The fact that this is a label is indicated by the trailing colon. You typically apply labels of this form to the opening loop statements: `while()`, `do`, or `for()`.

Here, when the processing of the second array comes across a 0 value, it abandons the whole processing not just for the inner loop, but for the current object in the main array. This is equivalent to jumping to the statement `i++` in the first `for()` statement.

You might still think this is not really any advantage over using `if()` statements, but imagine that further processing was done between lines 6 and 7, and that finding the 0 character in the array was required to avoid that further processing. To achieve that without using `continue`, you would have to set a flag in the inner loop and use it to abandon the outer loop processing. It can be done, but it is rather messy.

Using *break*

The `break` statement, when applied to a loop, is somewhat similar to the `continue` statement. However, instead of prematurely completing the current iteration of a loop, `break` causes the entire loop to be abandoned. Consider this example:

```
1. for (int j = 0; j < array.length; j++) {
2.     if (array[j] == null) {
3.         break; //break out of inner loop
4.     }
5.     // process array[j]
6. }
```

In this case, instead of simply skipping some processing for `array[j]` and proceeding directly to processing `array[j+1]`, this version quits the entire inner loop as soon as a `null` element is found.

You can also use labels on `break` statements, and as before, you must place a matching label on one of the enclosing blocks. The `break` and `continue` statements provide a convenient way to make parts of a loop conditional, especially when used in their labeled formats.

> **TIP** In fact, labels may be applied to any statements, and break can be used to jump out of any labeled block, whether that block is the body of a loop statement or not. Thus the break statement is a close imitation of a full-fledged goto. In the Certification Exam, you will not be expected to use break for any purpose other than jumping out of loops. In daily programming, you should probably avoid using it for any other purpose, too.

The next section discusses the `if()`/`else` and `switch()` constructions, which provide the normal means of implementing conditional code.

The Selection Statements

Java provides a choice of two selection constructs: the if()/else and switch() mechanisms. You can easily write simple conditional code for a choice of two execution paths based on the value of a boolean expression using if()/else. If you need more complex choices between multiple execution paths, and if an integral argument is available to control the choice, then you can use switch(); otherwise you can use either nests or sequences of if()/else.

The *if()/else* Construct

The if()/else construct takes a boolean argument as the basis of its choice. Often you will use a comparison expression to provide this argument. For example:

```
1. if (x > 5) {
2.    System.out.println("x is more than 5");
3. }
```

This sample executes line 2, provided the test (x > 5) in line 1 returns true. Notice that we used a block even though there is only a single conditional line, just as we suggested you should generally do with the loops discussed earlier.

You can use an else block to give code that is executed under the conditions that the test returns false. For example:

```
1. if (x > 5) {
2.    System.out.println("x is more than 5");
3. }
4. else {
5.    System.out.println("x is not more than 5");
6. }
```

You can also use if()/else in a nested fashion, refining conditions to more specific, or narrower, tests at each point.

The if()/else construction makes a test between only two possible paths of execution. However, you can also use the if()/else construction to choose between multiple possible execution paths by using the if()/else if() varation of the construction. For example:

```
1. if (hours > 1700) {
2.    System.out.println("good evening");
3. }
4. else if (hours > 1200){
```

```
5.    System.out.println("good afternoon");
6. }
7. else {
8.    System.out.println("good morning");
9. }
```

The code snippet above can be rewritten using the `switch()` statement. The next section discusses the `switch()` statement, which allows a single value to select between multiple possible execution paths.

The *switch()* Construct

If you need to make a choice between multiple alternative execution paths, and the choice can be based upon an `int` value, you can use the `switch()` construct. Consider this example:

```
1. switch (x) {
2.    case 1:
3.       System.out.println("Got a 1");
4.       break;
5.    case 2:
6.    case 3:
7.       System.out.println("Got 2 or 3");
8.       break;
9.    default:
10.      System.out.println("Not a 1, 2, or 3");
11.      break;
12. }
```

Note that, although you cannot determine the fact by inspection of this code, the variable x must be either `byte`, `short`, `char`, or `int`. It must not be `long`, either of the floating-point types, `boolean`, or an object reference. Strictly, the value must be "assignment compatible" with `int`.

The comparison of values following `case` labels with the value of the expression supplied as an argument to `switch()` determines the execution path. The arguments to `case` labels must be constants, or at least constant expressions that can be fully evaluated at compile time. You cannot use a variable or an expression involving variables.

Each `case` label takes only a single argument, but when execution jumps to one of these labels, it continues downward until it reaches a `break` statement. This occurs even if execution passes another `case` label or the `default` label. So, in the previous example, if x has the value 2, execution goes through lines 1, 5, 6, 7, and 8, and continues beyond line 12. This requirement for `break` to indicate the completion of the `case` part is important. More often than not, you do not want to omit the `break`, because you do not want execution to "fall through." However, to achieve the effect shown in the example, where more than one particular value of x causes execution of the same block of code, you use multiple `case` labels with only a single `break`.

The `default` statement is comparable to the `else` part of an `if()/else` construction. Execution jumps to the `default` statement if none of the explicit `case` values matches the argument provided to `switch()`. Although the `default` statement is shown at the end of the `switch()` block in the example (and this is both a conventional and reasonably logical place to put it), no rule requires this placement.

Now that you have examined the constructions that provide for iteration and selection under normal program control, let's look at the flow of control under exception conditions—that is, conditions when some runtime problem has arisen.

Exceptions

Sometimes when a program is executing, something occurs that is not quite normal from the point of view of the goal at hand. For example, a user might enter an invalid filename; a file might contain corrupted data; a network link could fail; or a bug in the program might cause it to try to make an illegal memory access, such as referring to an element beyond the end of an array.

Circumstances of this type are called *exception* conditions in Java and are represented using objects. A subtree of the class hierarchy starting with the class `java.lang.Throwable` is dedicated to describing them.

The process of an exception "appearing" either from the immediate cause of the trouble, or because a method call is abandoned and passes the exception up to its caller, is called *throwing* an exception in Java. You will hear other terms used, particularly an exception being *raised*.

If you take no steps to deal with an exception, execution jumps to the end of the current method. The exception then appears in the caller of that method, and execution jumps to the end of the calling method. This process continues until execution reaches the "top" of the affected thread, at which point the thread dies.

Flow of Control in Exception Conditions

When you write your own exception-based code, and when you prepare for the exam, it is vital to understand exactly how control proceeds, whether or not an exception gets thrown. The following sections examine control in the common `try/catch` case, when a `finally` block is included, and when multiple exception handlers are provided.

Using *try{} catch() {}*

To intercept, and thereby control, an exception, you use a `try/catch/finally` construction. You place lines of code that are part of the normal processing sequence in a *try* block. You then add code to deal with an exception that might arise during execution of the try block in a *catch* block. If multiple exception classes might arise in the try block, then several catch blocks are allowed to handle them. Code that must be executed no matter what happens can be placed in a finally block. Let's take a moment to consider an example:

```
1.  int x = (int)(Math.random() * 5);
2.  int y = (int)(Math.random() * 10);
3.  int [] z = new int[5];
4.  try {
5.    System.out.println("y/x gives " + (y/x));
6.    System.out.println("y is "es " + (y/x));
7.      + y + " z[y] is " + z[y]);
8.  }
9.  catch (ArithmeticException e) {
10.   System.out.println("Arithmetic problem " + e);
11. }
12. catch (ArrayIndexOutOfBoundsException e) {
13.   System.out.println("Subscript problem " + e);
14. }
```

In this example, an exception is possible at line 5 and at line 6. Line 5 has the potential to cause a division by 0, which in integer arithmetic results in an ArithmeticException being thrown. Line 6 will sometimes throw an ArrayIndexOutOfBoundsException.

If the value of x happens to be 0, then line 5 will result in the construction of an instance of the ArithmeticException class that is then thrown. Execution continues at line 9, where the variable e takes on the reference to the newly created exception. At line 10, the message printed includes a description of the problem, which comes directly from the exception itself. A similar flow occurs if line 5 executes without a problem but the value of y is 5 or greater, causing an out-of-range subscript in line 6. In that case, execution jumps directly to line 12.

In either of these cases, where an exception is thrown in a try block and is caught by a matching catch block, the exception is considered to have been handled: Execution continues after the last catch block as if nothing had happened. If, however, no catch block names either the class of exception that has been thrown or a class of exception that is a parent class of the one that has been thrown, then the exception is considered to be unhandled. In such conditions, execution generally leaves the method directly, just as if no try had been used.

> **NOTE** You cannot write a catch block for exceptions that would never be thrown in the try block. This will generate a compiler error.

Table 5.1 summarizes the flow of execution that occurs in the exception-handling scenarios discussed up to this point. You should not rely on this table for exam preparation, because it only describes the story so far.

TABLE 5.1 Outline of Flow in Simple Exception Conditions

Exception	*try {}*	Matching *catch() {}*	Behavior
No	N/A	N/A	Normal flow
Yes	No	N/A	Method terminates
Yes	Yes	No	Method terminates
Yes	Yes	Yes	1. Terminate `try {}` block
			2. Execute body of matching `catch` block
			3. Continue normal flow after `catch` blocks

Using *finally*

The generalized exception-handling code has one more part to it than you saw in the last example. This is the `finally` block. If you put a `finally` block after a `try` and its associated `catch` blocks, then once execution enters the `try` block, the code in that `finally` block will definitely be executed whatever the circumstances—well, nearly definitely. If an exception arises with a matching `catch` block, then the `finally` block is executed after the `catch` block. If no exception arises, the `finally` block is executed after the `try` block. If an exception arises for which there is no appropriate `catch` block, then the `finally` block is executed after the `try` block.

The circumstances that can prevent execution of the code in a `finally` block are

- An exception arising in the `finally` block itself
- The death of the thread
- The use of `System.exit()`
- Turning off the power to the CPU

Notice that an exception in the `finally` block behaves exactly like any other exception; it can be handled via a `try/catch`. If no `catch` is found, then control jumps out of the method from the point at which the exception is raised, perhaps leaving the `finally` block incompletely executed.

Catching Multiple Exceptions

When you define a `catch` block, that block will catch exceptions of the class specified, including any exceptions that are subclasses of the one specified. In this way, you can handle categories of exceptions in a single `catch` block. If you specify one exception class in one particular `catch` block and a parent class of that exception in another `catch` block, you can handle the more specific exceptions—those of the subclass—separately from others of the same general parent class. Under such conditions these rules apply:

- A more specific `catch` block must precede a more general one in the source. Failure to meet this ordering requirement causes a compiler error.
- Only one `catch` block, the first applicable one, will be executed.

Now let's look at the overall framework for `try`, multiple `catch` blocks, and `finally`:

```
1. try {
2.    // statements
3.    // some are safe, some might throw an exception
4. }
5. catch (SpecificException e) {
6.    // do something, perhaps try to recover
7. }
8. catch (OtherException e) {
9.    // handling for OtherException
10. }
11. catch (GeneralException e) {
12.    // handling for GeneralException
13. }
14. finally {
15.    // code that must be executed under
16.    // successful or unsuccessful conditions.
17. }
18. // more lines of method code
```

In this example, `GeneralException` is a parent class of `Specific Exception`. Several scenarios can arise under these conditions:

- No exceptions occur.
- A `SpecificException` occurs.
- A `GeneralException` occurs.
- An entirely different exception occurs, which we will call an `UnknownException`.

If no exceptions occur, execution completes the `try` block, lines 1–4, and then proceeds to the `finally` block, lines 14–17. The rest of the method, line 18 onward, is then executed.

If a `SpecificException` occurs, execution abandons the `try` block at the point the exception is raised and jumps into the `SpecificException catch` block. Typically, this might result in lines 1 and 2, then 5, 6, and 7 being executed. After the `catch` block, the `finally` block and the rest of the method are executed, lines 14–17 and line 18 onward.

If a `GeneralException` that is not a `SpecificException` occurs, then execution proceeds out of the `try` block, into the `GeneralException catch` block at lines 11–13. After that `catch` block, execution proceeds to the `finally` block and the rest of the method, just as in the last example.

If an `UnknownException` occurs, execution proceeds out of the `try` block directly to the `finally` block. After the `finally` block is completed, the rest of the method is abandoned. This is an uncaught exception; it will appear in the caller just as if there had never been any `try` block in the first place.

Now that we have discussed what happens when an exception is thrown, let's proceed to how exceptions are thrown and the rules that relate to methods that might throw exceptions.

Throwing Exceptions

The last section discussed how exceptions modify the flow of execution in a Java program. We will continue by examining how exceptions are issued in the first place and how you can write methods that use exceptions to report difficulties.

The *throw* Statement

Throwing an exception, in its most basic form, is simple. You need to do two things. First, you create an instance of an object that is a subclass of `java.lang.Throwable`. Next you use the `throw` keyword to actually throw the exception. These two are normally combined into a single statement like this:

```
throw new IOException("File not found");
```

There is an important reason why the `throw` statement and the construction of the exception are normally combined. The exception builds information about the point at which it was created, and that information is shown in the stack trace when the exception is reported. It is convenient if the line reported as the origin of the exception is the same line as the `throw` statement, so it is a good idea to combine the two parts; `throw new xxx()` becomes the norm.

The *throws* Statement

You saw how easy it is to generate and throw an exception; however, the overall picture is more complex. First, as a general rule, Java requires that any method that might throw an exception must declare the fact. In a way, this is a form of enforced documentation, but you will see that there is a little more to it than that.

If you write a method that might throw an exception (and this includes unhandled exceptions that are generated by other methods called from your method), then you must declare the possibility using a `throws` statement. For example, the (incomplete) method shown here can throw a `MalformedURLException` or an `EOFException`:

```
1.  public void doSomeIO(String targetUrl)
2.    throws MalformedURLException, EOFException {
3.    // new URL might throw MalformedURLException
4.    URL url = new URL(targetUrl);
5.    // open the url and read from it...
6.    // set flag 'completed' when IO is successful
7.    //....
8.    // so if we get here with completed == false,
9.    // we got unexpected end of file.
10.   if (!completed) {
11.     throw new EOFException("Invalid file contents");
12.   }
13. }
```

Line 11 demonstrates the use of the `throw` statement—it is usual for a `throw` statement to be conditional in some way; otherwise the method has no way to complete successfully. Line 2 shows the use of the `throws` statement. In this case, two distinct exceptions are listed that the method might throw under different failure conditions. The exceptions are given as a comma-separated list.

The section "Catching Multiple Exceptions" earlier in this chapter explained that the class hierarchy of exceptions is significant in `catch` blocks. The hierarchy is also significant in the `throws` statement. In this example, line 2 could be shortened to `throws IOException`, because both `MalformedURLException` and `EOFException` are subclasses of `IOException`.

It is important to recognize that declaring that a method throws an exception does not mean the method will fail with that exception, only that it might do so. In fact, it is perfectly legitimate—and in some situations that you will see later, actually necessary—to make such declarations, even though they appear to be redundant.

Checked Exceptions

So far we have discussed throwing exceptions and declaring methods that might throw exceptions. We have stated that any method that throws an exception should use the `throws` statement to declare the fact. The whole truth is slightly subtler.

The class hierarchy that exists under the class `java.lang.Throwable` is divided into three parts. One part contains the errors, which are `java.lang.Error` and all subclasses. Another part is called the runtime exceptions, which are `java.lang.RuntimeException` and all its subclasses. The third part contains the checked exceptions, which are all subclasses of `java.lang.Exception` (except for `java.lang.RuntimeException` and its subclasses). Figure 5.1 shows this diagrammatically.

FIGURE 5.1 Categories of exceptions

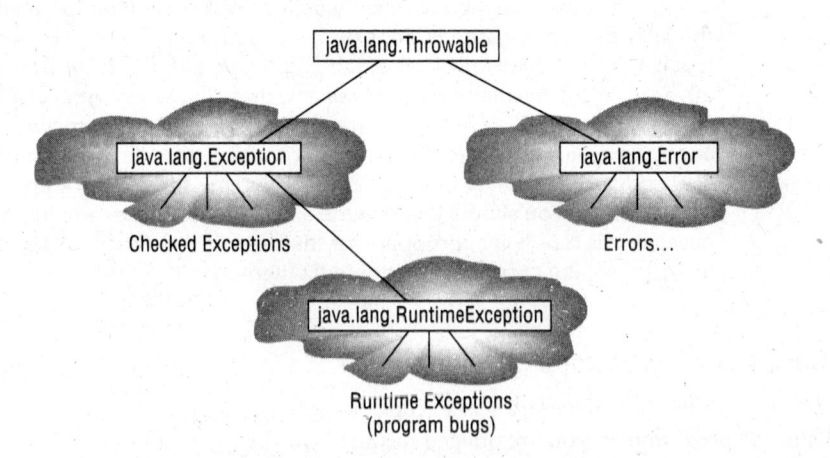

You might well ask why the hierarchy is divided up and what these various names mean.

The *checked exceptions* describe problems that can arise in a correct program—typically, difficulties with the environment such as user mistakes or I/O problems. For example, attempting to open a socket can fail if the remote machine does not exist, is not responding, or is not providing the requested service. Neither of these problems indicates a programming error; it's more likely to be a problem with the machine name (the user mistyped it) or with the remote machine (perhaps it is incorrectly configured). Because these conditions can arise at any time, in a commercial-grade program you must write code to handle and recover from them. In fact, the Java compiler checks that you have indeed stated what is to be done when they arise, and because of this checking, they are called checked exceptions.

Runtime exceptions typically describe program bugs. You could use a runtime exception as deliberate flow control, but it would be an odd way to design code and rather poor style. Runtime exceptions generally arise from things like out-of-bounds array accesses, and normally a correctly coded program would avoid them. Because runtime exceptions should never arise in a correct program, you are not required to handle them. After all, it would only clutter your program if you had to write code that your design states should never be executed.

Errors generally describe problems that are sufficiently unusual and sufficiently difficult to recover from that you are not required to handle them. They might reflect a program bug, but more commonly they reflect environmental problems, such as running out of memory. As with runtime exceptions, Java does not require that you state how these are to be handled. Although errors behave just like exceptions, they typically should not be caught, because it is impossible to recover from them.

> An approach to program design and implementation that is highly effective in producing robust and reliable code is known as *programming by contract*. Briefly, this approach requires clearly defined responsibilities for methods and the callers of those methods. For example, a square-root method could require that it must be called only with a non-negative argument. If called with a negative argument, the method would react by throwing an exception, because the contract between it and its caller has been broken. This approach simplifies code, because methods only attempt to handle properly formulated calls. It also brings bugs out into the open as quickly as possible, thereby ensuring that they get fixed. You should use runtime exceptions to implement this approach because it is clearly inappropriate for the caller to have to check for programming errors; the programmer should fix them.

Checking Checked Exceptions

We stated that of the three categories of exceptions, the checked exceptions make certain demands of the programmer: you are obliged to state how the exception is to be handled. In fact, you have two choices. You can put a `try` block around the code that might throw the exception and provide a corresponding `catch` block that will apply to the exception in question. Doing so handles the exception so it effectively goes away. Alternatively, you might decide that if this exception occurs, your method cannot proceed and should be abandoned. In this case, you do not need to provide the `try/catch` construction, but you must instead make sure the method declaration includes a `throws` part that informs potential callers that the exception might arise. Notice that by insisting the method be declared in this way, the responsibility for handling the exception is explicitly passed to the caller of the method, which must then make the same choice—whether to declare or handle the exception. The following example demonstrates this choice:

```
1.  public class DeclareOrHandle {
2.    // This method makes no attempt to recover from the
3.    // exception, rather it declares that it might
4.    // throw it and uses no try block
5.    public void declare(String s) throws IOException {
6.      URL u = new URL(s); // might throw IOException
7.      // do things with the URL object u...
8.    }
9.
10.   // This method handles the exception that might
11.   // arise when it calls the method declare().
12.   // Therefore, it does not throw any exceptions
13.   // and so does not use any throws declaration
14.   public void handle(String s) {
```

```
15.     boolean success = false;
16.     while (!success) {
17.       try {
18.         declare(s);  // might throw an IOException
19.         // execute this if declare() succeeded
20.         success = true;
21.       }
22.       catch (IOException e) {
23.         // Advise user that String s is somehow
24.         // unusable and ask for a new one
25.       }
26.     } // end while loop, exits when success is true
27.   }
28. }
```

The method `declare()` does not attempt to handle the exception that might arise during construction of the URL object. Instead, the `declare()` method states that it might throw the exception. By contrast, the `handle()` method uses a `try/catch` construction to ensure that control remains inside the `handle()` method itself until it becomes possible to recover from the problem.

We have now discussed the handling of exceptions and the constructions that allow you to throw exceptions of your own. Before we finish with exceptions, you must consider a rule relating to overriding methods and exceptions. The next section discusses this rule.

Exceptions and Overriding

When you extend a class and override a method, the Java compiler insists that all exception classes thrown by the new method must be the same as, or subclasses of, the exception classes thrown by the original method. Consider these examples (assume they are declared in separate source files; the line numbers are simply for reference):

```
1. public class BaseClass {
2.   public void method() throws IOException {
3.   }
4. }
5.
6. public class LegalOne extends BaseClass {
7.   public void method() throws IOException {
8.   }
9. }
10.
11. public class LegalTwo extends BaseClass {
12.   public void method() {
13.   }
```

```
14.  }
15.
16.  public class LegalThree extends BaseClass {
17.     public void method()
18.     throws EOFException, MalformedURLException {
19.     }
20.  }
21.
22.  public class IllegalOne extends BaseClass {
23.     public void method()
24.     throws IOException, IllegalAccessException {
25.     }
26.  }
27.
28.  public class IllegalTwo extends BaseClass {
29.     public void method()
30.     throws Exception {
31.     }
32.  }
```

Notice that the original method() in BaseClass is declared as throwing IOException. This declaration allows it, and any overriding method defined in a subclass, to throw an IOException or any object that is a subclass of IOException. Overriding methods cannot, however, throw any checked exceptions that are not subclasses of IOException.

Given these rules, you will see that line 7 in LegalOne is correct, because method() is declared exactly the same way as the original that it overrides. Similarly, line 18 in LegalThree is correct, because both EOFException and MalformedURLException are subclasses of IOException—so this adheres to the rule that nothing may be thrown that is not a subclass of the exceptions already declared. Line 12 in LegalTwo is correct, because it throws no exceptions and therefore cannot throw any exceptions that are not subclasses of IOException.

The methods at lines 23 and 29 are not permissible, because both of them throw checked exceptions that are not subclasses of IOException. In IllegalOne, IllegalAccessException is a subclass of Exception; in IllegalTwo, Exception itself is a superclass of IOException. Both IllegalAccessException and Exception are checked exceptions, so the methods that attempt to throw them are illegal as overriding methods of method() in BaseClass.

The point of this rule relates to the use of base class variables as references to objects of subclass type. Chapter 4, "Converting and Casting," explains that you can declare a variable of a class X and then use that variable to refer to any object that is of class X or any subclass of X.

Imagine that in the examples just described, you declared a variable myBaseObject of class BaseClass; you can use it to refer to objects of any of the classes LegalOne, LegalTwo, and LegalThree. (You can't use it to refer to objects of class IllegalOne or IllegalTwo, because those objects cannot be created in the first place: their code won't compile.) The compiler imposes checks on how you call `myBaseObject.method()`. Those checks ensure that for each call, you have either enclosed the call in a `try` block and provided a corresponding `catch` block, or you have declared that the calling method itself might throw an `IOException`. Now suppose that at runtime, the variable `myBaseObject` was used to refer to an object of class `IllegalOne`. Under these conditions, the compiler would still believe that the only exceptions that must be dealt with are of class `IOException`, because it believes that `myBaseObject` refers to an object of class `BaseClass`. The compiler would therefore not insist that you provide a `try/catch` construct that catches the `IllegalAccessException`, nor that you declare the calling method as throwing that exception. Thus if the class `IllegalOne` were permitted, overriding methods would be able to bypass the enforced checks for checked exceptions.

It is important to consider the likely needs of subclasses whenever you define a class. Recall from the earlier section "The `throws` Statement" that it is entirely permissible to declare that a method throws an exception even if no code exists to actually throw that exception. Now that you know an overriding method cannot throw exceptions that were not declared in the parent method, you will recognize that some parent classes need to declare exceptions in methods that do not in fact throw any exceptions. For example, the `InputStream` class cannot, of itself, actually throw any exceptions, because it doesn't interact with real devices that could fail. However, it is used as the base class for a whole hierarchy of classes that do interact with physical devices: `FileInputStream` and so forth. It is important that the `read()` methods of those subclasses be able to throw exceptions, so the corresponding `read()` methods in the `InputStream` class itself must be declared as throwing `IOException`.

We have now looked at all the aspects of exception handling that you will need to prepare for the Certification Exam and to make effective use of exceptions in your programs.

Assertions

The Java 1.4 release includes a new facility called *assertion*. Assertions provide a convenient mechanism for verifying that a class's methods are called correctly. This mechanism can be enabled or disabled at runtime. The intention is that assertions typically will be enabled during development and disabled in the field.

The new `assert` keyword has the following syntax:

`assert` *Expression1*;
`assert` *Expression1*:*Expression2*;

Expression1 must have `boolean` type. *Expression2* may have any type. If assertions are disabled at runtime (the default state), the `assert` statement does absolutely nothing. If assertions are enabled at runtime (via a command-line argument to the JVM), then *Expression1* is evaluated. If its value is true, no further action is taken. If its value is false, then an `AssertionError` is thrown. If *Expression2* is present, it is passed into the constructor of the `AssertionError`, where it is converted to a `String` and used as the error's message.

Assertions and Compilation

Sun is generally reluctant to expand the Java language, and with good reason. Unbridled language expansion would compromise Java's simplicity, and could also create compatibility problems with existing code.

For example, the introduction of the `assert` keyword is inconvenient for developers who have used `assert` as an identifier in pre-1.4 code (perhaps to implement their own home-grown assertion facility). Thus it was necessary to introduce a compiler flag to control whether `assert` should be treated as an identifier or as a keyword. To treat it as a keyword (that is, to take advantage of the new facility), compile with `-source 1.4` as in the following example:

```
javac -source 1.4 UsefulApplication.java
```

If the flag is omitted, the 1.4 compiler treats source code as if the `assert` keyword did not exist; thus `assert` can be used as an identifier.

Runtime Enabling of Assertions

Assertions are disabled by default. To enable assertions at runtime, use the `-enableassertions` or `-ea` flag on the Java command line as in the following example:

```
java -ea UsefulApplication
```

Additional runtime flags enable or disable assertions at the class level, but they are beyond the scope of the exam and of this book. If assertions are disabled, `assert` statements have no effect.

The `-ea` flag means that code can be developed with heavy reliance on assertions for debugging. The code can be shipped without removing the `assert` statements; they will have negligible effect on performance in the field, where the code is run with assertions disabled. This functionality demonstrates the benefit of incorporating assertions into the Java language. Assertion support could certainly have been built from scratch based on pre-1.4 platforms (and indeed it probably has been, in many different forms at many different sites). However, it would be difficult to field-disable the facility. The new Java 1.4 functionality ensures that assertions are simple and consistent.

Using Assertions

Assertions are commonly used to check *preconditions*, *postconditions*, and *class invariants*. Before going further, we should define these terms.

A precondition is a constraint that must be met on entry of a method. If a method's preconditions are not met, the method should terminate at once before it can do any damage. A method's preconditions are typically functions of its arguments and the state of its object. Argument range checking at the start of a method is a common form of precondition testing.

A postcondition is a constraint that must be met on return from a method. If a method's postconditions are not met, the method should not be allowed to return. A method's postconditions are typically functions of its return value and the state of its object. In a general sense, if a precondition fails, the problem lies in the method's caller, whereas if a postcondition fails, the problem lies in the method itself.

A class invariant is a constraint on a class's state that must be met before and after execution of any non-private method of a class. (Private methods might be used to restore the required state after execution of a non-private method.)

To see how assertions can be used to enforce pre- and postconditions, imagine a class called `Library` that models a library (not a software library, but the kind where you can borrow books). Such a class might have a method called `reserveACopy()` that reserves a copy of a book on behalf of a library member. This method might look as follows, assuming the existence of classes `Member` (representing a person who is a member of the library) and `Book` (representing a single copy of a book):

```
1.  private Book reserveACopy(String title, Member member) {
2.      assert isValidTitle(title);
3.
4.      Book book = getAvailableCopy(title);
5.      reserve(book, member);
6.
7.      assert bookIsInStock(book);
8.      return book;
9.  }
```

Line 2 enforces a precondition. If the title is not valid (perhaps someone accidentally typed "Moby-Duck"), then the method should terminate as soon as possible, before any damage can be done. In fact, if the precondition fails, the failure indicates that the class needs more work. The code that called `reserveACopy()` with bad arguments needs to be fixed. The assertion failed (we hope) during in-house testing. Eventually the `Library` class would be debugged so that `reserveACopy()` would never be called with bad arguments. At this point (and not before this point), the class would be ready for shipment to the field, where assertions would be disabled.

Line 7 enforces a postcondition. The body of the method is supposed to find an available copy of the desired book. If the book that was found is not available after all, then a problem exists with the method's algorithm. The method should be terminated immediately before the library's data gets hopelessly corrupted, and the method should be debugged. When the author of the method has faith in the algorithm's correctness, the method can be shipped to an environment where assertions can be disabled.

There is a subtle point to be made about the appropriateness of using assertions to check preconditions of public methods. Note that the method in our example was private, so it could be called only from within its own class. Thus if the assertion on line 2 failed, you could only point the finger of blame at yourself or at a colleague down the hall; nobody else could call `reserveACopy()`. However, if the method were public, it could be called by anyone, including a customer who bought the class for re-use in a separate product. Such a programmer is beyond the control of your quality assurance system. A call to `reserveACopy()` with bad arguments would not necessarily indicate an internal problem with the `Library` class. So, if the `reserveACopy()` method were public, preconditions would have to be checked without the assertion mechanism, because the bad call would happen in the field with assertions disabled. The following code shows how to use an exception to indicate precondition failure:

```
1. public Book reserveACopy(String title, Member member) {
2.    if (!isValidTitle(title))
3.       throw new IllegalArgumentException("Bad title: "tle: + title);
4.
5.    Book book = getAvailableCopy(title);
6.    reserve(book, member);
7.
8.    assert bookIsInStock(book);
9.    return book;
10. }
```

`IllegalArgumentException` is a runtime exception, so `reserveACopy()` does not need a `throws` clause and callers do not need to use the `try/catch` mechanism.

This example demonstrates that assertions are not appropriate for checking preconditions in public methods.

Summary

This chapter covered various aspects of flow control in Java, including loop constructs, selection statements, exception handling and throwing, and assertions. The main points of flow control are summarized here.

Early in the chapter we touched on Java's three loop constructions: `while()`, `do`, and `for()`. Recall that each loop provides the facility for repeating the execution of a block of code until some condition occurs.

The `continue` statement causes the current iteration of the loop to be abandoned, and flow restarts at the top of the loop. The `break` statement abandons the loop altogether. Both `break` and `continue` can take a label that causes them to skip out of multiple levels of a nested loop.

After we covered loop constructions, we discussed Java's two selection constructs: the `if()/else` and `switch()` statements. Both the `if()/else` and `switch()` statements provide a way to conditionally execute code. The `if()` statement takes a `boolean` argument, and the optional `else` statement is executed if the value of that `boolean` argument is false.

The `switch()` statement takes an argument that is compatible to `int` (that is, one of `byte`, `short`, `char`, or `int`). The argument to `case` must be a constant or constant expression that can be calculated at compile time.

As we neared the end of the chapter, we discussed flow in exception handling. An exception causes a jump to the end of the enclosing `try` block even if the exception occurs within a method called from the `try` block (in which case the called method is abandoned). If no appropriate `catch` block is found, the exception is considered unhandled.

Regardless of whether an exception occurred, or whether it was handled, execution proceeds next to the `finally` block associated with the `try` block, if such a `finally` block exists. If no exception occurred, or if the exception was handled, execution continues after the `finally` block.

If the exception was not handled, then the thread is killed and a message and stack trace are dumped to `System.err`.

Finally, we examined how exceptions are issued in the first place, and how you can write methods that use exceptions to report problems. Any object that is of class `java.lang.Exception`, or any subclass of `java.lang.Exception` (except subclasses of `java.lang.RuntimeException`) is a checked exception. A method cannot throw any `Throwable` other than `RuntimeException`, `Error`, and subclasses of these, unless a `throws` declaration is attached to the method to indicate that this might happen. An overriding method may not throw a checked exception unless the overridden method also throws that exception or a superclass of that exception.

Exam Essentials

Understand the operation of Java `while`, `do`, and `for` loops. Understand labeled loops, labeled breaks, and labeled continues in these loops. You should be able to construct each kind of loop and know when blocks are executed and conditions are evaluated. Know how flow control proceeds in each of these structures.

Know the legal argument types for `if` and `switch()` statements. The argument of an `if` statement must be of type `boolean`. The argument of a `switch()` must be of type `byte`, `short`, `char`, or `int`.

Recognize and create correctly constructed `switch()` statements. You should be able to create regular and default cases, with or without `break` statements.

Analyze code that uses a `try` block, and understand the flow of control no matter what exception types are thrown. You should be completely familiar with all the functionality of the `try`, `catch`, and `finally` blocks.

Understand the difference between checked exceptions and runtime exceptions Know the inheritance of these families of exception types and know which kinds must be explicitly handled in your code.

Understand all of your exception-handling options when calling methods that throw checked exceptions. You should know how to create `try` blocks and how to declare that a method throws exceptions.

Know what exception types may be thrown when you override a method that throws exceptions. You need to be familiar with the required relationships between the superclass version's exception types and the subclass version's exception types.

Know how to use the assertions facility. You need to know the syntax of `assert` statements, and behavior when the `boolean` statement is true or false. You also need to know how to enable assertions at compile- and runtime.

Key Terms

Before you take the exam, be certain you are familiar with the following terms:

assertion	postcondition
catch	precondition
checked exception	raised
class invariant	runtime exception
condition	statement
error	throw
exception	try
expression	

Review Questions

1. Consider the following code:
   ```
   1. for (int i = 0; i < 2; i++) {
   2.    for (int j = 0; j < 3; j++) {
   3.       if (i == j) {
   4.          continue;
   5.       }
   6.       System.out.println("i = " + i + " j = " + j);
   7.    }
   8. }
   ```

   Which lines would be part of the output? (Choose all that apply.)
   A. i = 0 j = 0
   B. i = 0 j = 1
   C. i = 0 j = 2
   D. i = 1 j = 0
   E. i = 1 j = 1
   F. i = 1 j = 2

2. Consider the following code. Assume that i and j have been declared as ints and initialized.
   ```
   1. outer: for (int i = 0; i < 2; i++) {
   2.    for (int j = 0; j < 3; j++) {
   3.       if (i == j) {
   4.          continue outer;
   5.       }
   6.       System.out.println("i = " + i + " j = " + j);
   7.    }
   8. }
   ```

   Which lines would be part of the output? (Choose all that apply.)
   A. i = 0 j = 0
   B. i = 0 j = 1
   C. i = 0 j = 2
   D. i = 1 j = 0
   E. i = 1 j = 1
   F. i = 1 j = 2

3. Which of the following are legal loop constructions? (Choose all that apply.)

    A. 1. while (int i < 7) {
       2.   i++;
       3.   System.out.println("i is " + i);
       4. }

    B. 1. int i = 3;
       2. while (i) {
       3.   System.out.println("i is " + i);
       4. }

    C. 1. int j = 0;
       2. for (int k = 0; j + k != 10; j++, k++) {
       3.   System.out.println("j is " + j + " k is " + k);
       4. }

    D. 1. int j = 0;
       2. do {
       3.   System.out.println("j is " + j++);
       4.   if (j == 3) { continue loop; }
       5. } while (j < 10);

4. What would be the output from this code fragment?

    1. int x = 0, y = 4, z = 5;
    2. if (x > 2) {
    3.   if (y < 5) {
    4.   System.out.println("message one");
    5.   }
    6.   else {
    7.   System.out.println("message two");
    8.   }
    9. }
    10. else if (z > 5) {
    11.   System.out.println("message three");
    12. }
    13. else {
    14.   System.out.println("message four");
    15. }

    A. message one
    B. message two
    C. message three
    D. message four

5. Which statement is true about the following code fragment?
   ```
   1. int j = 2;
   2. switch (j) {
   3.    case 2:
   4.       System.out.println("value is two");
   5.    case 2 + 1:
   6.       System.out.println("value is three");
   7.       break;
   8.    default:
   9.       System.out.println("value is " + j);
   10.      break;
   11. }
   ```

   A. The code is illegal because of the expression at line 5.
   B. The acceptable types for the variable j, as the argument to the switch() construct, could be any of byte, short, int, or long.
   C. The output would be the text value is two.
   D. The output would be the text value is two followed by the text value is three.
   E. The output would be the text value is two, followed by the text value is three, followed by the text value is 2.

6. Consider the following class hierarchy and code fragment:

   ```
                    java.lang.Exception
                            \
                     java.io.IOException
                     /                  \
   java.io.StreamCorruptedException   java.net.MalformedURLException
   ```

   ```
   1. try {
   2.    // assume s is previously defined
   3.    URL u = new URL(s);
   4.    // in is an ObjectInputStream
   5.    Object o = in.readObject();
   6.    System.out.println("Success");
   7. }
   8. catch (MalformedURLException e) {
   9.    System.out.println("Bad URL");
   10. }
   11. catch (StreamCorruptedException e) {
   12.    System.out.println("Bad file contents");
   13. }
   14. catch (Exception e) {
   ```

```
15.     System.out.println("General exception");
16. }
17. finally {
18.     System.out.println("Doing finally part");
19. }
20. System.out.println("Carrying on");
```

What lines are output if the constructor at line 3 throws a `MalformedURLException`? (Choose all that apply.)

A. Success

B. Bad URL

C. Bad file contents

D. General exception

E. Doing finally part

F. Carrying on

7. Consider the following class hierarchy and code fragment:

```
                   java.lang.Exception
                            \
                       java.io.IOException
                      /                    \
    java.io.StreamCorruptedException    java.net.MalformedURLException
```

```
1.  try {
2.      // assume s is previously defined
3.      URL u = new URL(s);
4.      // in is an ObjectInputStream
5.      Object o = in.readObject();
6.      System.out.println("Success");
7.  }
8.  catch (MalformedURLException e) {
9.      System.out.println("Bad URL");
10. }
11. catch (StreamCorruptedException e) {
12.     System.out.println("Bad file contents");
13. }
14. catch (Exception e) {
15.     System.out.println("General exception");
16. }
17. finally {
18.     System.out.println("Doing finally part");
```

19. }
20. System.out.println("Carrying on");

What lines are output if the methods at lines 3 and 5 complete successfully without throwing any exceptions? (Choose all that apply.)

A. Success
B. Bad URL
C. Bad file contents
D. General exception
E. Doing finally part
F. Carrying on

8. Consider the following class hierarchy and code fragment:

```
              java.lang.Throwable
             /                    \
    java.lang.Error            java.lang.Exception
        /                              \
java.lang.OutOfMemoryError       java.io.IOException
                                  /              \
              java.io.StreamCorruptedException   java.net.MalformedURLException
```

```
1.  try {
2.      // assume s is previously defined
3.      URL u = new URL(s);
4.      // in is an ObjectInputStream
5.      Object o = in.readObject();
6.      System.out.println("Success");
7.  }
8.  catch (MalformedURLException e) {
9.      System.out.println("Bad URL");
10. }
11. catch (StreamCorruptedException e) {
12.     System.out.println("Bad file contents");
13. }
14. catch (Exception e) {
15.     System.out.println("General exception");
16. }
17. finally {
18.     System.out.println("Doing finally part"),
19. }
20. System.out.println("Carrying on");
```

154 Chapter 5 · Flow Control, Assertions, and Exception Handling

What lines are output if the method at line 5 throws an OutOfMemoryError? (Choose all that apply.)

A. Success
B. Bad URL
C. Bad file contents
D. General exception
E. Doing finally part
F. Carrying on

9. The method risky() might throw a java.io.IOException, java.lang.RuntimeException, or java.net.MalformedURLException (which is a subclass of java.io.IOException). Appropriate imports have been declared for each of those exceptions. Which of the following classes and sets of classes are legal? (Choose all that apply.)

A.
```
1. public class SomeClass {
2.     public void aMethod() {
3.         risky();
4.     }
5. }
```

B.
```
1. public class SomeClass {
2.     public void aMethod() throws
3.         IOException {
4.         risky();
5.     }
6. }
```

C.
```
1. public class SomeClass {
2.     public void aMethod() throws
3.         RuntimeException {
4.         risky();
5.     }
6. }
```

D.
```
1.  public class SomeClass {
2.      public void aMethod() {
3.          try {
4.              risky();
5.          }
6.          catch (IOException e) {
7.              e.printStackTrace();
8.          }
9.      }
10. }
```

E.
```
1.  public class SomeClass {
2.    public void aMethod()
3.      throws MalformedURLException {
4.      try { risky(); }
5.      catch (IOException e) {
6.        // ignore it
7.      }
8.    }
9.  }
10.
11. public class AnotherClass
12.   extends SomeClass {
13.   public void aMethod()
14.     throws java.io.IOException {
15.     super.aMethod();
16.   }
17. }
```

10. Consider the following code:

```
1. public class Assertification {
2.   public static void main(String[] args) {
3.     assert args.length == 0;
4.   }
5. }
```

Which of the following conditions must be true in order for the code to throw an AssertionError? (Choose all that apply.)

A. The source code must be compiled with the -source 1.4 flag.

B. The application must be run with the -enableassertions flag or another assertion-enabling flag.

C. The args array must have exactly zero elements.

D. The args array must have one or more elements.

Answers to Review Questions

1. **B, C, D, F.** The loops iterate i from 0 to 1 and j from 0 to 2. However, the inner loop executes a `continue` statement whenever the values of i and j are the same. Because the output is generated inside the inner loop, after the `continue` statement, no output is generated when the values are the same. Therefore, the outputs suggested by answers A and E are skipped.

2. **D.** It seems that the variable i will take the values 0 and 1, and for each of these values, j will take values 0, 1, and 2. However, whenever i and j have the same value, the outer loop is continued before the output is generated. Because the outer loop is the target of the `continue` statement, the whole of the inner loop is abandoned. So, for the value pairs, this table shows what happens:

i	j	Effect
0	0	Continues at line 4
1	0	Prints at line 6
1	1	Continues at line 4
2	1	Exits loops at line 1

   Therefore, the only line to be output is that shown in D.

3. **C.** In A, the variable declaration for i is illegal. This type of declaration is permitted only in the first part of a `for()` loop. The absence of initialization should also be a clue here. In B, the loop control expression—the variable i in this case—is of type `int`. A `boolean` expression is required. C is valid. Despite the complexity of declaring one value inside the `for()` construction and one outside (along with the use of the comma operator in the end part), this code is entirely legitimate. D would be correct, except that the label has been omitted from line 2, which should read `loop: do {`.

4. **D.** The first test at line 2 fails, which immediately causes control to skip to line 10, bypassing both the possible tests that might result in the output of `message one` or `message two`. So, even though the test at line 3 would be true, it is never made; A is not correct. At line 10, the test is again false, so the message at line 11 is skipped, but `message four`, at line 14, is output.

5. **D.** A is incorrect because the code is legal despite the expression at line 5; the expression itself is a constant. B is incorrect because it states that the `switch()` part can take a `long` argument. Only `byte`, `short`, `char`, and `int` are acceptable. The output results from the value 2 like this: first, the option `case 2:` is selected, which outputs `value is two`. However, there is no `break` statement between lines 4 and 5, so the execution falls into the next `case` and outputs `value is three` from line 6. The `default:` part of a `switch()` is executed only when no other options have been selected, or if no `break` precedes it. In this case, neither of these situations holds true, so the output consists only of the two messages listed in D.

Answers to Review Questions 157

6. **B, E, F.** The exception causes a jump out of the `try` block, so the message `Success` from line 6 is not printed. The first applicable `catch` is at line 8, which is an exact match for the thrown exception. This results in the message at line 9 being printed, so B is one of the required answers. Only one `catch` block is ever executed, so control passes to the `finally` block, which results in the message at line 18 being output; so E is part of the correct answer. Because the exception was caught, it is considered to have been handled, and execution continues after the `finally` block. This results in the output of the message at line 20, so F is also part of the correct answer.

7. **A, E, F.** With no exceptions, the `try` block executes to completion, so the message `Success` from line 6 is printed and A is part of the correct answer. No `catch` is executed, so B, C, and D are incorrect. Control then passes to the `finally` block, which results in the message at line 18 being output, so E is part of the correct answer. Because no exception was thrown, execution continues after the `finally` block, resulting in the output of the message at line 20; so, F is also part of the correct answer.

8. **E.** The thrown error prevents completion of the `try` block, so the message `Success` from line 6 is not printed. No `catch` is appropriate, so B, C, and D are incorrect. Control then passes to the `finally` block, which results in the message at line 18 being output; so option E is part of the correct answer. Because the error was not caught, execution exits the method and the error is rethrown in the caller of this method; so, F is not part of the correct answer.

9. **B, D.** A does not handle the exceptions, so the method aMethod() might throw any of the exceptions that risky() might throw. However, the exceptions are not declared with a `throws` construction. In B, declaring `throws IOException` is sufficient; because `java.lang.RuntimeException` is not a checked exception and because `IOException` is a superclass of `MalformedURLException`, it is unnecessary to mention the `MalformedURLException` explicitly (although it might make better "self-documentation" to do so). C is unacceptable because its `throws` declaration fails to mention the checked exceptions—it is not an error to declare the runtime exception, although it is strictly redundant. D is also acceptable, because the `catch` block handles `IOException`, which includes `MalformedURLException`. `RuntimeException` will still be thrown by the method aMethod() if it is thrown by risky(), but because `RuntimeException` is not a checked exception, this is not an error. E is not acceptable, because the overriding method in anotherClass is declared as throwing `IOException`, whereas the overridden method in aClass was only declared as throwing `MalformedURLException`. It would have been correct for the base class to declare that it throws `IOException` and then the derived class to throw `MalformedURLException`, but as it is, the overriding method is attempting to throw exceptions not declared for the original method. The fact that the only exception that can arise is the `MalformedURLException` is not enough to rescue this code—the compiler only checks the declarations, not the semantics of the code.

10. **A, B, D.** If the source is not compiled with the -source 1.4 flag, `assert` will be treated as an identifier rather than as a keyword. If the application is not run with assertions explicitly enabled, all `assert` statements will be ignored. If the args array does not have exactly zero arguments, no `AssertionError` will be thrown.

Chapter 6

Objects and Classes

JAVA CERTIFICATION EXAM OBJECTIVES COVERED IN THIS CHAPTER:

- ✓ 1.4 Identify legal return types for any method given the declarations of all related methods in this or parent classes.

- ✓ 6.1 State the benefits of encapsulation in object-oriented design and write code that implements tightly encapsulated classes and the relationships "is a" and "has a".

- ✓ 6.2 Write code to invoke overridden or overloaded methods and parental or overloaded constructors; and describe the effect of invoking these methods.

- ✓ 6.3 Write code to construct instances of any concrete class including normal top-level classes and nested classes.

This chapter discusses the object-oriented features of Java. Good coding in Java requires a sound understanding of the object-oriented (OO) paradigm, and this in turn requires a good grasp of the language features that implement objects and classes. The many benefits of object orientation have been the subject of considerable public debate, but for many programmers these benefits have not been realized. In most cases, the reason the promise has not been fulfilled is simply that programmers have not been writing objects. Instead, many programmers have been writing hybrid applications with a mixture of procedural and object-oriented code. Unfortunately, while such an approach has given rise to *some* of the benefits of OO, it has also engendered *all* the disadvantages of both styles.

Benefits of Object-Oriented Implementation

The Programmer's and Developer's Exams require you to understand the benefits of object-oriented design. These benefits accrue from two particular features of the OO paradigm. The first of these, and perhaps the most important, is the notion of *encapsulation*; the second and perhaps better known is the extensibility provided by *inheritance*.

Encapsulation

Encapsulation is really just a fancy name for the aggregation of data and behavior. Consider the primitive data types of any programming language you have ever used. You do not know how these data items are stored and, for the most part, you do not care. What matters are the operations that you can perform on these data items and the boundary conditions within which you can expect those operations to properly work. These primitive types are in fact reference types, albeit not user-defined.

Your first goal in defining a good class should be to clearly define the data members that describe instances of that class, keeping in mind that this should be done only with variables of private accessibility. Next, consider how to represent the behavior associated with these data. All behavior should be accessed only via methods. By insisting that the variables inside an object are inaccessible outside the object, you ensure that the nature of those variables is irrelevant outside the object. This in turn means that you can freely change the nature of the storage for maintenance purposes, performance improvement, or any other reason. This is the essence of encapsulation.

Sometimes, perhaps as a consequence of the way you have stored the state in a class, boundary conditions must be applied to its methods. A *boundary condition* is a limit on the range of arguments for which a method can operate properly. As examples, a square-root function cannot operate on a negative number unless imaginary numbers are included in its range; an add operation cannot operate if both of its arguments are more than half the maximum value for the operation's return type.

When you encounter a boundary condition that results from your choice of storage format, you must make a choice. If you consider that the boundary conditions are reasonable, then you should do two things. First, document the boundary condition. Next, test the boundary conditions at the entry to the method and, if the boundary condition has been exceeded, throw a runtime exception of some kind. Alternatively, you might decide that the boundary condition is not acceptable, in which case you should redesign the storage used in the class.

Now, consider this: if you had allowed access to any of the variables used to represent the object state, then redefining the way the object's state is stored would immediately cause any other code that uses these variables to have to be rewritten. However, by using only private member variables, you have insisted that all interaction with this object is made through methods and never by direct variable access—so you have eliminated this problem. In consequence, you are able to redesign your internal storage freely and, provided the signatures of all the methods remain the same, no other code needs to change.

Encapsulation and Perceived Efficiency

Many programmers have such deep-seated concerns about performance that they cannot bring themselves to force all access to their objects to be made through methods, and they resist creating classes with entirely private member variables. This approach is unwise for several reasons. First, fully encapsulated classes are more likely to be used correctly, especially if boundary conditions are properly flagged with exceptions—therefore, code using them is more likely to be correct. Second, bug fixes and maintenance changes are less likely to break the program as a whole, because the effects of the change are confined to the affected class. These reasons fall under the broad heading, "Would your customer prefer a slow program that works and is delivered on time (and that can be made faster later) or a program that is delivered late, works incorrectly, but runs quickly?"

There are more reasons fully encapsulated classes are the right way to begin a design. An optimizing virtual machine such as Sun's HotSpot can transparently optimize simple variable access methods by "inlining." This approach allows the program all the robustness, reliability, and maintainability that results from full encapsulation, while giving the runtime performance associated with direct variable access. Furthermore, if you decide that a program's slow performance is attributable to the use of private variables and accessor/mutator methods, then changing the variable to be more accessible does not require any changes to the rest of the code, either inside or outside the class. On the other hand, if you have code that fails to run properly as a result of making direct variable access, you will find that reducing the accessibility of the relevant variable will require considerable collateral changes in many other pieces of code (all code that makes such direct access).

Re-use

We discussed how tight encapsulation can make code that is more reliable and robust. Now we will consider the second most significant advantage of object-oriented programming: code re-use.

Writing good, encapsulated classes usually requires more work in the initial stages than would be required to produce the same functionality with a traditional programming approach. However, you will normally find that using rigorous OO techniques will actually reduce the overall time required to produce finished code. This is the case for two reasons. First, the robust classes you produce require less time to integrate into the final program and less time to fix bugs. Second, with careful design, you can re-use classes even in some circumstances that are different from the original intent of the class.

This re-use is possible in two ways, using either composition (the "has a" relation) or inheritance (the "is a" relation). Composition is probably safer and easier to control, although inheritance—perhaps because it is perceived as "pure OO"—seems to be more interesting and appealing to most programmers.

The Java Certification Exam does not require you to discuss details of object-oriented design techniques or the relative merits and weaknesses of composition versus inheritance. However, you should appreciate one significant sequence of facts: if a class is well-encapsulated, it will be easier to re-use successfully. The more a class is re-used, the better tested it will be and the fewer bugs it will have. Better-tested, less-buggy classes are easier to re-use. This sequence leads to a positive spiral of quality because the better the class, the easier and safer it becomes to re-use. All these benefits come from tight encapsulation.

Now that we've discussed why you would want to write object-oriented code, let's look at how this is achieved.

Implementing Object-Oriented Relationships

This section is not intended to discuss object-oriented design; rather, it considers the implementation of classes for which you have been given a basic description.

Two clauses are commonly used when describing a class in plain English: "is a" and "has a." As a working simplification, they are used to describe the superclass and member variables, respectively. For example, consider this description:

"A home is a house that has a family and a pet."

This description would give rise to the outline of a Java class in this form:

```
1. public class Home extends House {
2.    Family inhabitants;
3.    Pet thePet;
4. }
```

Notice the direct correspondence between the "is a" clause and the **extends** clause. In this example, a direct correspondence also exists between the items listed after "has a" and the member variables. Such a correspondence is representative in simple examples and in a test situation; however, you should be aware that in real examples, there are other ways you can provide a class with attributes. Probably the most important of these alternatives is the approach taken by JavaBeans, which is to supply accessor and mutator methods that operate on private data members.

> **TIP** The example shown is simplified to focus on the knowledge and understanding that is required by the exam. In a real situation, the variables should generally be private (or at least some specific rationale should apply to whatever accessibility they have), and some methods will be needed in the class.

Overloading and Overriding

As you construct classes and add methods to them, in some circumstances you will want to re-use the same name for a method. You can do so two ways with Java. Re-using the same method name with different arguments and perhaps a different return type is known as *overloading*. Using the same method name with identical arguments and return type is known as *overriding*.

A method name can be re-used anywhere, as long as certain conditions are met:

- In an unrelated class, no special conditions apply, and the two methods are not considered related in any way.

- In the class that defines the original method, or a subclass of that class, the method name can be re-used if the argument list differs in terms of the type of at least one argument. This is overloading. It is important to realize that a difference in return type or list of thrown exceptions is insufficient to constitute an overload and is illegal.

- In a strict subclass of the class that defines the original method, the method name can be re-used with identical argument types and order and with identical return type. This is overriding. In this case, additional restrictions apply to the accessibility of, and exceptions that may be thrown by, the method.

> **NOTE** In general, a class is considered to be a subclass of itself. That is, if classes A, B, and C are defined so that C extends B and B extends A, then the subclasses of A are A, B, and C. The term *strict subclass* is used to describe the subclasses excluding the class itself. So the strict subclasses of A are only B and C.

Now let's take a look at these ideas in detail. First, we will consider overloading method names.

Overloading Method Names

In Java, a method is uniquely identified by the combination of its fully qualified class name, the method name, and the exact sequence of its argument types. Overloading is the re-use of a method name in the one class or subclass for a different method. It is not related to object orientation, although a purely coincidental correlation shows that object-oriented languages are more likely to support overloading. Notice that overloading is essentially a trick with names; hence this section's title is "Overloading Method Names" rather than "Overloading Methods." The following are all different methods:

1. `public void aMethod(String s) { }`
2. `public void aMethod() { }`
3. `public void aMethod(int i, String s) { }`
4. `public void aMethod(String s, int i) { }`

These methods all have identical return types and names, but their argument lists are different either in the types of the arguments that they take or in the order. Only the argument *types* are considered, not their names, so a method such as

`public void aMethod(int j, String name) { }`

would *not* be distinguished from the method defined in line 3.

What Is Overloading For?

Why is overloading useful? Sometimes you will be creating several methods that perform closely related functions under different conditions. For example, imagine methods that calculate the area of a triangle. One such method might take the Cartesian coordinates of the three vertices, and another might take the polar coordinates. A third method might take the lengths of all three sides, whereas a fourth might take three angles and the length of one side. These methods would all be performing the same essential function, so it is entirely proper to use the same name for the methods. In languages that do not permit overloading, you would have to think up four different method names, such as:

```
areaByCoord(Point p, Point q, Point r)
areaByPolarCoord(PolarPt p, PolarPt q, PolarPt r)
areaBySideLengths(int l1, int l2, int l3)
areaByAnglesAndASide(int l1, int angle1, int angle2, int angle3)
```

Overloading is really nothing new. Almost every language that has a type system has used overloading in a way, although most have not allowed the programmer free use of it. Consider the arithmetic operators +, -, *, and /. In most languages, they can be used with integer or floating-point operands. The implementation of, say, multiplication for integer and floating-point operands generally involves completely different code, and yet the compiler permits the same symbol to be used. Because the operand types are different, the compiler can decide which version of the operation

Overloading and Overriding

should be used. This process is known as *operator overloading* and is the same principle as method overloading.

It is quite useful, for thinking up method names and for improving program readability, to be able to use one method name for several related methods requiring different implementations. However, you should restrict your use of overloaded method names to situations where the methods really are performing the same basic function with different data sets. Methods that perform different jobs should have different names.

One last point to consider is the return type of an overloaded method. The language treats methods with overloaded names as totally different methods, and as such they *can* have different return types (you will see shortly that overriding methods do not have this freedom).

Invoking Overloaded Methods

When you write multiple methods that perform the same basic function with different arguments, you often find that it would be useful to call one of these methods as support for another version. Consider a method called printRJ() that is to be provided in versions that take a String or an int value. The version that takes an int could most easily be coded so that it converts the int to a String and then calls the version that operates on String objects.

You can do this easily. Remember that the compiler decides which method to call simply by looking at the argument list, and that the various overloaded methods are in fact unrelated. All you have to do is write the method call exactly as normal—the compiler will do the rest. Consider this example:

```
1.  public class RightJustify {
2.      // Declare a String of 80 spaces
3.      private static final String padding =
4.          "                    " +
5.          "                    " +
6.          "                    " +
7.          "                    ";
8.      public static void printRJ(String s, int w) {
9.          System.out.print(
10.             padding.substring(0, w - s.length()));
11.         System.out.print(s);
12.     }
13.     public static void printRJ(int i, int w) {
14.         printRJ("" + ", w);
15.     }
16. }
```

At line 14, the int argument is converted to a String object by adding it to an empty String. The method call at this same line is then seen by the compiler as a call to a method called print() that takes a String as the first argument, which results in selection of the method at line 8.

To summarize, these are the key points about overloading methods:

- The identity of a method is determined by the combination of its fully qualified class; its name; and the type, order, and count of arguments in the argument list.
- Two or more methods in the same class (including methods inherited from a superclass) with the same name but different argument lists are called *overloaded*.
- Methods with overloaded names are effectively independent methods—using the same name is really just a convenience to the programmer. Return type, accessibility, and exception lists may vary freely.

Now that we have considered overloading thoroughly, let's look at overriding.

Method Overriding

You have just seen that overloading is essentially a trick with names, effectively treating the argument list as part of the method identification. Overriding is somewhat more subtle, relating directly to subclassing and hence to the object-oriented nature of a language.

When you extend one class to produce a new one, you inherit and have access to certain nonprivate methods of the original class (as dictated by access modifiers and package relationships). Sometimes, however, you might need to modify the behavior of one of these methods to suit your new class. In this case, you actually want to redefine the method, and this is the essential purpose of overriding.

There are a number of key distinctions between overloading and overriding:

- Overloaded methods supplement each other; an overriding method replaces the method it overrides.
- Overloaded methods can exist, in any number, in the same class. Each method in a parent class can be overridden at most once in any one subclass.
- Overloaded methods must have *different* argument lists; overriding methods must have argument lists of *identical* type and order (otherwise they are simply treated as overloaded methods).
- The return type of an overloaded method may be chosen freely; the return type of an overriding method must be *identical* to that of the method it overrides.
- The exception list of an overloaded method may be chosen according to the rules defined earlier in this chapter.
- The access modifiers of an overloaded method may be chosen according to the rules defined earlier in this chapter.

What Is Overriding For?

Overloading allows multiple implementations of the same essential functionality to use the same name. Overriding, on the other hand, modifies the implementation of a particular piece of behavior for a subclass.

Consider a class that describes a rectangle. Imaginatively, we'll call it `Rectangle`. We're talking about an abstract rectangle here, so no visual representation is associated with it. This class has a method called `setSize()`, which is used to set width and height values. In the `Rectangle` class, the implementation of the `setSize()` method simply sets the value of the private width and height variables for later use. Now, imagine you create a `DisplayedRectangle` class that is a subclass of the original `Rectangle`. When the `setSize()` method is called, you need to arrange a new behavior. Specifically, the width and height variables must be changed, but also the visual representation must be redrawn. This is achieved by overriding.

If you define a method that has exactly the same name and exactly the same argument types as a method in a parent class, then you are overriding the method. Under these conditions, the method must also have the identical return type and follow the accessibility and exception list rules for that of the method it overrides. Consider this example:

```
1.  class Rectangle {
2.      int x, y, w, h;
3.
4.      public void setSize(int w, int h) {
5.          this.w = w; this.h = h;
6.      }
7.  }
8.  class DisplayedRectangle extends Rectangle {
9.      public void setSize(int w, int h) {
10.         this.w = w; this.h = h;
11.         redisplay(); // implementation
12.     }
13.     public void redisplay() {
14.         // implementation not shown
15.     }
16. }
17.
18. public class TestRectangle {
19.     public static void main(String args[]) {
20.         Rectangle [] recs = new Rectangle[4];
21.         recs[0] = new Rectangle();
22.         recs[1] = new DisplayedRectangle();
23.         recs[2] = new DisplayedRectangle();
24.         recs[3] = new Rectangle();
25.         for (int r=0; r<4; r++) {
26.             int w = ((int)(Math.random() * 400));
27.             int h = ((int)(Math.random() * 200));
28.             recs[r].setSize(w, h);
29.         }
30.     }
31. }
```

Clearly this example is incomplete, because no code exists to cause the display of the `DisplayedRectangle` objects, but it is complete enough for us to discuss.

At line 20, the array `recs` is created as an array of `Rectangle` objects; yet at lines 21–24, the array is used to hold not only two instances of `Rectangle` but also two instances of `DisplayedRectangle`. Subsequently, when the `setSize()` method is called, it will be important that the executed code be the code associated with the actual object referred to by the array element, rather than always being the code of the `Rectangle` class. This is exactly what Java does, and this is the essential point of overriding methods. It is as if you ask an object to perform certain behavior, and that object makes its own interpretation of the request. C++ programmers should take particular note of this point, because it differs significantly from the default behavior of overriding methods in that language.

In order for any particular method to override another correctly, some requirements must be met. Some of them have been mentioned before in comparison with overloading, but all are listed here for completeness:

- The method name and the type and order of arguments must be identical to those of a method in a parent class. If this is the case, then the method is an attempt to override the corresponding parent class method and the remaining points listed here must be adhered to, or a compiler error arises. If these criteria are not met, then the method is not an attempt to override and the following rules are irrelevant.
- The return type must be identical.
- Methods marked `final` may not be overridden.
- The accessibility must not be more restrictive than that of the original method.
- The method must not throw new or broader checked exceptions of classes than are thrown by the original method.

The first three points have been covered, but the last two are new. The accessibility of an overriding method must not be less than that of the method it overrides, simply because it is considered to be the replacement method in conditions like those of the rectangles example earlier. So, imagine that the `setSize()` method of `DisplayedRectangle` was inaccessible from the `main()` method of the `TestRectangle` class. The calls to `recs[1].setSize()` and `recs[2].setSize()` would be illegal, but the compiler would be unable to determine this because it only knows that the elements of the array are `Rectangle` objects. The `extends` keyword literally requires that the subclass be an extension of the parent class: if methods could be removed from the class or made less accessible, then the subclass would not be a simple extension but would potentially be a reduction. Under those conditions, the idea of treating `DisplayedRectangle` objects as being `Rectangle` objects when used as method arguments or elements of a collection would be severely flawed.

A similar logic gives rise to the final rule relating to checked exceptions. Checked exceptions are those that the compiler ensures are handled in the source you write. As with accessibility, it must be possible for the compiler to make correct use of a variable of the parent class even if that variable really refers to an object of a derived class. For checked exceptions, this requirement means that an overriding method must not be able to throw exceptions that would not be thrown by the original method. Chapter 5, "Flow Control, Assertions, and Exception Handling," discusses checked exceptions and this rule in more detail.

Late Binding

Normally, when a compiler for a non-object-oriented language comes across a method (or function or procedure) invocation, it determines exactly what target code should be called and builds machine language to represent that call. In an object-oriented language, this behavior is not possible because the proper code to invoke is determined based upon the class of the object being used to make the call, not the type of the variable. Instead, code is generated that will allow the decision to be made at runtime. This delayed decision-making is variously referred to as *late binding* (*binding* is one term for the job a linker does when it glues various bits of machine code together to make an executable program file).

The Java Virtual Machine (JVM) has been designed from the start to support an object-oriented programming system, so there are machine-level instructions for making method calls. The compiler only needs to prepare the argument list and produce one method invocation instruction; the job of identifying and calling the proper target code is performed by the JVM.

If the JVM is to be able to decide what code should be invoked by a particular method call, it must be able to determine the class of the object upon which the call is based. Again, the JVM design has supported this process from the beginning. Unlike traditional languages or runtime environments, every time the Java system allocates memory, it marks that memory with the type of the data that it has been allocated to hold. So, given any object, and without regard to the type associated with the reference variable acting as a handle to that object, the runtime system can determine the real class of that object by inspection. This process is the basis of the `instanceof` operator, which allows you to program a test to determine the actual class of an object at runtime. The `instanceof` operator is described in Chapter 2, "Operators and Assignments."

Invoking Overridden Methods

When we discussed overloading methods, you saw how to invoke one version of a method from another. It is also useful to be able to invoke an overridden method from the method that overrides it. Consider that when you write an overriding method, that method entirely replaces the original method. However, sometimes you wish only to add a little extra behavior and want to retain all the original behavior. This goal can be achieved, although it requires a small trick of syntax to perform. Look at this example:

```
1.  class Rectangle {
2.      private int x, y, w, h;
3.      public String toString() {
4.          return "x = " + x + ", y = " + y +
5.              ", w = " + w + ", h = " + h;
6.      }
7.  }
8.  class DecoratedRectangle extends Rectangle {
9.      private int borderWidth;
10.     public String toString() {
11.         return super.toString() + ", borderWidth = " +
```

```
12.         borderWidth;
13.     }
14. }
```

At line 11, the overriding method in the `DecoratedRectangle` class uses the parental `toString()` method to perform the greater part of its work. Because the variables x, y, w, and h in the `Rectangle` class are marked as `private`, it would have been impossible for the overriding method in `DecoratedRectangle` to achieve its work directly.

A call of the form `super.xxx()` always invokes the behavior that would have been used if the current overriding method had not been defined. It does not matter whether the parental method is defined in the immediate superclass or in some ancestor class further up the hierarchy: `super` invokes the version of this method that is "next up the tree."

To summarize, these are the key points about overriding methods:

- A method that has an identical name and identical number, types, and order of arguments as a method in a parent class is an overriding method.
- Each parent class method may be overridden once at most in any one subclass. (That is, you cannot have two identical methods in the same class.)
- An overriding method must return exactly the same type as the method it overrides.
- An overriding method must not be less accessible than the method it overrides.
- An overriding method must not throw any checked exceptions (or subclasses of those exceptions) that are not declared for the overridden method.
- An overridden method is completely replaced by the overriding method unless the overridden method is deliberately invoked from within the subclass.

This is quite a lot to think about, so you might like to take a break before you move on to the next topic: constructors.

Constructors and Subclassing

Inheritance generally makes the code and data defined in a parent class available for use in a subclass. This is subject to accessibility controls so that, for example, private items in the parent class are not directly accessible in the methods of the subclass, even though they exist. In fact, constructors are not inherited in the normal way but must be defined for each class in the class itself.

A constructor is invoked with a call of the form `new MyClass(arg1, arg2, ...)`. If the argument list is empty, the constructor is called a *no-arguments* (or *no-args*) *constructor*. If you do not explicitly code any constructors for a class, the compiler automatically creates a default constructor that does nothing except invoke the superclass's default constructor, via a mechanism described in the next section. This "freebie" constructor is called the *default constructor*. It has public access if the class is public; otherwise its access mode is default.

Often you will define a constructor that takes arguments and will want to use those arguments to control the construction of the parent part of the object. You can pass control to a constructor in the parent class by using the keyword **super**. To control the particular constructor that is used, you simply provide the appropriate arguments. Consider this example:

```
1.  class Base {
2.    public Base(String s) {
3.      // initialize this object using s
4.    }
5.    public Base(int i) {
6.      // initialize this object using i
7.    }
8.  }
9.
10. class Derived extends Base {
11.   public Derived(String s) {
12.     // pass control to Base constructor at line 2
13.     super(s);
14.   }
15.   public Derived(int i) {
16.     // pass control to Base constructor at line 5
17.     super(i);
18.   }
19. }
```

The code at lines 13 and 17 demonstrates the use of **super()** to control the construction of the parent class part of an object. The definitions of the constructors at lines 11 and 15 select an appropriate way to build their inherited part by invoking **super()** with an argument list that matches one of the constructors for the parent class. It is important to know that the superclass constructor must be called before any reference is made to any part of this object. This rule is imposed to guarantee that nothing is ever accessed in an uninitialized state. Generally, the rule means that if **super()** is to appear at all in a constructor, then it must be the first statement.

Although the example shows the invocation of parental constructors with argument lists that match those of the original constructor, this is not a requirement. It would be perfectly acceptable, for example, if line 17 read:

```
17.     super("Value is " + i);
```

This would have caused control to be passed to the constructor at line 2, which takes a String argument, rather than the one at line 5.

Overloading Constructors

Although you just saw that constructors are not inherited in the same way as methods, the overloading mechanisms apply quite normally. In fact, the example discussing the use of super() to control the invocation of parental constructors showed overloaded constructors. You saw earlier how you could invoke one method from another that overloads its name simply by calling the method with an appropriate parameter list. There are also times when it's useful to invoke one constructor from another. Imagine you have a constructor that takes five arguments and does considerable processing to initialize the object. You wish to provide another constructor that takes only two arguments and sets the remaining three to default values. It would be nice to avoid re-coding the body of the first constructor and instead simply set up the default values and pass control to the first constructor. You can do so using a small trick of syntax.

Usually, you would invoke a method by using its name followed by an argument list in parentheses, and you would invoke a constructor by using the keyword new, followed by the name of the class, followed again by an argument list in parentheses. Thus you might try to use the new ClassName(args) construction to invoke another constructor of your own class. Unfortunately, although this is legal syntax, it results in an entirely separate object being created. The approach Java takes is to provide another meaning for the keyword this. Look at this example:

```
1. public class AnyClass {
2.    public AnyClass(int a, String b, float c, Date d) {
3.       // complex processing to initialize
4.       // based on arguments
5.    }
6.    public AnyClass(int a) {
7.       this(a, "default", 0.0F, new Date());
8.    }
9. }
```

The constructor at line 6 takes a single argument and uses that, along with three other default values, to call the constructor at line 2. The call is made using the this() construction at line 7. As with super(), this() must be positioned as the first statement of the constructor.

We have said that any use of either super() or this() in a constructor must be placed at the first line. Clearly, you cannot put both on the first line. If you write a constructor that has neither a call to super() nor a call to this(), then the compiler automatically inserts a call to the parent class constructor with no arguments. If an explicit call to another constructor is made using this(), then the superclass constructor is not called until the other constructor runs. It is permitted for that other constructor to start with a call to either this() or super(), if desired. Java insists that the object is initialized from the top of the class hierarchy downward; that is why the call to super() or this() must occur at the start of a constructor. This point has an important consequence. We just said that if there is no call to either this() or super(), then the compiler puts in a call to the no-argument constructor in the parent. As a result, if you try to extend a class that does not have a no-argument constructor, then you *must* explicitly call super() with one of the argument forms that are supported by constructors in the parent class.

Let's summarize the key points about constructors before we move on to inner classes:

- Constructors are not inherited in the same way as normal methods. You can only create an object if the class defines a constructor with an argument list that matches the one your new call provides.

- If you define no constructors in a class, then the compiler provides a default that takes no arguments. If you define even a single constructor, this default is not provided.

- It is common to provide multiple overloaded constructors—that is, constructors with different argument lists. One constructor can call another using the syntax this(arguments).

- A constructor delays running its body until the parent parts of the class have been initialized. This commonly happens because of an implicit call to super() added by the compiler. You can provide your own call to super(arguments) to control the way the parent parts are initialized. If you do so, it must be the first statement of the constructor.

- A constructor can use overloaded constructor versions to support its work. These are invoked using the syntax this(arguments) and if supplied, this call must be the first statement of the constructor. In such conditions, the initialization of the parent class is performed in the overloaded constructor.

Inner Classes

The material we have looked at so far has been part of Java since its earliest versions. Inner classes are a feature added with the release of JDK 1.1. *Inner classes*, which are sometimes called *nested classes*, can give your programs additional clarity and make them more concise.

Fundamentally, an inner class is the same as any other class, but is declared inside (that is, between the opening and closing curly braces of) some other class. In fact, you can declare nested classes in any block, including blocks that are part of a method. Classes defined inside a method differ slightly from the more general case of inner classes that are defined as members of a class; we'll look at these differences in detail later. For now, when we refer to a "member class," we mean a class that is *not* defined in a method but rather in a class. In this context, the use of the term member is closely parallel to its use in the context of member variables and member methods.

The complexity of inner classes relates to scope and access—particularly access to variables in enclosing scopes. Before we consider these matters, let's look at the syntax of a basic inner class, which is really quite simple. Consider this example:

```
1. public class OuterOne {
2.     private int x;
```

```
3.    public class InnerOne {
4.       private int y;
5.       public void innerMethod() {
6.          System.out.println("y is " + y);
7.       }
8.    }
9.    public void outerMethod() {
10.      System.out.println("x is " + x);
11.   }
12.   // other methods...
13. }
```

In this example, there is no obvious benefit in having declared the class called `InnerOne` as an inner class; so far we are only looking at the syntax. When an inner class is declared like this, the enclosing class name becomes part of the fully qualified name of the inner class. In this case, the two classes' full names are `OuterOne` and `OuterOne.InnerOne`. This format is reminiscent of a class called `InnerOne` declared in a package called `OuterOne`. This point of view is not entirely inappropriate, because an inner class belongs to its enclosing class in a fashion similar to the way a class belongs to a package. It is illegal for a package and a class to have the same name, so there can be no ambiguity.

> **WARNING** Although the dotted representation of inner class names works for the declaration of the type of an identifier, it does not reflect the filename of the class. If you try to load this class using the `Class.forName()` method, the call will fail. On the disk, and from the point of view of the `Class` class and class loaders, the name of the class is `OuterOne$InnerOne`. The dollar-separated name is also used if you print out the class name by using the methods `getClass().getName()` on an instance of the inner class. You probably recall that classes are located in directories that reflect their package names. The dollar-separated convention is adopted for inner class names to ensure that there is no ambiguity on the disk between inner classes and package members. It also reduces conflicts with file systems and shell interpreters that treat the dot character as special, perhaps limiting the number of characters that can follow it.

Although for the purpose of naming, being able to define a class inside another class provides some organizational benefit, this is not the end of the story. Objects that are instances of the inner class generally retain the ability to access the members of the outer class. This behavior is discussed in the next section.

> **Real World Scenario**
>
> **Inner Class Details**
>
> Write an application that answers the following two questions:
>
> 1. Suppose an enclosing class contains a private nonanonymous inner class, which implements a particular interface. Suppose a method of the enclosing class returns an instance of the inner class. Can that method be called from code outside the enclosing class?
>
> 2. What if the inner class in Question 1 is anonymous?
>
> Think about how the code that calls the method will reference the return value. The reference type clearly cannot be the inner class, because the inner class is invisible to the calling class. But remember that the inner class implements an interface.

The Enclosing *this* Reference and Construction of Inner Classes

When an instance of an inner class is created, normally a preexisting instance of the outer class must act as context. This instance of the outer class will be accessible from the inner object. Consider this example, which is expanded from the earlier one:

```
1.  public class OuterOne {
2.    private int x;
3.    public class InnerOne {
4.      private int y;
5.      public void innerMethod() {
6.        System.out.println("enclosing x is " + x);
7.        System.out.println("y is " + y);
8.      }
9.    }
10.   public void outerMethod() {
11.     System.out.println("x is " + x);
12.   }
13.   public void makeInner() {
14.     InnerOne anInner = new InnerOne();
15.     anInner.innerMethod();
16.   }
17.   // other methods...
18. }
```

You will see two changes in this code when you compare it to the earlier version. First, `innerMethod()` now not only outputs the value of y, which is defined in `InnerOne`, but also, at line 6, outputs the value of x, which is defined in `OuterOne`. The second change is that in lines 13–16, the code creates an instance of the `InnerOne` class and invokes `innerMethod()` upon it.

The accessibility of the members of the enclosing class is crucial and very useful. It is possible because the inner class has a hidden reference to the outer class instance that was the current context when the inner class object was created. In effect, it ensures that the inner class and the outer class belong together, rather than the inner instance being just another member of the outer instance.

Sometimes you might want to create an instance of an inner class from a static method, or in some other situation where no `this` object is available. The situation arises in a `main()` method or if you need to create the inner class from a method of some object of an unrelated class. You can achieve this by using the new operator as though it were a member method of the outer class. Of course, you still must have an instance of the outer class. The following code, which is a `main()` method in isolation, could be added to the code seen so far to produce a complete example:

```
1. public static void main(String args[]) {
2.    OuterOne.InnerOne i = new OuterOne().new InnerOne();
3.    i.innerMethod();
4. }
```

From the point of view of the inner class instance, this use of two new statements on the same line is a compacted way of doing the following:

```
1. public static void main(String args[]) {
2.    OuterOne o = new OuterOne();
3.    OuterOne.InnerOne i = o.new InnerOne();
4.    i.innerMethod();
5. }
```

If you attempt to use the new operation to construct an instance of an inner class without a prefixing reference to an instance of the outer class, the implied prefix `this.` is assumed. This behavior is identical to that which you find with ordinary member accesses and method invocations. As with member access and method invocation, it is important that the `this` reference be valid when you try to use it. A `static` method contains no `this` reference, which is why you must take special efforts in these conditions.

Member Classes

To this point, we have not distinguished between classes defined directly in the scope of a class—that is, *member classes*—and classes defined inside of methods. There are important distinctions between these two scopes that you will need to have clear in your mind when you sit for the Certification Exam. First, we'll look at the features that are unique to member classes.

Access Modifiers

Members of a class, whether they are variables, methods, or nested classes, may be marked with modifiers that control access to those members. This means that member classes can be marked `private`, `public`, `protected`, or default access. The meaning of these access modifiers is the same for member classes as it is for other members, and therefore we won't spend time on those issues here. Instead, refer to Chapter 3, "Modifiers," if you need to revisit these concepts.

Static Inner Classes

Just like any other member, a member inner class may be marked `static`. When applied to a variable, `static` means that the variable is associated with the class, rather than with any particular instance of the class. When applied to an inner class, the meaning is similar. Specifically, a static inner class does *not* have any reference to an enclosing instance. As a result, methods of a static inner class cannot use the keyword `this` (either implied or explicit) to access instance variables of the enclosing class; those methods can, however, access static variables of the enclosing class. This is just the same as the rules that apply to static methods in ordinary classes. As you would expect, you can create an instance of a static inner class without the need for a current instance of the enclosing class. The syntax for this construction is very simple; just use the long name of the inner class—that is, the name that includes the name of the outer class, as in the highlighted part of line 5:

```
1. public class MyOuter {
2.   public static class MyInner {
3.   }
4.   public static void main(String [] args) {
5.     MyInner aMyInner = new MyOuter.MyInner();
6.   }
7. }
```

The net result is that a static inner class is really just a top-level class with a modified naming scheme. In fact, you can use static inner classes as an extension to packaging.

Not only can you declare a class inside another class, but you can also declare a class inside a method of another class. We will discuss this next.

Classes Defined Inside Methods

In the opening of this chapter, we said that nested classes can be declared in any block, and that this means you can define a class inside a method. This is superficially similar to what you have already seen, but in this case there are three particular points to be considered.

The first point is that anything declared inside a method is not a member of the class but is local to the method. The immediate consequence is that classes declared in methods are private to the method and cannot be marked with any access modifier; neither can they be marked as `static`. If you think about this, you'll recognize that these are just the same rules as for any variable declaration you might make in a method.

The second point is that an object created from an inner class within a method can have some access to the variables of the enclosing method. We'll look at how this is done and the restrictions that apply to this access in a moment.

Finally, it is possible to create an anonymous class—literally, a class with no specified name—and doing so can be very eloquent when working with event listeners. We will discuss this technique after covering the rules governing access from an inner class to method variables in the enclosing blocks.

Accessing Method Variables

The rule that governs access to the variables of an enclosing method is simple. Any variable, either a local variable or a formal parameter, can be accessed by methods within an inner class, provided that variable is marked `final`. A final variable is effectively a constant, so this might seem to be quite a severe restriction, but the point is simply this: an object created inside a method is likely to outlive the method invocation. Because local variables and method arguments are conventionally destroyed when their method exits, these variables would be invalid for access by inner class methods after the enclosing method exits. By allowing access only to final variables, it becomes possible to copy the values of those variables into the object, thereby extending their lifetimes. The other possible approaches to this problem would be writing to two copies of the same data every time it was changed or putting method local variables onto the heap instead of the stack. Either of these approaches would significantly degrade performance.

Let's look at an example:

```
1.  public class MOuter {
2.     private int m = (int)(Math.random() * 100);
3.     public static void main(String args[]) {
4.        MOuter that = new MOuter();
5.        that.go((int)(Math.random() * 100),
6.           (int)(Math.random() * 100));
7.     }
8.
9.     public void go(int x, final int y) {
10.       int a = x + y;
11.       final int b = x - y;
12.       class MInner {
13.          public void method() {
14.             System.out.println("m is " + m);
15. //           System.out.println("x is " + x); //Illegal!
16.             System.out.println("y is " + y);
17. //           System.out.println("a is " + a); //Illegal!
18.             System.out.println("b is " + b);
19.          }
20.       }
21.
```

```
22.        MInner that = new MInner();
23.        that.method();
24.    }
25. }
```

In this example, the class `MInner` is defined in lines 12–20 (in bold). Within it, `method()` has access to the member variable m in the enclosing class (as with the previous examples) but also to the final variables of `go()`. The commented-out code on lines 15 and 17 would be illegal, because it attempts to refer to nonfinal variables in `go()`; if these lines were included in the source proper, they would cause compiler errors.

Anonymous Classes

Some classes that you define inside a method do not need a name. A class defined in this way without a name is called an *anonymous class*. Anonymous classes can be declared to extend another class or to implement a single interface. The syntax does not allow you to do both at the same time, nor to implement more than one interface explicitly (of course, if you extend a class and the parent class implements interfaces, then so does the new class). If you declare a class that implements a single explicit interface, then it is a direct subclass of `java.lang.Object`.

Because you do not know the name of an anonymous inner class, you cannot use the new keyword in the usual way to create an instance of that class. In fact, the definition, construction, and first use (often in an assignment) of an anonymous class all occur in the same place. The next example shows a typical creation of an anonymous inner class that implements a single interface, in this case `ActionListener`. The essential parts of the declaration and construction are in bold on lines 3–7:

```
1. public void aMethod() {
2.    theButton.addActionListener(
3.       new ActionListener() {
4.          public void actionPerformed(ActionEvent e) {
5.             System.out.println("The action has occurred");
6.          }
7.       }
8.    );
9. }
```

In this fragment, the variable used at line 2, `theButton`, is a reference to a `Button` object. Notice that the action listener attached to the button is defined in lines 3–7. The entire declaration forms the argument to the `addActionListener()` method call at line 2; the closing parenthesis that completes this method call is on line 8.

The declaration and construction both start on line 3. Notice that the name of the interface is used immediately after the new keyword. This pattern is used for both interfaces and classes. The class has no visible name of its own in the source but is referred to simply using the class or interface name from which the new anonymous class is derived. The effect of this syntax is to state that you are defining a class and you do not want to think up a name for that class. Further, the class implements the specified interface or extends the specified class without using the either the `implements` or `extends` keyword.

An anonymous class gives you a convenient way to avoid having to think up trivial names for classes, but the facility should be used with care. Clearly, you cannot instantiate objects of this class anywhere except in the code shown. Further, anonymous classes should be small. If the class defines methods other than those of a simple, well-known interface such as an AWT event listener, it probably should not be anonymous. Similarly, if the class has methods containing more than one or two lines of straightforward code or if the entire class has more than about 10 lines, it probably should not be anonymous. These are not absolute rules; rather, the point here is that if you do not give the class a name, you have only the "self-documenting" nature of the code to explain what it is for. If, in fact, the code is not simple enough to be genuinely self-documenting, then you probably should give it a descriptive name.

When the compiler comes across an anonymous inner class, it creates a separate class file for it called *EnclosingClassName$n*.class, where *EnclosingClassName* is the name of the class that contains the anonymous inner class, and *n* is the integer counter for the anonymous inner classes in the enclosing class (starting at 1).

Construction and Initialization of Anonymous Inner Classes

You need to understand a few points about the construction and initialization of anonymous inner classes to succeed in the Certification Exam and in real life. Let's look at these issues.

As you have already seen, the class is instantiated and declared in the same place. This means that anonymous inner classes are unique to method scopes; you cannot have anonymity with a member class.

You cannot define any specific constructor for an anonymous inner class. This is a direct consequence of the fact that you do not specify a name for the class, and therefore you cannot use that name to specify a constructor. However, an inner class can be constructed with arguments under some conditions, and an inner class can have an initializer if you wish.

Anonymous Class Declarations

As you have already seen, the central theme of the code that declares and constructs an anonymous inner class is

```
new Xxxx() { /* class body. */ }
```

where Xxxx is a class or interface name. It is important to grasp that code of this form is an *expression* that returns a reference to an object. Thus the previous code is incomplete by itself but can be used wherever you can use an object reference. For example, you might assign the reference to the constructed object into a variable, like this:

```
Xxxx AnXxxx = new Xxxx () { /* class body. */ };
```

Notice that you must be sure to make a complete statement, including the closing semicolon. Alternatively, you might use the reference to the constructed object as an argument to a method call. In that case, the overall appearance is like this:

```
someMethod(new Xxxx () { /* class body. */ });
```

Passing Arguments into the Construction of an Anonymous Inner Class

If the anonymous inner class extends another class, and that parent class has constructors that take arguments, then you can arrange for one of these constructors to be invoked by specifying the argument list to the construction of the anonymous inner class. An example follows:

```
// Assume this code appears in some method
Button b = new Button("Anonymous Button") {
    // behavior for the button
};
// do things with the button b...
...
```

In this situation, the compiler will build a constructor for your anonymous inner class that effectively invokes the superclass constructor with the argument list provided, something like this:

```
// This is not code you write! This exemplifies what the
// compiler creates internally when asked to compile
// something like the previous anonymous example
class AnonymousButtonSubclass extends Button {
    public AnonymousButtonSubclass(String s) {
        super(s);
    }
}
```

Note that this isn't the actual code that would be created—specifically, the class name is made up—but it conveys the general idea.

Initializing an Anonymous Inner Class

Sometimes you will want to perform some kind of initialization when an inner class is constructed. In normal classes, you would create a constructor. In an anonymous inner class, you cannot do this, but you can use the initializer feature that was added to the language at JDK 1.1. If you provide an unnamed block in class scope, then it will be invoked as part of the construction process, like this:

```
public MyClass {
    { // initializer
        System.out.println("Creating an instance");
    }
}
```

This is true of any class, but the technique is particularly useful with anonymous inner classes, where it is the only tool you have that provides some control over the construction process.

A Complex Example of Anonymous Inner Classes

Now let's look at a complete example following the pattern of the earlier example using a Button. This example uses two anonymous inner classes, one nested inside the other; an initializer; and a constructor that takes an argument:

```
1.  import java.awt.*;
2.  import java.awt.event.*;
3.
4.  public class X extends Frame {
5.    public static void main(String args[]) {
6.      X x = new X();
7.      x.pack();
8.      x.setVisible(true);
9.    }
10.
11.   private int count;
12.
13.   public X() {
14.     final Label l = new Label("Count = " + count);
15.     add(l, BorderLayout.SOUTH);
16.
17.     add(
18.       new Button("Hello " + 1) {
19.         { // initializer
20.           addActionListener(
21.             new ActionListener() {
22.               public void actionPerformed(
23.                 ActionEvent ev) {
24.                 count++;
25.                 l.setText("Count = " + count);
26.               }
27.             }
28.           );
29.         }
30.       }, BorderLayout.NORTH
31.     );
32.   }
33. }
```

Lines 19–29 form the initializer and set up a listener on the Button. The listener is another anonymous inner class; as we said earlier, you can arbitrarily nest these things. Notice how the label variable declared at line 14 is final; this allows it to be accessed from the inner classes, and specifically, from the listener defined in the initializer of the first anonymous inner class.

Summary

We have covered a lot of material in this chapter, but all of it is important. Let's look again at the key points.

We began by covering object-oriented design and implementation. The benefits of object-oriented design and implementation include reusability (through composition and inheritance) and data protection (through encapsulation). We discussed the concept of overloading methods, which allows the programmer to write several methods by the same name in the same class with different argument lists, return types, accessibility modifiers, and lists of exceptions to be thrown. We also discussed overriding methods, which allows the programmer to define new behavior in a subclass method that differs from that of the superclass method. Late binding ensures that the correct behavior is executed at runtime.

We defined when and how constructors are defined with respect to subclassing. Constructors are not inherited, but a single default constructor is provided by the compiler for all classes, including subclasses. A constructor in a subclass can call a constructor in its superclass (by using the super() reference) or another constructor in the same class (by using the this() reference).

Inner classes is an updated feature in the JDK 1.1 release. Because they can be declared in any scope, they can give your programs additional clarity and make them more concise. An inner class in class scope can have any accessibility, including private. Inner classes defined as local to a block may not be static. However, an inner class declared local to a block (for example, in a method), must not have any access modifier. Such a class is effectively private to the block. Classes defined in methods can be anonymous, in which case they must be instantiated at the same point they are defined. Anonymous inner classes can implement an interface or extend a class, but they cannot have any explicit constructors.

Exam Essentials

Be familiar with the way the Java language realizes the "is a" and "has a" relationships. The "is a" relationship implies class extension. The "has a" relationship implies ownership of a reference to a different object.

Be able to identify legally overloaded methods and constructors. The methods/constructors must have different argument lists.

Be able to identify legally overridden methods. The methods must have the same name, argument list, and return type.

Know the legal return types for overloaded and overridden methods. There are no restrictions for an overloaded method; an overriding method must have the same return type as the overridden version.

Know that the compiler generates a default constructor when a class has no explicit constructors. When a class has constructor code, no default constructor is generated.

Understand the chain of calls to parental constructors. Each constructor invocation begins by invoking a parental constructor.

Know how to create a constructor that invokes a nondefault parental constructor. Understand the use of the `super` keyword.

Be able to identify correctly constructed inner classes, including inner classes in methods and anonymous inner classes. The syntax for each of these forms is explained in previous sections of this chapter.

Know which data and methods of an enclosing class are available to an inner class. Understand that the inner class can access all data and methods of its enclosing class.

Understand the restrictions on static inner classes. Understand that a static inner class cannot access nonstatic features of its enclosing class.

Know how to use a nonstatic inner class from a static method of the enclosing class. Be able to recognize the `new Outer().new Inner()` format.

Key Terms

Before you take the exam, be certain you are familiar with the following terms:

anonymous class	late binding
default constructor	member class
encapsulation	overloading
inheritance	overriding
inner class	

Review Questions

1. Consider this class:

   ```
   1. public class Test1 {
   2.    public float aMethod(float a, float b) {
   3.    }
   4.
   5. }
   ```

   Which of the following methods would be legal if added (individually) at line 4? (Choose all that apply.)

   A. `public int aMethod(int a, int b) { }`
   B. `public float aMethod(float a, float b) { }`
   C. `public float aMethod(float a, float b, int c) throws Exception { }`
   D. `public float aMethod(float c, float d) { }`
   E. `private float aMethod(int a, int b, int c) { }`

2. Consider these classes, defined in separate source files:

   ```
   1. public class Test1 {
   2.    public float aMethod(float a, float b) throws
   3.       IOException {...
   4.    }
   5. }
   ```

   ```
   1. public class Test2 extends Test1 {
   2.
   3. }
   ```

   Which of the following methods would be legal (individually) at line 2 in class Test2? (Choose all that apply.)

   A. `float aMethod(float a, float b) {...}`
   B. `public int aMethod(int a, int b) throws Exception {...}`
   C. `public float aMethod(float a, float b) throws Exception {...}`
   D. `public float aMethod(float p, float q) {...}`

3. You have been given a design document for a veterinary registration system for implementation in Java. It states:

   "A pet has an owner, a registration date, and a vaccination-due date. A cat is a pet that has a flag indicating whether it has been neutered, and a textual description of its markings."

   Given that the Pet class has already been defined, which of the following fields would be appropriate for inclusion in the Cat class as members? (Choose all that apply.)

   A. `Pet thePet;`
   B. `Date registered;`
   C. `Date vaccinationDue;`
   D. `Cat theCat;`
   E. `boolean neutered;`
   F. `String markings;`

4. You have been given a design document for a veterinary registration system for implementation in Java. It states:

   "A pet has an owner, a registration date, and a vaccination-due date. A cat is a pet that has a flag indicating if it has been neutered, and a textual description of its markings."

   Given that the Pet class has already been defined and you expect the Cat class to be used freely throughout the application, how would you make the opening declaration of the Cat class, up to but not including the first opening brace? Use only these words and spaces: boolean, Cat, class, Date, extends, Object, Owner, Pet, private, protected, public, String.

   A. `protected class Cat extends Owner`
   B. `public class Cat extends Object`
   C. `public class Cat extends Pet`
   D. `private class Cat extends Pet`

5. Consider the following classes, declared in separate source files:

```
1. public class Base {
2.    public void method(int i) {
3.       System.out.print("Value is " + i);
4.    }
5. }
```
```
1. public class Sub extends Base {
2.    public void method(int j) {
3.       System.out.print("This value is " + j);
4.    }
5.    public void method(String s) {
```

```
6.      System.out.print("I was passed " + s);
7.    }
8.    public static void main(String args[]) {
9.        Base b1 = new Base();
10.       Base b2 = new Sub();
11.       b1.method(5);
12.       b2.method(6);
13.    }
14. }
```

What output results when the main method of the class Sub is run?

A. Value is 5Value is 6
B. This value is 5This value is 6
C. Value is 5This value is 6
D. This value is 5Value is 6
E. I was passed 5I was passed 6

6. Consider the following class definition:

```
1. public class Test extends Base {
2.    public Test(int j) {
3.    }
4.    public Test(int j, int k) {
5.        super(j, k);
6.    }
7. }
```

Which of the following are legitimate calls to construct instances of the Test class? (Choose all that apply.)

A. Test t = new Test();
B. Test t = new Test(1);
C. Test t = new Test(1, 2);
D. Test t = new Test(1, 2, 3);
E. Test t = (new Base()).new Test(1);

7. Consider the following class definition:

```
1. public class Test extends Base {
2.    public Test(int j) {
3.    }
```

```
4.    public Test(int j, int k) {
5.       super(j, k);
6.    }
7. }
```

Which of the following forms of constructor must exist explicitly in the definition of the **Base** class? Assume **Test** and **Base** are in the same package. (Choose all that apply.)

A. Base() { }

B. Base(int j) { }

C. Base(int j, int k) { }

D. Base(int j, int k, int l) { }

8. Which of the following statements are true? (Choose all that apply.)

   A. An inner class may be declared `private`.

   B. An inner class may be declared `static`.

   C. An inner class defined in a method should always be anonymous.

   D. An inner class defined in a method can access all the method local variables.

   E. Construction of an inner class may require an instance of the outer class.

9. Consider the following definition:

```
1. public class Outer {
2.    public int a = 1;
3.    private int b = 2;
4.    public void method(final int c) {
5.       int d = 3;
6.       class Inner {
7.          private void iMethod(int e) {
8.
9.          }
10.      }
11.   }
12. }
```

   Which variables can be referenced correctly at line 8? (Choose all that apply.)

   A. a

   B. b

   C. c

   D. d

   E. e

10. Which of the following statements are true? (Choose all that apply.)
    A. Given that Inner is a nonstatic class declared inside a public class Outer and that appropriate constructor forms are defined, an instance of Inner can be constructed like this: new Outer().new Inner()
    B. If an anonymous inner class inside the class Outer is defined to implement the interface ActionListener, it can be constructed like this: new Outer().new ActionListener()
    C. Given that Inner is a nonstatic class declared inside a public class Outer and that appropriate constructor forms are defined, an instance of Inner can be constructed in a static method like this: new Inner()
    D. An anonymous class instance that implements the interface MyInterface can be constructed and returned from a method like this:
    ```
    1. return new MyInterface(int x) {
    2.     int x;
    3.     public MyInterface(int x) {
    4.         this.x = x;
    5.     }
    6. };
    ```

Answers to Review Questions

1. **A, C, E.** In each of these answers, the argument list differs from the original, so the method is an overload. Overloaded methods are effectively independent, and there are no constraints on the accessibility, return type, or exceptions that may be thrown. B would be a legal overriding method, except that it cannot be defined in the same class as the original method; rather, it must be declared in a subclass. D is also an override, because the *types* of its arguments are the same: changing the parameter names is not sufficient to count as overloading.

2. **B, D.** A is illegal because it is less accessible than the original method; the fact that it throws no exceptions is perfectly acceptable. B is legal because it overloads the method of the parent class, and as such it is not constrained by any rules governing its return value, accessibility, or argument list. The exception thrown by C is sufficient to make that method illegal. D is legal because the accessibility and return type are identical, and the method is an override because the types of the arguments are identical—remember that the names of the arguments are irrelevant. The absence of an exception list in D is not a problem: An overriding method may legitimately throw fewer exceptions than its original, but it may not throw more.

3. **E, F.** The Cat class is a subclass of the Pet class, and as such should extend Pet, rather than containing an instance of Pet. B and C should be members of the Pet class and as such are inherited into the Cat class; therefore, they should not be declared in the Cat class. D would declare a reference to an instance of the Cat class, which is not generally appropriate inside the Cat class (unless, perhaps, you were asked to give the Cat a member that refers to its mother). Finally, the neutered flag and markings descriptions, E and F, are the items called for by the specification; these are correct items.

4. **C.** The class should be public, because it is to be used freely throughout the application. The statement "A cat is a pet" tells you that the Cat class should subclass Pet. The other words offered are required for the body of the definitions of either Cat or Pet—for use as member variables—but are not part of the opening declaration.

5. **C.** The first message is produced by the Base class when b1.method(5) is called and is therefore Value is 5. Despite the fact that variable b2 is declared as being of the Base class, the behavior that results when method() is invoked upon it is the behavior associated with the class of the actual object, not with the type of the variable. Because the object is of class Sub, not of class Base, the second message is generated by line 3 of class Sub: This value is 6.

6. **B, C.** Because the class has explicit constructors defined, the default constructor is suppressed, so A is not possible. B and C have argument lists that match the constructors defined at lines 2 and 4 respectively, and so are correct constructions. D has three integer arguments, but there are no constructors that take three arguments of any kind in the Test class, so D is incorrect. Finally, E is a syntax used for construction of inner classes and is therefore wrong.

7. **A, C.** The constructor at lines 2 and 3 includes no explicit call to either `this()` or `super()`, which means that the compiler will generate a call to the zero-argument superclass constructor, as in A. The explicit call to `super()` at line 5 requires that the `Base` class must have a constructor as in C. This requirement has two consequences. First, C must be one of the required constructors and therefore one of the answers. Second, the `Base` class must have at least that constructor defined explicitly, so the default constructor is not generated, but must be added explicitly. Therefore the constructor of A is also required and must be a correct answer. At no point in the `Test` class is there a call to either a superclass constructor with one or three arguments, so B and D need not explicitly exist.

8. **A, B, E.** Member inner classes may be defined with any accessibility, so `private` is entirely acceptable and A is correct. Similarly, the `static` modifier is permitted on a member inner class, which causes it not to be associated with any particular instance of the outer class; thus B is also correct. Inner classes defined in methods may be anonymous—and indeed often are—but this is not required, so C is wrong. D is wrong because it is not possible for an inner class defined in a method to access the local variables of the method, except for those variables that are marked as `final`. Constructing an instance of a static inner class does not need an instance of the enclosing object, but all nonstatic inner classes do require such a reference, and that reference must be available to the new operation. The reference to the enclosing object is commonly implied as `this`, which is why it is commonly not explicit. These points make E true.

9. **A, B, C, E.** Because `Inner` is not a static inner class, it has a reference to an enclosing object, and all the variables of that object are accessible. Therefore A and B are correct, despite the fact that b is marked `private`. Variables in the enclosing method are accessible only if those variables are marked `final`, so the method argument c is correct, but the variable d is not. Finally, the parameter e is of course accessible, because it is a parameter to the method containing line 8.

10. **A.** Construction of a normal (that is, a named and nonstatic) inner class requires an instance of the enclosing class. Often this enclosing instance is provided via the implied `this` reference, but an explicit reference can be used in front of the `new` operator, as shown in A. Anonymous inner classes can be instantiated only at the same point they are declared, like this:

```
return new ActionListener() {
  public void actionPerformed(ActionEvent e) { }
}
```

Hence, B is illegal; it attempts to instantiate the interface `ActionListener` as if that interface were an inner class inside `Outer`. C is illegal because `Inner` is a nonstatic inner class, and so it requires a reference to an enclosing instance when it is constructed. The form shown suggests the implied `this` reference, but because the method is `static`, there is no `this` reference and the construction is illegal. D is illegal because it attempts to use arguments to the constructor of an anonymous inner class that implements an interface. The clue is in the attempt to define a constructor at line 3. This would be a constructor for the interface `MyInterface`, not for the inner class—this is wrong on two counts. First, interfaces do not define constructors, and second, you need a constructor for your anonymous class, not for the interface.

Chapter 7

Threads

JAVA CERTIFICATION EXAM OBJECTIVES COVERED IN THIS CHAPTER:

- ✓ 4.2 Identify classes that correctly implement an interface where that interface is either `java.lang.Runnable` or a fully specified interface in the question.

- ✓ 7.1 Write code to define, instantiate, and start new threads using both `java.lang.Thread` and `java.lang.Runnable`. Recognize conditions that might prevent a thread from executing.

- ✓ 7.2 Write code using synchronized `wait`, `notify`, and `notifyAll` to protect against concurrent access problems and to communicate between threads.

- ✓ 7.3 Define the interaction among threads and object locks when executing synchronized `wait`, `notify`, or `notifyAll`.

- ✓ 7.4 Define the interaction among threads and object locks when executing synchronized `wait`, `notify` or `notifyAll`.

Threads are Java's way of making a single Java Virtual Machine (JVM) look like many machines, all running at the same time. This effect, usually, is an illusion: there is only one JVM and usually only one CPU, but the CPU switches among the JVM's various threads to give the impression that there are multiple CPUs. JVM threads work behind the scenes on your behalf, listening for user input, managing garbage collection, and performing a variety of other tasks.

As a Java programmer, you can choose between a *single-threaded* and a *multithreaded* programming paradigm. A single-threaded Java program has one entry point (the `main()` method) and one exit point. All instructions are run serially, from start to finish. A multi-threaded program has a *first* entry point (the `main()` method), followed by multiple entry and exit points for other methods that may be scheduled to run concurrently with the `main()` method.

Java provides you with tools for creating and managing threads. Threads are valuable tools for allowing unrelated, loosely related, or tightly related work to be programmed separately and executed concurrently.

The Certification Exam objectives require that you be familiar with Java's thread support, including the mechanisms for creating, controlling, and communicating between threads.

Thread Fundamentals

Java's thread support resides in three places:
- The `java.lang.Thread` class
- The `java.lang.Object` class
- The Java language and JVM

Most (but definitely not all) support resides in the `Thread` class. In Java, every thread corresponds to an instance of the `Thread` class. These objects can be in various states: at any moment, at most one object is executing per CPU, while others might be waiting for resources, waiting for a chance to execute, sleeping, or dead.

In order to demonstrate an understanding of threads, you need to be able to answer a few questions:
- When a thread executes, what code does it execute?
- What states can a thread be in?
- How does a thread's state get changed?

The next few sections will look at each of these questions in turn.

What a Thread Executes

To make a thread execute, you call its `start()` method. Doing so registers the thread with a piece of system code called the *thread scheduler*. The scheduler might be part of the JVM or of the host operating system. The scheduler determines which thread is running on each available CPU at any given time. Note that calling your thread's `start()` method doesn't immediately cause the thread to run; it just makes the thread *eligible* to run. The thread must still contend for CPU time with all the other threads. If all is well, then at some point in the future the thread scheduler will permit your thread to execute.

During its lifetime, a thread spends some time executing and some time in any of several non-executing states. In this section, you can ignore (for the moment) the question of how the thread is moved between states. The question at hand is this: When the thread gets to execute, what does it execute?

The simple answer is that it executes a method called `run()`. But which object's `run()` method? You have two choices:

- The thread can execute its own `run()` method.
- The thread can execute the `run()` method of some other object.

If you want the thread to execute its own `run()` method, you need to subclass the `Thread` class and implement the `run()` method. For example:

```
1. public class CounterThread extends Thread {
2.   public void run() {
3.     for (int i = 1; i <= 10; i++) {
4.       System.out.println("Counting: " + i);
5.     }
6.   }
7. }
```

This `run()` method prints out the numbers from 1 to 10. To do this in a thread, you first construct an instance of `CounterThread` and then invoke its `start()` method:

```
1. CounterThread ct = new CounterThread();
2. ct.start();        // start(), not run()
```

What you *don't* do is call `run()` directly; that would just count to 10 in the current thread. Instead, you call `start()`, which the `CounterThread` class inherits from its parent class, `Thread`. The `start()` method registers the thread `ct` with the thread scheduler; eventually the thread will execute, and at that time its `run()` method will be called.

If you want your thread to execute the `run()` method of some object other than itself, you still need to construct an instance of the `Thread` class. The only difference is that when you call the `Thread` constructor, you have to specify which object owns the `run()` method that you want. To do this, you invoke an alternate form of the `Thread` constructor:

```
public Thread(Runnable target)
```

The `Runnable` interface describes a single method:

```
public void run();
```

Thus you can pass any object you want into the `Thread` constructor, provided it implements the `Runnable` interface (so that it really does have a `run()` method for the thread scheduler to invoke).

Having constructed an instance of `Thread`, you proceed as before: you invoke the `start()` method. As before, doing so registers the thread with the scheduler, and eventually the `run()` method of the target will be called.

For example, the following class has a `run()` method that counts down from 10 to 1:

```
1. public class DownCounter implements Runnable {
2.    public void run() {
3.       for (int i = 10; i >= 1; i--) {
4.          System.out.println("Counting Down: " + i);
5.       }
6.    }
7. }
```

This class does not extend `Thread`. However, it has a `run()` method, and it declares that it implements the `Runnable` interface. Thus any instance of the `DownCounter` class is eligible to be passed into the alternative (nondefault) constructor for `Thread`:

```
1. DownCounter dc = new DownCounter();
2. Thread t = new Thread(dc);
3. t.start();
```

This section has presented two strategies for constructing threads. Superficially, the only difference between these two strategies is the location of the `run()` method. The second strategy, where a runnable target is passed into the constructor, is perhaps a bit more complicated in the case of the simple examples we have considered. However, there are good reasons why you might choose to make this extra effort. The `run()` method, like any other member method, is allowed to access the private data, and call the private methods, of the class of which it is a member. Putting `run()` in a subclass of `Thread` may mean that the method cannot access features it needs (or cannot access those features in a clean, reasonable manner).

Another reason that might persuade you to implement your threads using runnables rather than subclassing `Thread` is the single implementation inheritance rule. If you write a subclass of `Thread`, it cannot be a subclass of anything else; but using `Runnable`, you can subclass whatever other parent class you choose.

Finally, from an object-oriented point of view, a subclass of `Thread` combines two unrelated functionalities: support for multithreading inherited from the `Thread` superclass, and execution behavior provided by the `run()` method. These functionalities are not closely related, so good object-oriented discipline suggests that they exist in two separate classes. In the jargon of object-oriented analysis, if you create a class that extends `Thread`, you're saying that your class "is a" thread. If you create a class that implements `Runnable`, you're saying that your class "is associated with" a thread.

To summarize, you can use two approaches to specify which run() method will be executed by a thread:

- Subclass Thread. Define your run() method in the subclass.
- Write a class that implements Runnable. Define your run() method in that class. Pass an instance of that class into your call to the Thread constructor.

When Execution Ends

When the run() method returns, the thread has finished its task and is considered *dead*. There is no way out of this state. Once a thread is dead, it cannot be started again; if you want the thread's task to be performed again, you have to construct and start a new thread instance. The dead thread continues to exist; it is an object like any other object, and you can still access its data and call its methods. You just can't make it run again. In other words:

- You *can't* restart a dead thread by calling it's start() or run() methods.
- You *can* call other methods (besides start() and run()) of a dead thread.

The Thread methods include a method called stop(), which forcibly terminates a thread, putting it into the dead state. This method is deprecated since JDK 1.2, because it can cause data corruption or deadlock if you kill a thread that is in a critical section of code. The stop() method is therefore no longer part of the Certification Exam. Instead of using stop(), if a thread might need to be killed from another thread, you should call interrupt() on it from the killing method.

> Although you can't restart a dead thread, if you use runnables, you can submit the old Runnable instance to a new thread. However, it is generally poor design to constantly create, use, and discard threads, because constructing a Thread is a relatively heavyweight operation, involving significant kernel resources. It is better to create a pool of reusable worker threads that can be assigned chores as needed.

Thread States

When you call start() on a thread, the thread does not run immediately. It goes into a "ready-to-run" state and stays there until the scheduler moves it to the "running" state. Then the run() method is called. In the course of executing run(), the thread may temporarily give up the CPU and enter some other state for a while. It is important to be aware of the possible states a thread might be in and of the triggers that can cause the thread's state to change.

The thread states are

Running   The state that all threads aspire to

Various nonrunning states   Monitor states, Sleeping, Suspended, Blocked

Ready   Not waiting for anything except the CPU

Dead   All done

Figure 7.1 shows the nondead states. Notice that the figure does not show the dead state.

FIGURE 7.1   Living thread states

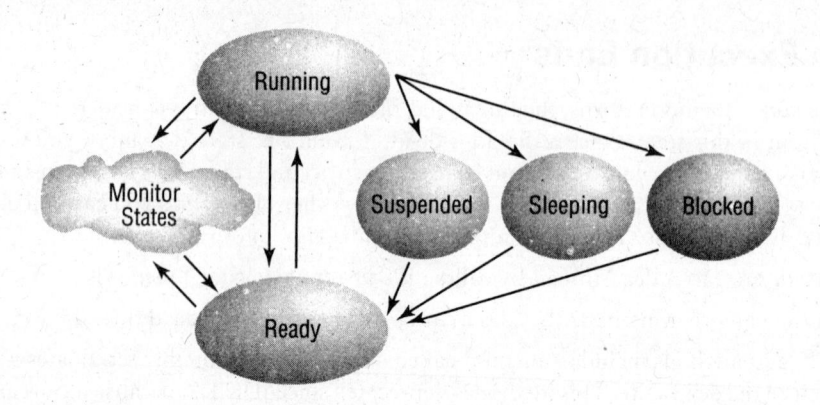

At the top of Figure 7.1 is the Running state. At the bottom is the Ready state. In between are the various not-ready states. A thread in one of these intermediate states is waiting for something to happen; when that something eventually happens, the thread moves to the Ready state, and eventually the thread scheduler will permit it to run again. Note that the methods associated with the Suspended state are now deprecated; you will not be tested on this state or its associated methods in the exam. For this reason, we will not discuss them in any detail in this book.

The arrows between the bubbles in Figure 7.1 represent state transitions. Be aware that only the thread scheduler can move a ready thread into the CPU.

Later in this chapter, you will examine in detail the various waiting states. For now, the important thing to observe in Figure 7.1 is the general flow: a running thread enters an intermediate state for some reason; later, whatever the thread was waiting for comes to pass, and the thread enters the Ready state; later still, the scheduler grants the CPU to the thread. The exceptions to this general flow involve synchronized code and the `wait()` / `notify()` sequence—the corresponding portion of Figure 7.1 is depicted as a vague bubble labeled "Monitor States." These monitor states are discussed later in this chapter, in the section "Monitors, `wait()`, and `notify()`."

Thread Priorities

Every thread has a *priority*, which is an integer from 1 to 10; threads with higher priority should get preference over threads with lower priority. The priority is considered by the thread scheduler when it decides which ready thread should execute. The scheduler generally chooses the highest-priority waiting thread. If more than one thread is waiting, the scheduler chooses one of them. There is no guarantee that the thread chosen will be the one that has been waiting the longest.

The default priority is 5, but all newly created threads have their priority set to that of the creating thread. To set a thread's priority, call the `setPriority()` method, passing in the desired new priority. The `getPriority()` method returns a thread's priority. The following code fragment increments the priority of thread `theThread`, provided the priority is less than 10. Instead of hard-coding the value 10, the fragment uses the constant `MAX_PRIORITY`. The `Thread` class also defines constants for `MIN_PRIORITY` (which is 1), and `NORM_PRIORITY` (which is 5).

1. `int oldPriority = theThread.getPriority();`
2. `int newPriority = Math.min(oldPriority+1,`
3. `    Thread.MAX_PRIORITY);`
4. `theThread.setPriority(newPriority);`

> **WARNING** The specifics of how thread priorities affect scheduling are platform dependent. The Java specification states that threads must have priorities, but it does not dictate precisely what the scheduler should do about priorities. This vagueness is a problem: algorithms that rely on manipulating thread priorities might not run consistently on all platforms.

Controlling Threads

Thread control is the art of moving threads from state to state. You control threads by triggering state transitions. This section examines the various pathways out of the Running state. These pathways are

- Yielding
- Suspending and then resuming
- Sleeping and then waking up
- Blocking and then continuing
- Waiting and then being notified

Yielding

A thread can offer to move out of the virtual CPU by *yielding*. A call to the `yield()` method causes the currently executing thread to move to the Ready state if the scheduler is willing to run any other thread in place of the yielding thread. The state transition is shown in Figure 7.2.

FIGURE 7.2 Yield

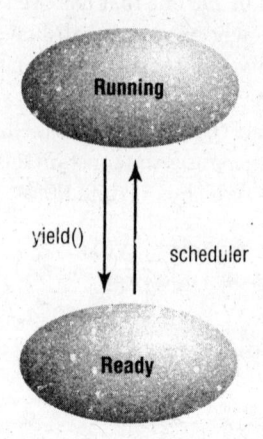

[Diagram: Running state and Ready state connected by arrows — yield() from Running to Ready, scheduler from Ready to Running]

A thread that has yielded goes into the Ready state. There are two possible scenarios. If any other threads are in the Ready state, then the thread that just yielded might have to wait a while before it gets to execute again. However, if no other threads are waiting, then the thread that just yielded will get to continue executing immediately. Note that most schedulers do not stop the yielding thread from running in favor of a thread of lower priority.

The `yield()` method is a static method of the `Thread` class. It always causes the currently executing thread to yield.

Yielding allows a time-consuming thread to permit other threads to execute. For example, consider an applet that computes a 300 × 300 pixel image using a ray-tracing algorithm. The applet might have a Compute button and an Interrupt button. The action event handler for the Compute button would create and start a separate thread, which would call a `traceRays()` method. A first cut at this method might look like this:

```
1. private void traceRays() {
2.   for (int j = 0; j < 300; j++) {
3.     for (int i = 0; i < 300; i++) {
4.       computeOnePixel(i, j);
5.     }
6.   }
7. }
```

There are 90,000 pixel color values to compute. If it takes 0.1 second to compute the color value of one pixel, then it will take two and a half hours to compute the complete image.

Suppose after half an hour the user looks at the partial image and realizes that something is wrong. (Perhaps the viewpoint or zoom factor is incorrect.) The user will then click the Interrupt button, because there is no sense in continuing to compute the useless image. Unfortunately, the thread that handles GUI input might not get a chance to execute until the thread that is executing `traceRays()` gives up the CPU. Thus the Interrupt button will not have any effect for another two hours.

If priorities are implemented meaningfully in the scheduler, then lowering the priority of the ray-tracing thread will have the desired effect, ensuring that the GUI thread will run when it has something useful to do. However, this mechanism is not reliable between platforms (although it is a good course of action anyway, because it will do no harm). The reliable approach is to have the ray-tracing thread periodically yield. If no input is pending when the yield is executed, then the ray-tracing thread will not be moved off the CPU. If, on the other hand, there is input to be processed, the input-listening thread will get a chance to execute.

The ray-tracing thread can have its priority set like this:

```
rayTraceThread.setPriority(Thread.NORM_PRIORITY-1);
```

The `traceRays()` method listed earlier can yield after each pixel value is computed, after line 4. The revised version looks like this:

```
1. private void traceRays() {
2.    for (int j = 0; j < 300; j++) {
3.       for (int i = 0; i < 300; i++) {
4.          computeOnePixel(i, j);
5.          Thread.yield();
6.       }
7.    }
8. }
```

Suspending

Suspending a thread is a mechanism that allows any arbitrary thread to make another thread unready for an indefinite period of time. The suspended thread becomes ready when some other thread resumes it. This might feel like a useful technique, but it is very easy to cause deadlock in a program using these methods—a thread has no control over when it is suspended (the control comes from outside the thread) and it might be in a critical section, holding an object lock at the time. The exact effect of `suspend()` and `resume()` is much better implemented using `wait()` and `notify()`.

The `suspend()` and `resume()` methods are deprecated as of the Java 2 release and do not appear in the Certification Exam, so we will not discuss them any further.

Sleeping

A *sleeping* thread passes time without doing anything and without using the CPU. A call to the `sleep()` method requests the currently executing thread to cease executing for (approximately) a specified amount of time. You can call this method two ways, depending on whether you want to specify the sleep period to millisecond precision or to nanosecond precision:

- `public static void sleep(long milliseconds) throws InterruptedException`
- `public static void sleep(long milliseconds, int nanoseconds) throws InterruptedException`

> **NOTE:** `sleep()`, like `yield()`, is static. Both methods operate on the currently executing thread.

The state diagram for Sleeping is shown in Figure 7.3. Notice that when the thread has finished sleeping, it does not continue execution. As you would expect, it enters the Ready state and will execute only when the thread scheduler allows it to do so. For this reason, you should expect that a `sleep()` call will block a thread for at least the requested time, but it might block for much longer. This behavior suggests that you should give very careful thought to your design before you expect any meaning from the nanosecond accuracy version of the `sleep()` method.

FIGURE 7.3 The Sleeping state

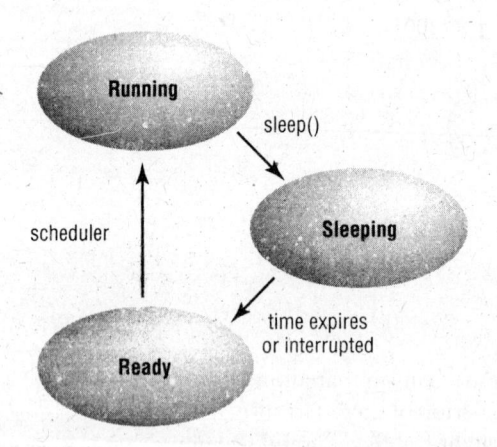

The `Thread` class has a method called `interrupt()`. A sleeping thread that receives an `interrupt()` call moves immediately into the Ready state; when it gets to run, it will execute its `InterruptedException` handler.

Blocking

Many methods that perform input or output have to wait for some occurrence in the outside world before they can proceed; this behavior is known as *blocking*. A good example is reading from a socket:

```
1. try {
2.    Socket sock = new Socket("magnesium", 5505);
3.    InputStream istr = sock.getInputStream();
4.    int b = istr.read();
5. }
```

```
6. catch (IOException ex) {
7.    // Handle the exception
8. }
```

It looks like line 4 reads a byte from an input stream that is connected to port 5505 on a machine called "magnesium." Actually, line 4 *tries* to read a byte. If a byte is available (that is, if magnesium has previously written a byte), then line 4 can return immediately and execution can continue. If magnesium has not yet written anything, however, the `read()` call has to wait. If magnesium is busy doing other things and takes half an hour to get around to writing a byte, then the `read()` call has to wait for half an hour.

Clearly, it would be a serious problem if the thread executing the `read()` call on line 4 remained in the Running state for the entire half hour. Nothing else could get done. In general, if a method needs to wait an indeterminable amount of time until some I/O occurrence takes place, then a thread executing that method should graciously step out of the Running state. All Java I/O methods behave this way. A thread that has graciously stepped out in this fashion is said to be *blocked*. Figure 7.4 shows the transitions of the Blocked state.

FIGURE 7.4   The Blocked state

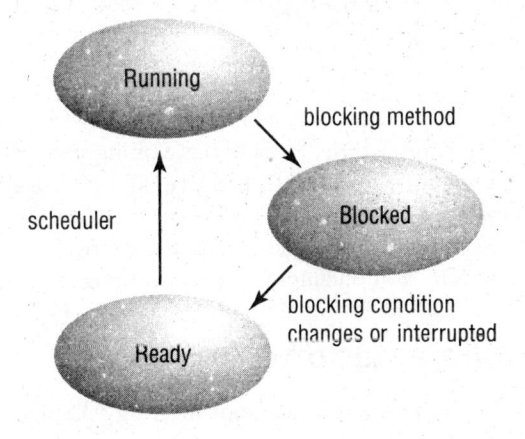

> In general, if you see a method with a name that suggests that it might do nothing until something becomes ready—for example, waitForInput() or waitForImages()—you should expect that the caller thread might be blocked, thus losing the CPU, when the method is called. You do not need to know about all APIs to make this assumption; this is a general principle of APIs, both core and third party, in a Java environment.

A thread can also become blocked if it fails to acquire the lock for a monitor or if it issues a `wait()` call. Locks and monitors are explained in detail later in this chapter, beginning in the section "Monitors, `wait()`, and `notify()`." Internally, most blocking for I/O, like the `read()` calls just discussed, is implemented using `wait()` and `notify()` calls.

Monitor States

Figure 7.5 (which is a rerun of Figure 7.1) shows all the thread-state transitions. The intermediate states on the right side of the figure (Suspended, Sleeping, and Blocked) have been discussed in previous sections. The monitor states are drawn all alone on the left side of the figure to emphasize that they are very different from the other intermediate states.

FIGURE 7.5 Thread states (reprise)

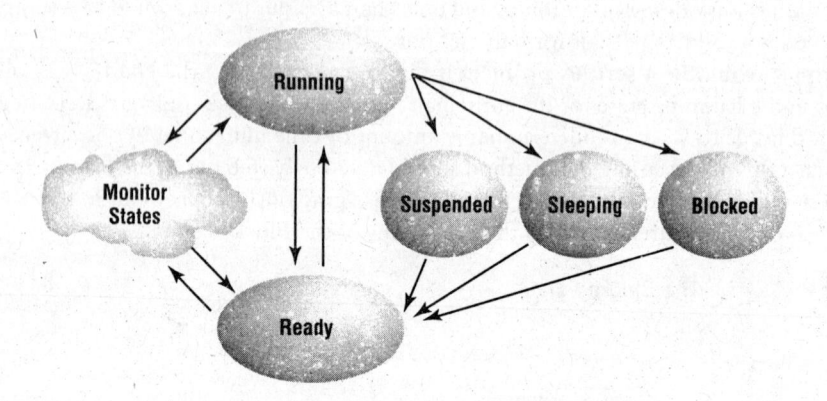

The `wait()` method puts an executing thread into the *Waiting* state, and the `notify()` and `notifyAll()` methods move waiting threads out of the Waiting state. However, these methods are very different from `suspend()`, `resume()`, and `yield()`. For one thing, they are implemented in the `Object` class, not in `Thread`. For another, they can only be called in synchronized code. The Waiting state and its associated issues and subtleties are discussed in the final sections of this chapter. But first, let's look at one more topic concerning thread control.

Scheduling Implementations

Historically, two approaches have emerged for implementing thread schedulers:

- *Preemptive scheduling*
- *Time-sliced scheduling* or *round-robin scheduling*

So far, the facilities described in this chapter have been preemptive. In preemptive scheduling, there are only two ways for a thread to leave the Running state without explicitly calling a thread-scheduling method such as `wait()` or `suspend()`:

- It can cease to be ready to execute (by calling a blocking I/O method, for example).
- It can get moved out of the CPU by a higher-priority thread that becomes ready to execute.

With time-slicing, a thread is allowed to execute only for a limited amount of time. It is then moved to the Ready state, where it must contend with all the other ready threads. Time-slicing ensures against the possibility of a single high-priority thread getting into the Running state and never getting out, preventing all other threads from doing their jobs. Unfortunately, time-slicing creates a nondeterministic system; you can't be certain at any moment which thread is executing or for how long it will continue to execute.

> **NOTE** It is natural to ask which implementation Java uses. The answer is that it depends on the platform; the Java specification gives implementations a lot of leeway.

Monitors, *wait()*, and *notify()*

A *monitor* is an object that can block and revive threads. The concept is simple, but it takes a bit of work to understand what monitors are good for and how to use them effectively.

The reason for having monitors is that sometimes a thread cannot perform its job until an object reaches a certain state. For example, consider a class that handles requests to write to standard output:

```
1. class Mailbox {
2.     public boolean    request;
3.     public String     message;
4. }
```

The intention of this class is that a client can set `message` to some value, and then set `request` to true:

```
1. myMailbox.message = "Hello everybody.";
2. myMailbox.request = true;
```

There must be a thread that checks `request`; on finding it true, the thread should write `message` to `System.out`, and then set `request` to false. (Setting `request` to false indicates that the mailbox object is ready to handle another request.) It is tempting to implement the thread like this:

```
1.  public class Consumer extends Thread {
2.      private Mailbox myMailbox;
3.
4.      public Consumer(Mailbox box) {
5.          this.myMailbox = box;
6.      }
7.
8.      public void run() {
9.          while (true) {
10.             if (myMailbox.request) {
```

```
11.         System.out.println(myMailbox.message);
12.         myMailbox.request = false;
13.     }
14.
15.     try {
16.         sleep(50);
17.     }
18.     catch (InterruptedException e) { }
19. }
20. }
```

The consumer thread loops forever, checking for requests every 50 milliseconds. If there is a request (line 10), the consumer writes the message to standard output (line 11) and then sets `request` to false to show that it is ready for more requests.

The `Consumer` class may look fine at first glance, but it has two serious problems:

- The `Consumer` class accesses data internal to the `Mailbox` class, introducing the possibility of corruption. On a time-sliced system, the consumer thread could just possibly be interrupted between lines 10 and 11. The interrupting thread could just possibly be a client that sets `message` to its own message (ignoring the convention of checking `request` to see if the handler is available). The consumer thread would send the wrong message.

- The choice of 50 milliseconds for the delay can never be ideal. Sometimes 50 milliseconds will be too long, and clients will receive slow service; sometimes 50 milliseconds will be too frequent, and cycles will be wasted. A thread that wants to send a message has a similar dilemma if it finds the `request` flag set: the thread should back off for a while, but for how long? There is no good answer to this question.

Ideally, these problems would be solved by making some modifications to the `Mailbox` class:

- The mailbox should be able to protect its data from irresponsible clients.
- If the mailbox is not available—that is, if the `request` flag is already set—then a client consumer should not have to guess how long to wait before checking the flag again. The handler should tell the client when the time is right.

Java's monitor support addresses these issues by providing the following resources:

- A lock for each object
- The `synchronized` keyword for accessing an object's lock
- The `wait()`, `notify()`, and `notifyAll()` methods, which allow the object to control client threads

The following sections describe locks, synchronized code, and the `wait()`, `notify()`, and `notifyAll()` methods and show how these can be used to make thread code more robust.

The Object Lock and Synchronization

Every object has a *lock*. At any moment, that lock is controlled by, at most, one single thread. The lock controls access to the object's *synchronized code*. A thread that wants to execute an object's synchronized code must first attempt to acquire that object's lock. If the lock is available—that is, if it is not already controlled by another thread—then all is well. If the lock is under another thread's control, then the attempting thread goes into the Seeking Lock state and becomes ready only when the lock becomes available. When a thread that owns a lock passes out of the synchronized code, the thread automatically gives up the lock. All this lock-checking and state-changing is done behind the scenes; the only explicit programming you need to do is to declare code to be synchronized.

Figure 7.6 shows the Seeking Lock state. This figure is the first state in our expansion of the monitor states, as depicted in Figure 7.5.

FIGURE 7.6 The Seeking Lock state

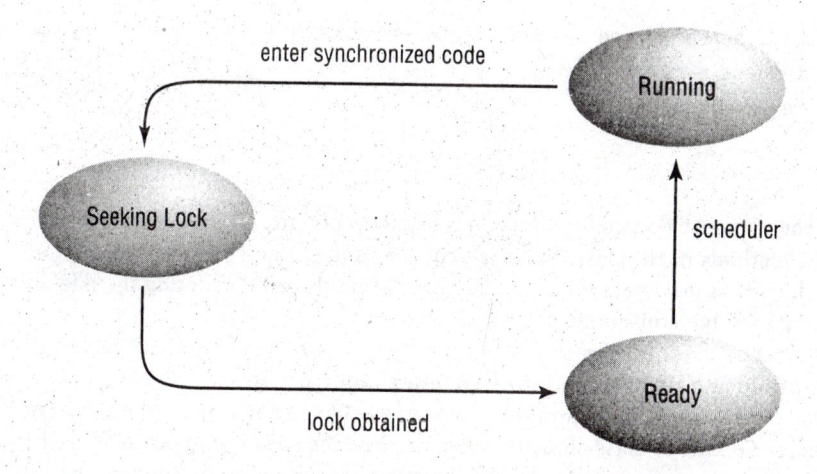

You can mark code as synchronized two ways:

- Synchronize an entire method by putting the `synchronized` modifier in the method's declaration. To execute the method, a thread must acquire the lock of the object that owns the method.

- Synchronize a subset of a method by surrounding the desired lines of code with curly brackets (`{}`) and inserting the expression `synchronized(someObject)` before the opening curly. This technique allows you to synchronize the block on the lock of any object at all, not necessarily the object that owns the code.

The first technique is by far the more common; synchronizing on any object other than the object that owns the synchronized code can be extremely dangerous. The Certification Exam requires you to know how to apply the second technique, but the exam does not make you think through complicated scenarios of synchronizing on external objects. The second technique is discussed at the end of this chapter.

Synchronization makes it easy to clean up some of the problems with the `Mailbox` class:

```
1.  class Mailbox {
2.     private boolean   request;
3.     private String    message;
4.
5.     public synchronized void
6.     storeMessage(String message) {
7.        request = true;
8.        this.message = message;
9.     }
10.
11.    public synchronized String retrieveMessage() {
12.       request = false;
13.       return message;
14.    }
15. }
```

Now the `request` flag and the message string are private, so they can be modified only via the public methods of the class. Because `storeMessage()` and `retrieveMessage()` are synchronized, there is no danger of a message-producing thread corrupting the flag and spoiling things for a message-consuming thread, or vice versa.

The `Mailbox` class is now safe from its clients, but the clients still have problems. A message-producing client should call `storeMessage()` only when the `request` flag is false; a message-consuming client should call `retrieveMessage()` only when the `request` flag is true. In the `Consumer` class of the previous section, the consuming thread's main loop polled the `request` flag every 50 milliseconds. (Presumably a message-producing thread would do something similar.) Now the `request` flag is private, so you must find another way.

It is possible to come up with any number of clever ways for the client threads to poll the mailbox, but the whole approach is backward. The mailbox becomes available or unavailable based on changes of its own state. The mailbox should be in charge of the progress of the clients. Java's `wait()` and `notify()` methods provide the necessary controls, as you will see in the next section.

wait() and *notify()*

The `wait()` and `notify()` methods provide a way for a shared object to pause a thread when it becomes unavailable to that thread and to allow the thread to continue when appropriate. The threads themselves never have to check the state of the shared object.

Monitors, wait(), and notify()

An object that controls its client threads in this manner is known as a monitor. In strict Java terminology, a monitor is any object that has some synchronized code. To be really useful, most monitors make use of `wait()` and `notify()` methods. So, the `Mailbox` class is already a monitor; it just is not quite useful yet.

Figure 7.7 shows the state transitions of `wait()` and `notify()`.

FIGURE 7.7 The monitor states

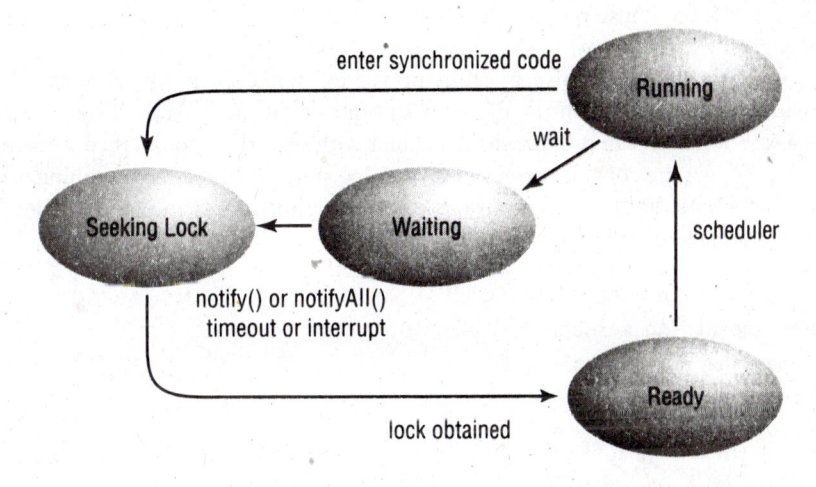

Both `wait()` and `notify()` must be called in synchronized code. A thread that calls `wait()` releases the virtual CPU; at the same time, it releases the lock. It enters a pool of waiting threads, which is managed by the object whose `wait()` method got called. Every object has such a pool. The following code shows how the `Mailbox` class's `retrieveMessage()` method could be modified to begin taking advantage of calling `wait()`:

```
1.  public synchronized String retrieveMessage() {
2.     while (request == false) {
3.        try {
4.           wait();
5.        } catch (InterruptedException e) { }
6.     }
7.     request = false;
8.     return message;
9.  }
```

Now consider what happens when a message-consuming thread calls this method. The call might look like this:

```
myMailbox.retrieveMessage();
```

When a message-consuming thread calls this method, the thread must first acquire the lock for myMailbox. Acquiring the lock could happen immediately, or it could incur a delay if some other thread is executing any of the synchronized code of myMailbox. One way or another, eventually the consumer thread has the lock and begins to execute at line 2. The code first checks the request flag. If the flag is not set, then myMailbox has no message for the thread to retrieve. In this case the wait() method is called at line 4 (it can throw an InterruptedException, so the try/catch code is required, and the while will retest the condition). When line 4 executes, the consumer thread ceases execution; it also releases the lock for myMailbox and enters the pool of waiting threads managed by myMailbox.

The consumer thread has been successfully prevented from corrupting the myMailbox monitor. Unfortunately, it is stuck in the monitor's pool of waiting threads. When the monitor changes to a state where it can provide the consumer with something to do, then something will have to be done to get the consumer out of the Waiting state. This is done by calling notify() when the monitor's request flag becomes true, which happens only in the storeMessage() method. The revised storeMessage() looks like this:

```
1. public synchronized void
2. storeMessage(String message) {
3.   this.message = message;
4.   request = true;
5.   notify();
6. }
```

On line 5, the code calls notify() just after changing the monitor's state. The notify() method arbitrarily selects one of the threads in the monitor's waiting pool and moves it to the Seeking Lock state. Eventually that thread will acquire the mailbox's lock and can proceed with execution.

Now imagine a complete scenario. A consumer thread calls retrieveMessage() on a mailbox that has no message. It acquires the lock and begins executing the method. It sees that the request flag is false, so it calls wait() and joins the mailbox's waiting pool. (In this simple example, no other threads are in the pool.) Because the consumer has called wait(), it has given up the lock. Later, a message-producing thread calls storeMessage() on the same mailbox. It acquires the lock, stores its message in the monitor's instance variable, and sets the request flag to true. The producer then calls notify(). At this moment, only one thread is in the monitor's waiting pool: the consumer. So the consumer gets moved out of the waiting pool and into the Seeking Lock state. Now the producer returns from storeMessage(); because the producer has exited from synchronized code, it gives up the monitor's lock. Later the patient consumer reacquires the lock and gets to execute; once this happens, it checks the request flag and (finally!) sees that a message is available for consumption. The consumer returns the message; upon return it automatically releases the lock.

To briefly summarize this scenario: a consumer tried to consume something, but there was nothing to consume, so the consumer waited. Later a producer produced something. At that point there was something for the consumer to consume, so the consumer was notified; once the producer was done with the monitor, the consumer consumed a message.

Monitors, wait(), and notify()

> **NOTE**
> As Figure 7.7 shows, a waiting thread has ways to get out of the Waiting state that do not require being notified. One version of the wait() call takes an argument that specifies a timeout in milliseconds; if the timeout expires, the thread moves to the Seeking Lock state, even if it has not been notified. No matter what version of wait() is invoked, if the waiting thread receives an interrupt() call, it moves immediately to the Seeking Lock state.

This example protected the consumer against the possibility that the monitor might be empty; the protection was implemented with a wait() call in retrieveMessage() and a notify() call in storeMessage(). A similar precaution must be taken in case a producer thread wants to produce into a monitor that already contains a message. To be robust, storeMessage() needs to call wait(), and retrieveMessage() needs to call notify(). The complete Mailbox class looks like this:

```
1.  class Mailbox {
2.    private boolean   request;
3.    private String    message;
4.
5.    public synchronized void
6.    storeMessage(String message) {
7.      while(request == true) {
8.        // No room for another message
9.        try {
10.         wait();
11.       } catch (InterruptedException e) { }
12.     }
13.     request = true;
14.     this.message = message;
15.     notify();
16.   }
17.
18.   public synchronized String retrieveMessage() {
19.     while(request == false) {
20.       // No message to retrieve
21.       try {
22.         wait();
23.       } catch (InterruptedException e) { }
24.     }
25.     request = false;
26.     notify();
27.     return message;
28.   }
29. }
```

> **NOTE** By synchronizing code and judiciously calling wait() and notify(), monitors such as the Mailbox class can ensure the proper interaction of client threads and protect shared data from corruption.

Here are the main points to remember about wait():

- The calling thread gives up the CPU.
- The calling thread gives up the lock.
- The calling thread goes into the monitor's waiting pool.

Here are the main points to remember about notify():

- One arbitrarily chosen thread gets moved out of the monitor's waiting pool and into the Seeking Lock state.
- The thread that was notified must re-acquire the monitor's lock before it can proceed.

Real World Scenario

Order of Notification

If an object has multiple threads waiting for it, there is no guarantee about the order in which those threads will be revived when the object receives a notifyAll() call. In this exercise, you'll observe the order of notification.

Create a class called NotifyLab, with two inner classes. (You will probably want the inner classes to be static, because instances of them will be constructed in the main() method.) The first inner class, called Rendezvous, should provide a method called hurryUpAndWait(), which performs any necessary housekeeping and then calls wait(). The main() method will construct a single instance of this inner class. The second inner class, called Waiter, extends Thread; its run() method calls hurryUpAndWait() on the instance of Rendezvous, and then prints out a message to report that notification has happened. Each instance of Waiter should have a unique serial number, assigned at creation time and printed out after notification, so that you will be able to know the order in which threads were notified.

This exercise is mostly straightforward, but one part is tricky: you have to make sure that the threads call wait() in serial order. If you just create and start several waiter threads, you won't know the order in which they call wait(), so the output from your program won't be meaningful. One way to take care of this issue is to add a little housekeeping functionality to the hurryUpAndWait() method of Rendezvous. The rest is for you to work out!

The solution appears on the CD-ROM in the file NotifyLab.java. Here is a sample of its output:

```
>java NotifyLab 5
Thread #0 just got notified.
```

```
Thread #2 just got notified.
Thread #3 just got notified.
Thread #4 just got notified.
Thread #1 just got notified.
```

Be aware that the results you observe are anecdotal and should not be interpreted as predictors of general JVM behavior. Other JVMs may behave differently. The only way to write reliable code using notifyAll() is to be indifferent to order of notification.

The Class Lock

It is clear by now that every object (that is, every instance of every class) has a lock. Every class also has a lock. The class lock controls access to all synchronized static code in the class. Consider the following example:

```
class X {
  static int x, y;
  static synchronized void foo() {
    x++;
    y++;
  }
}
```

When the foo() method is called (for example, with the code X.foo()), the invoking thread must acquire the class lock for the X class. Ordinarily, when a thread attempts to call a nonstatic synchronized method, the thread must acquire the lock of the current object; the current object is referenced by this in the scope of the method. However, there is no this reference in a static method because there is no current object.

If Java did not provide class locks, there would be no built-in way to synchronize static code and no way to protect shared static data such as x and y in the previous example.

Beyond the Pure Model

The mailbox example of the previous few sections is a very simple example of a situation involving one producer and one consumer. In real life, things are not always so simple. You might have a monitor that has several methods that do not purely produce or purely consume. All you can say in general about such methods is that they cannot proceed unless the monitor is in a certain state, and they themselves can change the monitor's state in ways that could be of vital interest to the other methods.

The notify() method is not precise: You cannot specify which thread is to be notified. In a mixed-up scenario such as the one just described, a thread might alter the monitor's state in a way that is useless to the particular thread that gets notified. In such a case, the monitor's methods should take two precautions:

- Always check the monitor's state in a `while` loop rather than an `if` statement.
- After changing the monitor's state, call `notifyAll()` rather than `notify()`.

The first precaution means that you should *not* do the following:

```
1. public synchronized void mixedUpMethod() {
2.    if (i<16 || f>4.3f || message.equals("UH-OH") {
3.       try { wait(); } catch (InterruptedException e) { }
4.    }
5.
6.    // Proceed in a way that changes state, and then...
7.    notify();
8. }
```

The danger is that sometimes a thread might execute the test on line 2 and then notice that i is (for example) 15, and have to wait. Later, another thread might change the monitor's state by setting i to −23444 and then call `notify()`. If the original thread is the one that gets notified, it will pick up where it left off, even though the monitor is not in a state where it is ready for `mixedUpMethod()`.

The solution is to change `mixedUpMethod()` as follows:

```
1. public synchronized void mixedUpMethod() {
2.    while (i<16 || f>4.3f || message.equals("UH-OH") {
3.       try { wait(); } catch (InterruptedException e) { }
4.    }
5.
6.    // Proceed in a way that changes state, and then...
7.    notifyAll();
8. }
```

The monitor's other synchronized methods should be modified in a similar manner. Now when a waiting thread gets notified, it does not assume that the monitor's state is acceptable. It checks again, in the `while`-loop check on line 2. If the state is still not conducive, the thread waits again.

On line 7, having made its own modifications to the monitor's state, the code calls `notifyAll()`; this call is like `notify()`, but it moves *every* thread in the monitor's waiting pool to the Seeking Lock state. Presumably every thread's `wait()` call happened in a loop like the one on lines 2–4, so every thread will once again check the monitor's state and either wait or proceed. Note that if a monitor has a large number of waiting threads, calling `notifyAll()` can cost a lot of time.

> Using a while loop to check the monitor's state is a good idea even if you are coding a pure model of one producer and one consumer. After all, you can never be sure that somebody won't try to add an extra producer or an extra consumer.

Deadlock

The term *deadlock* describes another class of situations that might prevent a thread from executing. In general terms, if a thread blocks because it is waiting for a condition, and something else in the program makes it impossible for that condition to arise, then the thread is said to be deadlocked.

Deadlock conditions can arise for many reasons, but there is one classic example of the situation that is easy to understand. Because it is used as the standard example, this situation has a special name of its own: "deadly embrace."

Imagine a thread is trying to obtain exclusive use of two locks that are encapsulated in objects a and b. First the thread gets the lock on object a, and then it proceeds to try to get the lock on object b. This process sounds innocent enough, but now imagine that another thread already holds the lock on object b. Clearly, the first thread cannot proceed until the second thread releases the lock on object b.

Now for the nasty part: imagine that the other thread, while holding the lock on object b, is trying to get the lock on object a. This situation is now hopeless. The first thread holds the lock on object a and cannot proceed without the lock on object b. Further, the first thread cannot release the lock on object a until it has obtained the lock on object b. At the same time, the second thread holds the lock on object b and cannot release it until it obtains the lock on object a.

Let's have a look at code that could cause this situation:

```
1.  public class Deadlock implements Runnable {
2.      public static void main(String [] args) {
3.          Object a = "Resource A";
4.          Object b = "Resource B";
5.          Thread t1 = new Thread(new Deadlock(a, b));
6.          Thread t2 = new Thread(new Deadlock(b, a));
7.          t1.start();
8.          t2.start();
9.      }
10.
11.     private Object firstResource;
12.     private Object secondResource;
13.
14.     public Deadlock(Object first, Object second) {
```

```
15.        firstResource = first;
16.        secondResource = second;
17.      }
18.
19.      public void run() {
20.        for (;;) {
21.          System.out.println(
22.            Thread.currentThread().getName() +
23.            " Looking for lock on " + firstResource);
24.
25.          synchronized (firstResource) {
26.            System.out.println(
27.              Thread.currentThread().getName() +
28.              " Obtained lock on " + firstResource);
29.
30.            System.out.println(
31.              Thread.currentThread().getName() +
32.              " Looking for lock on " + secondResource);
33.
34.            synchronized (secondResource) {
35.              System.out.println(
36.                Thread.currentThread().getName() +
37.                " Obtained lock on " + secondResource);
38.              // simulate some time consuming activity
39.              try { Thread.sleep(100); }
40.              catch (InterruptedException ex) {}
41.            }
42.          }
43.        }
44.      }
45.    }
```

In this code, the resources are locked at lines 25 and 34. Notice that, although the same code executes in both threads, the references firstResource and secondResource actually refer to different objects in both threads. This is the case because of the way the two DeadLock instances are constructed on lines 5 and 6.

When you run the code, the exact behavior is nondeterministic, because of differences in thread scheduling between executions. Commonly, however, the output will look something like this:

Thread-1 Looking for lock on Resource A
Thread-1 Obtained lock on Resource A

Monitors, wait(), and notify()

```
Thread-2 Looking for lock on Resource B
Thread-1 Looking for lock on Resource B
Thread-2 Obtained lock on Resource B
Thread-2 Looking for lock on Resource A
```

If you study this output, you will see that the first thread (Thread-1) holds the lock on Resource A and is trying to obtain the lock on Resource B. Meanwhile, the second thread (Thread-2) holds the lock on Resource B—which prevents the first thread from ever executing. Further, the second thread is waiting for Resource A and can never proceed because that object will never be released by the first thread.

It is useful to realize that if both threads were looking for the locks in the same order, then the deadly embrace situation would never occur. However, it can be very difficult to arrange for this ordering solution in situations where the threads are disparate parts of the program. Indeed, looking at the variables used in this example, you will see that it can sometimes be difficult to recognize an ordering problem like this even if the code is all in one place.

Another Way to Synchronize

There is an additional way to synchronize code. It is hardly common and generally should not be used without a compelling reason. This approach is to synchronize on the lock of a different object.

We briefly mentioned in an earlier section ("The Object Lock and Synchronization") that you can synchronize on the lock of any object. Suppose, for example, that you have the following class, which is admittedly a bit contrived:

```
1. class StrangeSync {
2.     Rectangle rect = new Rectangle(11, 13, 1100, 1300);
3.     void doit() {
4.         int x = 504;
5.         int y = x / 3;
6.         rect.width -= x;
7.         rect.height -= y;
8.     }
9. }
```

If you add the synchronized keyword at line 3, then a thread that wants to execute the doit() method of some instance of StrangeSync must first acquire the lock for that instance. That may be exactly what you want. However, perhaps you only want to synchronize lines 6 and 7, and perhaps you want a thread attempting to execute those lines to synchronize on the lock of rect, rather than on the lock of the current executing object. The way to do this is shown here:

```
1. class StrangeSync {
2.     Rectangle rect = new Rectangle(11, 13, 1100, 1300);
3.     void doit() {
```

```
 4.    int x = 504;
 5.    int y = x / 3;
 6.    synchronized(rect) {
 7.        rect.width -= x;
 8.        rect.height -= y;
 9.    }
10.  }
11. }
```

This code synchronizes on the lock of some arbitrary object (specified in parentheses after the `synchronized` keyword on line 6), rather than synchronizing on the lock of the current object. Also, the code synchronizes just two lines, rather than an entire method.

It is difficult to find a good reason for synchronizing on an arbitrary object. However, synchronizing only a subset of a method can be useful; sometimes you want to hold the lock as briefly as possible, so that other threads can get their turn as soon as possible. The Java compiler insists that when you synchronize a portion of a method (rather than the entire method), you have to specify an object in parentheses after the `synchronized` keyword. If you put `this` in the parentheses, then the goal is achieved: you have synchronized a portion of a method, with the lock using the lock of the object that owns the method.

To summarize, your options are

- To synchronize an entire method, using the lock of the object that owns the method. To do this, put the `synchronized` keyword in the method's declaration.

- To synchronize part of a method, using the lock of an arbitrary object. Put curly brackets around the code to be synchronized, preceded by `synchronized(theArbitraryObject)`.

- To synchronize part of a method, using the lock of the object that owns the method. Put curly brackets around the code to be synchronized, preceded by `synchronized(this)`.

Summary

A Java thread scheduler can be preemptive or time-sliced, depending on the design of the JVM. No matter which design is used, a thread becomes eligible for execution (ready) when its `start()` method is invoked. When a thread begins execution, the scheduler calls the `run()` method of the thread's target (if there is a target) or the `run()` method of the thread itself (if there is no target). The target must be an instance of a class that implements the `Runnable` interface.

In the course of execution, a thread can become ineligible for execution for a number or reasons: A thread can suspend, sleep, block, or wait. In due time (we hope!), conditions will change so that the thread once more becomes eligible for execution; then the thread enters the Ready state and eventually can execute.

When a thread returns from its `run()` method, it enters the Dead state and cannot be restarted. You might find the following lists to be a useful summary of Java's threads.

- Scheduler implementations:
  - Preemptive
  - Time-sliced
- Constructing a thread:
  - `new Thread()`: no target; thread's own `run()` method is executed
  - `new Thread(Runnable target)`: target's `run()` method is executed
- Nonrunnable thread states:
  - Suspended: caused by `suspend()`, waits for `resume()`
  - Sleeping: caused by `sleep()`, waits for timeout
  - Blocked: caused by various I/O calls or by failing to get a monitor's lock, waits for I/O or for the monitor's lock
  - Waiting: caused by `wait()`, waits for `notify()` or `notifyAll()`
  - Dead: caused by `stop()` or returning from `run()`, no way out

Exam Essentials

Know how to write and run code for a thread by extending `java.lang.Thread`. Extend the Thread class, overriding the `run()` method. Create an instance of the subclass and call its `start()` method to launch the new thread.

Know how to write and run code for a thread by implementing the interface `java.lang.Runnable`. Create a class that implements Runnable. Construct the thread with the `Thread(Runnable)` constructor and call its `start()` method.

Know the mechanisms that suspend a thread's execution. These mechanisms include: entering any synchronized code, or calling `wait()`, `yield()`, or `sleep()`.

Recognize code that might cause deadly embrace. Deadlock conditions cause permanent suspension of threads, and deadly embrace is the classic example of this.

Understand the functionality of the `wait()`, `notify()`, and `notifyAll()` methods. These methods are explained in detail in the "`wait()` and `notify()`" section.

Know that the resumption order of threads that execute `wait()` on an object is not specified. The Java specification states that the resumption order for threads waiting on an object is unspecified.

Key Terms

Before you take the exam, be certain you are familiar with the following terms:

blocking	single-threaded
deadlock	sleeping thread
lock	suspending
monitor	synchronized code
multithreaded	thread scheduler
preemptive scheduling	time-sliced scheduling
priority	waiting state
round-robin scheduling	yielding

Review Questions

1. Which one statement is true concerning the following code?

    ```
    1.  class Greebo extends java.util.Vector
    2.      implements Runnable {
    3.      public void run(String message) {
    4.          System.out.println("in run() method: " +
    5.              message);
    6.      }
    7.  }
    8.
    9.  class GreeboTest {
    10.     public static void main(String args[]) {
    12.         Greebo g = new Greebo();
    13.         Thread t = new Thread(g);
    14.         t.start();
    15.     }
    16. }
    ```

    A. There will be a compiler error, because class `Greebo` does not correctly implement the Runnable interface.

    B. There will be a compiler error at line 13, because you cannot pass a parameter to the constructor of a Thread.

    C. The code will compile correctly but will crash with an exception at line 13.

    D. The code will compile correctly but will crash with an exception at line 14.

    E. The code will compile correctly and will execute without throwing any exceptions.

2. Which one statement is always true about the following application?

    ```
    1.  class HiPri extends Thread {
    2.      HiPri() {
    3.          setPriority(10);
    4.      }
    5.
    6.      public void run() {
    7.          System.out.println(
    8.              "Another thread starting up.");
    9.          while (true) { }
    10.     }
    11.
    12.     public static void main(String args[]) {
    ```

```
13.     HiPri hp1 = new HiPri();
14.     HiPri hp2 = new HiPri();
15.     HiPri hp3 = new HiPri();
16.     hp1.start();
17.     hp2.start();
18.     hp3.start();
19.   }
20. }
```

A. When the application is run, thread hp1 will execute; threads hp2 and hp3 will never get the CPU.

B. When the application is run, all three threads (hp1, hp2, and hp3) will get to execute, taking time-sliced turns in the CPU.

C. Either A or B will be true, depending on the underlying platform.

3. A thread wants to make a second thread ineligible for execution. To do this, the first thread can call the yield() method on the second thread.

A. True

B. False

4. A thread's run() method includes the following lines:

```
1. try {
2.     sleep(100);
3. } catch (InterruptedException e) { }
```

Assuming the thread is not interrupted, which one of the following statements is correct?

A. The code will not compile, because exceptions cannot be caught in a thread's run() method.

B. At line 2, the thread will stop running. Execution will resume in, at most, 100 milliseconds.

C. At line 2, the thread will stop running. It will resume running in exactly 100 milliseconds.

D. At line 2, the thread will stop running. It will resume running some time after 100 milliseconds have elapsed.

5. A monitor called mon has 10 threads in its waiting pool; all these waiting threads have the same priority. One of the threads is thr1. How can you notify thr1 so that it alone moves from the Waiting state to the Ready state?

A. Execute notify(thr1); from within synchronized code of mon.

B. Execute mon.notify(thr1); from synchronized code of any object.

C. Execute thr1.notify(); from synchronized code of any object.

D. Execute thr1.notify(); from any code (synchronized or not) of any object.

E. You cannot specify which thread will get notified.

6. If you attempt to compile and execute the following application, will it ever print out the message In xxx?

```
1.  class TestThread3 extends Thread {
2.    public void run() {
3.      System.out.println("Running");
4.      System.out.println("Done");
5.    }
6.
7.    private void xxx() {
8.      System.out.println("In xxx");
9.    }
10.
11.   public static void main(String args[]) {
12.     TestThread3 ttt = new TestThread3();
13.     ttt.xxx();
14.     ttt.start();
12.   }
13. }
```

A. Yes

B. No

7. A Java monitor must either extend Thread or implement Runnable.

A. True

B. False

8. Which of the following methods in the Thread class have been deprecated?

A. suspend() and resume()

B. wait() and notify()

C. start() and stop()

D. sleep() and yield()

9. Which of the following statements about threads is true?

A. Every thread starts executing with a priority of 5.

B. Threads inherit their priority from their parent thread.

C. Threads are guaranteed to run with the priority that you set using the setPriority() method.

D. Thread priority is an integer ranging from 1 to 100.

10. Which of the following statements about the wait() and notify() methods is true?
    A. The wait() and notify() methods can be called outside of synchronized code.
    B. The programmer can specify which thread should be notified in a notify() method call.
    C. The thread that calls wait() goes into the monitor's pool of waiting threads.
    D. The thread that calls notify() gives up the lock.

Answers to Review Questions

1. A. The `Runnable` interface defines a `run()` method with `void` return type and no parameters. The method given in the problem has a `String` parameter, so the compiler will complain that class `Greebo` does not define `void run()` from interface `Runnable`. B is wrong, because you can definitely pass a parameter to a thread's constructor; the parameter becomes the thread's target. C, D, and E are nonsense.

2. C. A is true on a preemptive platform, and B is true on a time-sliced platform. The moral is that such code should be avoided, because it gives such different results on different platforms.

3. B. The `yield()` method is static and always causes the current thread to yield. In this case, ironically, the first thread will yield.

4. D. The thread will sleep for 100 milliseconds (more or less, given the resolution of the JVM being used). Then the thread will enter the Ready state; it will not actually run until the scheduler permits it to run.

5. E. When you call `notify()` on a monitor, you have no control over which waiting thread gets notified.

6. A. The call to xxx() occurs before the thread is registered with the thread scheduler, so the question has nothing to do with threads.

7. B. A monitor is an instance of any class that has synchronized code.

8. A. The `suspend()` and `resume()` methods were deprecated in the Java 2 release.

9. B. A is not correct because, although the default priority for a thread is 5, it may be changed by the parent thread. C is not correct because Java does not make any promises about priority at runtime. Finally, D is incorrect because thread priorities range from 1 to 10.

10. C. Option A is incorrect because `wait()` and `notify()` must be called from within synchronized code. Option B is incorrect because the `notify()` call arbitrarily selects a thread to notify from the pool of waiting threads. Option D is incorrect because the thread that calls `wait()` is the thread that gives up the lock.

Chapter 8

The *java.lang* and *java.util* Packages

JAVA CERTIFICATION EXAM OBJECTIVES COVERED IN THIS CHAPTER:

- ✓ 8.1 Write code using the following methods of the java.lang.Math **class**: abs, ceil, floor, max, min, random, round, sin, cos, tan, sqrt.

- ✓ 8.2 Describe the significance of the immutability of String objects.

- ✓ 8.3 Describe the significance of wrapper classes, including making appropriate selections in the wrapper classes to suit specified behavior requirements, stating the result of executing a fragment of code that includes an instance of one of the wrapper classes, and writing code using the following methods of the wrapper classes (e.g., Integer, Double, **etc.**):
    - doubleValue()
    - floatValue()
    - intValue()
    - longValue()
    - parseXxx()
    - getXxx()
    - toString()
    - toHexString()

- ✓ 9.1 Make appropriate selection of collection classes/interfaces to suit specified behavior requirements.

- ✓ 9.2 Distinguish between correct and incorrect implementations of the hashcode methods.

The `java.lang` package contains classes that are central to the operation of the Java language and environment. Very little can be done without the `String` class, for example, and the `Object` class is completely indispensable. The Java compiler automatically imports all the classes in the `java.lang` package into every source file.

This chapter examines some of the most important classes of the `java.lang` package:

- `Object`
- `Math`
- The wrapper classes
- `String`
- `StringBuffer`

In addition, this chapter also covers the collection classes of the `java.util` package.

The *Object* Class

The `Object` class is the ultimate ancestor of all Java classes. If a class does not contain the `extends` keyword in its declaration, the compiler builds a class that extends directly from `Object`.

All the methods of `Object` are inherited by every class. Three of these methods (`wait()`, `notify()`, and `notifyAll()`) support thread control, and they are discussed in detail in Chapter 7, "Threads." Two other methods, `equals()` and `toString()`, provide little functionality on their own. The intention is that programmers who develop reusable classes can override `equals()` and `toString()` in order to provide useful class-specific functionality.

The signature of `equals()` is

```
public boolean equals(Object object)
```

The method is supposed to provide "deep" comparison, in contrast to the "shallow" comparison provided by the `==` operator. To see the difference between the two types of comparison, consider the `java.util.Date` class, which represents a moment in time. Suppose you have two references of type `Date`: `d1` and `d2`. One way to compare them is with the following line of code:

```
if (d1 == d2)
```

The comparison will be true if the *reference* in d1 is equal to the *reference* in d2. Of course, this is the case only when both variables refer to the same object.

Sometimes you want a different kind of comparison. Sometimes you don't care whether d1 and d2 refer to the same `Date` object. Sometimes you *know* they are different objects. What you care about is whether the two objects, which encapsulate day and time information, represent the same moment in time. In this case, you don't want the shallow reference-level comparison of ==; you need to look deeply into the objects themselves. The way to do that is with the `equals()` method:

```
if (d1.equals(d2))
```

The version of `equals()` provided by the `Object` class is not very useful because it just does an == comparison. All classes should override `equals()` so that it performs a useful comparison. That is just what most of the standard Java classes do: they compare the relevant instance variables of two objects.

The purpose of the `toString()` method is to provide a string representation of an object's state. This method is especially useful for debugging.

The `toString()` method is similar to `equals()` in that the version provided by the `Object` class is not especially useful—it just prints out the object's class name, followed by a hash code. Many JDK classes override `toString()` to provide more useful information. Java's string-concatenation facility makes use of this method, as you will see later in this chapter, in the "String Concatenation the Easy Way" section.

The *Math* Class

Java's `Math` class contains a collection of methods and two constants that support mathematical computation. The class is `final`, so you cannot extend it. The constructor is private, so you cannot create an instance. Fortunately, the methods and constants are static, so they can be accessed through the class name without having to construct a `Math` object. (See Chapter 3, "Modifiers," for an explanation of Java's modifiers, including `final`, `static`, and `private`.)

The two constants of the `Math` class are `Math.PI` and `Math.E`. They are declared to be public, static, final, and double.

The methods of the `Math` class cover a broad range of mathematical functionality, including trigonometry, logarithms and exponentiation, and rounding. The intensive number-crunching methods are often written as native methods to take advantage of any math-acceleration hardware that might be present on the underlying machine.

The Certification Exam requires you to know about the methods shown in Table 8.1.

TABLE 8.1 Methods of the *Math* Class

Method	Returns
int abs(int i)	Absolute value of i
long abs(long l)	Absolute value of l
float abs(float f)	Absolute value of f
double abs(double d)	Absolute value of d
double ceil(double d)	The smallest integer that is not less than d (returns as a double)
double floor(double d)	The largest integer that is not greater than d (returns as a double)
int max(int i1, int i2)	Greater of i1 and i2
long max(long l1, long l2)	Greater of l1 and l2
float max(float f1, float f2)	Greater of f1 and f2
double max(double d1, double d2)	Greater of d1 and d2
int min(int i1, int i2)	Smaller of i1 and i2
long min(long l1, long l2)	Smaller of l1 and l2
float min(float f1, float f2)	Smaller of f1 and f2
double min(double d1, double d2)	Smaller of d1 and d2
double random()	Random number >= 0.0 and < 1.0
int round(float f)	Closest int to f
long round(double d)	Closest long to d
double `(double d)	Sine of d
double cos(double d)	Cosine of d
double tan(double d)	Tangent of d
double sqrt(double d)	Square root of d

The Wrapper Classes

Each Java primitive data type has a corresponding *wrapper class*. A wrapper class is simply a class that encapsulates a single, immutable value. For example, the Integer class wraps up an int value, and the Float class wraps up a float value. The wrapper class names do not perfectly match the corresponding primitive data type names. Table 8.2 lists the primitives and wrappers.

TABLE 8.2 Primitives and Wrappers

Primitive Data Type	Wrapper Class
boolean	Boolean
byte	Byte
char	Character
short	Short
int	Integer
long	Long
float	Float
double	Double

All the wrapper classes can be constructed by passing the value to be wrapped into the appropriate constructor. The following code fragment shows how to construct an instance of each wrapper type:

```
1. boolean   primitiveBoolean = true;
2. Boolean   wrappedBoolean =
3.              new Boolean(primitiveBoolean);
4.
5. byte      primitiveByte = 41;
6. Byte      wrappedByte = new Byte(primitiveByte);
7.
8. char      primitiveChar = 'M';
9. Character wrappedChar = new Character(primitiveChar);
10.
11. short     primitiveShort = 31313;
```

Chapter 8 · The java.lang and java.util Packages

```
12. Short      wrappedShort = new Short(primitiveShort);
13.
14. int        primitiveInt = 12345678;
15. Integer    wrappedInt = new Integer(primitiveInt);
16.
17. long       primitiveLong = 12345678987654321L;
18. Long       wrappedLong = new Long(primitiveLong);
19.
20. float      primitiveFloat = 1.11f;
21. Float      wrappedFloat = new Float(primitiveFloat);
22.
23. double     primitiveDouble = 1.11111111;
24. Double     wrappedDouble =
25.                new Double(primitiveDouble);
```

There is another way to construct any of these classes, with the exception of Character: you can pass into the constructor a String that represents the value to be wrapped. Most of these constructors throw NumberFormatException, because there is always the possibility that the string will not represent a valid value. Only Boolean does not throw this exception; the constructor accepts any String input and wraps a true value if the string (ignoring case) is "true." The following code fragment shows how to construct wrappers from strings:

```
1.  Boolean wrappedBoolean = new Boolean("True");
2.  try {
3.      Byte wrappedByte = new Byte("41");
4.      Short wrappedShort = new Short("31313");
5.      Integer wrappedInt = new Integer("12345678");
6.      Long wrappedLong = new Long("12345678987654321");
7.      Float wrappedFloat = new Float("1.11f");
8.      Double wrappedDouble = new Double("1.11111111");
9.  }
10. catch (NumberFormatException e) {
11.     System.out.println("Bad Number Format");
12. }
```

The values wrapped inside two wrappers of the same type can be checked for equality by using the equals() method discussed in the previous section. For example, the following code fragment checks two instances of Double:

```
1. Double d1 = new Double(1.01055);
2. Double d2 = new Double("1.11348");
3. if (d1.equals(d2)) {
4.     // Do something.
5. }
```

After a value has been wrapped, you may eventually need to extract it. For an instance of `Boolean`, you can call `booleanValue()`. For an instance of `Character`, you can call `charValue()`. The other six classes extend from the abstract superclass `Number`, which provides methods to retrieve the wrapped value as a `byte`, a `short`, an `int`, a `long`, a `float`, or a `double`. In other words, the value of any wrapped number can be retrieved as any numeric type. The retrieval methods are

- `public byte byteValue()`
- `public short shortValue()`
- `public int intValue()`
- `public long longValue()`
- `public float floatValue()`
- `public double doubleValue()`

The wrapper classes are useful whenever it would be convenient to treat a piece of primitive data as if it were an object. A good example is the `Vector` class, which is a dynamically growing collection of objects of arbitrary type. The method for adding an object to a vector is

`public boolean add(Object ob)`

Using this method, you can add any object of any type to a vector; you can even add an array (you saw why in Chapter 4, "Converting and Casting"). You cannot, however, add an `int`, a `long`, or any other primitive to a vector. No special methods exist for doing so, and `add(Object ob)` will not work because there is no automatic conversion from a primitive to an object. Thus, the following code will not compile:

1. `Vector vec = new Vector();`
2. `boolean boo = false;`
3. `vec.add(boo);   // Illegal`

The solution is to wrap the `boolean` primitive, as shown here:

1. `Vector vec = new Vector();`
2. `boolean boo = false;`
3. `Boolean wrapper = new Boolean(boo);`
4. `vec.add(wrapper);   // Legal`

The wrapper classes are useful in another way: They provide a variety of utility methods, most of which are static. For example, the static method `Character.isDigit(char ch)` returns a `boolean` that tells whether the character represents a base-10 digit. All the wrapper classes except `Character` have a static method called `valueOf(String s)`, which parses a string and constructs and returns a wrapper instance of the same type as the class whose method was called. So, for example, `Long.valueOf("23")` constructs and returns an instance of the `Long` class that wraps the value 23.

One set of static wrapper methods are the `parseXXX()` methods. These are `Byte.parseByte()`, `Short.parseShort()`, `Integer.parseInt()`, `Long.parseLong()`, `Float.parseFloat()`, and

Double.parseDouble(). Each of these takes a String argument and returns the corresponding primitive type. They all throw NumberFormatException.

Other static methods that are mentioned in the exam objectives are the getXXX() methods. These are Boolean.getBoolean(), Integer.getInteger(), and Long.getLong(). Each of these takes a String argument that is the name of a system property and returns the value of the property. The return value is a primitive boolean or a wrapper Integer or Long that encapsulates the property value, provided the property is defined, is not empty, and is compatible with the respective type. Integer.getInteger() and Long.getLong() have overloaded forms that take a second argument, which is a primitive of the respective type. The second argument is a default value that is wrapped and returned in case the property is not defined, is empty, or is not compatible with the respective type.

All the wrapper classes provide toString() methods. Additionally, the Integer and Long classes provide toBinaryString(), toOctalString(), and toHexString(), which return strings in base 2, 8, and 16.

All wrapper classes have an inconvenient feature: The values they wrap are immutable. After an instance is constructed, the encapsulated value cannot be changed. It is tempting to try to subclass the wrappers, so that the subclasses inherit all the useful functionality of the original classes while offering mutable contents. Unfortunately, this strategy doesn't work because the wrapper classes are final.

To summarize the major facts about the primitive wrapper classes:

- Every primitive type has a corresponding wrapper class type.
- All wrapper types can be constructed from primitives. All except Character can also be constructed from strings.
- Wrapped values can be tested for equality with the equals() method.
- Wrapped values can be extracted with various *XXX*Value() methods. All six numeric wrapper types support all six numeric *XXX*Value() methods.
- Wrapper classes provide various utility methods, including the static valueOf() methods, which parse an input string.
- Wrapped values cannot be modified.

Strings

Java uses the String and StringBuffer classes to encapsulate strings of characters. Java uses 16-bit Unicode characters to support a broader range of international alphabets than would be possible with traditional 8-bit characters. Both strings and string buffers contain sequences of 16-bit Unicode characters. The next several sections examine these two classes, as well as Java's string-concatenation feature.

The *String* Class

The String class contains an immutable string. Once an instance is created, the string it contains cannot be changed. Numerous forms of constructor allow you to build an instance out of an array of bytes or chars, a subset of an array of bytes or chars, another string, or a string buffer. Many of these constructors give you the option of specifying a character encoding, specified as a string. However, the Certification Exam does not require you to know the details of character encodings.

Probably the most common string constructor simply takes another string as its input. This constructor is useful when you want to specify a literal value for the new string:

```
String s1 = new String("immutable");
```

An even easier abbreviation could be:

```
String s1 = "immutable";
```

It is important to be aware of what happens when you use a string literal ("immutable" in both examples). Every string literal is represented internally by an instance of String. Java classes may have a pool of such strings. When a literal is compiled, the compiler adds an appropriate string to the pool. However, if the same literal already appeared as a literal elsewhere in the class, then it is already represented in the pool. The compiler does not create a new copy. Instead, it uses the existing one from the pool. This process saves on memory and can do no harm. Because strings are immutable, a piece of code can't harm another piece of code by modifying a shared string.

Earlier in this chapter, you saw how the equals() method can be used to provide a deep equality check of two objects. With strings, the equals() method does what you would expect: it checks the two contained collections of characters. The following code shows how this is done:

```
1. String s1 = "Compare me";
2. String s2 = "Compare me";
3. if (s1.equals(s2)) {
4.     // whatever
5. }
```

Not surprisingly, the test at line 3 succeeds. Given what you know about how string literals work, you can see that if line 3 is modified to use the == comparison, as shown here, the test still succeeds:

```
1. String s1 = "Compare me";
2. String s2 = "Compare me";
3. if (s1 == s2) {
4.     // whatever
5. }
```

The == test is true because s2 refers to the String in the pool that was created in line 1. Figure 8.1 shows this graphically.

FIGURE 8.1 Identical literals

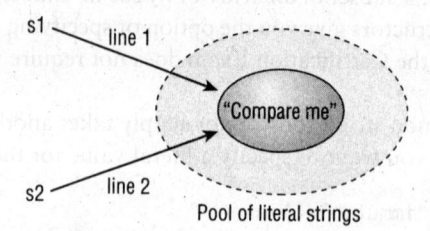

[Figure: s1 (line 1) and s2 (line 2) both pointing to "Compare me" in the Pool of literal strings]

You can also construct a String by explicitly calling the constructor, as shown next; however, doing so causes extra memory allocation for no obvious advantage:

```
String s2 = new String("Constructed");
```

When this line is compiled, the string literal "Constructed" is placed into the pool. At runtime, the new String() statement is executed and a fresh instance of String is constructed, duplicating the String in the literal pool. Finally, a reference to the new String is assigned to s2. Figure 8.2 shows the chain of events.

FIGURE 8.2 Explicitly calling the String constructor

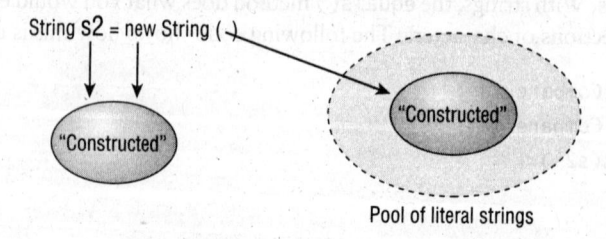

[Figure: String s2 = new String( ) pointing to "Constructed" object outside the Pool of literal strings, which contains another "Constructed"]

Figure 8.2 shows that explicitly calling new String() results in the existence of two objects, one in the literal pool and the other in the program's space.

You just saw that if you create a new String instance at runtime, it will not be in the pool but will be a new and distinct object. You can arrange for your new String to be placed into the pool for possible reuse, or to reuse an existing identical String from the pool, by using the intern() method of the String class. In programs that use a great many similar strings, this approach can reduce memory requirements. More importantly, in programs that make a lot of String equality comparisons, ensuring that all strings are in the pool allows you to use the == reference comparison in place of the equals() method. The equals() method runs slower because it must do a character-by-character comparison of the two strings, whereas the == operator only compares the two memory addresses.

The `String` class includes several convenient methods, some of which transform a string. For example, `toUpperCase()` converts all the characters of a string to uppercase. It is important to remember that the original string is not modified. That would be impossible, because strings are immutable. What really happens is that a new string is constructed and returned. Generally, this new string will not be in the pool unless you explicitly call `intern()` to put it there.

The methods in the following list are just some of the most useful methods of the `String` class. There are more methods than those listed here, and some of those listed have overloaded forms that take different inputs. This list includes all the methods that you are required to know for the Certification Exam, plus a few additional useful ones:

`char charAt(int index)`   Returns the indexed character of a string, where the index of the initial character is 0.

`String concat(String addThis)`   Returns a new string consisting of the old string followed by `addThis`.

`int compareTo(String otherString)`   Performs a lexical comparison; returns an `int` that is less than 0 if the current string is less than `otherString`, equal to 0 if the strings are identical, and greater than 0 if the current string is greater than `otherString`.

`boolean endsWith(String suffix)`   Returns true if the current string ends with `suffix`; otherwise returns false.

`boolean equals(Object ob)`   Returns true if `ob instanceof String` and the string encapsulated by `ob` matches the string encapsulated by the executing object.

`boolean equalsIgnoreCase(String s)`   Returns true if `s` matches the current string, ignoring upper- and lowercase considerations.

`int indexOf(int ch)`   Returns the index within the current string of the first occurrence of `ch`. Alternative forms return the index of a string and begin searching from a specified offset.

`int lastIndexOf(int ch)`   Returns the index within the current string of the last occurrence of `ch`.

`int length()`   Returns the number of characters in the current string.

`String replace(char oldChar, char newChar)`   Returns a new string, generated by replacing every occurrence of `oldChar` with `newChar`.

`boolean startsWith(String prefix)`   Returns true if the current string begins with `prefix`; otherwise returns false. Alternate forms begin searching from a specified offset.

`String substring(int startIndex)`   Returns the substring, beginning at `startIndex` of the current string and extending to the end of the current string. An alternate form specifies starting and ending offsets.

`String toLowerCase()`   Converts the executing object to lowercase and returns a new string.

`String toString()`   Returns the executing object.

`String toUpperCase()`   Converts the executing object to uppercase and returns a new string.

`String trim()`   Returns the string that results from removing whitespace characters from the beginning and ending of the current string.

The following code shows how to use two of these methods to modify a string. The original string is " 5 + 4 = 20". The code first strips off the leading blank space and then converts the addition sign to a multiplication sign:

1. `String s = " 5 + 4 = 20";`
2. `s = s.trim();`   // "5 + 4 = 20"
3. `s = s.replace('+', 'x');`   // "5 x 4 = 20"

After line 3, `s` refers to a string whose appearance is shown in the line 3 comment. Of course, the modification has not taken place within the original string. Both the `trim()` call in line 2 and the `replace()` call of line 3 construct and return new strings; the address of each new string in turn gets assigned to the reference variable `s`. Figure 8.3 shows this sequence graphically.

FIGURE 8.3 Trimming and replacing

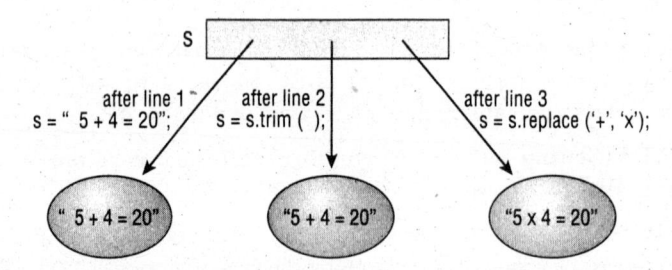

```
                              s
                    ┌──────────────────┐
                    └────────┬─────────┘
         after line 1    after line 2        after line 3
       s = " 5 + 4 = 20";  s = s.trim( );    s = s.replace ('+', 'x');
              ↓                ↓                    ↓
         ( " 5 + 4 = 20" ) ( "5 + 4 = 20" )   ( "5 x 4 = 20" )
```

Figure 8.3 shows that the original string seems to be only modified, but it is actually replaced, because strings are immutable. If much modification is required, then this process becomes very inefficient—it stresses the garbage collector cleaning up all the old strings, and it takes time to copy the contents of the old strings into the new ones. The next section discusses a class that helps alleviate these problems because it represents a mutable string: the `StringBuffer` class.

The *StringBuffer* Class

An instance of Java's `StringBuffer` class represents a string that can be dynamically modified.

The most commonly used constructor takes a `String` instance as input. You can also construct an empty string buffer (probably with the intention of adding characters to it later). An empty string buffer can have its initial capacity specified at construction time. The three constructors are

StringBuffer()   Constructs an empty string buffer

StringBuffer(int capacity)   Constructs an empty string buffer with the specified initial capacity

StringBuffer(String initialString)   Constructs a string buffer that initially contains the specified string

A string buffer has a *capacity*, which is the longest string it can represent without needing to allocate more memory. A string buffer can grow beyond this capacity as necessary, so usually you do not have to worry about it. However, it is more efficient to declare a large initial capacity when instantiating a string buffer to avoid the system calls required to allocate more memory.

The following list presents some of the methods that modify the contents of a string buffer. All of them return the original string buffer:

StringBuffer append(String str) Appends `str` to the current string buffer. Alternative forms support appending primitives and character arrays which are converted to strings before appending.

StringBuffer append(Object obj) Calls `toString()` on `obj` and appends the result to the current string buffer.

StringBuffer insert(int offset, String str) Inserts `str` into the current string buffer at position `offset`. There are numerous alternative forms.

StringBuffer reverse() Reverses the characters of the current string buffer.

StringBuffer setCharAt(int offset, char newChar) Replaces the character at position `offset` with `newChar`.

StringBuffer setLength(int newLength) Sets the length of the string buffer to `newLength`. If `newLength` is less than the current length, the string is truncated. If `newLength` is greater than the current length, the string is padded with null characters.

The following code shows the effect of using several of these methods in combination:

```
1. StringBuffer sbuf = new StringBuffer("12345");
2. sbuf.reverse();          // "54321"
3. sbuf.insert(3, "aaa");   // "543aaa21"
4. sbuf.append("zzz");      // "543aaa21zzz"
```

The method calls actually modify the string buffer they operate on (unlike the `String` class example of the previous section). Figure 8.4 graphically shows what this code does.

FIGURE 8.4 Modifying a string buffer

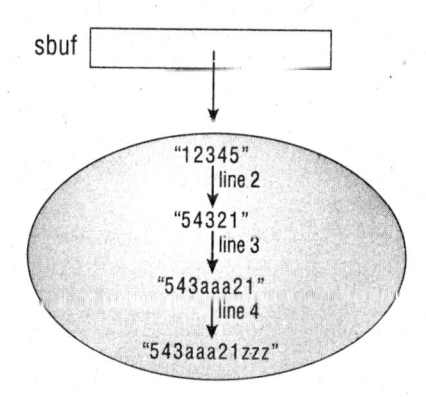

The `StringBuffer` class does not override the version of `equals()` that it inherits from `Object`. Thus the method returns `true` only when comparing references to the same single object. If two distinct instances encapsulate identical strings, `equals()` will return false.

One last string buffer method that bears mentioning is `toString()`. You saw earlier in this chapter that every class has one of these methods. Not surprisingly, the string buffer's version just returns the encapsulated string as an instance of class `String`. You will see in the next section that this method plays a crucial role in string concatenation.

String Concatenation the Easy Way

The `concat()` method of the `String` class and the `append()` method of the `StringBuffer` class glue two strings together. Another way to concatenate strings is to use Java's overloaded + operator. Similarly, another way to append a string is to use Java's overloaded += operator. However, don't forget that you, the programmer, cannot define additional operator overloads.

String concatenation is useful in many situations—for example, in debugging print statements. So, to print the value of a `double` called `radius`, all you have to do is this:

```
System.out.println("radius = " + radius);
```

This technique also works for object data types. To print the value of a `Dimension` called `dimension`, all you need is

```
System.out.println("dimension = " + dimension);
```

It is important to understand how the technique works. At compile time, if either operand of a + operator (that is, what appears on either side of a + sign) is a `String` object, then the compiler recognizes that it is in a *string context*. In a string context, the + sign is interpreted as calling for string concatenation rather than arithmetic addition.

A string context is simply a run of additions, where one of the operands is a string. For example, if variable a is a string, then the following partial line of code is a string context, regardless of the types of the other operands:

```
a + b + c
```

The Java compiler treats the previous code as if it were the following:

```
new StringBuffer().append(a).append(b).append(c).toString();
```

If any of the variables (a, b, or c) is a primitive, the `append()` method computes an appropriate string representation. For an object variable, the `append()` method uses the string returned from calling `toString()` on the object. The conversion begins with an empty string buffer, then appends each element in turn to the string buffer, and finally calls `toString()` to convert the string buffer to a string.

The following code implements a class with its own `toString()` method:

```
1.  class Abc {
2.      private int a;
3.      private int b;
4.      private int c;
5.
6.      Abc(int a, int b, int c) {
7.          this.a = a;
8.          this.b = b;
9.          this.c = c;
10.     }
11.
12.     public String toString() {
13.         return "a = " + a + ", b = " + b + ", c = " + c;
14.     }
15. }
```

Now the `toString()` method (lines 12–14) can be used by any code that wants to take advantage of string concatenation. For example:

```
Abc theAbc = new Abc(11, 13, 48);
System.out.println("Here it is: " + theAbc);
```

The output is

```
Here it is: a = 11, b = 13, c = 48
```

To summarize the sequence of events for a string context:

1. An empty string buffer is constructed.
2. Each argument in turn is concatenated to the string buffer, using the `append()` method.
3. The string buffer is converted to a string with a call to `toString()`.

That is all you need to know about string manipulation for the Certification Exam, and it's probably all you need to know to write effective and efficient code, too. Next, we're going to look at collections.

The Collections API

Many programs need to keep track of groups of related data items. The most basic mechanism for doing this is the array. Although they are extremely useful for many purposes, arrays have some inherent limitations. They provide only a very simple mechanism for storing and accessing data. Moreover, their capacity must be known at construction time because there is no way to make an array bigger or smaller. Java has always had arrays and also some additional classes, such as the Vector and Hashtable classes, to allow you to manipulate groups of objects. Since JDK 1.2, however, a significant feature supports much more generalized collection management: the Collections API. The Certification Exam objectives now require that you have a grasp of the concepts of this new functionality.

> **NOTE** The Collections API is a mechanism for manipulating object references. Although arrays are capable of storing primitives or references, collections are not. If you need to take advantage of collection functionality to manipulate primitives, you have to wrap the primitives in the wrapper classes that were presented earlier in this chapter.

The Collections API is often referred to as a *framework*. That is, the classes have been designed with a common abstraction of data container behavior in mind, ensuring uniform semantics wherever possible. At the same time, each implemented collection type is free to optimize its own operations. The factory class java.util.Collections supplements support for these types, which are discussed next, with a variety of static helper methods. These methods support operations such as synchronizing the container, establishing immutability, and executing binary searches. With these classes in place, programmers are no longer required to build their own basic data structures from scratch.

A class or group of classes is considered *threadsafe* if any thread can call any method of any instance at any time. The collections framework as a whole is not threadsafe. If you use collections in a multithreaded environment, you are generally responsible for protecting the integrity of the encapsulated data. One way to accomplish this is to use certain static factory methods of the java.util.Collections class. The names of these methods begin with "synchronized" (such as synchronizedList() and synchronizedMap()); they are well documented in the API.

Collection Types

There are several different collections. They vary, for example, in the storage mechanisms used, in the way they can access data, and in the rules about what data can be stored. The Collections API provides a variety of interfaces and some concrete implementation classes covering these variations.

A general interface, java.util.Collection, defines the basic framework for collections. This interface stipulates the methods that allow you to add items, remove items, determine if items are in the collection, and count the number of items in the collection. A collection is sometimes known as a *bag* or a *multiset*. A simple collection places no constraints on the type, order, or repetition of elements within the collection.

Some collections are ordered; that is, there is a clear notion of one item following another. A collection of this kind is commonly known as a *list* or a *sequence*. In some lists, the order is the order in which items are added to the collection; in others, the elements themselves are assumed to have a natural order, and that order is understood by the list. In the Java Collections API, the interface `java.util.List` defines a basic framework for collections of this sort.

If a collection imposes the specific condition that it cannot contain the same value more than once, then it is known as a *set*. The interface `java.util.Set` defines the basic framework for this type of collection. In some sets, the `null` value is a legitimate entry; but if it is allowed, `null` can occur only once in a set.

The final type of specialized behavior directly supported by the Collections API is known as a *map*. A map uses a set of key values to look up, or index, the stored data. For example, if you store an object representing a person, then as the key value you could either use that person's name or some other unique identifier such as a social security number or employee ID number. Maps are particularly appropriate for implementing small online databases, especially if the data being stored will usually be accessed via the unique identifier. It is a requirement for a map that the key be unique, and for this reason if you were storing data about a person in a map, the name would not make a very good key—it is quite possible for two people to have the same name.

Let's take a moment to recap these points:

- A collection has no special order and does not reject duplicates.
- A list is ordered and does not reject duplicates.
- A set has no special order but rejects duplicates.
- A map supports searching on a key field, values of which must be unique.

Of course, it is possible for combinations of these behaviors to be meaningful. For example, a map might also be ordered. However, the Certification Exam only requires you to understand these four fundamental types of collection.

The storage associated with any one collection can be implemented in many ways, but the Collections API implements the four methods that are most widely used: an array, a linked list, a tree, or a hash table. Each of these techniques has benefits and constraints. Let's consider these benefits and constraints for each storage technique in turn.

Array *Array* storage tends to be fast to access, but it is relatively inefficient as the number of elements in the collection grows or if elements need to be inserted or deleted in the middle of a list. These limitations occur because the array itself is a fixed sequence. Adding or removing elements in the middle requires that all the elements from that point onward must be moved up or down by one position. Adding more data once the array is full requires a whole new array to be allocated and the entire contents to be copied over to the new array. Another limitation of an array is that it provides no special search mechanism. Despite these weaknesses, an array can still be an appropriate choice for data that is ordered, does not change often, and does not need to be searched much.

Linked list A *linked list* allows elements to be added to or removed from the collection at any location in the container, and it allows the size of the collection to grow arbitrarily without the penalties associated with array copying. This improvement occurs because each element is an individual object that refers to the next (and sometimes previous, in a double-linked list) element in the list. However, it is significantly slower to access by index than an array, and it still provides no special search mechanism. Because linked lists can insert new elements at arbitrary locations, however, they can apply ordering very easily, making it a simple (if not always efficient) matter to search a subset, or range, of data.

Tree A *tree*, like a linked list, allows easy addition and deletion of elements and arbitrary growth of the collection. Unlike lists, trees insist on a means of ordering. In fact, constructing a tree requires that there be some comparison mechanism to the data being stored—although this can be created artificially in some cases. A tree will usually provide more efficient searching than either an array or a linked list, but this benefit may be obscured if unevenly distributed data is being stored.

Hash table A *hash table* requires that some unique identifying key can be associated with each data item, which in turn provides efficient searching. Hashes still allow a reasonably efficient access mechanism and arbitrary collection growth. Hashing may be inappropriate for small data sets, however, because some overhead typically is associated with calculating the hash values and maintaining the more complex data structure associated with this type of storage. Without a sufficiently large number of elements that would justify the operational costs, the overhead of a hashing scheme may cancel out or outweigh the benefits of indexed access.

Collections, Equality, and Sorting

Sets maintain uniqueness of their elements. Maps maintain uniqueness of their keys. It is important to understand how uniqueness is defined. Set elements and map keys are considered unique if they are unequal, and equality is tested with the equals() method, not with the == operator. (The difference between these two concepts of equality is discussed in Chapter 1, "Language Fundamentals.")

Consider the following code fragment (assume that the set is initially empty):

```
1.   Integer aSix = new Integer(6);
2.   Integer anotherSix = new Integer(6);
3.   mySet.add(aSix);
4.   mySet.add(anotherSix);
```

When line 3 executes, the instance of Integer referenced by aSix is added to the set. When line 4 executes, the instance of Integer referenced by anotherSix is compared to the set's contents using the equals() method. Although the two instances of Integer are distinct objects, the equals() call returns true and so the two objects are considered equal. Thus line 4 has no effect on the set.

Certain collection implementations are ordered. To work properly, the elements of these collections must implement the interface java.lang.Comparable, which defines compareTo(), a method for determining the inherent order of two items of the same type. Most implementations of Map will also require a correct implementation of the hashCode() method.

> It is advisable to keep these three methods in mind whenever you define a new class, even if you do not anticipate storing instances of this class in collections.

The *hashCode()* Method

Many maps rely on hashing algorithms to provide efficient implementations. The Programmer's Exam does not require you to know the details of how this is accomplished. However, maps can only hash effectively if the objects they manage implement reasonable hashCode() methods. The exam tests your ability to write correct hashCode() methods.

The purpose of hashCode() is to provide a single integer to represent an object. Two objects that are equal (as determined by the equals() method) should return the same hashcode; otherwise hashing maps will not be able to reliably store and retrieve those objects. Note that the reverse is not required; that is, it is not necessary that two unequal objects must return different hashcodes. However, a hashcode() method that really does return different values for unequal objects is likely to result in better hashing map performance. This requirement and its corollaries are know as the hashcode "contract." The contract is spelled out formally on the API page for java.lang.Object under the hashcode() method's entry.

Any time you create a class that might be inserted into a hashing map, you should give your class a hashCode() method. A reasonable approach is to return a value that is a function of those variables that are scrutinized by the equals() method. Consider the following simple class:

```
class HashMe {
  private int a, b, c;
  public boolean equals(Object that) {
    if (!(that instanceof HashMe))
      return false;
    HashMe h = (HashMe)that;
    return (a == h.a  &&  b == h.b);
  }
}
```

Note that the equals() method considers the values of a and b but ignores c. We will look at three alternative ways to provide this class with a hashcode() method.

A very simple approach is

```
public int hashCode() { return 49; }
```

This method returns a constant value. Certainly any two instances of HashMe will generate identical hashcodes, so the contract is obeyed, but a map that contains many instances of this class could perform very slowly.

A more reasonable version would be

```
public int hashCode() { return a+b; }
```

This version returns a value that is a function of the two variables that are scrutinized by the equals() method. There will be times when unequal instances will return equal hashcodes. For example, one instance might have a=1 and b=2, while another instance has a=-5 and b=8. Both objects will return a hashcode of 3. Presumably this will be rare enough that maps will be able to function efficiently.

A third approach is the following:

```
public int hashCode() { return (int)(Math.pow(2,a) + Math.pow(3,b)); }
```

This version will only return equal hashcodes on equal objects. Thus the hashing inefficiency of the first example is completely ignored. However, this `hashcode()` method is itself not very efficient because it involves three double-precision operations and a number of type conversions.

Collection Implementations in the API

A variety of concrete implementation classes are supplied in the Collections API to implement the interfaces `Collection`, `List`, `Set`, and `Map`, using different storage types. Some of them are listed here:

HashMap/Hashtable These two classes are very similar; both use hash-based storage to implement a map. `Hashtable` has been in the Java API since the earliest releases, and `HashMap` was added at JDK 1.2. The main difference between the two is that `Hashtable` does not allow the `null` value to be stored, although it makes some efforts to support multithreaded use.

> **TIP** The `List` and `Set` interfaces extend the `Collection` interface. The `Map` interface does not extend `Collection`.

HashSet This is a set, so it does not permit duplicates and it uses hashing for storage.

LinkedList This is an implementation of a list, based on a linked list storage.

TreeMap This class provides an ordered map. The elements must be orderable, either by implementing the `Comparable` interface or by providing a `Comparator` class to perform the comparisons.

TreeSet This class provides an ordered set, using a tree for storage. As with the `TreeMap`, the elements must have an order associated with them.

Vector This class, which has been in the Java API since the first release, implements a list using an array internally for storage. The array is dynamically reallocated as necessary, as the number of items in the vector grows.

Stack This class implements a last-in, first-out (LIFO) collection of objects.

> **Real World Scenario**
>
> **A Sortable, Reversible Stack**
>
> Here's a scenario in which you will write a class that implements a stack with additional properties.
>
> The class should have a constructor that populates the stack with a specified number of instances of the Character class. These Characters should be random and unique. Provide methods called sort() and reverse(), which should respectively sort and reverse the contents of the stack. Provide a main() method that demonstrates the functionality of the constructor and of the sort() and reverse() methods. Here is a sample:
>
> ```
> >java CleverStack
> Initial State: CZqnWSNMyu
>        Sorted: CMNSWZnquy
>      Reversed: yuqnZWSNMC
> ```
>
> A second run produces different output because the stack is initialized with different random Characters:
>
> ```
> >java CleverStack
> Initial State: DZBpUlPMbI
>        Sorted: BDIMPUZblp
>      Reversed: plbZUPMIDB
> ```
>
> Without collections, initializing, sorting, and reversing would require a lot of original code. With the proper use of the classes in the `java.util` package, these operations require only a few lines each.
>
> As an additional exercise, consider what would happen if the Characters in the stack did not have to be unique. (Thus, for example, it would be legal to have an initial state of AAAqwertyu.) Construction would become easier because the constructor would no longer need to prevent duplication, and reversing would not be affected. However, sorting would be profoundly affected. Think about why this is the case, and think about ways to implement sorting of nonunique elements. The solution is beyond the scope of this chapter.

Collections and Code Maintenance

There is no such thing as the "best implementation" of a collection. Using any kind of collection involves several kinds of overhead penalty: memory usage, storage time, and retrieval time. No implementation can optimize all three of these features. So, instead of looking for the best list or the best hash table or the best set, it is more reasonable to look for the most appropriate list, set, or hash table implementation for a particular programming situation.

Chapter 8 · The java.lang and java.util Packages

As a program evolves, its data collections tend to grow. A collection that was created to hold a little bit of data may later be required to hold a large amount of data, while still providing reasonable response time. It is prudent from the outset to design code in such a way that it is easy to substitute one collection implementation type for another. Java's collections framework makes this easy because of its emphasis on interfaces. This section presents a typical scenario.

Imagine a program that maintains data about shoppers who are uniquely identified by their e-mail addresses. Such a program might use a Shopper class, with instances of this class stored in some kind of hash table, keyed by e-mail address. Suppose that when the program is first written, it is known that there are and always will be only three shoppers. The following code fragment constructs one instance for each shopper and stores the data in a hash map; then the map is passed to various methods for processing:

```
1.  private void getShoppers() {
2.      Shopper sh1 = getNextShopper();
3.      String email1 = getNextEmail();
4.      Shopper sh2 = getNextShopper();
5.      String email2 = getNextEmail();
6.      Shopper sh3 = getNextShopper();
7.      String email3 = getNextEmail();
8.
9.      Map map = new HashMap();    // Very important!
10.     map.put(email1, sh1);
11.     map.put(email2, sh2);
12.     map.put(email3, sh3);
13.
14.     findDesiredProducts(map);
15.     shipProducts(map);
16.     printInvoices(map);
17.     collectMoney(map);
18. }
```

Note the declaration of map on line 9. The reference type is Map, not HashMap (the interface, rather than the class). This is a very important difference whose value will become clear later on. The four processing methods do not much concern us here. Just consider their declarations:

```
private void findDesiredProducts(Map map) { ... }
private void shipProducts (Map map) { ... }
private void printInvoices (Map map) { ... }
private void collectMoney (Map map) { ... }
```

Imagine that each of these methods passes the hash map to other subordinate methods, which pass it to still other methods; our program has a large number of processing methods. Note that the argument types will be Map, not HashMap (again, the interface, rather than the class).

As development proceeds, suppose it becomes clear that the `getShoppers()` method should return the map's keys (which are the shoppers' e-mail addresses) in a sorted array. Because there are and always will be only three shoppers, there are and always will be only three keys to sort; the easiest implementation is therefore as follows:

```
1.  private String[] getShoppers() {   // New return type
2.     Shopper sh1 = getNextShopper();
3.     String email1 = getNextEmail();
4.     Shopper sh2 = getNextShopper();
5.     String email2 = getNextEmail();
6.     Shopper sh3 = getNextShopper();
7.     String email3 = getNextEmail();
8.
9.     Map map = new HashMap();
10.    map.put(email1, sh1);
11.    map.put(email2, sh2);
12.    map.put(email3, sh3);
13.
14.    findDesiredProducts(map);
15.    shipProducts(map);
16.    printInvoices(map);
17.    collectMoney(map);
18.
19.    // New sorting code.
20.    String[] sortedKeys = new String[3];
21.    if (email1.compareTo(email2) < 0  &&
22.        email1.compareTo(email3) < 0) {
23.       sortedKeys[0] = email1;
24.       if (email2.compareTo(email3) < 0)
25.          sortedKeys[1] = email2;
26.       else
27.          sortedKeys[2] = email3;
28.    }
29.    else if (email2.compareTo(email3) < 0) {
30.       sortedKeys[0] = email2;
31.       if (email1.compareTo(email3) < 0)
32.          sortedKeys[1] = email1;
33.       else
34.          sortedKeys[2] = email3;
35.    }
36.    else {
```

```
37.         sortedKeys[0] = email3;
38.         if (email1.compareTo(email2) < 0)
39.             sortedKeys[1] = email1;
40.         else
41.         sortedKeys[2] = email2;
42.     }
43.     return sortedKeys;
44. }
```

The added code is fairly lengthy: 26 lines.

> **TIP** Beware of specs claiming that the size of anything is and always will be small.

Predictably, as soon as the code is developed and debugged, someone will decide that the program needs to be expanded to accommodate 20 shoppers instead of the original 3. The new requirement suggests the need for a separate sorting algorithm, in its own separate method. The new method will be called sortStringArray(). The next evolution of getShoppers() looks like this:

```
1.  private String[] getShoppers() {
2.      String[] keys = new String[20];
3.      Map map = new HashMap()
4.      for (int i=0; i<20; i++) {
5.          Shopper s = getNextShopper();
6.          keys[i] = getNextEmail();
7.          map.put(keys[i], s);
8.      }
9.
10.     findDesiredProducts(map);
11.     shipProducts(map);
12.     printInvoices(map);
13.     collectMoney(map);
14.
15.     sortStringArray(keys);
16.     return keys;
17. }
```

This code is much more modular and compact. However, it is still not mature. The next requirement is that it has to be able to handle any number of shoppers, even a very large number.

At first glance, the solution seems very simple: just pass the number of shoppers in to the method, as shown here:

```
1.  private String[] getShoppers(int nShoppers) {
2.      String[] keys = new String[nShoppers];
3.      Map map = new HashMap()
4.      for (int i = 0; i < nShoppers; i++) {
5.          Shopper s = getNextShopper();
6.          keys[i] = getNextEmail();
7.          map.put(keys[i], s);
8.      }
9.
10.     findDesiredProducts(map);
11.     shipProducts(map);
12.     printInvoices(map);
13.     collectMoney(map);
14.
15.     sortStringArray(keys);
16.     return keys;
17. }
```

This code seems fine until the number of shoppers crosses some threshold. Then the amount of time spent sorting the keys (in method `sortStringArray()`, called on line 15) becomes prohibitive. Now is the time when the Collections framework shows its true value. In particular, you are about to see the value of referencing the map with variables of type Map, rather than HashMap (the interface, rather than the class).

Because the sorting method is now the bottleneck, it is reasonable to wonder whether a different kind of map can solve the performance problem. It is time for a quick look at the API pages for the classes that implement the Map interface. You'll find a suitable alternative: the TreeMap class. This implementation maintains its keys in sorted order and has a method for returning them in sorted order. Because the keys are always sorted, there seems to be zero overhead for sorting. Actually, the situation is not quite so good—there must be some extra overhead (which you can hope will be slight) in the put() method, when the tree map stores a new key. Before deciding that TreeMap is the right class to use, it is important to ascertain that storing and retrieving data in the new collection will not cost an unreasonable amount of time, even if the map is very large.

First, what is the current cost of storing and retrieving in a hash map? The API page for HashMap says that storage and retrieval take constant time, no matter what the size of the map might be. This is ideal; let's hope the performance of a tree map will also be constant. If it is not constant, it must still be acceptable when the data collection is large.

The API page for TreeMap says that the class "provides guaranteed $\log(n)$ time cost" for various operations, including storage and retrieval. This means that the time to store and retrieve data grows with the logarithm of the size of the data set. Figure 8.5 shows a graph of the logarithm function.

FIGURE 8.5 The logarithm function

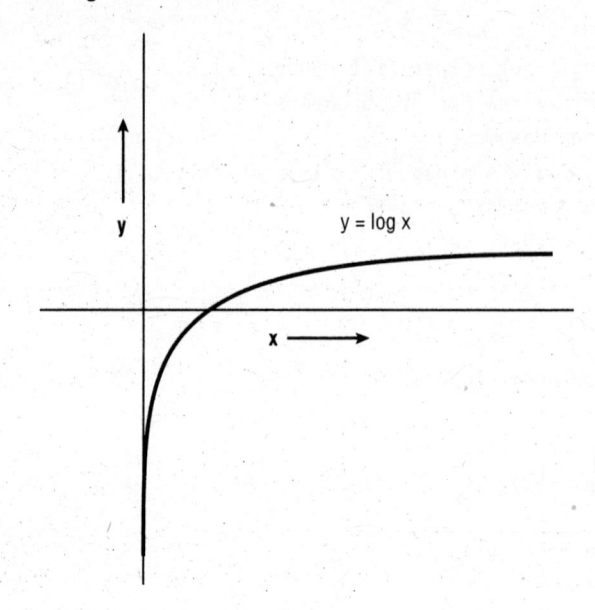

[Graph showing y = log x curve, rising steadily at a decreasing rate]

The graph in the figure rises steadily, but at an ever-decreasing rate. The cost for accessing a large tree map is only slightly greater than the cost for accessing a small one. Logarithmic overhead is almost as good as constant overhead; it is certainly acceptable for the current application.

Apparently, the `TreeMap` class is a very good substitute for the original `HashMap` class. Now you see how easy it is to replace one collection implementation with another. Because all references to the hash table are of type `Map` (the interface) rather than type `HashMap` (the class), only one line of code needs to be modified: the line in which the hash table is constructed. That line originally was

```
Map map = new HashMap();
```

All that is required is to call a different constructor:

```
Map map = new TreeMap();
```

Many data-processing methods pass references to the hash table back and forth among themselves. Not one of these methods needs to be modified at all. In fact, the only major change that needs to be made is to dispense with the `sortStringArray()` method and the call to it, substituting the tree map's intrinsic functionality. This modification is not directly relevant to the main point of this example, which is how easy it is to replace one collection type with another. However, it is instructive to see how the modification is accomplished. The final code looks like this:

```
1. private String[] getShoppers(int nShoppers) {
2.     Map map = new TreeMap();
3.     for (int i=0; i< nShoppers; i++) {
```

```
 4.       map.put(getNextEmail(), getNextShopper());
 5.     }
 6.
 7.     findDesiredProducts(map);
 8.     shipProducts(map);
 9.     printInvoices(map);
10.     collectMoney(map);
11.
12.     String[] keys = new String[nShoppers];
13.     Iterator iter = map.keySet().iterator();
14.     int i = 0;
15.     while (iter.hasNext())
16.        keys[i++] = (String)iter.next();
17.     return keys;
18. }
```

An *iterator* is an object that returns the elements of a collection one by one. Here the iterator on line 13 returns the elements of the hash table's key set. Because the hash table is an instance of `TreeMap`, the key set is guaranteed to be sorted.

This example shows the importance of referencing collections with variables of interface rather than class type. If you do this, replacing one collection type with another type becomes trivially easy.

Summary

The `java.lang` package contains classes that are indispensable to Java's operation, so all the classes of the package are automatically imported into all source files. Some of the most important classes in the package are

- Object
- Math
- The wrapper classes
- String
- StringBuffer

In a string context, addition operands are appended in turn to a string buffer, which is then converted to a string; primitive operands are converted to strings, and objects are converted by having their `toString()` methods invoked.

The `java.util` package contains many utilities, but for the Certification Exam, the Collections API is of primary interest. Collections provide ways to store and retrieve data in a program. Different types of collection provide different rules for storage, and different collection implementations optimize different access and update behaviors.

Summary of Collections

The essential points we've covered about collections are
- Collections impose no order nor restrictions on content duplication.
- Lists maintain an order (possibly inherent in the data, possibly externally imposed).
- Sets reject duplicate entries.
- Maps use unique keys to facilitate lookup of their contents.

For storage:
- Using arrays makes insertion, deletion, and growing the store more difficult.
- Using a linked list supports insertion, deletion, and growing the store, but makes indexed access slower.
- Using a tree supports insertion, deletion, and growing the list. Indexed access is slow, but searching is faster.
- Using hashing supports insertion, deletion, and growing the store. Indexed access is slow, but searching is particularly fast. However, hashing requires the use of unique keys for storing data elements.

Exam Essentials

Understand the common methods of the Math class. These methods are summarized in Table 8.1.

Understand the functionality of the wrapper classes. Each of the eight primitive types has a corresponding wrapper class.

Understand the functionality of the String class. The encapsulated text is immutable. Strings are supported by the string literal pool.

Understand the functionality of the StringBuffer class. The encapsulated text is mutable. String concatenation via the + operator is implemented with behind-the-scenes string buffers.

Know the main characteristics of each kind of Collections API: List, Set, and Map. Be aware that List maintains order, Set prohibits duplicate members, and Map associates keys with values.

Understand how collections test for duplication and equality. Collections use the equals() method rather than the == operator.

Understand that collection classes are not threadsafe. Most implementation classes are not threadsafe. You should assume that a collection class is not threadsafe unless its API documentation explicitly states otherwise.

Understand why it is preferable for references to collections to have interface type rather than class type. Be aware of the maintenance benefits when substituting one implementing class for another.

Key Terms

Before you take the exam, be certain you are familiar with the following terms:

array	sequence
framework	set
hash table	string context
iterator	threadsafe
linked list	tree
list	wrapper class
map	

Review Questions

1. Given a string constructed by calling s = new String("xyzzy"), which of the calls modify the string? (Choose all that apply.)

    A. s.append("aaa");

    B. s.trim();

    C. s.substring(3);

    D. s.replace('z', 'a');

    E. s.concat(s);

    F. None of the above

2. Which one statement is true about the following code?

    1. String s1 = "abc" + "def";
    2. String s2 = new String(s1);
    3. if (s1 == s2)
    4.   System.out.println("== succeeded");
    5. if (s1.equals(s2))
    6.   System.out.println(".equals() succeeded");

    A. Lines 4 and 6 both execute.

    B. Line 4 executes and line 6 does not.

    C. Line 6 executes and line 4 does not.

    D. Neither line 4 nor line 6 executes.

3. Suppose you want to write a class that offers static methods to compute hyperbolic trigonometric functions. You decide to subclass java.lang.Math and provide the new functionality as a set of static methods. Which one statement is true about this strategy?

    A. The strategy works.

    B. The strategy works, provided the new methods are public.

    C. The strategy works, provided the new methods are not private.

    D. The strategy fails because you cannot subclass java.lang.Math.

    E. The strategy fails because you cannot add static methods to a subclass.

4. Which one statement is true about the following code fragment?
   1. `import java.lang.Math;`
   2. `Math myMath = new Math();`
   3. `System.out.println("cosine of 0.123 = " +`
   4. `    myMath.cos(0.123));`

   A. Compilation fails at line 2.
   B. Compilation fails at line 3 or 4.
   C. Compilation succeeds, although the import on line 1 is not necessary. During execution an exception is thrown at line 3 or 4.
   D. Compilation succeeds. The import on line 1 is necessary. During execution, an exception is thrown at line 3 or 4.
   E. Compilation succeeds and no exception is thrown during execution.

5. Which one statement is true about the following code fragment?
   1. `String s = "abcde";`
   2. `StringBuffer s1 = new StringBuffer("abcde");`
   3. `if (s.equals(s1))`
   4. `    s1 = null;`
   5. `if (s1.equals(s))`
   6. `    s = null;`

   A. Compilation fails at line 1 because the `String` constructor must be called explicitly.
   B. Compilation fails at line 3 because `s` and `s1` have different types.
   C. Compilation succeeds. During execution, an exception is thrown at line 3.
   D. Compilation succeeds. During execution, an exception is thrown at line 5.
   E. Compilation succeeds. No exception is thrown during execution.

6. In the following code fragment, after execution of line 1, sbuf references an instance of the StringBuffer class. After execution of line 2, sbuf still references the same instance.
   1. `StringBuffer sbuf = new StringBuffer("abcde");`
   2. `sbuf.insert(3, "xyz");`

   A. True
   B. False

7. In the following code fragment, after execution of line 1, sbuf references an instance of the StringBuffer class. After execution of line 2, sbuf still references the same instance.
   1. `StringBuffer sbuf = new StringBuffer("abcde");`
   2. `sbuf.append("xyz");`

   A. True
   B. False

8. In the following code fragment, line 4 is executed.
   1. `String s1 = "xyz";`
   2. `String s2 = "xyz";`
   3. `if (s1 == s2)`
   4.   `System.out.println("Line 4");`

   A. True
   B. False

9. In the following code fragment, line 4 is executed.
   1. `String s1 = "xyz";`
   2. `String s2 = new String(s1);`
   3. `if (s1 == s2)`
   4.   `System.out.println("Line 4");`

   A. True
   B. False

10. Which would be most suitable for storing data elements that must not appear in the store more than once, if searching is not a priority?

    A. Collection
    B. List
    C. Set
    D. Map
    E. Vector

Answers to Review Questions

1. F. Strings are immutable.

2. C. Because s1 and s2 are references to two different objects, the == test fails. However, the strings contained within the two String objects are identical, so the equals() test passes.

3. D. The java.lang.Math class is final, so it cannot be subclassed.

4. A. The constructor for the Math class is private, so it cannot be called. The Math class methods are static, so it is never necessary to construct an instance. The import at line 1 is not required, because all classes of the java.lang package are automatically imported.

5. E. A is wrong because line 1 is a perfectly acceptable way to create a String and is actually more efficient than explicitly calling the constructor. B is wrong because the argument to the equals() method is of type Object; thus any object reference or array variable may be passed. The calls on lines 3 and 5 return false without throwing exceptions because s and s1 are objects of different types.

6. A. The StringBuffer class is mutable. After execution of line 2, sbuf refers to the same object, although the object has been modified.

7. A. The StringBuffer class is mutable. After execution of line 2, sbuf refers to the same object, although the object has been modified.

8. A. Line 1 constructs a new instance of String and stores it in the string pool. In line 2, "xyz" is already represented in the pool, so no new instance is constructed.

9. B. Line 1 constructs a new instance of String and stores it in the string pool. Line 2 explicitly constructs another instance.

10. C. A set prohibits duplication, whereas a list or collection does not. A map also prohibits duplication of the key entries, but maps are primarily for looking up data based on the unique key. So, in this case, you could use a map, storing the data as the key and leaving the data part of the map empty. However, you are told that searching is not a priority, so the proper answer is a set.

The Developer's Exam

PART II

Chapter 9

Taking the Developer's Exam

The most important thing to know about the Java 2 Developer's Exam is that it is practical rather than objective. In an industry where certification testing frequently boils down to multiple-choice questions, term/definition matching, short answers, and true/false statements—the mainstays of evaluating competence cost effectively—practical exams are rare. Beyond cost, however, there are good reasons for writing such exams. In a timed multiple-choice test, for example, the answer to each question can be *normalized*, or designed so it not only provides the correct answer but also elicits it, unambiguously, with the right question. The average response time (difficulty level) can be assessed in trials, so that the candidate faces a reasonable number of questions for the time allotted, receives the same opportunity as everyone else, and is evaluated fairly.

For people who prefer projects to knowledge-based examinations, the Developer's Exam is ideal (although you still must pass the Programmer's Exam as a prerequisite). Because it is broad in scope and because there are few industry exams like it, we will review the concepts and expectations of the exam in some detail. We'll discuss an example similar to the one the Developer's Exam offers to help you understand what is required and how to approach the test, by breaking down its component parts and building them into a working whole. The test costs a few hundred dollars, so it is certainly worth your while to assess your readiness.

Are You Ready for the Exam?

You can deduce from the guide to the Programmer's Exam in this book that Sun does not want to confer pro forma certifications. The candidates for that exam are expected to know the core libraries, operators, and compile-time and runtime behaviors well enough to recognize flawed code when they read it and to anticipate the errors such code will generate.

Again, this certification exam is a practical one. The test challenges your ability to use Java in conjunction with the skills, experience, and discipline required of a competent programmer. If Java has been your sole focus for more than a year and you have a bit more experience on development projects using Java or some other language—ideally an object-oriented one—little of what you see in the programming assignment or follow-up exam should be too surprising. Even if some requirements represent new territory, there's no time limit, so the opportunity to learn one or two things as you go should not represent a hardship.

It should therefore come as no surprise that getting the code to execute correctly merely *initiates* the grading process. Professional developers must be able to justify their designs, recognize strengths and weaknesses in their solutions, translate those principles correctly into code, and document their work clearly for the benefit of future programmers and maintainers of that code. In that spirit, this guide focuses on strategy and design choices more than fully coded solutions, in order to demonstrate the various tasks that the exam presents and provide a conceptual model for developing the solution. Your ability to write the code is assumed.

The exam itself has as many right answers as there are justifiable ways of solving them. The exam does not hint at or beg for an *ideal* solution. Rather, you must design and implement the assignment project in a manner that you will ultimately justify. The code must pass a functional test, which cannot verify all possible solutions. Finally, you must explain how your code works in two ways: by demonstrating knowledge of some other approaches and by explaining what benefits and penalties derive from the one applied.

Here are a few general questions to spur your thinking as you assess your readiness:

- Do you write Java code three or more days a week?
- How many applications have you completed based only on written instructions?
- Can you name one or two principles of effective user interface design?
- How many multithreaded applications have you written? Client-server? Database-oriented?
- Recall your last experience of being assigned an incomplete project, including undocumented code and missing source files. How did you work through those problems?
- What risks are involved with a remote client locking a record on a database?
- For storing data in memory, when does it make sense to use an array? A `Vector`? A `Hashtable`? A `List`?
- What are the relative merits of using Remote Method Invocation (RMI), object serialization, or some ad hoc data format for network communication?
- How is a two-tier client-server scheme different from three-tier?

Precise knowledge of Java's core operations and class libraries, which is required to pass the Programmer's Exam, will carry you some of the way. The single best preparation for getting certified as a developer, however, is meaningful experience with Java development, ideally by completing tasks put to you by someone else. We cannot emphasize enough the value of good programming habits and experience in taking on a moderately complex programming task with only written instructions for guidance and no real-world pressure to finish (other than forfeiting the registration fee).

> **NOTE** Sun offers a five-day course called Java Programming Language Workshop that is well suited to preparing students for this certification. The course is numbered SL-285; you can view the course description by pointing your browser to http://suned.sun.com. Sun also offers courses specific to major areas of the exam, but these are not defined as certification courses. You may also wish to browse SL-320, GUI Construction with Java Foundation Classes, and SL-301, Distributed Programming with Java Technology, which treats RMI in detail.

Formalities of the Exam

The Developer's Certification Exam has two parts: a project assignment and a follow-up exam. The assignment describes a programming task that starts with some code supplied with the project description; you are then asked to finish the intended project. Some portions of the final code are to be written from scratch, some must extend or apply provided interfaces or classes, and some must modify incomplete or rudimentary classes. The requirements will also indicate areas of the application that you are not required to finish. To keep the test within reasonable limits, no one will be asked to create a robust, user-tolerant, business-grade application. In fact, going beyond the scope of the assignment may actually create problems. You will not receive extra credit for implementing extra functionality, but you might lose points if problems are found in the extra functionality. To keep testing simple, the assignment constrains some areas by disallowing certain approaches (for example, CORBA) or by simply requiring them (say, RMI or object serialization). As further discouragement against going too far afield, a solution that works but duplicates resources readily available in the core libraries may be scored lower.

The follow-up exam, which takes place in a timed and proctored test facility, has at least three aspects. The *objective* aspect deals with knowledge of Java's features and libraries. For example, you might be asked to list some data structures useful for storing an indeterminate number of runtime objects and then to explain the advantages each of those structures offers relative to the others. The *practical* aspect of the exam focuses on your knowledge and understanding of your own code (yes, this is a check to make sure you've done the work), asking you to offer one or two cases where you made a certain choice and what you decided on. Finally, in the *subjective* aspect, you may be asked to justify that choice. Perhaps you did not pick the most efficient data structure. What did you pick, and why? The right answer, in this last case, will be one that demonstrates that your choices were made in a conscious and reasonable way, regardless of whether the grader of the test might have done the same thing. It's important to bear in mind that this is not an exercise in anticipating what Sun wants Java programmers to think. You should not second-guess your own judgment if your design suits you.

Nonetheless, the reality of open-ended practical exams is that grading is subjective. Process does matter. So, although getting your application to run properly doesn't guarantee certification, it's a bare minimum for getting to that point. But it isn't worthwhile to dwell for very long on the idea of subjective grading. There are a few compensating factors:

- The weight allotted to each part of the assignment evaluation, and the categories of evaluation, are included in the assignment.
- The time limit of the exam is the life of the exam's administration.
- This guide will help you to broaden your inquiry into the skills needed to succeed.

Downloading the Assignment

Once you pay the registration fee for the Developer's Exam, Sun will enter your name in their certification database. You may have to wait a day for it to process.

> **NOTE:** Full details on the Developer's Exam for Java 2 are available by browsing http://suned.sun.com/US/certification/java/java_devj2se.html or by calling Sun Educational Services at 800-422-8020.

Once the assignment is ready, you can download it by logging in to the database through your browser. Be sure to save the downloaded bundle to a backup right away; the site is not set up to allow repeated downloads. The bundle you receive will include the project description, some source and class files, and instructions for submitting the finished work back to Sun.

> **TIP:** You'll need your assigned student ID as a password. The login page is located at www.galton.com/~sun. You can verify your Programmer's Exam score and certification there as well. You may also want to check the contact information this database has for you and make sure it is correct.

Taking the Follow-up Exam

Sun does not review your assignment until you complete the follow-up examination. This portion requires an additional fee payable to Sun, which will issue you an exam voucher. The voucher is used to reserve testing space at any Sylvan Prometric center, which administers the exam. Because seating is limited in most centers, and the exams are scheduled ahead of time for download to a testing computer, reservations are essential (call 800-795-3926). The time limit for finishing the follow-up exam is 90 minutes.

The finished assignment will be relatively complex, and you will not have the luxury of bringing any notes into the exam room. It's a good idea to submit the assignment as soon as you have it working and to take the follow-up quickly thereafter, while the code is still fresh in your mind.

What the Assignment Covers

You'll be asked to take an existing database scheme and enhance its features by adding one or more new functions. The database may require support for user access (local, remote, or both), concurrent users, and a client GUI to facilitate ease of use. Accomplishing these tasks—integrating them and designing something flexible enough to make future improvements easy to implement—requires a practical command of these areas:

- I/O streams
- Swing
- The AWT event model
- Object serialization
- RMI
- javadoc

- Packages
- Threads
- Interfaces

Some of the elements listed here may not appear on the exam or may already be familiar to you; familiarity in that topic area may be all that you need. For example, one or two interfaces may be provided that you will be required to implement. In other cases, the assignment may dictate how you may apply elements to the project, typically to help standardize the grading process or to ensure that the finished code compiles.

How the Assignment and Exam Are Graded

Review of the assignment begins once the follow-up exam is completed and forwarded to a Sun-appointed grader. The grader tests the submitted application code by hand; failure to clear this phase automatically concludes the evaluation. If you have tested your code before submitting it, however, this step should be a formality. The grader then examines the source code along with the answers given in the follow-up exam. Good source-writing style, adequate documentation, clarity of design, judicious use of the core libraries, and the consistency of the follow-up essays with the assignment all fall under review.

Sun estimates that grading takes four weeks from the date it receives the follow-up exam. The values assigned to each part of the grading criteria are listed in the downloaded assignment documentation, but here are some general parameters:

- Assignment uses API-style documentation and uses comment code properly
- Code uses standard library features and algorithms
- Conventional object-oriented programming techniques are applied
- The GUI meets requirements and follows principles for effective human-computer interaction
- Error-handling mechanisms are appropriate
- Data operations are threadsafe
- Code layout is clear, maintainable, and consistent, and follows expected formatting guidelines

Structure of the Assignment

The project description of the Developer's Exam reads something like the following:

- Write an application program with the following component parts:
  - A user interface utilizing specified component elements and conforming to general principles of human interaction.
  - An RMI connection using a specified protocol to connect to an information server that supplies the data for display in the user interface.

- A multithreaded, threadsafe network server, which connects to a previously specified Java database.
- An application created by extending the functionality of a previously written piece of code, for which only limited documentation is available. This application may take the form of a flat-file database or some other application that can be modeled simply in pure Java.

- List some of the significant design choices to be made during the implementation of the application.
- List some of the main advantages and disadvantages of each of these design choices.
- Briefly justify choices made in terms of the comparison of design and implementation objectives with the advantages and disadvantages of each.

Our purpose here is to familiarize you with the conditions of the exam. It starts with some nearly completed code for a database scheme, based on a business scenario. Your job is broken down into a series of tasks, which may include some or all of the following:

- Supply the "missing feature" to the database scheme; this may be a field-level search capability, a sort routine to support advanced queries, or a record-locking mechanism.
- Implement the network connection.
- Write a GUI-based client to access the database. Count on using only Swing components. Because you can certainly expect to display records, a `JTable` is an obvious consideration.

Certain variations will occur from one assignment to the next, and certain underlying files may vary accordingly. This step is a check against sharing with or receiving assignment files and tasks from other candidates because there is no time limit and no way to monitor the work before submission.

In short, the assignment's test of functional proficiency lies in completing a project with multiple, interrelated tasks, despite any limitations imposed by the initial code. The test of overall proficiency is in writing code that is clear, concise, and relatively easy to interpret through its generated API documentation. One aim you should have in mind is to produce code that a less-experienced programmer could read and maintain with a working knowledge of the language and the use of standard Java references and conventions.

Code and APIs Provided

The code supplied with the project assignment will largely consist of concrete code, rather than a skeletal design that must first be implemented. With respect to the database scheme, this means that certain choices, such as the underlying Collections type, will be predetermined, along with the fundamental methods for reading from and writing to the database. Method signatures for the enhancements you are required to add may already be defined as well. You may have to subclass the code provided or add the missing code to it.

An implementation-independent schema might look like this:

```
public interface DataBase {
    public Field[] getFields();
    public int recordTotal();
    public Record getRecord(int recID);
    public Record[] find(String matchItem);
    public void addRecord(String [] newData);
    public void modifyRecord(Record changes);
    public void deleteRecord(Record delete);
    public void close();
}
```

This prototype view is for the sake of illustration. Obviously, we cannot define important constructors or protected methods—which could nonetheless be designed independent of implementation—in an interface; but we wanted to keep this preview tight and defer fleshing out an abstract or concrete. Even though you won't have to develop schema code of your own, you can see in this interface what a simple Java schema might amount to. The object types' names are self-explanatory. Those who want more flexibility may balk at defining an `int` for a record number in `getRecord()`. You could, of course, specify `recID` as an `Object`, and argue that it makes more sense to use a wrapper class to get an `int`. Alternatively, you might overload `getRecord()` in a concrete subclass and call the provided method signature from there. These are both useful observations to apply to the follow-up exam, so keep a critical eye toward such factors as you consider how you will complete the project.

The project will also incorporate a package structure to logically divide the functional areas of the project. Packaging should pose no particular difficulties with respect to the scope of existing code; you should observe the vanilla rules of encapsulation unless there is an unavoidable reason to do otherwise (performance or the ease of direct field access are not good reasons to offer). Certain classes that must be developed may already be named in the assignment to assure consistent grading.

Example Assignment: Build a Trouble-Ticket System

Let's say you have been working with several start-up companies, and they all seem to have a common need: none of them has a systematic process for resolving internal technical support problems. To get support, staff members must call an engineer whose primary roles are development, external customer support, and monitoring production systems. In other words, solving problems that do not directly affect customer satisfaction is often a matter of competing for already strained resources.

Maintaining responsiveness to such problems, as a result, is typically governed by political rather than technical priorities. The focus of the response, once arranged, is to quickly restore the individual's ability to be productive; no one tracks whose time is required or how much is used. Tracking tech support is viewed as simply another secondary assignment.

Because there is no formal record-keeping of problems, assignments, or resolution—much less a centralized way to enter, modify, or view such records—hiring additional engineers to fulfill technical support needs is difficult to justify (except during an ongoing crisis). To establish and maintain an efficient operation, the resource managers of these companies must find a way to:

- Match the right expert to technical problems to improve turnaround time
- Correlate widely reported symptoms to their source, thereby reducing duplication of effort
- Sort the outstanding problems by priority and allocate resources first to the most important ones
- Allow for distributed record entry into the database, relying on each person's responsibility to report problems

Most start-ups, however, can't afford and don't want complex trouble-ticket systems for internal use. The organization's staffing can change rapidly, along with ownership of various projects. One of the few remedies available is to distribute the responsibility (and benefits) of the system. Start-up groups are also more inclined to use tools that require little learning, achieve specific objectives, and impose few requirements. They are more likely to use a tool if they can adapt it to their needs quickly.

You decide to prototype a trouble-ticket system that will work on all of your customers' existing systems, that you can modify as their needs are better identified, and that you can enhance without significant rewrites. You do not want to compromise your own rapid time-to-market objectives by simply adding flexibility (that is, complexity)—you just want your code to be open to future requirements.

Your solution requires a simple client-server structure. Naturally, the server itself must allow for concurrent user connections, accommodate searches for specific data, and, of course, protect against concurrent writes to the same record. You also want to keep the client-server connection scheme generic, for two reasons. First, you want to maintain a single communications model for all customers so that a change to the data set does not change the code that connects the client and server. You must abstract the data from the data transport model. Second, you want to promote centralization. Start-up companies want to outsource or contract technical support whenever they can. If you leave open the possibility of using your client as a *monitor*, you will be able to add features that let you manage several of these databases, regardless of their individual schema, from one location. If your clients like the tool and use it, the next thing they need is technical support that doesn't take away from their business focus. You will already know how they see their data, a crucial advantage in pursuing other consulting opportunities.

After surveying several of these companies for interest, you decide on a simple, generalized data scheme for our prototype, depicted in the following table:

Field	Data Type
Record Number	Integer
Reporting Person	String
Location	String
Time of Report	String (Date)
Engineer	String
Category	String
Complaint	String
Status	String

You will use fundamental data types and start out with an internally delimited ASCII file to help model the graphic client interface. Once the logical elements are set, the ASCII data can be converted into a format that suits our server code. For now, follow this form:

RECNUM|REPORT|LOCAT|TIME|ENGIN|CATEG|COMPLT|STATUS

Sample records would look like this in file:

```
001|Sayers|DEN|03/28/00 10:21|Wort|Network|T-1 is down|CLOSED
002|Padula|EDI|04/01/00 13:30|Markson|Office|No cookies|PENDING
003|Hunter|DEN|04/03/00 10:15|Brown|Server|Backups failing|CLOSED
004|Cramer|MPT|04/09/00 08:59|Ramirez|Workstation|U-10 down|IN-PRO
005|Lewis|BRM|04/11/00 21:48|Unassigned|Database|Locked table|OPEN
006|Gant|SFO|04/15/00 14:15|Unassigned|Office|Loud whining|CRITICAL
```

GUI Development

The centerpiece of your graphic interface will naturally be a table—a JTable, that is, because you are using Swing components. For the sake of depicting a monitor-oriented approach to the client, you'll also include a JTree in the prototype, as shown in Figure 9.1. This experiment will give you a chance to:

- Consider another graphic model to use for viewing multiple databases
- Connect actions to tree nodes for use as stored procedures
- Help you think about alternative layouts as the GUI develops

FIGURE 9.1 A simple box diagram to show relative position and layout

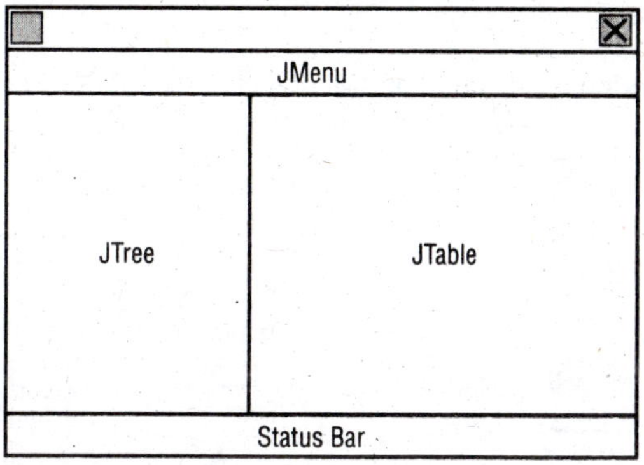

```
┌─────────────────────────────────────┐
│ ▫                                 ☒ │
│              JMenu                  │
├──────────────┬──────────────────────┤
│              │                      │
│              │                      │
│   JTree      │      JTable          │
│              │                      │
│              │                      │
│              │                      │
├──────────────┴──────────────────────┤
│            Status Bar               │
└─────────────────────────────────────┘
```

All Swing components inherit from `java.awt.Container`. Thus it is possible to contain other components inside any `JComponent`—which is ample motivation to look past AWT widgets. This feature comes to mind because some of the data fields described so far, such as Location, Engineer, or Status, might have a fixed or constrained list of values. The graphic client can simplify data entry and validation in those cases by displaying a choice list instead of a text field. Furthermore, if you can get the data scheme to carry this information, you can adjust the graphic table to reflect not only the header and field length, but also the most suitable component for displaying it. Swing was built to meet these kinds of needs, so take the opportunity to learn how to do that while building the client code.

The visual aspect, or *view*, is easy to represent, but you are just scratching the surface of the code you'll need. You should put more thought into the *model*, or the way you expect to contain your data. A `JTable` Model is defined by an implementation of the `TableModel` interface. If you want to exploit more capability than the `DefaultTableModel` provides—a simple `Vector` of `Vectors`—you can specify your own `TableColumnModels`. In short, plenty of work can be developed on the client side even before the actual data is determined. If you exercise a little forethought and focus on modular design, you might be able to handle even substantive changes in the data structure without altering the basic design of your GUI code.

Database/Server Development

The bulk of your back-end project consists of serving your data over the network; we'll start this discussion at the design level, using Java's Remote Method Invocation (RMI) API. You could also use object serialization to develop a protocol for conversing in objects between client and server—the exam allows either approach—but using RMI will give us a reason to talk about interfaces.

RMI simplifies programming the client-side logic by requiring you to define the remote interface to the server in advance. Actual implementations can vary from client to client. One way to think about this is to have a single RMI server that exports multiple interfaces to the same database—in short, continue adding features to the database, but make them available through multiple interfaces. Then, add them to clients in the form of an interface collection. Figure 9.2 illustrates this approach.

FIGURE 9.2 Serving a collection of RMI objects to a remote client

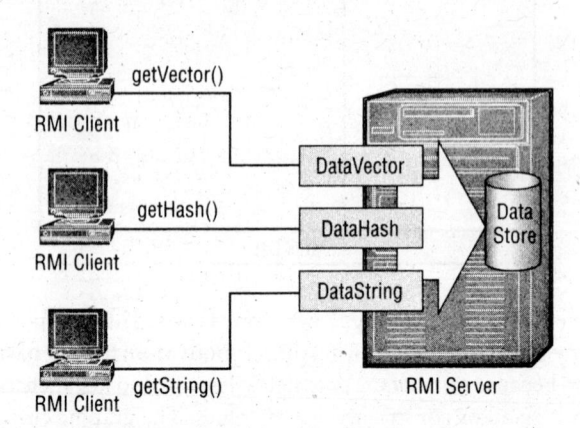

This approach isn't any faster to code; it's simply more flexible. You're far less likely to get locked in to one way of doing things. In any event, the key is what happens to the client code. A client that accesses remote resources through RMI initiates the process through an RMI request. As long as the connection request works, remote method calls look the same as local calls: the programmer sees no difference in writing an implementation. That's all there is to it—to avoid the problem of everyone generating their own protocols, RMI provides a generic transport for serialized objects. You don't have to worry about the *order* of communication as much, but you do have to consider whether the remote service provides a *complete* interface. As long as you're thinking about flexibility for the future—perhaps creating a database of databases in a later phase—implementing RMI is good practice.

Begin your server development with a basic schema and include the functions necessary to support data entry and retrieval. Our discussion will center on incorporating search and record-locking features and on dealing with concurrent access. As instructors, we have found that multithreading is new territory for many students when they take Sun's preparatory Java courses, and we assume that this is generally true among programmers as a whole. Those who are familiar with multithreaded programming sometimes struggle with Java's nondeterministic thread scheduling, which we'll touch on as well.

Client-Server Logic

With the graphic end of the client roughed out, and the server code in place, all that remains is to tie the graphic client to your RMI client logic. As mentioned earlier, remote method call semantics are no different from local method calls once the server connection is made. Simply tie the data given by the user via the GUI to a client request and then pass the response from the server back up. The overall model is the same: the user manipulates a Controller (graphic widget) to change the Model (data table), which makes the requested changes and updates the View (as illustrated in Figure 9.3). Aside from network latency or other performance aspects, there's no functional difference to the user—the local data model is merely being updated by a data source on another computer.

FIGURE 9.3 A data transaction using a remote data source

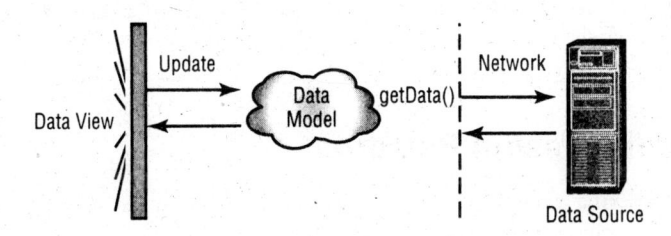

Coding Tips

The following elements address how the grader appointed by Sun will review the source code and documentation submitted with your working program. The assignment documentation you receive will provide the relative weight of each category.

Adhere to Supplied Naming

Following the naming scheme given for packages, classes, and methods primarily ensures that the grader will check the code properly. Beyond that, there is no set limit on the number of support classes you create for the finished assignment. Choose names for any such classes you supply that evoke their purpose or type. Naming subclasses so that they refer to the parent helps to create an immediate association for the code reader and is good policy where it is practical.

Stress Readability

Java software recommends a few conventions for programmers to follow. These guidelines promote a common visual appearance for source code that makes it easier for other programmers to identify the elements and form a clear impression of the code's operation. Some guidelines to bear in mind are as follows:

- Begin all class names with an uppercase letter.
- Begin all method and field names with a lowercase letter.
- Use mixed case for multiple-word names (like `getResourceAsStream()`).
- Avoid one-character field names except as temporary variables in a loop. The identifiers O and 1 (uppercase "oh" and lowercase "ell") are always undesirable because they look too much like zero and one.

- Indent three or four spaces per code block. (We use smaller indents in this book to avoid line breaks.)
- Avoid using multiple `System.out.print()` calls to concatenate a long string. Use the + operator instead and span the strings over multiple lines.

As with any coding style, the key is a consistent application of form the intended readers know. One habit we have seen in sample code on the Web is beginning class names with a lowercase letter. Although legal, doing so can make a class reference hard to distinguish from a variable in a long code list. Avoid this practice.

Use Standard Design Patterns

Design patterns describe a relation within a class or among several classes that serve a fundamental purpose to applications without regard to their "domain." The JDK makes ample use of design patterns throughout its core libraries: Swing uses a variation of the MVC pattern to support multiple graphic views of one data model. The `Applet` class uses an Observer pattern to monitor any `Image` instances it may contain. These abstractions also allow developers to communicate their ideas in terms of architecture, rather than implementation. Once consensus is achieved on the structure of an application, the individual programmers can then focus on building the elements needed to complete it.

Design patterns by themselves are not magic; they simply express a consistently useful approach to some common problem. It's quite likely that some experienced programmers use them without knowing their given names. But knowing these patterns by name and structure can greatly reduce the time it takes to recognize the tools that use them. Classes like `java.net.ContentHandlerFactory`, for example, embed the design model directly in their names. If you know what a Factory design is good for, you'll be able to identify a factory class's role quickly and put it to use. Other classes, such as `java.util.Observer` and `Observable`, get their names directly from the patterns they implement, so the pattern-aware programmer can save time otherwise spent researching classes and reading method lists. It is worth your while to research the patterns most commonly used and learn to apply them to your projects.

Submission Requirements

The final Developer's Exam submission to Sun must be packaged as a single JAR file. The rules for correct packaging listed in the exam assignment are strict but not complex. In concluding this second scenario, this chapter models a sample submission by reviewing the tools needed (`jar` and `javadoc`) and by adding a few pointers on keeping a submission clean and easy to read. The topics included are

- Using `javadoc`
- Adhering to file structure rules
- Using the JAR tool

> **NOTE:** The written instructions don't specify how or where to upload the assignment. Instructions at http://suned.sun.com/US/certification/ state that the upload should be done at the same location from which you initiated the download. The page is located on www.galton.com/~sun and is restricted by password access. Make sure to record the login and password given to you for the download!

The completed assignment must include the following elements:

- All source code: new, modified, or unchanged
- All compiled class code
- HTML documentation on all source code
- Notes on each working program
- A top-level README file

All elements must be bundled together in a single JAR file, with an "appropriate" directory structure. The main JAR may contain other JAR files, which is how we recommend the client/GUI and server/database applications be presented.

You must run all source code through javadoc so the examiner can verify through a browser your proper application of comments. The assignment also requires you to supply a text or HTML file for each working program in the submission. There should be three of these files altogether: one for the GUI, one for the server program, and one for a data-conversion utility you're asked to write. This utility must accept a flat table of records, provided in the assignment instructions, and store it to a file format that can be used by the code Sun provides.

> **NOTE:** The flat-file format used for the assignment is similar to the one we described as your practice data. We avoided following Sun's data format, however, to preserve the integrity of the exercise. You must deduce and apply the correct binary format only by reading the details of the data routines—a task that is as real-world as it gets.

The most important piece of documentation is the README file. It must be a single file in ASCII format. Your project instructions will tell you the exact name for this file; do not use any other filename. Depending on which assignment you receive, your README may be required to include the following information:

- How to execute each program, including command-line syntax
- A list of the files submitted, along with directory location and brief purpose for each
- The location of files that document the design of the submission, including any justifications

If you omit a required element, the submission fails, so it's well worth the effort to cover these guidelines carefully and take your time on the packaging process. Sun does allow you to submit twice under the same fee, but it would be a waste to fail because you didn't follow instructions.

278   Chapter 9 · Taking the Developer's Exam

You will be graded on your project's ease of use. Bear in mind that a major factor of ease of use is ease of invocation. If it is difficult to figure out how to start your programs, you will definitely be marked down. Before you submit your project, review your README file and ask yourself how much sense it will make to someone who is completely unfamiliar with your project. If your instructions seem complicated, there are two possibilities:

- Your implementation is complicated.
- Your program is simple, but your documentation is complicated.

If your implementation is complicated, you have accurately documented the implementation, complications and all. Consider changing your program because you will be graded on maintainability, and a simple approach is always more maintainable than a complicated approach. For example, consider the following instructions:

```
The data file is in the data.jar archive, in the /data/mydata/jars subdirectory.
Go into /data/mydata/jars and type ìjar xvf data.jarî. The data file will be
extracted to datafiles/db.db. Invoke the server by typing ìjava suncertify.
server.Server - datafilepath data/mydata/jars/ datafiles/db.dbî.
```

This paragraph is possibly the most concise way to describe the location of the database file and the server's command-line invocation. The implementation is clearly overly complicated, because putting the data file in a JAR in a subdirectory provides no benefit.

If your program is simple but your documentation is complicated, rewrite your documentation. It seems unfair to require you to be a good writer as well as a good software developer, but sometimes that's the way it works out.

The philosopher C. S. Lewis, known for the clarity of his prose, used to give his students the following advice about writing: "Know precisely what you want to say, and say precisely that." In other words, documentation—like software—should be designed and thought through before you begin writing. Don't start a sentence before you figure out what the sentence ought to say.

Another good principle is that writing should be both truthful and helpful. In the context of documentation, this means that it is not enough to be accurate. Everything you say not only should be true, but should also advance the reader's understanding.

Using *javadoc*

Table 9.1 presents a select overview of javadoc options.

TABLE 9.1   *javadoc* Options for Standard HTML Output

Option	Comment
-overview <file>	Reads in an HTML overview file.
-[public | protected | package | private]	Sets the level of scope to the document.
-1.1	Creates 1.1-style documentation.

TABLE 9.1 *javadoc* Options for Standard HTML Output *(continued)*

Option	Comment
-sourcepath <pathlist>	Location of the source code. Useful for references to classes in other package structures or JAR files.
-classpath <pathlist>	Location of the user class files. Useful for references to classes in other package structures or JAR files.
-verbose	Provides more information on javadoc processing (mostly process time on loading reference classes and parsing the source files).

The `javadoc` command verifies the compilability of all the source files indicated as a necessary precondition for parsing the comments. Not only will it fail to produce documentation if the source can't compile, `javadoc` will abort if any one source file in the list is not correct. Warnings are issued for bad tag information, such as `@see` and `@link` tags that don't link up to qualified class names, and so on.

Among the helper files that `javadoc` generates is what's known as a *cascading style sheet*, `stylesheet.css`. This document provides the default values for fonts and colors in all the HTML pages generated. It plugs into every page by way of a <LINK> reference, so changes made in `stylesheet.css` will affect all pages in the same directory. Thus if you want the default document structure but possibly different cosmetic values, you can make changes in a single file and have those changes "cascade" to every associated HTML page.

Run the following command to install documentation pages in your current directory (use a backslash in place of the slash for Windows platforms, of course):

```
$ javadoc -sourcepath <path_to_source>/*.java
```

File Structure

If you principally work with Java at the command line, you may have run into some annoying problems with the CLASSPATH environment variable. Dealing with this value is often a headache for novices and for good reason: how CLASSPATH works is not always intuitive.

The usual obstacle is an entity known as the *default package*. It applies to every Java class that does not declare its own package structure and appears to resolve to the current directory—except when the source is in the same location. When a class that explicitly declares a package shares the same directory as its source, strange things happen. The effect is to collapse the "unnamed" package (the current directory) and the CLASSPATH pointer (locations of all "named" packages) together, forcing a name collision that the runtime interpreter won't try to resolve.

You can easily resolve this conflict by locating the source directory and the root package directory within a common parent. This way, no package-name collision will interfere with runtime execution. This scheme facilitates runtime and compilation use as well. The command-line invocation here assumes `Code.java` has declared package `this.that`:

```
$ javac -d .. Code.java
```

This command creates the class file `../this/that/Code.class`, relative to the `src` directory, as shown in Figure 9.4.

FIGURE 9.4 Directories for source and compiled code

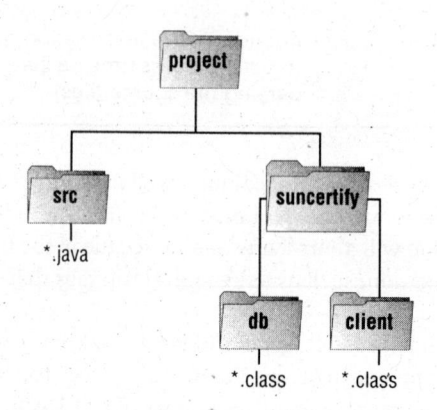

```
              project
             /      \
           src     suncertify
           |       /       \
         *.java  db       client
                 |          |
              *.class    *.class
```

From the same directory, the code can be run as follows:

```
$ java -cp .. this.that.Code
```

This same approach works well under the submission requirements. The JAR file acts as a directory point of its own, under which you can create `src` and `suncertify` (the top-level package name for the exam source). Add a `docs` directory at this level to store the class and application notes. If you want to take advantage of the Java 2 runtime's ability to execute a JAR file directly, create `server.jar`, `client.jar`, and `converter.jar` and place them here as well. Finally, if RMI is the mechanism for connecting client and server over the network, you should also include a `policy` file at this directory level. Figure 9.5 shows the complete file layout.

FIGURE 9.5 File distribution for the submission

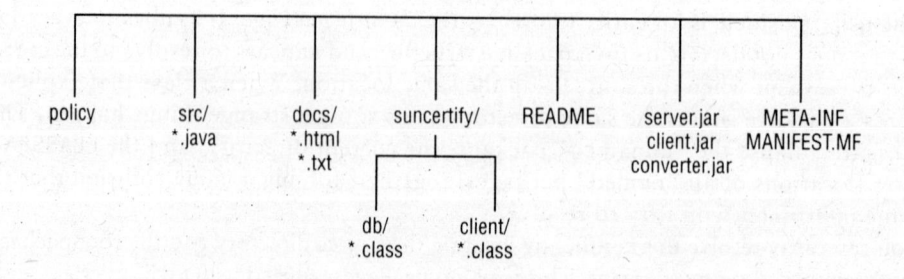

```
   policy   src/      docs/     suncertify/   README   server.jar    META-INF
            *.java    *.html                           client.jar    MANIFEST.MF
                      *.txt                            converter.jar
                                /        \
                              db/       client/
                              *.class   *.class
```

Writing the README file

README.TXT doesn't have to be fancy, just clear and to the point. Possibly, the submission rules are so insistent on proper form because the file might be extracted programmatically; in any case, it's a good idea to be thorough. Here's a mockup of a submission given as a guide:

```
Java 2 Developer's Submission
Candidate: Cuppa, Joe
This JAR contains the following files:

server.jar - an executable JAR file that launches an RMI
   data server.

   Please read the notes on this application in the docs
   directory before executing.  This application will run
   with the command-line invocation:

   $ java -jar server.jar

client.jar - a Swing client that connects to the server.
   Run this application with the following command-line
   invocation:

   $ java -jar client.jar <server_name>

   See the notes on client.jar in the docs directory for
   more details.

converter.jar - a tool that takes the flat file record
   format given in the Exam and converts it to a file the
   server code can read.  Run this application with the
   following command-line invocation:

   $ java -jar converter.jar records.txt

docs/ - .html files for the source, and text notes on the
   design of these applications.

src/ - All .java files for new and modified code, as well
   as unmodified code that was provided with the exam.
```

suncertify/ - top-level directory package. All class
files are contained in the subdirectories db/ and
client/.

policy - sets the permissions for the RMI server. Do not
move this file.

records.txt - a flat file of records ready for conversion
using converter.jar. This file should reside in the
same directory as the application.

Using the JAR Tool

The jar binary is a bridge between two worlds: the syntax of the Unix tar command, and the file storage mechanics of PKZip. Because traditional tar doesn't offer compression but has always been free, this is a nice combination of virtues, at least for Unix users already familiar with the syntax. The jar command now represents a single-image compression utility for any platform that Java can run on, making it a nearly universal file format. Command options are listed in Table 9.2.

TABLE 9.2 *jar* Command Options

Option	Comment
-c | -x | -u	Create, extract from, update
-v	Verbose
-m	Named manifest file
-f	Named JAR file
-t	Create a table of contents
-0	Use zero (no) compression
-M	Do not create a manifest
-C *dir*	Find files in the *dir* directory

> **TIP** The jar command requires the manifest file (-m) and JAR file (-f) to appear on the command line in the same order as their respective option flags are declared.

A key selling point for the JAR format is its *manifest* specification. By providing certain tags in the manifest, you can signal a particular kind of usage or delivery. For example, there is a tag to specify whether a contained class file is a Java Bean. Other tags are used to "sign" the JAR for purposes of authentication and to assign it a control number used for version checking. Yet another tag supports a feature known as *package sealing*. With package sealing in place, the JAR itself mandates that all associated classes working with the JAR must be contained in it as a control against class-spoofing.

The tag we want to discuss allows any Java 2 interpreter to execute a `main` method within the JAR, without extracting the associated class file or even knowing its name. Furthermore, execution of the class is treated as though it resided in the current directory, so the syntax for adding command-line arguments is maintained. Here's a simple demonstration:

```
public class JARTest
{
  public static void main(String args[]) {
    System.out.println(args[0]);
  }
}
```

After compiling this code, write one line into a file called `manifest`:

```
Main-Class: JARTest
<empty line in the file here>
```

Include that file in the JAR image, and then execute the JAR using the runtime interpreter's `-jar` flag:

```
$ jar cfm test.jar manifest JARTest.class
$ java -jar test.jar Hello
Hello
$
```

Applying this technique to your deliverables keeps the structure of your submission clean and keeps the necessary files the examiner must handle to a minimum.

Preparation for the Follow-up Exam

Rather than attempt to mirror the exam questions, we created a list of questions that we hope will broaden your sense of what you should be prepared to discuss. Some of the discussion here will raise your awareness on points that, strictly speaking, aren't tested in the project assignment, but may provide an explicit way to justify a design choice or two that you, the developer, have intuitively grasped.

What Are the Choices for Data Structures?

Review the classes in `java.util` and consider using arrays where practical. The conventional wisdom is that the better you understand your data, the clearer the choices become for a type of storage. With the addition of the `Collections` framework to Java 2, however, switching container types to meet new requirements has become very simple. The `Collections` framework are described in Chapter 8, "The `java.lang` and `java.util` Packages." You can now move data from one kind of container to another with a minimum of conversion work. Knowing the benefits of each container type aids the selection process, but it's also important to know that such decisions can be changed more readily if necessary.

Each container type has its own most suitable usage. Arrays are fast, but once their length is set, they're fixed for the life of the program run. You can copy from one array to another with more room using `System.arraycopy()`, but if that turns out to be a common operation, a vector, which does the copying for you, is a tidier choice. Vectors will acquire memory space for more elements each time they reach capacity, but they don't trim themselves automatically; in a storage environment with high activity, vectors may require a lot of checking, and tuning for capacity and expansion may prove problematic.

Key-value structures like `HashMap` offer constant-time performance, meaning the time needed to add or access records doesn't scale along with the size of the table, assuming it is proportioned correctly. As long as operations against the table are predominantly simple ones, `HashMap`s perform well. Upon a nonkey search, however, you must typically iterate through the entire structure, which does take time proportional to the number of elements. A structure such as a linked list may take time up front to sort elements as they are added. This work greatly speeds up the time taken to iterate over the list. Presorting elements lets you select a small range of the list's contents in cases where the search follows the sorting criteria of the structure itself.

Although each container type has specific advantages, it may not always be clear that one is a better choice than another. In such cases, the best defense is to know the strengths of each type and justify your choice based on the features you find most useful for the task at hand. Simplicity is a reasonable justification too, provided you acknowledge that simplicity is important to you and the performance price you might have to pay is acceptable. Ease of maintenance is an even better reason in many situations.

Is Implementing *Runnable* Better Than Extending *Thread*?

Because threading is built into Java, you may be confused about the relationship between the `Thread` class and the `Runnable` interface. It's not uncommon to come across classes that extend

Thread and do nothing more than override the run() method. Compared to classes that merely implement Runnable and provide a code body for run(), these operations may seem synonymous in every important regard.

However, consider that you normally subclass to alter or specialize the function of a parent class. In cases where you extend JDK classes just to override a method or two, it's typically because the class is designed to be used that way (such as an exception or the Applet class). With respect to Thread, which merely houses a null implementation of the Runnable interface, there's no practical motivation to extend the class if all that's intended is to add run() code. It's just one method and, if no other behavior in Thread will be changed, it's not worth sacrificing the one opportunity you have to extend a parent class.

How Elaborate Should an Exception Class Structure Get?

It's possible to create as many shell exceptions as you want as a cheap and easy way to describe the variant conditions that represent nonroutine code execution for an application. It might be easy to infer from the cumbersome naming of certain JDK classes, such as ArrayIndexOutOfBoundsException, that naming is important enough to support, and that the expense of developer convenience is not too high a price to pay for it. Bearing in mind that some of these classes were never intended to be caught or managed by users—all exceptions that extend RuntimeException fall into this category—you have to take any emphasis on naming with a grain of salt. Yes, you want to know what an exception is about, and ideally you can get the idea from the name alone. A more substantive policy, however, might be to simply name unique exceptions when there is a potential need to catch them and write alternate code to execute when it occurs.

Provide new exceptions whenever the application should, under unusual conditions, inform the user, save current data, and offer alternate ways to continue or exit. Doing so helps to define exceptions by necessity rather than using them merely to spell out a problem through a class name. Also, consider the possibility that the exception class itself might add methods to enable context-specific processing, thus avoiding rewrites of the same catch code over several related classes.

How Many Ways Can You Set Up "Listener" Relationships? Which One Is Best?

Several patterns are already implemented in Java, including:

- Observer/Observable
- Event handling, as implemented in the AWT package
- "Model-delegate" (an MVC variant) in Swing, which is 50 percent event handling
- Beans-style change listeners, which are nothing more than a standardized set of event handlers

The proliferation of these patterns in Java reveals the increased use of objects that rely on event notification to monitor changes. Three of these listener schemes deal primarily with GUI components in one form or another, although Model-View-Controller as a pattern needn't be strictly defined as having a visual component. Views can just as easily be called filters when they offer a narrow perspective on the model at hand, and the filter can just as easily be an interpreter or parser. Whatever the case, several strategies are available to incorporate listening in one form or another; if you're persuaded that they work well enough that the graphic components won't hog all the fun, a little research will show you how these techniques work.

You may be inclined to experiment with *callbacks*, as they are often informally called, between the client and server in your project assignment. Assuming the assignment's main objectives don't prohibit doing so, it's easiest to experiment with the `Observer/Observable` interface/class pair in `java.util`. The class that implements `Observable` does most of the work, tying its inherited methods to state changes elsewhere in the class so that ultimately a call to its own `notifyObservers()` method is made. This method then calls `update()` in any class that implements `Observer` and has registered interest in the notifying `Observable`. However, this pattern has two knocks against it: the observed class must extend `Observable`, which may not be feasible if it must subclass something else; and the use of events and listeners is more widely accepted and accomplishes the same goal.

The event-handling model for the AWT and the change-listener format for Beans follow the same model as the `Observer/Observable` pattern. Swing, with its model-delegate structure, also takes advantage of the Beans specification by instituting change listeners and event-firing mechanisms as a way to bind changes in one part of a component's supporting tools to another. The nice part about the Beans model (which is essentially the AWT's) is that you don't have to create full-fledged Beans to take advantage of it. At the same time, the features that allow you to create modular components are easy enough to adopt that maintaining compatibility with Bean adaptation is usually a good idea. If there is no best way to establish listening between classes, there certainly seems to be a most popular one: the Beans model.

How Do I Know Which Layout Manager to Use?

Consider the type of behavior each layout manager supports, and consider the possibilities of mixing each with the behavior of different components. Then consider the additional permutations of nesting one container within another, each with its own layout manager. There are lots of variations, some of which ultimately produce the same effect. As far as the end user is concerned, whatever brings the GUI to its most effective presentation is suitable. However, although end-user satisfaction should be a developer goal, also remember that someone has to maintain the resulting code.

The only recommendation we can make is to offer all the required functionality in the most maintainable form possible for applications that may be in service a while. The overlap in behavior between one layout manager and another is often accounted for by the constrained situation in which a choice will be made. Border layouts are ideal where each set of components should occupy a fixed peripheral space and "serve" what's going on in the center. Flow layouts are best when each component should be laid out in the order it is specified and a single layout rule (such as "center everything") is sufficient. Grid layouts offer a quick "control console" feeling and automatic equal-weight distribution to every column and row. The Card layout is clearly different; it's useful for information that may stack well, but don't overlook the `JTabbedPane` in Swing, which gives the user control of the tabs. GridBag offers a great deal of flexibility, but its behavior is by far the most challenging of the five layout managers.

If the topmost layout strategy is unclear, one simple strategy is to build up to the containing frame. Components that share space or work together in some cohesive way will typically suggest by their function an appropriate layout scheme. As you place these groups in panels, it may make sense to combine two or more panels into another panel; nesting multiple containers is honorable. Once the major panels are assembled, it's very likely that one of two schemes will apply to the topmost container: Border or GridBag. GridBag, in a nutshell, allows you to vary components' dimensions by the rows and columns they reside in; if you have no need for this kind of flexibility, use Border.

Which Design Patterns Are Most Useful in This Kind of Project?

At the risk of sounding evasive, whichever design patterns help you get the job done are most useful. Although using design patterns competently to complete the project assignment will most likely lead to tighter code that an experienced programmer can readily appreciate, it's hard to say abstractly when to apply one. Using design patterns in a formal sense requires you to play around with them and work up your own practical uses for them. In much the same way that it's difficult to teach someone an application when they have no need for it, design patterns are far more useful when they can provide a solution for problems you already have in mind. If you know what they are, how they're commonly referred to, and how they solve specific problems, that is a good start. With some preparation and experience, it's more likely that articulating a specific objective may lead to a design pattern you know about and can apply to the situation.

Looking for a place to plug one probably won't help produce better code, but you can find plenty of opportunities just by reading some source in the JDK itself. `Observer/Observable` represents a class design pattern, as does MVC. Any time you come across a class with the term *factory* in its name, you're looking at a class built with that pattern in mind. Studying these classes along with a primer on design patterns will help you understand what's going on: Design patterns are simply solutions to very common problems in object-oriented programming.

That said, it's not necessarily true that formal schooling with design patterns is the only way to learn how to use them. For experienced programmers, many design patterns may seem to be generic articulations of code they've had in their toolboxes for years. Giving the patterns specific names simply makes it easier to talk about them; the proper application of design patterns in code makes them powerful.

Some knowledge of the formal conventions for design patterns may make it easier for you to discuss your programming rationale on the follow-up exam. A working knowledge of the patterns mentioned earlier will go a long way toward preparing you, because they are among the most prevalent patterns in the JDK. Look for signs of often-repeated words in class names: it's your best hint that a pattern is lurking underneath.

When Does It Make Sense to Use *protected* and *default* Scope?

Look for a compelling need to use either. Even though the project assignment may employ a package structure for the code provided, it's unlikely you'll be looking at a problem in choosing the best scope for a certain variable or method. Variables and methods that are protected are accessible only to subclasses and other classes sharing the same package. Members and variables that have no scope modifier are visible only to other package members. Subclasses outside the package do not have access to package-private resources, but subclasses inside the package do.

The value of these scopes is to allow direct access for "local" classes into important package resources, while blocking access to out-of-package programmers altogether, or blocking those who aren't extending the class in question. Typically, a package-private identifier is available within a package to allow some package-specific operations to take place more readily than they could through the normal public interface.

A good place to study the use of `protected` identifiers is the AWT, which includes a lot of class interrelations. You might want to begin investigating this for yourself in the `Component` class. Unless you intend to write something as complex as a windowing toolkit or similar package, chances are you won't have a real need for either scope. Good design starts with enforcing encapsulation wherever possible and breaking encapsulation (an evil) only when doing so allows a greater good to prevail. If it shouldn't be public, goes the general rule, make it private. If private seems restrictive, *keep* it private; resist the urge to open things up until a truly compelling need exists. If being private prevents related classes from doing their job without adding a lot of code, consider whether access outside the package would ever be warranted. If so, then use `protected`. Otherwise, choose `default` scope.

You should really challenge the nature of the question. Learning programmers want to know how best to use the tools they encounter, and so they ask questions in the form of the one that heads this section. The better question to ask is, "Why should I make all fields private?"

The first objective in developing new classes is to preserve encapsulation. A class is properly encapsulated when its data is available only through the class's public interface. When we say *interface* in this context, we mean the methods that permit access to the state of a class instance or object. Consider what happens to a class that uses a vector for internal storage and allows direct access to it, possibly in the name of greater performance. Along comes a better type of storage for the class developer's purpose. Now, if the developer wants to swap out the vector for this new type, all the subsequent code that relies on this class will break. If, instead, methods such as `getContainer()` and `setContainer()` are used to govern access to the data container, the developer is free to internally implement fields at will, leaving other programmers with a consistent, unchanging interface.

Encapsulation promotes maintenance. You can find several Java articles that demonstrate how much faster a field access is than a method call, but if you want to keep code maintenance simple, you'll acknowledge the difference and stick to proper encapsulation. A class can add methods to the interface without breaking its contract to existing users, and it can change the body of a method. As long as method signatures remain consistent, encapsulated classes provide the greatest protection to their users.

Why would you take a hit in performance, especially if your code seems to run unacceptably slowly? First, of course, you must determine whether method calls really are holding things up. Knowing that field accesses are faster than method calls is a dangerous bit of information if it's regarded in a vacuum. You must determine through profiling or other analysis where your cycles are being spent. Even if method calls prove to be your biggest expense, you still must consider whether breaking the public interface—a drastic step—is warranted. But it's a simple matter if access is initially more restrictive. You can simply change a private member to the appropriate scope and document this variance. If fields start out as public or protected, however, and you make them private, you'll break the public interface, and your users to date will have to address the consequences. Maintenance is easier if you begin with a conservative view of encapsulating fields.

In various portions of this guide, we've stated that you can't overestimate the importance of using interfaces to declare method calls when designing your application. Assuming you've been persuaded, you're also aware that an interface has no support for instance variables because an interface bears no relation to any one instance. The point of an interface is to separate design from the details of implementation. Once you've fixed on a specific field type and given access to other classes, you've anchored your design in a specific implementation. If you never need to change that specific field type, there's no problem. In this situation, you must admit that performance outweighs flexibility of design.

In short, keep fields private. If the application runs correctly but is too slow and performance is critical, consider allowing field access. If you can afford to wait, however, the best of all worlds is coming in the form of improved Virtual Machines (VMs), which include a just-in-time (JIT) compiler to execute code more quickly. Sun's HotSpot includes features such as the ability to "inline" simple accessor/mutator methods. From a design point of view, the long-term problem is creating an engine that runs with proper efficiency, rather than "tricking out" the design to achieve better performance by forsaking ease of maintenance.

Doesn't an Abstract Class Let the Developer Specify More Behavior Than an Interface?

If specific behavior is what you want, yes. The point of an interface, in one respect, is that it doesn't tie you down to much. Earlier in this chapter, we discussed the `run()` method in `Thread`, which is merely a null implementation of the `Runnable` interface. The fact is, `run()` has next to nothing to do with the `Thread` class. You can implement `run()` in any class you want. You can also call any object's `run()` method directly from another thread; bypassing `Thread.start()` simply means that you don't set this process off on its own execution context. In other words, nothing about the `run()` method by itself carries threaded behavior with it; it's just a hook, a method that when used as directed taps into the VM's multithreaded engine. If you don't honor the proper form for using the `run()` method, it's just a name. An abstract class, on the other hand, has at least some concrete behavior, some real definition.

One view of the abstract class is that it should contain the code that will be common to every subclass, but you should leave abstract those methods that rely on a local implementation to fulfill its commitments to other implemented methods in that class. If you have an abstract class `Currency`, for example, all methods pertaining to exchange for goods or services may be implemented. The methods that describe the local currency, however, which are called by the methods that describe exchange, still must be implemented locally for the class to be useful. This is the idea behind classes like the AWT's `Container` and `Component`, which define the vast majority of AWT operation but leave some important methods to be defined by actual components. Outside of toolkit development, abstract classes can also be used as convenience classes to capture information that interfaces cannot—implementations of nonpublic methods, constructors, overrides of inherited methods, for example—and could be useful as a kind of concrete reference for an intended subset of extending classes.

But this type of use should not necessarily be construed as affording the kind of control that interfaces lack. The true power of interfaces lies in remaining as abstract as possible. Consider this:

```
public interface Payment {
  public Double getAmount();
  public Account getAccountInfo();
}
public interface Account {
  public Double getBalance();
  public String getName();
}
public interface Payable {
  public Account deductPayment(Payment pmtOut);
}
public interface Receivable {
  public Account addPayment(Payment pmtIn);
}
```

With three exceptions, these preliminary interfaces rely completely on abstract definitions to describe a rudimentary ledger-entry system. If you need to add behavior as you further define the details, all you have to do is add the name of that method to the interface list, and you will have broken no code and set the stage to describe relationships for the classes that implement these interfaces. You will have also begun declaring their responsibilities for participating in this framework appropriately in a minimum of time. In this manner, you could go through a couple of design passes without ever worrying about updating concrete code as you make potentially sweeping changes.

Abstract classes are convenient for conveying ideas that are more concrete than design-oriented. Interfaces, by contrast, keep details from bogging down the design effort. Chances are, an interface that seems to do nothing but name methods simply hasn't been developed aggressively enough. Some schools of thought go so far as to propose that *every* parameter and return type in a method be represented by an interface, both for maximum flexibility and to preserve the precious single opportunity each class has to inherit from another.

Summary

The follow-up exam determines whether candidates can demonstrate their command of Java's core libraries and submitted code well enough to defend it in a series of essay questions. Candidates might be expected to offer several alternatives to a problem that is posed generally and to state the various attractions and drawbacks of each alternative. They might then be asked to correlate the previous question to a situation in the exam itself, detail how the problem was solved, and explain why they chose that approach.

The best preparation for this kind of exam is to have a reasonably broad overview of how the project assignment might be solved, as well as a particular interest in completing it in a manner that suits the candidate's style. The easiest way to answer subjective questions is to stick to your natural inclination for problem solving. In the context of an exam like this, there are wrong factual answers; it would be bad to conclude that synchronized methods are faster than synchronized blocks, or that arrays take up more memory than vectors. But in justifying an approach that has proven to work, the remaining element is whether the code as it appears on paper corresponds to the candidate's accounting for it, and whether its implementation remains consistent with their judgment.

Exam Essentials

Remember that the Developer's Exam is practical rather than objective. The test challenges your ability to use Java in conjunction with the skills, experience, and discipline required of a competent programmer.

The Developer's Certification Exam has two parts: a project assignment and a follow-up exam. The assignment describes a programming task that starts with some code supplied with the project description; you are then asked to finish the intended project. The follow-up exam, which takes place in a timed and proctored test facility, asks you to justify the choices you made when you wrote the code for the assignment.

Write code that adheres to standard naming conventions, uses standard design patterns, and is readable. You want the grader to be able to quickly and easily read your code. Use standard conventions wherever possible.

Key Terms

Before you take the exam, be certain you are familiar with the following terms:

callbacks	interface
cascading style sheet	manifest
default package	package sealing

Review Questions

1. How long do you have to complete the programming assignment once you've downloaded it?
   A. One day
   B. One week
   C. One month
   D. One year
   E. There is no time limit for the submission of the programming assignment.

2. How long do you have to take the follow-up exam once your test starts at the testing facility?
   A. One hour
   B. One and a half hours
   C. Two hours
   D. Three hours

3. Which of the following topics is not covered in the Developer's Exam?
   A. RMI
   B. Packages
   C. Threads
   D. JDBC

4. Which of the following is not required in your upload of the programming assignment?
   A. All compiled class code
   B. HTML documentation on all source code
   C. A README file
   D. A reference manual for how to install and use your code.

5. What are the three principal components of the application software that comprises the programming assignment?
   A. A front-end GUI, a back-end database server, and a method of connecting the front end to the back end.
   B. A front-end application portal, a back-end database server, and a method of connecting the front-end to the back-end.
   C. A front-end command-line interface, a back-end database server, and a method of connecting the front-end to the back-end.
   D. A front-end GUI, a middle-tier using Enterprise Java Beans, and a back-end database server.

Answers to Review Questions

1. E. You don't have a time limit for completing the assignment. However, it is recommended you finish the project and take the follow-up exam in as short a time as possible so that the code is fresh in your mind when you have to describe and defend it.

2. B. Even though the programming assignment has no time limit, the follow-up exam does.

3. D. The programming assignment may ask you to implement some sort of backend database server, but you will not use an industrial database (for example, Oracle). Therefore, there is no need for you to use JDBC to connect to it.

4. D. Any information that is required for the user to determine how to compile, install, or use the software should be documented in the README file.

5. A. The programming assignment does not require writing an application portal or a command-line interface, nor does it required using Enterprise Java Beans.

Chapter 10
Creating the User Interface with Swing

Lots of programmers who focus on writing business applications like to write the user interface first. The simple fact is that most people can absorb far more information in less time from a well-designed picture than they can from a well-written technical document. End users, particularly those who are removed from the process of programming, usually see a program's effectiveness in the form of the interaction it offers.

The GUI doesn't mean much, of course, unless it helps get the work done. Nor does it make sense to write application logic based on how the presentation will be structured. Java's Swing library addresses this issue by decoupling the responsibilities of data presentation and manipulation into two different class groups. One outcome is that the data model, once developed, places no real constraints on the potential views of it, and vice versa. Because the cohesion between data and graphic elements has already been spelled out, development of the GUI in Swing could begin with either part or progress in parallel in a team environment, without generating any fundamental concern for bringing the two together.

Another beauty of Swing is that this fundamental design pattern, often described as being loosely based on Model-View-Controller (MVC), is repeated throughout the library. We'll discuss the MVC design pattern in Chapter 13, "Connecting Client and Server." Don't worry about a comprehensive class review; exhaustive treatments of Swing are available elsewhere. We will focus instead on defining the GUI requirements and describing how to build Swing components. Once you have the basics down, you can reference the Swing library as necessary and absorb the details you need to develop the client you want.

Assuming you'll have to build from the ground up, we'll address a few points that will assist you in writing your GUI and defending it on the follow-up exam:

- Defining the GUI's requirements
- Common Swing methods
- Basic Swing components
- How to build a `JTable`
- How to build a `JTree`
- JMenus and actions
- Panes

Defining the GUI's Requirements

There's an even better tool for modeling a graphical user interface than a drag-and-drop code builder: pencil and paper. The single best recommendation we can make on designing your program's appearance is to draw what you'd like to see on the screen. You can create a sketch for one or two GUI layouts in the time it takes your computer to boot, and a sketch is likely to capture more of your requirements and create less of a distraction than finding the proper widget in a draw program (unless, of course, you are already expert with one). Because there is usually less investment in designing on paper, it's easier to throw away bad ideas (one of the more important design principles we know). Unless you already have the digital art skills or an existing template for the kind of display you want, a legible drawing makes a very reasonable initial reference document.

Here's a simple, four-step plan:

1. Identify needed components.
2. Sketch the GUI and a resizing.
3. Isolate regions of behavior.
4. Choose layout managers.

Identifying Needed Components

However austere the AWT's list of components might seem, it does have the advantage of economically describing the graphic objects in use on the most popular windowing systems today—Motif, Windows, and MacOS. It's therefore quite simple for virtually all GUI developers to express basic visual ideas in those terms: buttons for actions, check boxes for toggles, lists for specified choices, text fields for arbitrary input, and so on.

It can be difficult, having identified the needed pieces, to verbalize how they should lie on the page and how they should respond to a window resizing. The menu belongs at the top. Generally speaking, if there is a primary display area—whether graphic, tabular, or document oriented in presentation—you should devote any extra available space to it on a resize. Beyond those two principles, you need more information about what your application is. Assume for the sake of an illustration that you want to build a mail client in Java, and your first design review will concern the visual layout for a large number of departmental users. You know you will want to display a directory structure for sorting stored mail. Users will expect a table or list element to show mail items in the current directory, a text display for the current item being read, and a status area for updates on the client's background actions—downloading new messages, signaling new mail, and so forth.

Sketching the GUI

In the example in Figure 10.1, we profile the appearance of a typical mail client. The interface requires an area where you can review your directory tree of sorted mail in folders, which we placed to the left. You also need an area at the bottom of the frame for displaying status messages on the client's current attempt to send or retrieve mail. A dynamic display area for the list of pending incoming mail is located to the right of the tree structure and on top of another dynamic area that displays the current mail item. The detailed list of pending mail should be laid out by column with the column names in a button. We expect that experienced users will know to click a column name and infer from the results that a sort has taken place. As a provision for user preferences, we also want to allow the column size to be modified by dragging the column button's border.

FIGURE 10.1   Mail client window

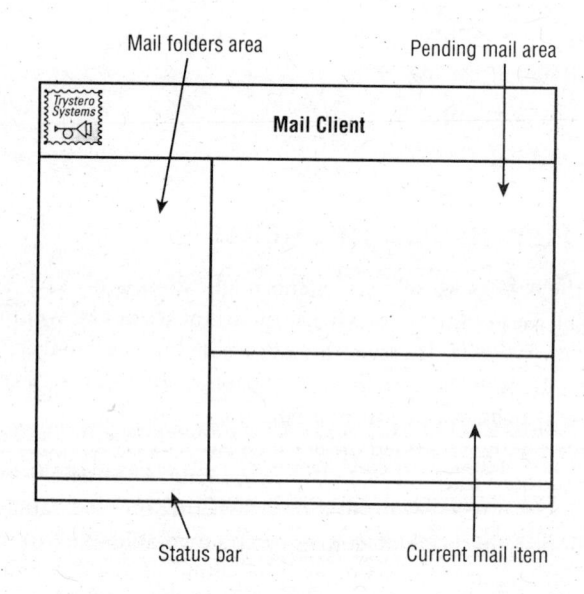

To get these ideas on paper, we sketched a diagram with a menu bar on top, a flush-left panel with a tree-like figure drawn in, and a bottom bar with some sample text. The dynamic space we split in two regions, showing multiple-column support for the pending mail list but a blank border area for the current mail item: we split this area into equal parts so that a resize will better demonstrate who is acquiring the new space and in which direction.

Figure 10.2 shows the intended effect of the resize. In the example, we wanted the mail item currently being read to assume as much available area as it could, on the presumption that the user resizes the window to get as much text to show as possible. Although some users may in fact want a larger font for status messages or a dynamic font for the menu, we chose not to tie such preferences to the default behavior of dragging a window corner.

FIGURE 10.2 Mail client window resized

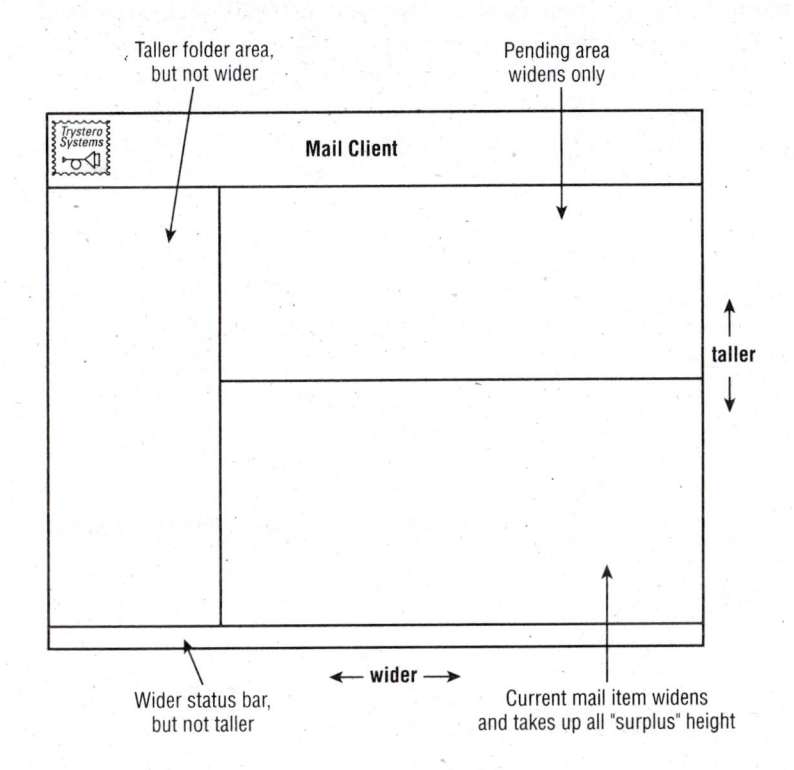

Figure shows a Mail Client window layout with annotations:
- Taller folder area, but not wider
- Pending area widens only
- taller (vertical arrow on right)
- wider (horizontal arrow at bottom)
- Wider status bar, but not taller
- Current mail item widens and takes up all "surplus" height

Along the horizontal axis, we want the bottom section to allow the status message area to use as much space as available, but without usurping the minimum space needed by the small icons. In the menu, we followed the convention that the Help or About menu list appears flush right on the frame (the menu components are not illustrated in Figure 10.2). The displays of both the current mail item and the pending mail list could grow to the right but won't impinge on the tree (folders) view. Along the vertical axis, the tree area could take all the space the menu and status bars will allow. In the display area, the intention is to allow the current mail item view to resize as needed; the pending mail list will, however, remain fixed.

Isolating Regions of Behavior

The description of the behavior shown in the figures, combined with your knowledge of the AWT layout managers, should already have tipped you off to some appropriate layout choices. There is, of course, no single answer or "right" choice to make for the entire screen. Any reasonably sophisticated interface requires multiple layout managers and panels to contain the management behavior to its prescribed area, and there is no one formula for ordering or nesting those panels to get the desired effect. Yet neither is there a completely neutral way to describe the behavior you want. It probably wasn't hard to tell we were already thinking in terms of

BorderLayout when we wrote the earlier description, particularly given our attempt to avoid saying "north," "south," "center," and so on. And this result is, in fact, exactly what you should expect: if you can articulate the screen behavior you want, the isolation of one region from the next and the tool needed to achieve the intent should be virtually self-evident.

This mail client breaks down very cleanly into the geographical areas provided by the Border layout manager—the default management scheme for an AWT frame—or Swing frame or window. The south will contain a status bar and small icons, and the tree will go in the west, leaving the center with the two dynamic areas. The center and south need a little more work to negotiate space allocation among the contained elements. In the south, the message bar and icons can first be contained by a panel. The panel, which is then added to the south, can adopt its own Border layout (instead of its default Flow layout), putting the message element in the panel's center and the icons in the east. Putting the icons in the east ensures that the icons get as much horizontal space as they require, and the center grabs all remaining space for messages. In the center, we added another panel with a Border layout manager, putting the mail list in its north and mail item in the center.

The west can hold the tree you want without further help, but adding a panel first and then adding the tree to the panel is not a bad idea. It is one way of leaving options open to modifying that area of the border scheme rather than just the contained component itself. Getting in the habit of composing graphic areas this way, so that they can be added to a larger component-container frame and hooked in—we're whispering a loose definition for a Java Bean here—is an honorable way to build task-specific, reusable components. As we're about to discuss, however, Swing components already do that work for us.

Choosing Layout Managers

When you do come across limitations in the layout model, it's not a time to worry. The default layout managers, along with Grid, are widely applicable to several visual design objectives and are relatively simple to use. Whether they will suffice to handle a particular requirement well is a good first question to ask. In most cases, you should probably consider several alternative layout schemes to ensure that you are choosing a simple approach that provides enough flexibility for some foreseeable changes. It's nice to have choices for future improvements, but there is also a limit to how much versatility is a benefit. For example, if a programmer is required to survey a variety of open-ended alternatives that could have just as easily been left static, the benefit of flexibility may be wiped out by the cost of too many subtle decisions.

Layout management is covered in detail in Chapter 11, "Layout Managers."

Common Swing Methods

Some properties are common to nearly all component types. These include size, location, foreground and background color, font, and enabled state. The methods that support these properties are described in the following sections. AWT programmers will recognize these methods from the java.awt.Component class, because the Swing components inherit from java.awt.Component.

getSize() and *setSize()*

The getSize() method returns the size of a component. The return type is Dimension, which has public data members height and width whose units are pixels.

The setSize() method takes two int arguments: width and height; an overloaded form takes a single Dimension object. If you have tried calling this method, you know that doing so is usually futile. A layout manager generally overrides the size and position you attempt to give a component. In fact, the setSize() method exists mostly for the use of layout managers. The major exceptions to this rule are the JFrame and JDialog classes, which are not under the thumb of a layout manager and are perfectly willing to have you set their size or bounds.

getLocation() and *setLocation()*

These methods access and set the location of a component in pixel units relative to the top-left corner of the component. The return type of getLocation() is Point. The setLocation() method's argument list requires either width and height ints or a single Point object.

Calling setLocation() is like calling setSize(): usually a layout manager overrides the location you try to set, but you can always set the location of a JFrame or JDialog.

setForeground() and *setBackground()*

These methods set a component's foreground and background color. The argument is an instance of java.awt.Color. The foreground color is used for rendering the component's decorations and text label (if the component uses any text). The background color is used for rendering the component's background.

setFont()

The setFont() method dictates which font a component will use for rendering any text it might display. The setFont() method takes one argument of type Font whose constructor takes three arguments: a font family, a style, and a size. The family is a string. Different platforms offer different fonts, but you can always count on Serif (a Times-Roman font), SansSerif (a Helvetica font), and Monospaced (a fixed-width Courier font). The style may be Font.PLAIN, Font.BOLD, Font.ITALIC, or the bitwise combination Font.BOLD|Font.ITALIC. The size argument defines the point size of the font.

setEnabled()

The setEnabled() method determines whether a component may respond to user input. The method takes a single boolean argument. A disabled component changes its appearance to a slightly grayed-out look. A component should be disabled if the application is in a state that cannot accept input from the component.

Disabling is preferable to the two commonly seen alternatives:

- Leave the component enabled. When the user uses the component, display some sort of "unavailable" message.
- Remove unusable components from the screen until they become usable, thus creating a visually unstable control area.

Judicious use of `setEnabled()` calls helps create a GUI that clearly reflects the application's state to the user.

Basic Swing Components

The Swing component classes can be found in the `javax.swing` package. The component class names all begin with the letter "J". The remainder of the class name is the name of the component, with each word starting with a capital letter. For example, a scroll bar is represented by the `javax.swing.JScrollBar` class.

Swing components cannot be combined with AWT components. However, certain non-component AWT classes are essential to Swing. All Swing components are subclasses of `java.awt.Container`, and most of them emit events from the `java.awt.event` package. Additionally, all the AWT layout managers work perfectly well with Swing components.

One way to approach the daunting number of components is to divide them into three categories:

- Container components
- Ordinary components
- Menu components

Before discussing these categories, we will look at some methods that are common to all the component classes, and then we will review events.

Container Components

Container components are components that can contain other components (including other containers). Containers use layout managers to determine the size and position of their child components. The code examples in this chapter all use the very basic `FlowLayout` manager. If you are unfamiliar with this class, for now just be aware that it arranges contained components in an evenly spaced row.

The container components that we will cover here are

- `JFrame`
- `JPanel`

JFrame

A JFrame is an independent window that can be moved around on the screen independently of any other GUI windows. Any application that requires a GUI must use one or more frames to contain the desired components. The following code displays an empty JFrame:

```
1. import javax.swing.*;
2.
3. public class FrameDemo {
4.   public static void main(String[] args) {
5.     JFrame f = new JFrame("Frame Demo");
6.     f.setSize(350, 250);
7.     f.setVisible(true);
8.   }
9. }
```

Line 5 demonstrates a constructor whose argument is a string that is to appear in the frame's banner. Line 6 is necessary because a newly constructed JFrame has zero width and zero height and must be given a nonzero size before it can be seen. You can set the size explicitly, as in line 6, or you can call the pack() method, which sizes the frame to fit the preferred sizes and layouts of its contained components. Line 7 is necessary because a newly constructed JFrame is not visible on the screen. If, at some point, you want to remove a visible frame from the screen, you can call setVisible(false).

Figure 10.3 shows the frame created by this application.

FIGURE 10.3   A simple, empty JFrame

Of course, an empty frame is not very useful. Frames are intended to be populated with child components. Readers familiar with Java's AWT know that the AWT frame implementation (the java.awt.Frame class) is a container to which child components can be directly added. The JFrame class is different in that it is not a container. You access the container portion of the frame by calling the JFrame's getContentPane() method. The following application displays a frame whose content pane contains three buttons. (In order to demonstrate the content pane, we have to get a bit ahead of ourselves by using a layout manager and the JButton class. We will explain these soon.)

```
1.  import java.awt.*;
2.  import javax.swing.*;
3.
4.  public class ContentDemo {
5.    public static void main(String[] args) {
6.      JFrame f = new JFrame("Content Pane Demo");
7.      f.setSize(350, 250);
8.      Container cont = f.getContentPane();
9.      cont.setLayout(new FlowLayout());
10.     for (int i=1; i<=3; i++)
11.       cont.add(new JButton("Button #" + i));
12.     f.setVisible(true);
13.   }
14. }
```

Note line 9, which sets a layout manager for the content pane rather than for the frame, and line 11, which adds buttons to the content pane rather than to the frame. Figure 10.4 shows the result of running this application.

FIGURE 10.4 Using a JFrame's content pane

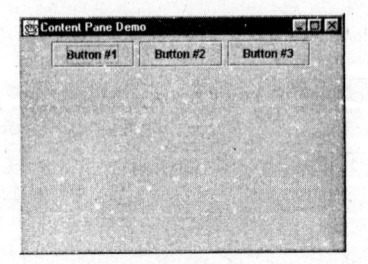

JFrame emits Window events to notify listeners when the frame iconifies, de-iconifies, is first displayed, and so on. Clicking a frame's "close" button (the X button in the upper-right corner on a Windows platform) does not automatically cause the frame to close. Instead, the click invokes the windowClosing() method to all of the frame's Window listeners. One listener must explicitly remove the frame from the screen; otherwise the user's click will have no effect.

JPanel

A JPanel is a blank rectangular component that can contain other components. Each panel uses a layout manager to determine the position and size of its child components. The following application adds two panels to a frame. Each panel contains three buttons. For better visibility, the upper panel is light gray and the lower panel is white. The application uses a Grid layout manager, which is covered in detail in the next chapter:

```java
import java.awt.*;
import javax.swing.*;
public class PanelDemo {
  public static void main(String[] args) {
    JFrame f = new JFrame("Content Pane Demo");
    f.setSize(350, 250);
    Container cont = f.getContentPane();
    cont.setLayout(new GridLayout(2,1));
    for (int i=0; i<2; i++) {
      JPanel pan = new JPanel();
      pan.setBackground(i==0 ? Color.lightGray : Color.white);
      for (int j=0; j<3; j++)
        pan.add(new JButton("Button"));
      cont.add(pan);
    }
    f.setVisible(true);
  }
}
```

Figure 10.5 shows this application's frame.

FIGURE 10.5 JPanel example

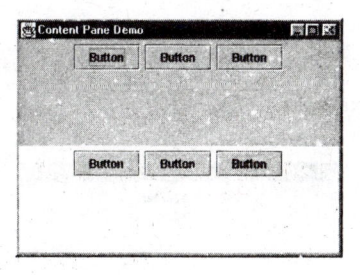

JPanels do not emit any important events.

Ordinary Components

In this section, we'll discuss eight *ordinary components*. They are ordinary in the sense that they are the components in which the user directly inputs data, in contrast to containers. We will review the following component types:

- JLabel
- JButton

Chapter 10 · Creating the User Interface with Swing

- JCheckBox
- JRadioButton
- JScrollBar
- JTextField
- JTextArea
- JComboBox

JLabel

The simplest component type is the JLabel, which displays a single line of text and/or an image. JLabels do not respond to user input and do not emit events. The following application displays a label in a frame, as shown in Figure 10.6.

```
import java.awt.*;
import javax.swing.*;

public class LabelDemo {
  public static void main(String[] args) {
    JFrame f = new JFrame("Label Demo");
    f.setSize(350, 250);
    Container cont = f.getContentPane();
    cont.setLayout(new FlowLayout());
    cont.add(new Label("This is a JLabel"));
    f.setVisible(true);
  }
}
```

FIGURE 10.6 JLabel example

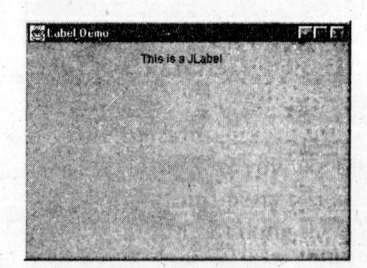

JButton

The JButton class implements a simple pushbutton. The button can display a text label, an icon, or both. When the user clicks the button, Action events are sent to all registered Action listeners.

The following application builds a frame that contains two buttons:

```java
import java.awt.*;
import java.awt.event.*;
import javax.swing.*;

public class ButtonDemo extends JFrame {
  private JButton helloBtn, goodbyeBtn;

  public static void main(String[] args) {
    (new ButtonDemo()).setVisible(true);
  }

  ButtonDemo() {
    super("Button Demo");
    setSize(350, 250);
    Container cont = getContentPane();
    cont.setLayout(new FlowLayout());
    helloBtn = new JButton("Hello");
    goodbyeBtn = new JButton("Goodbye");
    cont.add(helloBtn);
    cont.add(goodbyeBtn);
    ButtonListener listener = new ButtonListener();
    helloBtn.addActionListener(listener);
    goodbyeBtn.addActionListener(listener);
  }

  class ButtonListener implements ActionListener {
    public void actionPerformed(ActionEvent e) {
      if (e.getSource() == helloBtn)       // Which
        System.out.println("Hello");       // button
      else                                  // was
        System.out.println("Goodbye");     // pushed?
    }
  }
}
```

JButtons send Action events. The ActionListener interface contains only one method: public void actionPerformed(ActionEvent). This example creates a single Action listener and registers it with each of two buttons. Note the convenience of defining ButtonListener as an inner class. Its functionality is isolated, but it can still access the helloBtn private variable of the creating instance of the enclosing class. This makes it easy for the listener to determine which button was pressed.

Figure 10.7 shows the output of this application.

FIGURE 10.7 JButton example

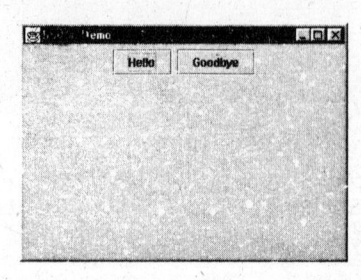

JCheckBox

The JCheckBox class implements a check box that can be selected and deselected. The following code creates a frame that contains two check boxes:

```
import java.awt.*;
import javax.swing.*;

public class CheckBoxDemo {
  public static void main(String[] args) {
    JFrame frame = new JFrame("CheckBox Demo");
    frame.setSize(350, 250);
    Container cont = frame.getContentPane();
    cont.setLayout(new FlowLayout());
    cont.add(new JCheckBox("Charge my acct"));
    cont.add(new JCheckBox("Gift wrap"));
    cont.add(new JButton("Submit"));
    frame.setVisible(true);
  }
}
```

This application does not register any listeners with the check boxes, even though the JCheckBox class emits Action and Item events; it is usually unnecessary or inappropriate to catch check-box events. Usually check boxes are used to input a number of binary options, which are later submitted to the application using a button. The example application shows two check boxes that might appear in the GUI for any online shopping application. The user decides whether to charge the order to an account and whether the order should be gift wrapped. After these decisions have been made, the user clicks the Submit button to indicate that the application should process the order. In general, the actionPerformed() method of some button will read the state of a GUI's check boxes.

Figure 10.8 shows the GUI built by this application.

FIGURE 10.8 JCheckBox example

JRadioButton

Radio buttons are typically used in groups to present exclusive selection. The name comes from the station buttons of older car radios: at any moment, exactly one button is pushed in, and pushing in a new button causes the old button to pop out. The `JRadioButton` class is generally used with the `ButtonGroup` class, which has an `add(AbstractButton)` method. When a radio button is selected, any other button in the same button group is automatically deselected.

The following application creates three radio buttons:

```
1.  import java.awt.*;
2.  import javax.swing.*;
3.
4.  public class RadioDemo {
5.
6.    public static void main(String[] args) {
7.      JFrame frame = new JFrame("Radio Demo");
8.      frame.setSize(350, 250);
9.      Container cont = frame.getContentPane();
10.     cont.setLayout(new FlowLayout());
11.     ButtonGroup btnGroup = new ButtonGroup();
12.     JRadioButton rbtn = new JRadioButton("Rare", true);
13.     btnGroup.add(rbtn);
14.     cont.add(rbtn);
15.     rbtn = new JRadioButton("Medium");
16.     btnGroup.add(rbtn);
17.     cont.add(rbtn);
18.     rbtn = new JRadioButton("Well Done");
19.     btnGroup.add(rbtn);
20.     cont.add(rbtn);
```

```
21.      frame.setVisible(true);
22.   }
23. }
```

Figure 10.9 shows this application's GUI. Because the three radio buttons are added to a button group (lines 13, 16, and 19), they exhibit radio behavior: Selecting one of them causes the previously selected one to become deselected.

FIGURE 10.9   JRadioButton example

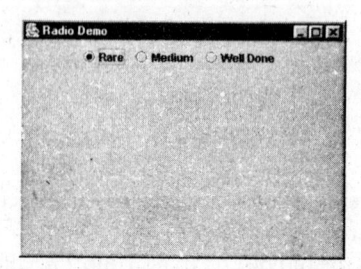

Radio buttons, like check boxes, can send `Action` and `Item` events. However, as with check boxes, listening for these events is generally not appropriate. A group of radio buttons is often found near an Apply button; the appropriate approach is to read the state of the radio buttons when the user clicks Apply.

JScrollBar

A `JScrollBar` is a component that lets the user enter an adjustable pseudo-analog value. Scroll bars can be oriented horizontally or vertically; the constants `JScrollBar.HORIZONTAL` and `JScrollBar.VERTICAL` can be passed into various constructor forms to determine orientation.

The following application creates one horizontal scroll bar. The simple Flow layout manager that we have used so far in this chapter does not do a very good job of displaying scroll bars, so we will use the more sophisticated Border layout manager. If you are not familiar with it, stay tuned until Chapter 11:

```
import java.awt.*;
import java.awt.event.*;
import javax.swing.*;

public class ScrollBarDemo extends JFrame {
  public static void main(String[] args) {
    (new ScrollBarDemo()).setVisible(true);
  }
  ScrollBarDemo() {
    super("Scroll Bar Demo");
```

```
    setSize(350, 250);
    Container cont = getContentPane();
    JScrollBar sbar = new JScrollBar(JScrollBar.HORIZONTAL);
    cont.add(sbar, BorderLayout.NORTH);
    BarListener listener = new BarListener();
    sbar.addAdjustmentListener(listener);
  }

  class BarListener implements AdjustmentListener {
    public void adjustmentValueChanged(AdjustmentEvent e) {
      System.out.println("Val = " + e.getValue());
    }
  }
}
```

Scroll bars send `Adjustment` events to registered `Adjustment` listeners. In this example, the listener is an instance of the `BarListener` inner class.

The `ScrollBarDemo` application produces the GUI shown in Figure 10.10.

FIGURE 10.10 JScrollBar example

JTextField and *JTextArea*

The `JTextField` and `JTextArea` components support single-line and multiline text entry. Both classes extend `javax.swing.text.JTextComponent`, which provides methods for accessing and modifying the component's text. The API page for `JTextComponent` includes a good description of text functionality.

Both `JTextField` and `JTextArea` send Key events when they receive keyboard input. Additionally, `JTextField` sends Action events when the user presses Enter. The following application contains one of each component; the `JTextArea` displays information about events in the `JTextField`. Once again, the Flow layout manager is inappropriate for the components we want to demonstrate, so we use a Border layout manager:

```
import java.awt.*;
import java.awt.event.*;
```

Chapter 10 · Creating the User Interface with Swing

```
import javax.swing.*;

public class TextDemo extends JFrame
  implements ActionListener, KeyListener {
  private JTextField    field;
  private JTextArea     area;
  public static void main(String[] args) {
    (new TextDemo()).setVisible(true);
  }

  TextDemo()
    super("TextDemo");
    setSize(350, 250);
    Container cont = getContentPane();
    field = new JTextField("Type here");
    field.addKeyListener(this);
    field.addActionListener(this);
    cont.add(field, BorderLayout.NORTH);
    area = new JTextArea();
    cont.add(area, BorderLayout.CENTER);
  }

  public void keyPressed(KeyEvent e)  { }
  public void keyReleased(KeyEvent e) { }
  public void keyTyped(KeyEvent e) {
    area.append("KEY: " + e.getKeyChar() + '

  }

  public void actionPerformed(ActionEvent e) {
    area.append("ACTION: " + field.getText() + '

  }
}
```

Figure 10.11 shows this application's frame after several keystrokes have been typed into the JTextField.

FIGURE 10.11 JTextField and JTextArea example

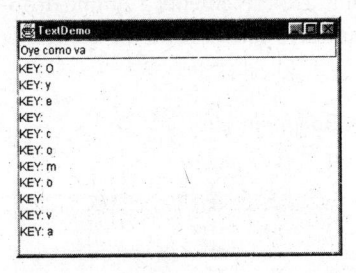

```
TextDemo
Oye como va
KEY: O
KEY: y
KEY: e
KEY:
KEY: c
KEY: o
KEY: m
KEY: o
KEY:
KEY: v
KEY: a
```

JComboBox

The JComboBox component combines the functionality of a text field and a drop-down list. With a JComboBox, you can present users with a preset list of options while giving them the alternative of entering an option that does not appear on the list. This component emits Action events when the user presses the Enter key and Item events when the user selects a preset item.

The following application displays a simple JComboBox:

```
1.  import java.awt.*;
2.  import javax.swing.*;
3.
4.  public class ComboDemo extends JFrame {
5.    public static void main(String[] args) {
6.      (new ComboDemo()).setVisible(true);
7.    }
8.
9.    ComboDemo() {
10.     super("ComboDemo");
11.     setSize(350, 250);
12.     Container cont = getContentPane();
13.     cont.setLayout(new FlowLayout());
14.     String[] initialVals = {"Dragon", "Ghost", "Unicorn"};
15.     JComboBox combo = new JComboBox(initialVals);
16.     combo.setEditable(true);
17.     cont.add(combo);
18.   }
19. }
```

Note line 16, which calls `setEditable()` on the combo box. Without this call, the component does not support typing but just implements a simple drop-down list. Figure 10.12 shows this application's GUI. Note that the figure shows the value "Centaur", which has been typed in by the user.

FIGURE 10.12   JComboBox example

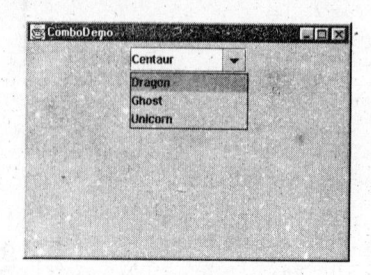

Menu Components

Menu components allow the programmer to organize Swing components in menus instead of placing all the components in the user's view. The `JMenuBar` component implements a menu bar that occupies the top portion of a `JFrame` and can contain drop-down menus. To insert a `JMenuBar` into a `JFrame`, call `setJMenuBar(theMenuBar)` on the `JFrame`.

To populate a menu bar, construct a number of instances of `JMenu` and install them in the menu bar by calling `theMenuBar.add(theMenu)`. The `JMenu` constructor takes as an argument the string that will appear on the menu bar.

The menus in a menu bar must themselves be populated with menu items. The most common type of menu item is the `JMenuItem`, which is a simple text item. You can also add separators, check boxes, radio buttons, and submenus to a menu. If you want check boxes or radio buttons, however, don't use `JCheckBox` or `JRadioButton`—instead use the `JCheckBoxMenuItem` and `JRadioButtonMenuItem` classes.

The following application creates two menus, populates them, and installs them into a menu bar. The second menu contains a plain menu item, a separator, a check box item, two radio items, and a submenu:

```
1. import java.awt.*;
2. import javax.swing.*;
3.
4. public class MenuDemo {
5.
```

```java
6.   public static void main(String[] args) {
7.       JFrame frame = new JFrame("Menu");
8.
9.       JMenuBar mbar = new JMenuBar();            // Create menu bar
10.
11.      JMenu fileMenu = new JMenu("File");        // Create file menu
12.      fileMenu.add(new JMenuItem("New"));
13.      fileMenu.add(new JMenuItem("Exit"));
14.      mbar.add(fileMenu);
15.
16.      JMenu sampleMenu = new JMenu("Sample");    // Create sample menu
17.      sampleMenu.add(new JMenuItem("Plain"));
18.      sampleMenu.insertSeparator(1);
19.      sampleMenu.add(new JCheckBoxMenuItem("Check"));
20.      ButtonGroup group = new ButtonGroup();
21.      JRadioButtonMenuItem radioMI;
22.      for (int i=0; i<2; i++) {
23.          radioMI = new JRadioButtonMenuItem("Radio" + i);
24.          group.add(radioMI);
25.          sampleMenu.add(radioMI);
26.      }
27.      JMenu subMenu = new JMenu("SubOptions");
28.      subMenu.add(new JMenuItem("AAA"));
29.      subMenu.add(new JMenuItem("BBB"));
30.      subMenu.add(new JMenuItem("CCC"));
31.      sampleMenu.add(subMenu);
32.      mbar.add(sampleMenu);
33.
34.      frame.setJMenuBar(mbar);                   // Install menu bar
35.      frame.setSize(350, 250);
36.      frame.setVisible(true);
37.  }
38. }
```

Note the ButtonGroup that is created at line 20. This class can accommodate both radio buttons and radio button menu items.

Figure 10.13 shows this application's GUI.

FIGURE 10.13 Menu example

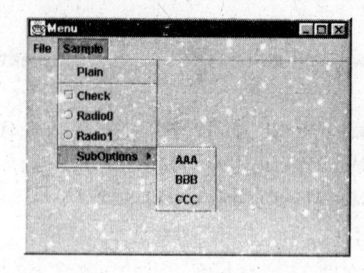

Building a *JTable*

Swing seems to lend itself to writing a lot of "glue" code. There is a temptation to take advantage of the library as it is, combine the available components as needed, and rely on the fact that the important hookups between models and views have been done for you.

A JTable, for example, has three core internal models, dealing with its data structure (TableModel), the state of its column order and the column members (TableColumnModel), and list selection behavior (ListSelectionModel). A JTable updates its view by capturing the event objects these models fire. All told, a JTable listens to six different event types, through the following interfaces:

- TableModelListener
- TableColumnModelListener
- ListSelectionListener
- CellEditorListener
- Scrollable
- Accessible

Each of these listener types has an event object counterpart, which we'll briefly describe. There are five different TableModelEvent constructors, each of which requires arguments at varying levels of granularity, so a TableModel can issue notifications ranging from a complete table refresh down to a single cell update. TableColumnModelEvent objects specify changes to the column structure of the table, including changes in column order, added or removed columns, and width changes. A ListSelectionEvent object reports which rows are included (or excluded) after the user or program has selected a range of rows to highlight. For example, if a user chooses a range of records in order to sort or delete them, a ListSelectionEvent gathers that collection and provides an index for it.

A CellEditorEvent object is created when editing on a cell completes or is cancelled. The Scrollable interface allows a JTable to be manipulated by any scrolling container (JScrollPane, JScrollBar, JViewport). Finally, the Accessible interface gives all implementing Swing components means for returning an `AccessibleContext` object. These objects are hooks that support using a Swing interface through some form of assisting technology, such as a Braille reader or magnified-font monitor. Figure 10.14 depicts the requirements a `JTable` adheres to just by listening.

FIGURE 10.14 JTable's interface implementations

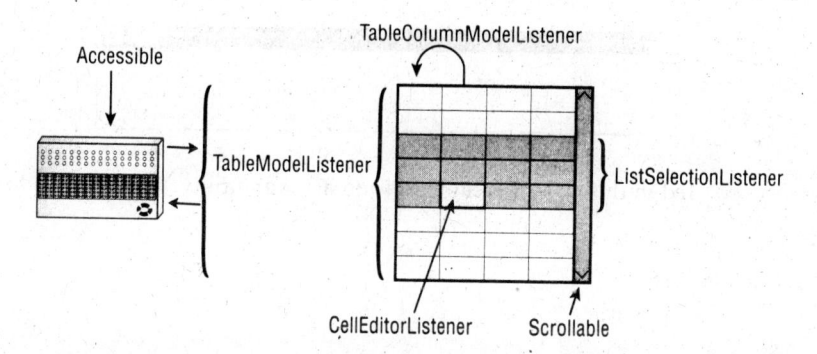

These interfaces are supported by various default classes located in `javax.swing.table`. They provide adequate behavior for many common uses so that implementing a simple subclass is not tedious work. For starters, here is a subclass that simply extends the list of available constructors:

```java
import java.awt.*;
import javax.swing.*;

public class VSTable extends JTable {

  public VSTable(int r, int c) {
    super(r,c);
  }

  public static void main(String args[]) {
    VSTable vst = new VSTable(3,6);
    JFrame jf = new JFrame();
    Panel pan = new Panel();
    pan.add(vst);
    jf.addWindowListener(new WindowCloser());
    jf.setContentPane(pan);
    jf.pack();
    jf.setVisible(true);
  }
}
```

This code produces the example shown in Figure 10.15. We've merely provided a constructor that requires a row and column integer pair. Under the premise that extending a class interface doesn't break it, we produced a form where `main()` only constructs and assembles objects. VSTable may change as you add features to it, and you can reuse the `main()` method for testing.

FIGURE 10.15 A JTable constructed with row and column values only

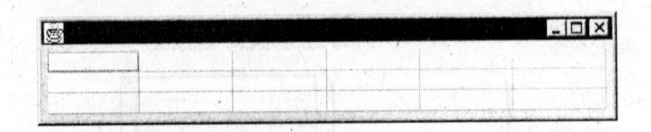

Also incorporated in this class is a simple `WindowCloser` utility, written as follows:

```
import java.awt.event.*;
import java.awt.*;

/**
 * Closes a window.
 * Subclass this to define more event handling.
 *
 * @author The CJ2CSG Guys
 */
public class WindowCloser extends WindowAdapter {
  public void windowClosing(WindowEvent wevt) {
    Window window = wevt.getWindow();
    window.setVisible(false);
    window.dispose();
    System.exit(0);
  }
}
```

This routine explicitly releases the system's windowing resources. There is a more direct way to do this, as explained in the following note, but we added this class to show a simple object with potential for reuse, either by itself or through subclassing.

> **TIP** You may have noticed in some applications that the `JFrame` window goes away when dismissed, but the session that spawned it may not return the prompt as expected. A `JFrame`'s closing behavior is defined by the `javax.swing.WindowConstants` interface. The default choice, HIDE_ON_CLOSE, accounts for this "hanging" behavior. You can change it to DISPOSE_ON_CLOSE or EXIT_ON_CLOSE with `JFrame`'s `setDefaultCloseOperation()`.

To make a table of less trivial value, you need to take hold of the models directly. Because the Developer's Exam focuses on data functions through the GUI, we'll concentrate on the key player for that: the `TableModel` interface and its all-purpose implementation, `AbstractTableModel`.

Using *AbstractTableModel*

As the driver for any `JTable` view, the `TableModel` incorporates all the behavior necessary to maintain data that is current and accurate. Developers who choose to implement the `TableModel` directly must also manage the event firing to all listeners, especially the `JTable` itself. Otherwise, it is far simpler to make a concrete subclass of `AbstractTableModel` and use it as a `JTable` constructor parameter. Default initialization code in the `JTable` takes care of the rest. At a bare minimum, you must implement:

- `public int getColumnCount()`
- `public int getRowCount()`
- `public Object getValueAt(int row, int col)`

Implementing these abstract methods makes for a concrete subclass, but it is not enough to make the table editable. Overriding the following methods as well will give you a more useful degree of control:

- `public boolean isCellEditable(int row, int col)`
- `public void setValueAt(Object obj, int row, int col)`
- `public String getColumnName(int index)`
- `public Class getColumnClass(int index)`

Overriding `setValueAt()` carries with it the responsibility of calling `fireTableCellUpdated()`, which in `AbstractTableModel` calls `fireTableChanged()` on the model's current listeners. Here's an example:

```
import javax.swing.table.*;

/**
 * A model for a trouble-ticket system using the
 * following schema and data representations:
 * <CODE>
 * <OL>
 * <LI>RECNUMBER int
 * <LI>REPORTER  java.lang.String
 * <LI>LOCATION  java.lang.String
 * <LI>TIMEOFRP  java.lang.String
 * <LI>ENGINEER  java.lang.String
 * <LI>CATEGORY  java.lang.String
 * <LI>COMPLAINT java.lang.String
```

```java
 * <LI>CTSTATUS  java.lang.String
 * </OL>
 * </CODE>
 *
 * @author The CJ2CSG Guys
 */
public class TroubleTicketModel
extends AbstractTableModel
{
  private String[] schema = { "Record Number",
    "Reporter", "Location", "Time of Report", "Engineer",
    "Category", "Complaint", "Status"};

  private String[][] rowData = {
    {"001", "Sayers", "Denver", "15:30 04/01/00", "Wort",
    "Network", "T-1 is down", "In Process"}
  };

  public TroubleTicketModel() {
  }

  /**
    * Returns the number of columns in the schema.
    */
  public int getColumnCount() {
    return schema.length;
  }

  /**
    * Returns the number of rows in the table.
    */
  public int getRowCount() {
    return rowData.length;
  }

  /**
    * Returns the value at the given cell as an Object.
    *
    * @return java.lang.Object
    */
```

```java
public Object getValueAt(int r, int c) {
  if (rowData[r] != null && schema[c] != null) {
    return rowData[r][c];
  }
  return null;
}

/**
 * Sets the value at a given cell and notifies
 * listeners.
 */
public void setValueAt(Object obj, int r, int c) {
  if (rowData[r] != null && schema[c] != null) {
    rowData[r][c] = obj.toString();
    fireTableCellUpdated(r,c);
  }
}

/**
 * Turns on editing for all cells, excepting the
 * column that holds the record number.
 */
public boolean isCellEditable(int r, int c) {
  if (c == 0) {
    return false;
  }
  return true;
}

/**
 * Returns the name of any column, given its
 * index in the model (not the current view).
 *
 * @return java.lang.String
 */
public String getColumnName(int index) {
  return schema[index];
}

/**
```

```
 * Returns a Class representation of the common
 * class of any column.
 *
 * @return java.lang.Class
 */
public Class getColumnClass(int index) {
  return String.class;
 }
}
```

With this in place, you can write a quick main() method to view the work so far:

```
import javax.swing.*;
import java.awt.*;

public class Test
{
  public static void main(String args[]) {
    JFrame jf = new JFrame("Trouble Ticket Table");
    JTable jt = new JTable(new TroubleTicketModel());
    JScrollPane jsp = new JScrollPane(jt);
    jf.getContentPane().add(jsp, BorderLayout.CENTER);
    jf.setDefaultCloseOperation(JFrame.EXIT_ON_CLOSE);
    jf.setSize(650,75);
    jf.setVisible(true);
  }
}
```

Figure 10.16 shows the output of this code.

FIGURE 10.16   Using JTable to display a TroubleTicketModel

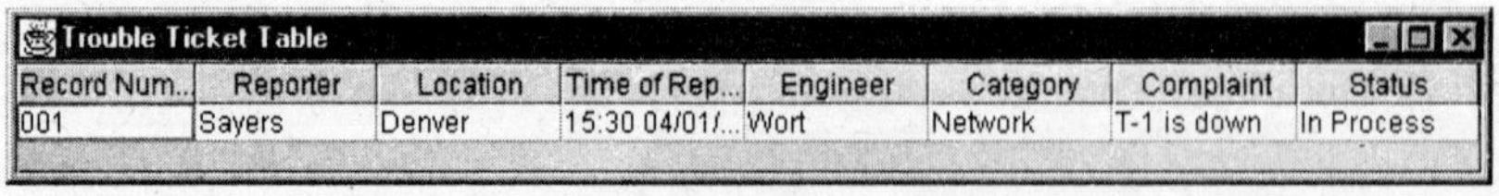

Record Num...	Reporter	Location	Time of Rep...	Engineer	Category	Complaint	Status
001	Sayers	Denver	15:30 04/01/...	Wort	Network	T-1 is down	In Process

We haven't yet worked on the cosmetics such as appropriately setting column widths. To manage that, you need a JTableHeader. Add a jt.setTableHeader(new JTableHeader()) call to the code and start experimenting. The beginning of a table prototype is in the works.

With that formula established, the real work remains: hooking a data feed into the model, and extending JTable to add view features you need. You're invited to create a more aesthetically pleasing table view and supplement the model with live data to see how things work.

Building a *JTree*

Like a `JTable`, a `JTree` is complex enough to warrant its own library of support classes. It is becoming more widely used in GUI designs, typically as a drill-down or focus-oriented controller, or as an indexing tool for things like e-mail messages and, of course, files.

But `JTree` is not as well-defined a listener as `JTable`, because it implements only the `Scrollable` and `Accessible` interfaces. The primary use for a `JTree` is outlining any data structure that lends itself to hierarchical order. It could be used to diagram, say, the operations of a recursive descent parser, but it is more readily useful as an indexing tool.

Trees consist of a series of nodes rooted in a single *root node*, from which other nodes called *child nodes* extend. A node that cannot have children is called a *leaf node*; otherwise it is called a *branch node*. A node is principally identified two ways: by its path, the route that links it back to the root; and by its row, the area it uses for display (similar to a `List` element).

Aside from defining user actions for adding and removing nodes, the most common event type associated with a tree is selection. In the trouble-ticket system, for example, you might want to associate a different display or action with each kind of node you present. If a user clicks a child of the Reporter node, you might want to display contact information for that person, or perhaps limit the table display to the trouble items reported by that person. To get the visual effect first, you can mock up a tree using the `DefaultMutableTreeNode` class.

It might also make sense for the table model to alter the node population of the tree using the data it receives to update the tabular view. A tree model could listen to property changes issued by the table model. The table model could filter the data before firing it, or the tree model could filter the table data. Or instead of adding this work to either class, where the fit is arbitrary, you could instead perform the translation work through an event adapter, whose only job is creating tree data out of table data. Keeping two models separated this way makes it possible to keep changes in the bootstrap code and out of the component code. Figure 10.17 is a logical diagram of this interaction.

FIGURE 10.17 Updating a tree outline with table data

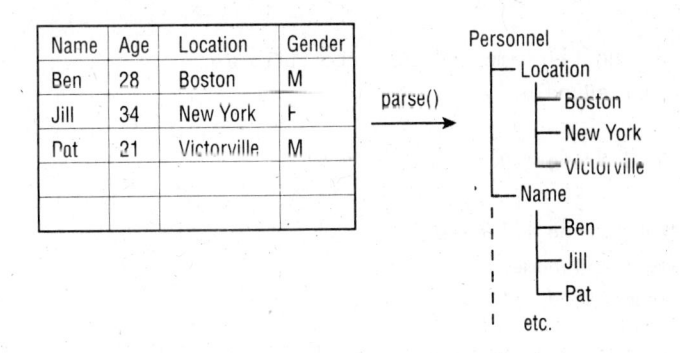

Name	Age	Location	Gender
Ben	28	Boston	M
Jill	34	New York	F
Pat	21	Victorville	M

parse() →

```
Personnel
  ├─ Location
  │    ├─ Boston
  │    ├─ New York
  │    └─ Victorville
  └─ Name
       ├─ Ben
       ├─ Jill
       └─ Pat
       etc.
```

Creating a reusable mock-up of a tree display can take a little doing. Rather than embed some static data in a demo class that makes a `JTree`, we decided to take an extra step and write one that could accept input in the form of a property file. Property files present data in the form

Chapter 10 · Creating the User Interface with Swing

of key-value pairs, where the key is always a String (and in the example, so are the values). Our file sample looks like this:

```
Location=Chicago New York Parkersburg
Reporter=Padula Hunter Gant Anonymous
Engineer=Wort Brown Carrigan None
Category=Network Office Workstation
```

You treat the key as a parent node and the values as children, once the file contents are read in. To do that, we created (in the following code) a class called TreeSetup to take any file that's written as a "bundle" of properties and convert it to a series of parent and children elements:

```java
import java.io.*;
import java.util.*;
import javax.swing.tree.*;

/**
 * TreeSetup converts a properties file into a set
 * of parent and child nodes. Each key in the file
 * becomes a parent, and each value is a child to its
 * key.
 *
 * @author The CJ2CSG Guys
 */
public class TreeSetup
{
  private PropertyResourceBundle prb;
  private String filename;

  /**
   * Accepts a String filename and converts it to a
   * PropertyResourceBundle.
   *
   * @see java.util.PropertyResourceBundle
   */
  public TreeSetup(String filename) {
    this.filename = filename;
    FileInputStream fis = null;
    try {
      fis = new FileInputStream(filename);
      prb = new PropertyResourceBundle(fis);
    }
    catch (FileNotFoundException fnfe) {
```

```
      System.err.println(filename + " was not found");
      System.exit(1);
    }
    catch (IOException ioe) {
      ioe.printStackTrace();
      System.err.println(
        "Error trying to open input stream");
      System.exit(1);
    }
  }

  /**
   * Returns a Vector of String values, given
   * a String key as a parameter.
   */
  public Vector getChildren(String node) {
    StringTokenizer st = null;
    Vector vec = new Vector();
    String children = prb.getString(node);
    st = new StringTokenizer(children);
    while (st.hasMoreTokens()) {
      vec.addElement(st.nextToken());
    }
    return vec;
  }

  /**
   * Returns a Vector of Strings representing
   * each key found.
   */
  public Vector getParents() {
    Enumeration enum = null;
    Vector vec = new Vector();
    enum = prb.getKeys();
    while (enum.hasMoreElements()) {
      Object key = (String)enum.nextElement();
      vec.addElement(key);
    }
    return vec;
  }
}
```

Chapter 10 • Creating the User Interface with Swing

The `Vector` returned by `getParents()` contains all the keys in the file. Passing each element of that `Vector`, as a `String`, into `getChildren()` will then return a `Vector` containing the key's values. Finally, we write (in the next code sample) a `SampleTree` class to create a `DefaultTreeModel` by passing the property file name as a parameter to the `TreeSetup` constructor, and using that object to create `DefaultMutableTreeNode` instances:

```
import java.util.*;
import javax.swing.*;
import javax.swing.tree.*;

public class SampleTree
{
  private DefaultMutableTreeNode[] nodes;
  private TreeSetup tsu;
  private DefaultMutableTreeNode root;
  private DefaultTreeModel dtm;

  public SampleTree(String schema) {
    root = new DefaultMutableTreeNode("Trouble Fields");
    tsu = new TreeSetup(schema);
    Enumeration enum = tsu.getParents().elements();

    while (enum.hasMoreElements()) {
      String category = (String)enum.nextElement();
      DefaultMutableTreeNode parent;
      parent = new DefaultMutableTreeNode(category);
      root.add(parent);
      Enumeration enum2;
      enum2 = tsu.getChildren(category).elements();

      while (enum2.hasMoreElements()) {
        String child = (String)enum2.nextElement();
        parent.add(new DefaultMutableTreeNode(child));
      }
    }

    dtm = new DefaultTreeModel(root, false);
  }

  public DefaultTreeModel getSampleTreeModel() {
    return dtm;
  }
}
```

```
  public static void main(String args[]) {
    if (args.length == 0) {
      System.out.println("Provide a valid property " +
        "file name and try again");
      System.exit(1);
    }
    SampleTree st = new SampleTree(args[0]);
    DefaultTreeModel tm = st.getSampleTreeModel();
    JTree jt = new JTree(tm);
    JScrollPane jsp = new JScrollPane(jt);
    JFrame jf = new JFrame("Sample Tree");
    jf.getContentPane().add(jsp);
    jf.setDefaultCloseOperation(JFrame.EXIT_ON_CLOSE);
    jf.pack();
    jf.setVisible(true);
  }
}
```

The resulting work takes the sample file listed earlier and displays it in a `JTree` like the one in Figure 10.18.

FIGURE 10.18 A JTree that displays the contents of the file sample

The work here was neither trivial nor difficult, but the result is a tool for creating any two-tier tree display quickly from a file—well worth the effort for a prototype tool.

JMenus and Actions

The Swing library seems particularly thoughtful when it comes to providing conveniences for common GUI-based tasks. It's easy to create a single action as an object and bind its behavior to a readymade Swing widget. `Action` objects encapsulate their behavior so that multiple widgets can reference them. An icon on a toolbar, a menu choice, or even a `KeyStroke` can all use the same object for processing. Using KeyStroke objects goes beyond the requirements of the Developer's Exam, but they can make the GUI friendlier for users who favor keyboard input over the mouse.

Classes must meet the same requirements as ActionListener in order to implement Action (or subclass AbstractAction). Action implementations are different in that they allow for direct containment by a JComponent, although only JMenu, JToolBar, and JPopupMenu know how to contain, display, and listen to them. Here's a simple look at creating an Action and binding it to a menu (the result of the following code is shown in Figure 10.19):

```java
import java.awt.event.*;
import javax.swing.*;

/**
 * This subclass of AbstractAction serves as a prototype
 * for creating simple Action objects. No provision is
 * made for icons - just a String value so the containing
 * component has something to display.
 *
 * @author The CJ2CSG Guys
 */
public class SampleAction extends AbstractAction
{
  private String message;

  /**
   * Passes the supplied String to the parent class;
   * also maintains a copy locally.
   */
  public SampleAction(String output) {
    super(output);
    message = output;
  }

  /**
   * Sends the Action message to stdout.
   */
  public void actionPerformed(ActionEvent ae) {
    System.out.println(message);
  }

  /**
```

```
 * A bootstrap test. Adds the object to a JMenu.
 */
public static void main(String args[]) {
  SampleAction sa = new SampleAction(args[0]);
  JFrame jf = new JFrame("Action Test");
  JMenuBar jmb = new JMenuBar();
  jf.setJMenuBar(jmb);
  JMenu jm = new JMenu("Sample");
  jmb.add(jm);
  jm.add(sa);
  jf.setSize(100,100);
  jf.setVisible(true);
  jf.setDefaultCloseOperation(JFrame.EXIT_ON_CLOSE);
  }
}
```

FIGURE 10.19 Adding an Action to a JMenu

Take another look at the `TreeSetup` class from the last section. This same code could be used to create a quick menu prototype, using a file that lists Menus as keys and MenuItems as values. It wouldn't have much interesting functionality, but it would provide a quick means for choosing how to visually arrange menu items.

It makes sense to rename `TreeSetup` to something more general, such as `WidgetSetup`, to suggest wider usage. As practice, write a `SampleMenu` class that reads from a menu property file and builds a GUI menu for you.

Panes

Swing panes all provide some form of containment service. The services they provide vary widely, from delegated layout managers (`content pane`) to specialized layout managers (`JSplitPane`, `JScrollPane`) and dialog boxes (`JOptionPane, JTabbedPane, JFileChooser`) to embedded layers that have no class of their own (the "glass pane" in the `JFrame`). The content pane is something everyone who writes a Swing application must use, and `JFileChooser` is a straightforward class, so we briefly discuss here two of the panes you might not think to use: `JSplitPane` and `JOptionPane`.

JSplitPane

As the name suggests, a `JSplitPane` holds two other components and provides an adjustable divider service. A `JSplitPane` is not a layout manager subclass, but it contains layout behavior just the same: it has its own rules regarding `minimumSize` and `preferredSize` requests from the components it contains. `JSplitPane` looks at `minimumSize` on a resize request, ensuring that one component does not encroach on the other's needed space. The range of the divider's location is normally fixed by the minimum sizes of the components in the pane, but it is adjustable.

Other properties of `JSplitPane` include

`orientation`   HORIZONTAL_SPLIT or VERTICAL_SPLIT

`dividerSize`   In pixels

`dividerLocation`   Current position

`minimumDividerLocation`   Left/bottom minimum size

`maximumDividerLocation`   Right/top minimum size

Now you're ready to put the tree, table, and simple menu together for a first look, which you can create with the following code:

```
import java.awt.*;
import java.awt.event.*;
import javax.swing.*;
import javax.swing.tree.*;

/** A bootstrap class that combines our table and tree,
 * in a split pane, along with a trivial menu that is
 * backed by an Action.
 *
 * @author The CJ2CSG Guys
 */
public class Prototype
{
  public static void main(String args[]) {
    JFrame jf = new JFrame("SplitPane Test");

    TroubleTicketModel ttm = new TroubleTicketModel();
    JTable jta = new JTable(ttm);

    SampleTree st = new SampleTree("sample");
```

```
    DefaultTreeModel tm = st.getSampleTreeModel();
    JTree jtr = new JTree(tm);

    SampleAction sa = new SampleAction("PROTOTYPE");
    JMenuBar jmb = new JMenuBar();
    jf.setJMenuBar(jmb);
    JMenu jm = new JMenu("Sample");
    jmb.add(jm);
    jm.add(sa);

    JSplitPane jsp = new
       JSplitPane(JSplitPane.HORIZONTAL_SPLIT, jtr, jta);

    jf.getContentPane().add(jsp, BorderLayout.WEST);
    jf.setDefaultCloseOperation(JFrame.EXIT_ON_CLOSE);
    jf.setSize(650,200);
    jf.setVisible(true);
  }
}
```

The result is shown in Figure 10.20. You didn't spend time refining appearances in this first round, but now you have a quick look at your elements. Most of the adjustments to appearance can be made in the bootstrap code, amounting to less focus on changing class behavior and more on experimenting with it.

FIGURE 10.20 Menu, table, and tree together in one JFrame

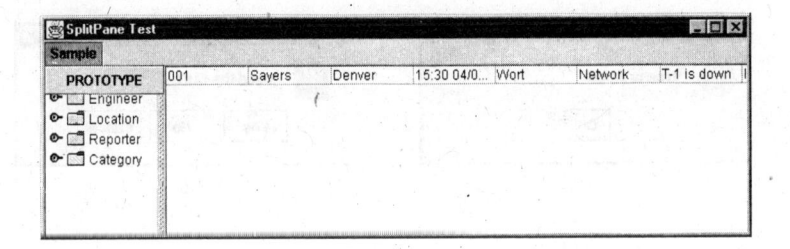

JOptionPane

The JOptionPane class encapsulates several conventional dialog-box formats, but with one clear advantage: You don't need to declare a Frame and bind to it (more on that in a moment).

Chapter 10 · Creating the User Interface with Swing

JOptionPane defines five message types:
- ERROR_MESSAGE
- INFORMATION_MESSAGE
- WARNING_MESSAGE
- QUESTION_MESSAGE
- PLAIN_MESSAGE

Each of these types maps to a prepared display format. These formats can be associated one of two ways: using a confirmation request that locks the underlying frame (a modal dialog), or using a dismiss-on-demand style that does not interfere with the application (a nonmodal dialog). These behaviors are respectively enabled by the static methods showConfirmDialog() and showMessageDialog().

Add the following code snippets to the Prototype class as a way to experiment, and compare your perception of speed before and after these changes. The dialogs that pop up are depicted in Figure 10.21:

```
...
JOptionPane.showMessageDialog(null, "Tree created",
     "Program Note", JOptionPane.INFORMATION_MESSAGE);
...
JOptionPane.showConfirmDialog(null, "Load the GUI?",
     "Roll Call!", JOptionPane.YES_NO_CANCEL_OPTION,
     JOptionPane.QUESTION_MESSAGE);
...
```

FIGURE 10.21   JOptionPane's information (a) and question (b) dialogs

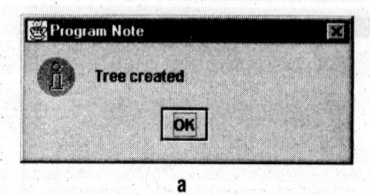

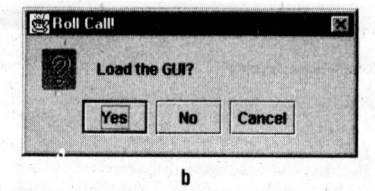

Summary

A simple, four-step plan to design a GUI includes identifying the needed components, sketching the GUI, isolating regions of behavior, and choosing layout managers.

Some properties are common to nearly all Swing components. These include size, location, foreground and background color, font, and enabled state. There are public methods for each component to set and get each of these properties.

The categories of Swing components are container components, ordinary components, and menu components. Containers include `JFrame`, `JPanel`, and `JPane`. Ordinary components include `JLabel`, `JButton`, `JCheckBox`, `JRadioButton`, `JScrollBar`, `JTextField`, `JTextArea`, and `JComboBox`. The menu components include `JMenu`, `JMenuBar`, `JMenuItem`, `JCheckBoxMenuItem`, and `JRadioButtonMenuItem`.

`JTables` have three core internal models, including `TableModel`, `TableColumnModel`, and `ListenerSelectionModel`. It's also possible (and simpler) to subclass `AbstractTableModel` and use it as a `JTable` constructor argument.

The primary use for a `JTree` is implementing any data structure that lends itself to a hierarchy. Trees consist of a root node and child nodes (leaf nodes and branch nodes).

Exam Essentials

Sketching a GUI using paper and pencil is sufficient when designing a GUI. It's not necessary to purchase a fancy illustration program when designing the GUI for the Developer's Exam.

The programming assignment requires that you use Swing to build the front-end GUI. You are not obligated to use any particular component in the Swing library, but the choices should be fairly straightforward.

Swing components can be classified in one of three ways. Swing components are either containers, ordinary components, or menu components.

Key Terms

Before you take the exam, be certain you are familiar with the following terms:

branch node	menu components
child node	ordinary components
container components	root node
leaf node	

Review Questions

1. The size of a Swing component is defined in which of the following units?
   A. Inches
   B. Centimeters
   C. Pixels
   D. Microns

2. Performing a selection in a GUI of which of the following Swing components will automatically trigger a deselection?
   A. JCheckBox
   B. JLabel
   C. JTextField
   D. JRadioButton

3. Select two properties that apply to all Swing components.
   A. Alignment
   B. Location
   C. Depth
   D. Font

4. Which of the following Swing components lends itself best to organizing data in a hierarchical fashion?
   A. JMenuItem
   B. JTable
   C. JTree
   D. JPane

5. Which of the following is not one of the three core internal models that a JTable uses for dealing with its data structure?
   A. TableModel
   B. TableColumnModel
   C. ListSelectionModel
   D. ColumnModel

Answers to Review Questions

1. **C.** All Swing components have a size property that is expressed in units of pixels.
2. **D.** A `JRadioButton` behaves like an older car radio button on which pressing one button pops the already selected button out.
3. **B, D.** Alignment and depth are not properties of any Swing component.
4. **C.** Tree structures (as implemented with a `JTree`) define a hierarchy of child nodes rooted in a single root node.
5. **D.** Option D is not a valid model in the Swing library.

Chapter 11

Layout Managers

In Chapter 10, "Creating the User Interface with Swing," we covered the basic look and feel of some of the basic Swing components. A sophisticated GUI, such as the one you will be required to create for your Developer's Exam project, consists of a number of interrelated components positioned so as to make the application easy to understand and use.

Java practically insists that you use layout managers to control the size and position of your GUI components. This requirement can be irritating, but it has the benefit of forcing programmers to think about the dynamic resizing behavior of their user interfaces. In this chapter we will examine the standard layout managers of the `java.awt` package: Flow, Grid, Border, Card, and GridBag. Note that these classes can lay out Swing components as well as AWT components.

Layout Manager Theory

The AWT toolkit includes five layout manager classes. You might expect that there would be a common abstract superclass, called something like `LayoutManager`, from which these five layout managers would inherit common functionality. In fact, the common ancestor is `java.awt.LayoutManager`. However, it is an interface, not a class, because the layout managers are so different from one another that they have nothing in common except a handful of method names. (There is also a `java.awt.LayoutManager2` subinterface, which the GridBag, Border, and Card layout managers implement.)

Layout managers work in partnership with containers. To understand layout managers, it is important to understand what a container is and what happens when a component gets inserted into a container. The next two sections explore these topics.

Swing GUIs reside in `JFrame`s or in `JApplet`s. For simple applications, you just add your components to your frame; for simple applets, you just put your components into your applet. (In both cases, you might wonder how the components end up where they do; layout managers are lurking in the background, taking care of details.) For more complicated GUIs, it is convenient to divide the frame or applet into smaller regions. These regions might constitute, for example, a toolbar or a matrix of radio buttons. In Java, GUI subregions are implemented most commonly with the `JPanel` container. Panels, like frames and applets, can contain other components: buttons, check boxes, scroll bars, text areas, text fields, and of course other panels. Complicated GUIs sometimes have very complicated containment hierarchies of panels within panels within panels, and so on, down through many layers of containment.

> **NOTE** In most object-oriented windowing systems, including Java, the term *hierarchy* is ambiguous. When discussing classes, hierarchy refers to the structure of inheritance from superclass to subclass. When discussing GUIs, hierarchy can refer to the containment structure of GUI components, such as applets, frames, panels, buttons and so on.

The GUI in Figure 11.1 is a moderate-size frame for specifying a color. You can see at a glance that the panel contains labels, scroll bars, text fields, and buttons. You have probably guessed that the frame also contains some panels, even though they cannot be seen. In fact, the frame contains five panels, not counting the frame's content pane. Each of the six containers (the five panels, plus the content pane) has its own layout manager: There are four instances of Grid layout managers, one Flow layout manager, and one Border layout manager.

FIGURE 11.1 A GUI with several levels of containment

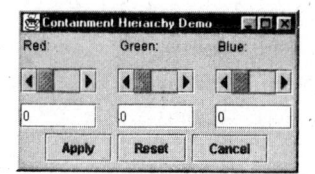

Figure 11.2 schematically shows the frame's containment hierarchy: A Java GUI programmer must master the art of transforming a proposed GUI into a workable and efficient containment hierarchy. This skill comes with experience, once the fundamentals are understood. The Java Developer's Certification Exam does not require you to develop any complicated containments, but it does require you to understand the fundamentals.

FIGURE 11.2 Containment hierarchy

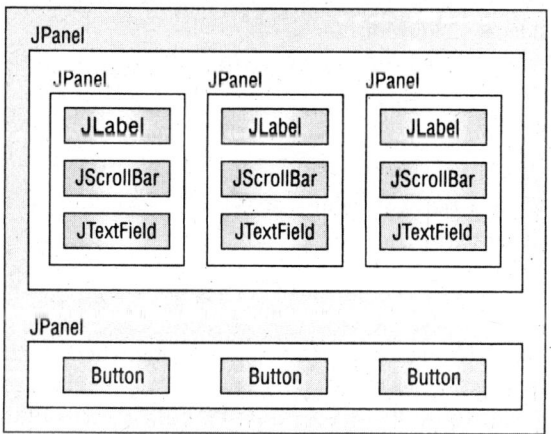

The code that implements the color chooser in Figure 11.1 is listed here:

```
1.  import java.awt.*;
2.  import javax.swing.*;
3.
4.  public class Hier extends JFrame {
5.    Hier() {
6.      super("Containment Hierarchy Demo");
7.      Container cont = getContentPane();
8.      // Build upper panel with 3 horizontal "strips".
9.      String strings[] = {"Red:", "Green:", "Blue:"};
10.     JPanel upperPan = new JPanel();
11.     upperPan.setLayout(new GridLayout(1, 3, 20, 0));
12.     for (int i=0; i<3; i++) {
13.       // Add strips.
14.       // Each strip is a panel within upperPan.
15.       JPanel levelPan = new JPanel();
16.       levelPan.setLayout(new GridLayout(3, 1, 0, 10));
17.       levelPan.add(new Label(strings[i]));
18.       levelPan.add(new
              JScrollBar(JScrollBar.HORIZONTAL));
19.       levelPan.add(new JTextField("0"));
20.       upperPan.add(levelPan);
21.     }
22.     cont.add(upperPan, BorderLayout.CENTER);
23.     // Build lower panel containing 3 buttons.
24.     JPanel lowerPan = new JPanel();
25.     lowerPan.add(new JButton("Apply"));
26.     lowerPan.add(new JButton("Reset"));
27.     lowerPan.add(new JButton("Cancel"));
28.     cont.add(lowerPan, BorderLayout.SOUTH);
29.     pack();
30.   }
31.
32.   public static void main(String[] args) {
33.     (new Hier()).setVisible(true);
34.   }
35. }
```

As you can see from the listing, no code specifies exactly where the labels, scroll bars, text fields, buttons, or panels should go, or what size they should be. Instead, each container (the content pane of the JFrame, as well as the various JPanels) uses its default layout manager or is specifically assigned a nondefault layout manager.

After each container is constructed and possibly assigned a new layout manager, the container is populated with the components it is to contain. For example, the lower `JPanel`, constructed in line 24, is populated with `JButton`s in lines 25, 26, and 27 (using its default layout manager).

Finally, the now-populated panel is added to the container that is to hold it (line 28).

Each panel in the sample code is built in four steps:

1. Construct the panel.
2. Give the panel a layout manager.
3. Populate the panel.
4. Add the panel to its own container.

When a container is constructed (step 1), it is given a default layout manager. For panels, the default is a Flow layout manager, and step 2 can be skipped if this is the desired manager. In step 3, populating the panel involves constructing components and adding them to the panel; if any of these components is itself a panel, steps 1–4 must be executed recursively.

A container delegates to its layout manager the job of determining where components will be placed and (optionally) how they will be resized. If the container is subsequently resized, the layout manager again lays out the container's components (probably with different results, because it has a different area to work with). This "conference" between the container and the layout manager is the subject of the next section.

Component Size and Position

Components know where they are and how big they are. That is to say, the `java.awt.Component` class, which is a superclass of all AWT and Swing components, has instance variables called x, y, width, and height. The x and y variables specify the position of the component's upper-left corner (as measured from the upper-left corner of the container that contains the component), and width and height are in pixels. Figure 11.3 illustrates the x, y, width, and height of a text area inside a panel inside a frame.

FIGURE 11.3 Position and size

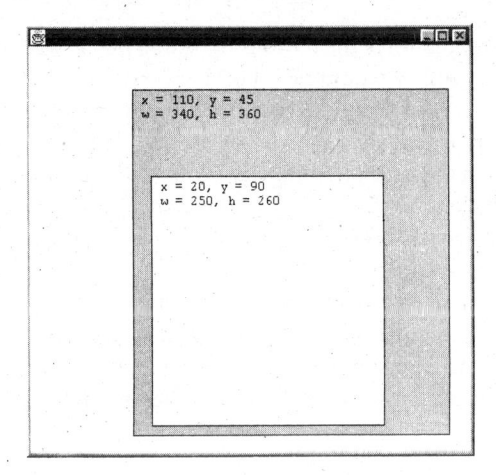

342 Chapter 11 · Layout Managers

A component's position and size can be changed by calling the component's `setSize()` method. It seems reasonable to expect that the following code, which calls `setSize()` on a button, would create two fairly big buttons:

```
1.  import java.awt.*;
2.  import javax.swing.*;
3.
4.  public class Disa extends JFrame {
5.      public static void main(String[] args) {
6.          JFrame frame = new JFrame();
7.          JPanel panel = new JPanel();
8.          for (int i=0; i<2; i++) {
9.              JButton btn = new JButton("We're enormous!");
10.             btn.setSize(300, 300);
11.             panel.add(btn);
12.         }
13.         frame.getContentPane().add(panel);
14.         frame.setSize(450, 70);
15.         frame.setVisible(true);
16.     }
17. }
```

If you have tried something like this, you know that the result is disappointing. A screen shot appears in Figure 11.4.

FIGURE 11.4   Disappointing buttons

It seems that line 10 should force the buttons to be 300 pixels wide by 300 pixels tall. In fact, the buttons are just the size they would be if line 10 were omitted or commented out.

Line 10 has no effect because after it executes, the button is added to a panel (line 11). Eventually (after a fairly complicated sequence of events), the panel calls on its layout manager to enforce its layout policy on the button. The layout manager decides where and how big the button should be; in this case, the layout manager wants the button to be just large enough to accommodate its label. When this size has been calculated, the layout manager calls `setBounds()` on the button, clobbering the work you did in line 10.

In general, it is futile to call `setBounds()` on a component, because layout managers always get the last word; that is, their call to `setBounds()` happens after yours. There are ways to defeat this functionality, but they tend to be complicated, difficult to maintain, and not in the spirit of Java. Java's GUI system wants you to let the layout managers do the layout work. In order to build a sophisticated GUI, you have to be familiar with the layout policies of the available layout managers. These policies are covered in the next several sections.

Layout Policies

Every Java component has a *preferred size* that expresses how big the component would like to be, barring conflict with a layout manager. Preferred size is generally the smallest size necessary to render the component in a visually meaningful way. For example, a button's preferred size is the size of its label text, plus a little border of empty space around the text, plus the shadowed decorations that mark the boundary of the button. Thus a button's preferred size is "just big enough."

When a layout manager lays out its container's child components, it has to balance two considerations: the layout policy and each component's preferred size. First priority goes to enforcing layout policy. If honoring a component's preferred size would mean violating the layout policy, then the layout manager overrules the component's preferred size.

Understanding a layout manager means understanding where it will place a component, and also how it will treat a component's preferred size. The next several sections discuss the layout managers: `FlowLayout`, `GridLayout`, `BorderLayout`, `CardLayout`, and `GridBagLayout`.

The Flow Layout Manager

The Flow layout manager arranges components in horizontal rows. It is the default manager type for panels and applets, so it is usually the first layout manager that programmers encounter. It is a common experience for new Java developers to add a few components to an applet and wonder how they came to be arranged so neatly. The following code is a good example:

```
1. import java.awt.*;
2. import javax.swing.*;
3.
4. public class Flow extends JFrame {
5.   public static void main(String[] args) {
6.     JFrame frame = new JFrame();
7.     Container cont = frame.getContentPane();
8.     cont.setLayout(new FlowLayout());
9.     cont.add(new JLabel("Name: "));
10.    cont.add(new JTextField("Beowulf    "));
11.    cont.add(new JButton("OK"));
12.    frame.setSize(450, 90);
13.    frame.setVisible(true);
14.  }
15. }
```

The resulting frame is shown in Figure 11.5.

FIGURE 11.5 Simple frame using the Flow layout manager

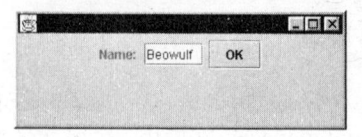

If the same three components appear in a narrower frame, as shown in Figure 11.6, there is not enough space for all three to fit in a single row.

FIGURE 11.6 A narrower frame using the Flow layout manager

The Flow layout manager fits as many components as possible into the top row and spills the remainder into a second row. The components always appear, left to right, in the order they were added to their container.

If the frame is thinner still, as in Figure 11.7, then the Flow layout manager creates still another row.

FIGURE 11.7 A very narrow frame using the Flow layout manager

Within every row the components are evenly spaced, and the cluster of components is centered. The alignment (sometimes called *justification*) of the clustering can be controlled by passing a parameter to the `FlowLayout` constructor. The possible values are `FlowLayout.LEFT`, `FlowLayout.CENTER`, and `FlowLayout.RIGHT`. The code that follows explicitly constructs a Flow layout manager to right-justify four buttons:

```
1. import java.awt.*;
2. import javax.swing.*;
3.
4. public class FlowRight extends JFrame {
5.   public static void main(String[] args) {
6.     JFrame frame = new JFrame();
```

```
7.      Container cont = frame.getContentPane();
8.      cont.setLayout(new FlowLayout(FlowLayout.RIGHT));
9.      for (int i=1; i<=4; i++)
10.        cont.add(new JButton("Button #" + i));
11.     frame.setSize(470, 90);
12.     frame.setVisible(true);
13.   }
14. }
```

Figure 11.8 shows the resulting frame.

FIGURE 11.8 A right-justifying Flow layout manager

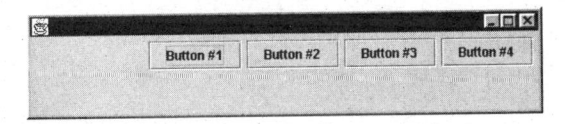

Figure 11.9 shows the frame of the previous figure, resized to be somewhat narrower.

FIGURE 11.9 A narrow right-justifying Flow layout manager

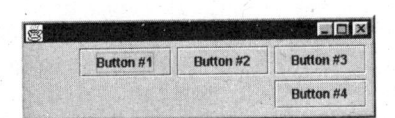

By default, the Flow layout manager leaves a gap of five pixels between components in both the horizontal and vertical directions. You can change this default by calling an overloaded version of the `FlowLayout` constructor, passing in the desired horizontal and vertical gaps. All layout managers have this capability.

The Grid Layout Manager

The Flow layout manager always honors a component's preferred size. The Grid layout manager takes the opposite extreme: when it performs a layout in a given space, it ignores a component's preferred size.

The Grid layout manager subdivides its territory into a matrix of rows and columns. The number of rows and number of columns are specified as parameters to the manager's constructor:

```
public GridLayout(int nRows, int nColumns)
```

Each row and each column in a Grid layout will be the same size; the overall area available to the layout is divided equally between the number of rows and between the number of columns.

Chapter 11 · Layout Managers

The following code uses a Grid layout manager to divide a frame into five rows and three columns, and then puts a component in each grid cell:

```
1.  import java.awt.*;
2.  import javax.swing.*;
3.
4.  public class Grid extends JFrame {
5.    public static void main(String[] args) {
6.      JFrame frame = new JFrame();
7.      Container cont = frame.getContentPane();
8.      cont.setLayout(new GridLayout(5, 3));
9.      for (int row=0; row<5; row++) {
10.       cont.add(new JLabel("Label " + row));
11.       cont.add(new JButton("Button " + row));
12.       cont.add(new JTextField("Text Field " + row));
13.     }
14.     frame.setSize(470, 140);
15.     frame.setVisible(true);
16.   }
17. }
```

Note that the constructor in line 8 creates five rows and three columns, not the other way around. After so many years of programming with Cartesian coordinates, it is probably second nature for most programmers to specify horizontal sorts of information before the comma, and vertical sorts of information after the comma. The `GridLayout` constructor uses "row-major" notation, which sometimes confuses people.

If you specify zero for either rows or columns, then the grid will size itself based on the number of components and the other dimension.

As you can see in Figure 11.10, every component is exactly the same size. Components appear in the order in which they were added, from left to right, row by row.

FIGURE 11.10 Grid layout

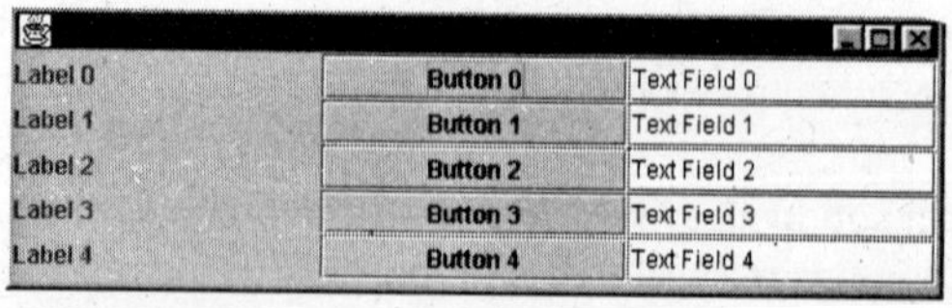

Label 0	Button 0	Text Field 0
Label 1	Button 1	Text Field 1
Label 2	Button 2	Text Field 2
Label 3	Button 3	Text Field 3
Label 4	Button 4	Text Field 4

If the same components are laid out in a taller, narrower frame, then every component is proportionally taller and narrower, as shown in Figure 11.11.

FIGURE 11.11 Tall, narrow Grid layout

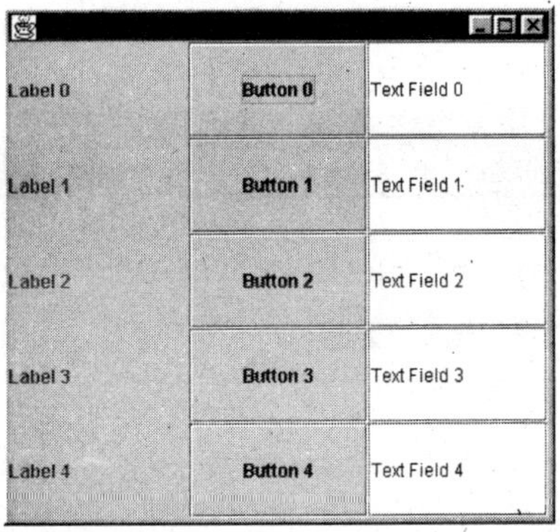

Grid layout managers behave strangely when they manage very few components (that is, significantly fewer than the number of rows times the number of columns) or very many components (that is, more than the number of rows times the number of columns).

The Border Layout Manager

The Border layout manager is the default manager for a JFrame's content pane, so sooner or later you must come to grips with it. It enforces a very useful layout policy, but it is less intuitive than either the Flow or Grid manager.

The Flow layout manager always honors a component's preferred size; the Grid layout manager never does. The Border layout manager does something in between.

The Border layout manager divides its territory into five regions: North, South, East, West, and Center. Each region may be empty or may contain one component (that is, no region is *required* to contain a component, but the regions can contain only one component).

The component at North gets positioned at the top of the container, and the component at South gets positioned at the bottom. The layout manager honors the preferred height of the North and South components and forces them to be exactly as wide as the container.

The North and South regions are useful for toolbars, status lines, and any other controls that ought to be as wide as possible but no higher than necessary. Figure 11.12 shows a frame that uses a Border layout manager to position a toolbar at North and a status line at South. The font of the status line is very large to illustrate that the height of each region is dictated by the preferred height of the component in the region. The panel that contains the

348 Chapter 11 • Layout Managers

toolbar buttons has its background set to black so you can see where it is. (For simplicity, the toolbar is just a panel containing a few buttons. Remember we said that you can only put a single component in each region? Well, if that component is a container, then you can get multiple components displayed.)

FIGURE 11.12 Border layout for a toolbar and a status line

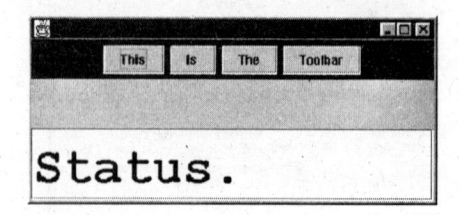

Figure 11.13 shows what happens if the same code is used but the frame is larger. Notice that the toolbar is still at the top and the status line is still at the bottom. The toolbar and the status line are as tall as they were in Figure 11.12, and they are automatically as wide as the frame.

FIGURE 11.13 Larger Border layout for a toolbar and a status line

The code that produced these screen shots is as follows:

```
1. import java.awt.*;
2. import javax.swing.*;
3.
4. public class Border extends JFrame {
5.   public static void main(String[] args) {
6.     JFrame frame = new JFrame();
7.     Container cont = frame.getContentPane();
8.
```

```
9.        // Build, populate, and add toolbar.
10.       JPanel toolbar = new JPanel();
11.       toolbar.setBackground(Color.black);
12.       toolbar.add(new JButton("This"));
13.       toolbar.add(new JButton("Is"));
14.       toolbar.add(new JButton("The"));
15.       toolbar.add(new JButton("Toolbar"));
16.       cont.add(toolbar, BorderLayout.NORTH);
17.
18.       // Add status line.
19.       JTextField status = new JTextField("Status.");
20.       Font font = new Font("Monospaced", Font.BOLD, 48);
21.       status.setFont(font);
22.       cont.add(status, BorderLayout.SOUTH);
23.
24.       frame.setSize(400, 375);
25.       frame.setVisible(true);
26.    }
27. }
```

Notice that in lines 16 and 22, an overloaded form of the add() method is used. The Border layout is not affected by the order in which you add components. Instead, you must specify which of the five regions will receive the component you are adding. The overloaded version of add() takes two parameters: first the component being added, and second an Object. Proper use of the Border layout manager requires that the second parameter be a constant defined in the BorderLayout class itself. The five constants that you should know about are:

- BorderLayout.NORTH
- BorderLayout.SOUTH
- BorderLayout.EAST
- BorderLayout.WEST
- BorderLayout.CENTER

These constants are of type String. You can use the string values rather than the constants, simply by passing in one of the literal strings "North", "South", "East", "West", or "Center". However, this approach is less robust than using the constants, because it does not protect you against spelling errors. For example, if you accidentally type "BorderLayout.SUOTH", the compiler will flag your error at compile time. If you use the literal value and make the corresponding typo, the compiler sees "Suoth", which is a valid string, and does not produce a compiler error.

The East and West regions are almost the opposite of North and South: in East and West, a component gets to be its preferred width but has its height constrained. Here a component extends vertically up to the bottom of the North component (if there is one) or to the top of the

350 Chapter 11 · Layout Managers

container (if there is no North component). A component extends down to the top of the South component (if there is one) or to the bottom of the container (if there is no South component). Figures 11.14 through 11.17 show frames that use a Border layout manager to lay out two scroll bars, one at East and one at West. In Figure 11.14, there are no components at North or South to contend with.

FIGURE 11.14 East and West

In Figure 11.15 there is a label at North.
In Figure 11.16 there is a label at South. The label has white text on a black background so that you can see exactly where the South region is.
In Figure 11.17, there are labels at both North and South. The labels have white text on a black background so that you can see exactly where the North and South regions are.

FIGURE 11.15 East and West, with North

FIGURE 11.16 East and West, with South

FIGURE 11.17 East and West, with both North and South

The code that generated these four images is listed here. There is only one application. The code, as shown, generates Figure 11.17 (both North and South); lines 17 and 24 were judiciously commented out to generate the other figures:

```
1. import java.awt.*;
2. import javax.swing.*;
3.
4. public class EastWest extends JFrame {
5.   public static void main(String[] args) {
6.     JFrame frame = new JFrame();
7.     Container cont = frame.getContentPane();
8.
9.     cont.add(new JScrollBar(), BorderLayout.WEST);
```

Chapter 11 · Layout Managers

```
10.      cont.add(new JScrollBar(), BorderLayout.EAST);
11.
12.      JLabel topLabel = new JLabel("This is North");
13.      topLabel.setOpaque(true);
14.      topLabel.setFont(new Font("Serif", Font.PLAIN, 36));
15.      topLabel.setForeground(Color.white);
16.      topLabel.setBackground(Color.black);
17.      cont.add(topLabel, BorderLayout.NORTH);
18.
19.      JLabel bottomLabel = new JLabel("This is South");
20.      bottomLabel.setOpaque(true);
21.      bottomLabel.setFont(new Font("Monospaced",
             Font.PLAIN, 18));
22.      bottomLabel.setForeground(Color.white);
23.      bottomLabel.setBackground(Color.black);
24.      cont.add(bottomLabel, BorderLayout.SOUTH);
25.
26.      frame.setSize(400, 375);
27.      frame.setVisible(true);
28.   }
29. }
```

The fifth region that a Border layout manager controls is called Center. Center is simply the part of a container that remains after North, South, East, and West have been allocated. Figure 11.18 shows a frame with buttons at North, South, East, and West and a text area at Center.

FIGURE 11.18   The Center region

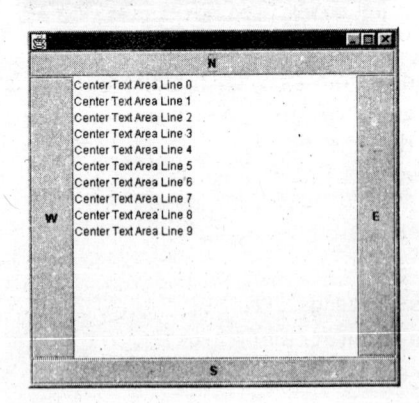

The code that generated Figure 11.18 is as follows:

```
1.  import java.awt.*;
2.  import javax.swing.*;
3.
4.  public class Center extends JFrame {
5.    public static void main(String[] args) {
6.      JFrame frame = new JFrame();
7.      Container cont = frame.getContentPane();
8.
9.      cont.add(new JButton("N"), BorderLayout.NORTH);
10.     cont.add(new JButton("S"), BorderLayout.SOUTH);
11.     cont.add(new JButton("E"), BorderLayout.EAST);
12.     cont.add(new JButton("W"), BorderLayout.WEST);
13.
14.     JTextArea ta = new JTextArea();
15.     for (int i=0; i<10; i++)
16.       ta.append("Center Text Area Line " + i + "

17.     cont.add(ta, BorderLayout.CENTER);
18.
19.     frame.setSize(400, 375);
20.     frame.setVisible(true);
21.   }
22. }
```

In line 17, the text area is added to the Center region. When adding a component to Center, it is legal, although unwise, to omit the second parameter to the add() call. In the Java 2 platform, the Border layout manager will assume that you mean Center; however, in older versions, the behavior was unpredictable and typically resulted in the component's being entirely invisible. Generally, it is easier for other people to understand your code if you explicitly specify the region, as in line 17.

Figures 11.19 and 11.20 show what happens to the Center region in the absence of various regions. The frames are generated by commenting out line 9 (for Figure 11.19) and lines 10–12 (for Figure 11.20). The figures show that Center (the text area) is simply the area that is left over after space has been given to the other regions.

FIGURE 11.19 Center, no North

FIGURE 11.20 Center, no South, East, or West

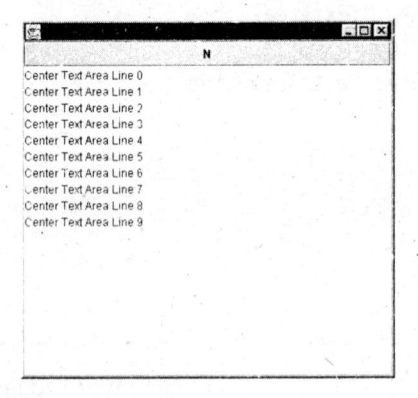

The Card Layout Manager

The Card layout manager lays out its components in time rather than in space. At any moment, a container using a Card layout manager is displaying one or another of its components; all the other components are unseen. A method call to the Card layout manager can tell it to display a different component. All the components (which are usually panels) are resized to occupy the entire container. The result is similar to a tabbed panel without the tabs.

When you use a Card layout, you have a couple of options for controlling which component is displayed and when. The Card layout gives the components that it manages a sequence, and you can ask it to display the first or last component in that sequence explicitly. In addition, you can ask for the next or previous component in the sequence. In this way, you can cycle through the components easily.

The second way to control component display is to give each component a name. If you take this approach, the Card layout allows you to select the component to be displayed using that name. This approach is much like an API equivalent of selecting a pane from a tabbed pane based on the label that it displays.

Adding Components to a Card Layout

To add components to a Card layout, you simply add them to the appropriate container. This process is like any other layout. You need to be aware of two things that influence the exact way that you add your components. First, the order in which you add the components determines the order in which they will be cycled by the Card layout, should you choose to use this feature. Second, if you want to select particular components for display using the "by name" feature mentioned in the previous paragraph, then you must supply a name when adding the component. (Obviously, the name should not be shared by any other component in the same container.)

To add a named component, simply use the `String` object that represents that name in the second argument of the add method, like this:

```
JPanel p = new JPanel();
p.setLayout(new CardLayout());
JButton b = new JButton("A Component");
p.add(b, "Button-B");
```

If you examine the API for the `Container` class, you'll see that there is another add method that takes a string as the first argument and the `Component` as the second. You can use this method, and it works. However, the API says that the add(*Component*, *Object*) version is "strongly preferred".

Selecting the Displayed Component

The Card layout manager provides five methods that can be used to select the component that is to be displayed:

- void first(*Container*)
- void last(*Container*)
- void next(*Container*)
- void previous(*Container*)
- void show(*Container*, *String*)

The first four of these methods are straightforward; `first` and `last` cause the display to select the first or last added component, respectively. Similarly, the methods `next` and `previous` cause the displayed component to be cycled based on the order in which the components were originally added to the container.

The final method, `show()`, selects a particular component based on the textual name that was given to the component when the component was added to the container. To use this method, naturally, you must provide a name for the component. You do so by using the method

add(*Component*, *Object*)

to add the component to its container and ensuring that the names given to the components are unique for that container.

Chapter 11 · Layout Managers

Let's look at an example. Note especially the lines in bold type, where components are added and displayed:

```java
import java.awt.*;
import java.awt.event.*;
import javax.swing.*;


public class CardDemo extends JPanel {
  private JPanel cardPanel = new JPanel();
  private CardLayout cardLayout = new CardLayout();

  private JPanel controlPanel = new JPanel();

  private JButton firstButton = new JButton("First");
  private JButton lastButton = new JButton("Last");
  private JButton nextButton = new JButton("Next");
  private JButton prevButton = new JButton("Prev");
  private JTextField selectText = new JTextField(" ");

  public CardDemo() {
    setLayout(new BorderLayout());

    cardPanel.setLayout(cardLayout);

    JPanel p = new JPanel();
    p.setLayout(new BorderLayout());
    p.add(new Label("This is panel One"),
        BorderLayout.CENTER);
    p.add(new Button("dummy button one"),
        BorderLayout.WEST);
    cardPanel.add(p, "1");

    p = new JPanel();
    p.setLayout(new BorderLayout());
    p.add(new Label("This is panel Two"),
        BorderLayout.CENTER);
    p.add(new Button("dummy button two"),
        BorderLayout.NORTH);
    cardPanel.add(p, "2");
```

```
p = new JPanel();
p.setLayout(new BorderLayout());
p.add(new Label("This is panel Three"),
     BorderLayout.CENTER);
p.add(new Button("dummy button three"),
     BorderLayout.SOUTH);
cardPanel.add(p, "3");

p = new JPanel();
p.setLayout(new BorderLayout());
p.add(new Label("This is panel Four"),
     BorderLayout.CENTER);
p.add(new Button("dummy button four"),
     BorderLayout.EAST);
cardPanel.add(p, "4");

add(cardPanel, BorderLayout.CENTER);

firstButton.addActionListener(
  new ActionListener() {
    public void actionPerformed(ActionEvent e){
      cardLayout.first(cardPanel);
    }
  }
);

lastButton.addActionListener(
  new ActionListener() {
    public void actionPerformed(ActionEvent e){
      cardLayout.last(cardPanel);
    }
  }
);

nextButton.addActionListener(
  new ActionListener() {
    public void actionPerformed(ActionEvent e){
      cardLayout.next(cardPanel);
    }
  }
);
```

```java
    prevButton.addActionListener(
      new ActionListener() {
        public void actionPerformed(ActionEvent e){
          cardLayout.previous(cardPanel);
        }
      }
    );

    selectText.addActionListener(
      new ActionListener() {
        public void actionPerformed(ActionEvent e) {
          cardLayout.show(cardPanel,
                          selectText.getText().trim());
        }
      }
    );

    JPanel cp1 = new JPanel();
    JPanel cp2 = new JPanel();
    cp1.add(firstButton);
    cp1.add(prevButton);
    cp1.add(nextButton);
    cp1.add(lastButton);

    cp2.add(new Label("Enter Panel Number: "));
    cp2.add(selectText);

    controlPanel.setLayout(new BorderLayout());
    controlPanel.add(cp1, BorderLayout.NORTH);
    controlPanel.add(cp2, BorderLayout.SOUTH);

    add(controlPanel, BorderLayout.SOUTH);
  }

  public static void main(String args[]) {
    JFrame f = new JFrame("CardLayout Example");
    CardDemo card = new CardDemo();
    f.getContentPane().add(card, BorderLayout.CENTER);
    f.pack();
```

```
        f.setVisible(true);
    }
}
```

The GridBag Layout Manager

GridBag is by far the most powerful layout manager. It can perform the work of the Flow, Grid, and Border layouts if appropriately programmed and is capable of much more, often without the need for nesting multiple panels as is so often required with the other layout managers.

The GridBag layout divides its container into an array of cells, but (unlike the cells of a Grid layout manager) different cell rows can have different heights, and different cell columns can have different widths. A component can occupy part or all of a region that is based on either a single cell or a rectangle made up of multiple cells. A GridBag layout manager requires a lot of information to know where to put a component. A helper class called `GridBagConstraints` is used to hold all the layout position information. When you add a component, you use the add(*Component*, *Object*) version of the add() method, passing an instance of `GridBagConstraints` as the *Object* parameter.

Designing a Layout with GridBag

Although the GridBag layout is powerful, it is sometimes considered hard to use. This perception stems mostly from two things. First, the supplied documentation, although precise and complete from a technical point of view, does not describe much more than the API. An explanation of the principles of operation is noticeably missing. Second, some aspects of the control of the GridBag layout are confusing. Specifically, you will notice that the row and column sizing controls are typically mixed in with the individual component controls. To make use the GridBag layout easily and confidently, you need to first understand the principles that drive it and then worry about the API that you must use.

Three levels of control are applied to a GridBag layout to make up the final layout in the container. The sizes of the various rows and columns, along with the way they stretch when the container is resized, must be considered. Also, the cell, or cells, that provides the target space for each component is determined. The final control determines how each component is stretched to fit or, if it isn't, how the component is positioned within the target space.

The API governing each of these aspects is built into a single mechanism based around the `GridBagConstraints` class. This class can be confusing, so we will discuss each of the principles of control separately as much as possible. As we do so, we will describe how the API controls this behavior. Finally, we will look at the interactions between these various controls and distill some generalizations that will be useful to you both when designing layouts and when answering examination questions.

Controlling the Rows and Columns

The row and column behavior of a GridBag layout has three aspects. The first is the number of rows and columns present. Typically, this total is determined by the number of rows and columns you ask to add components into. So, for example, if you place components at X coordinates 0, 1, 2, and 3, then you will find four columns in the container.

There is another way to specify that you want a particular number of rows or columns. The GridBag layout has two public variables called `columnWidths` and `rowHeights`. These are arrays of int values. If the `columnWidths` array contains four elements, then there will be (at least) four columns in the layout. The `rowHeights` affects the row count similarly. If you use these arrays, then the layout will contain at least as many rows as the size of the `rowHeights` array, and similarly the column count will be influenced by the size of the `columnWidths` array.

The second aspect is the default size of a row or column. The default height of a row is normally the preferred height of the tallest component in the row. Similarly, the default width of a column is the width of the widest component in the column. If you provided either or both of the `columnWidths` and `rowHeights` arrays, and if the value specified in the array for that particular row or column is greater than that calculated from the components, the array value will be used instead. That's easy enough, isn't it?

The final aspect of rows and columns is the stretchiness that occurs when the container is resized. It is governed by a property called *weight*. The rest of this section discusses row and column count, size, and weight.

Let's look at a trivial example that demonstrates controlling both the number of columns and the default size of those columns (it's hard to avoid having both at the same time, of course). The following example code creates a GridBag layout of three rows and three columns:

```
1.  import java.awt.*;
2.  import javax.swing.*;
3.
4.  public class GB1 extends JPanel {
5.     private JPanel tallPanel = new JPanel();
6.     private JPanel tallPanel2 = new JPanel();
7.
8.     public GB1() {
9.        tallPanel.setLayout(new GridLayout(3, 1));
10.       tallPanel.add(new Button("Press"));
11.       tallPanel.add(new Button("Any"));
12.       tallPanel.add(new Button("One"));
13.
14.       tallPanel2.setLayout(new GridLayout(3, 1));
15.       tallPanel2.add(new Button("Don't"));
16.       tallPanel2.add(new Button("Press"));
17.       tallPanel2.add(new Button("These"));
18.
19.       setLayout(new GridBagLayout());
20.
21.       GridBagConstraints c = new GridBagConstraints();
22.       c.gridx = 0; c.gridy = 0;
23.       add(new JButton("topleft"), c);
```

```
24.        c.gridx = 1;
25.        add(new JButton("topmiddle"), c);
26.        c.gridx = 2;
27.        add(new JButton("topright"), c);
28.
29.        c.gridx = 0; c.gridy = 1;
30.        add(new JButton("lefthandsidemiddle"), c);
31.        c.gridx = 1;
32.        add(tallPanel, c);
33.
34.        c.gridy = 2; // note, sets _y_
35.        add(new JButton("bottomcenter"), c);
36.        c.gridx = 2;
37.        add(tallPanel2, c);
38.    }
39.
40.    public static void main(String args[]) {
41.        JFrame f = new JFrame("GridBag 1 example");
42.        f.getContentPane().add(new GB1());
43.        f.pack();
44.        f.setVisible(true);
45.    }
46. }
```

This code results in a display like the one in Figure 11.21.

FIGURE 11.21   GridBag layout example

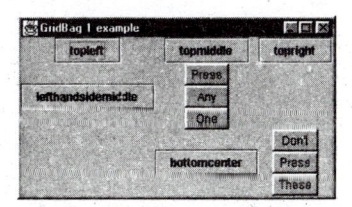

Notice how each component that is added is positioned using a `GridBagConstraints` object—actually the same object, but with different values. The `GridBagConstraints` object is used to specify all the controlling parameters for a GridBag layout and is provided each time a component is added. The GridBag layout itself copies the values, so it's quite all right to reuse the constraints object for each component you add.

Let's look at the behavior for a moment. We've said that this example produces three rows and three columns, and yet it might not be obvious where those row and column boundaries are. The diagram in Figure 11.22 shows these boundaries.

362 Chapter 11 · Layout Managers

FIGURE 11.22 Row and column boundaries in the GridBag layout example

You will see that two cells of the layout are unused, at 0, 2 (the bottom-left corner) and 2, 1 (right side, halfway down). This is not a problem, because the GridBag layout calculates the number of rows and columns required.

Each component in this layout was positioned explicitly using the `gridx` and `gridy` elements of the `GridBagConstraints` object. You do not always have to work quite this hard, but for now, it is easier to understand what is happening if you do. Therefore, we will continue to use this approach for a while longer.

Notice that each row has a height, determined by the tallest component that it contains; similarly, the width of each row is based on the widest component. For components that are smaller in one dimension or the other than the space available to them, you'll see that the component is left at its natural size and is placed in the middle of the available space. Although this behavior is the default, you will see later how to change it, too.

So, the remaining question to address is, what happens if the container is resized? We didn't specify any stretchiness for these rows and columns, so all that happens is that the space is wasted—actually, it is distributed evenly around the whole layout, as shown in Figure 11.23.

FIGURE 11.23 GridBag layout example with an enlarged window

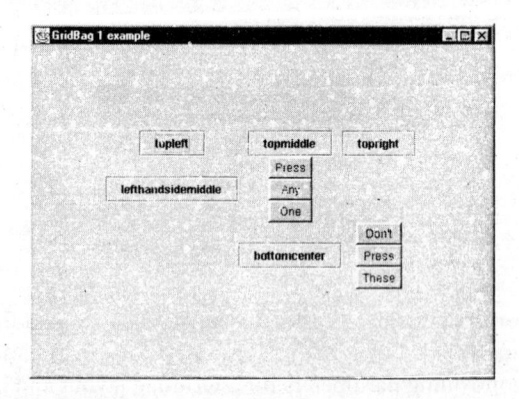

Often you will want to use this extra space, and doing so involves two steps. As we just said, components that are smaller than the available cell sit in the middle of the available space. If we

Layout Policies

enlarge the space, we must also change that behavior. We'll look at that technique shortly; for now. let's see how to enlarge the space. We will modify the program so that the center row and center column are allocated all the available space when the container is enlarged. To do this, we specify a nonzero value for the weight applied to the row and column.

The curious thing about weight is that it is specified using the members weightx and weighty in the GridBagConstraints object, so a value is specified for every component. This is odd because the value applies to the *row* or *column*, not to the individual component. To deal with this approach, be careful to specify a weightx in only one component in each column (weightx controls horizontal stretchiness) and a weighty in only one component in each row. We will modify our earlier example so that the right column and bottom row stretch to use up the available space. Rather than reprint the entire program to show the two areas of modification, we'll just show you the parts that relate to adding components to the layout:

```
21.     GridBagConstraints c = new GridBagConstraints();
22.     c.gridx = 0; c.gridy = 0;
23.     add(new JButton("topleft"), c);
24.     c.gridx = 1;
25.     add(new JButton("topmiddle"), c);
26.     c.gridx = 2;
27.     c.weightx = 1.0;   // This col is stretchy
28.     add(new JButton("topright"), c);
29.     c.weightx = 0.0;   // No other col stretches
30.
31.     c.gridx = 0; c.gridy = 1;
32.     add(new JButton("lefthandsidemiddle"), c);
33.     c.gridx = 1;
34.     add(tallPanel, c);
35.
36.     c.gridy = 2; // sets _y_
37.     add(new JButton("bottomcenter"), c);
38.     c.gridx = 2;
39.     c.weighty = 1.0;   // This row is stretchy
40.     add(tallPanel2, c);
41.     c.weighty = 0.0;   // No other row stretches
```

You'll see the components added at lines 28 and 40 have had weight applied to them. Don't forget: although this weight is carried on the back of a component, it applies to the row or column being added to and *not* to the component. So, at line 28, we're really setting a weightx value of 1 on *column* 2 (the last column), and similarly at line 40, we're setting a weighty value on *row* 2.

The effect of this change, after enlarging the window and adding the grid boundary lines, is shown in Figure 11.24.

FIGURE 11.24 GridBag layout example with weights applied and an enlarged window

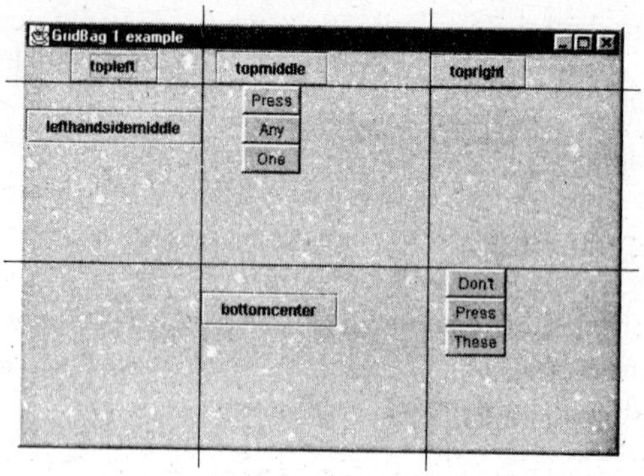

Two questions remain. First, what is the significance of the value "1.0" that was set as the weight—what would be the effect of other values? Second, how can you make more than one row or column stretch? It turns out that these two questions are related. If you apply weight values to more than one row or column, then the available space is divided among those rows or columns. Exactly how it is divided is determined by the weight values.

The weight values you specify represent a *proportion* of the whole space; the width (in the case of columns) gained is the ratio of a column's weight to the total of all column weights. If you have three columns with weights of 9, 9, and 18, respectively, then the first two will each get one-fourth of the total width gain: 9 / (9 + 9 + 18). The third column will get one-half of the extra space for itself. Similarly, if you specify the same weight for each (7, 7, and 7, for instance), then each column will gain one-third of the total space gained. The same calculations hold true for vertical stretch by rows.

Weights can be any number. They do not have to add to 1.0 or 100, but it is generally reasonable to use weights that add to 100 (or thereabouts) so that you can consider the values to be percentages. Just bear in mind that doing so is not required.

Although it is usual to set weights for rows and columns by using a `GridBagConstraints` object when a component is added, this is neither the only nor perhaps the best way to do so. Instead, you can use the public variables `rowWeights` and `columnWeights`. These variables are both arrays of `double` values and will act as minimum weights for each row or column. It makes little sense from a style point of view to specify weights for a row or column by means of data passed when adding a component to a cell.

Using the `rowWeights` and `columnWeights` arrays has two advantages. First, it makes much more sense to set the weights this way. Second, and more important, it lets you set a weight on a row or column that might not have any one component uniquely in that row or column. Using these arrays in conjunction with the `rowHeights` and `columnWidths` arrays allows you to simplify the code of many layouts and to avoid the use of dummy components (a technique you sometimes see used in complex GridBag layouts).

We have spent a long time on this discussion, so let's summarize what you've learned so far:
- The number of rows and columns in a GridBag layout is the greater of the number of cells that are used, or the size of the `rowHeights` and `columnWidths` arrays if these exist.
- The default size of each row and column is the size of its tallest or widest component, respectively, or the value in the relevant entry in the `rowHeights` or `columnWidths` array if the array exists and specifies a larger size than the default would otherwise be.
- Stretchiness of rows and columns is controlled by weight.
- Stretchiness is applied using the `weightx` (for a column) and `weighty` (for a row) values of the `GridBagConstraints` object, or by using the `rowWeights` and `columnWeights` arrays.
- Although `weightx` and `weighty` values exist for every component that is added, the values are meant for the row or column to which the component is added, not for the component itself. You should set a nonzero value for *at most* one component per row and one per column. (Note that you might have a component with both `weightx` and `weighty` set; rows and columns are independent things.) Using the `rowWeights` and `columnWeights` arrays can simplify this process considerably.
- The amount of stretch in a row or column is calculated as the total stretch divided in the same ratio as the individual weight values relative to the total weight for that axis. In math terms, if the weights are $w1$, $w2$, and $w3$, and the total stretch available is s, then the stretch applied to each column will be $s1$, $s2$, and $s3$ where $s1 = s \therefore w1 / (w1 + w2 + w3)$ and $s2 = s \therefore w2 / (w1 + w2 + w3)$ and $s3 = s \therefore w3 / (w1 + w2 + w3)$.

The next aspect we will look at is how a component is positioned when the target region in which it is located is larger than the component itself.

Controlling Component Position and Stretch in a Cell

You saw in the previous example that a component that occupies an oversized cell is normally placed in the center of the space, at its preferred size. Both these features are controllable. Using a feature called anchor, you can control where the component is placed within its available space. Using a feature called `fill`, you can determine whether a component stretches to fill the available space, either horizontally, vertically, or both. Let's look at several examples. We will start with this code:

```
1. import java.awt.*;
2. import java.awt.event.*;
3. import javax.swing.*;
4.
5. public class GB2 extends JPanel {
6.    public GB2() {
7.       Font bigfont = new Font("Serif", Font.PLAIN, 36);
8.       setLayout(new GridBagLayout());
9.       GridBagConstraints c = new GridBagConstraints();
10.
```

```
11.     c.gridx = 0; c.gridy = 0;
12.     addButton("TL", bigfont, c);
13.     c.gridx = 1;
14.     addButton("Top Middle", bigfont, c);
15.     c.gridx = 2;
16.     addButton("TR", bigfont, c);
17.
18.     c.gridx = 0; c.gridy = 1;
19.     addButton("ML", bigfont, c);
20.     c.gridx = 2;   // note skipped over x=1, y=1
21.     addButton("MR", bigfont, c);
22.
23.     c.gridx = 0; c.gridy = 2;
24.     addButton("BL", bigfont, c);
25.     c.gridx = 1;
26.     addButton("Bottom Middle", bigfont, c);
27.     c.gridx = 2;
28.     addButton("BR", bigfont, c);
29.
30.     Font smallfont = new Font("SansSerif", Font.PLAIN, 10);
31.     c.gridx = 1; c.gridy = 1;
32.     addButton("x", smallfont, c);
33.   }
34.
35.   private void addButton(String label, Font font,
36.                           GridBagConstraints gbc)
37.   {
38.     JButton btn = new JButton(label);
39.     btn.setFont(font);
40.     add(btn, gbc);
41.   }
42.
43.   public static void main(String args[]) {
44.     JFrame f = new JFrame("GridBag Example 2");
45.     f.getContentPane().add(new GB2(),
           BorderLayout.CENTER);
46.     f.pack();
47.     f.setVisible(true);
48.   }
49. }
```

When run, this code produces the output shown in Figure 11.25. Notice that the little button in the middle simply lies in the center of the space available to it.

FIGURE 11.25 GridBag layout example showing an unfilled, centered component

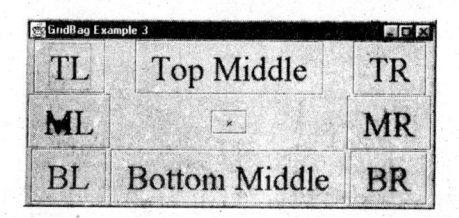

Let's look at the positions this component can occupy if we set different anchor values for it. The names of the anchor values are based on compass point names and are defined in the `GridBagConstraints` class as: NORTH, SOUTH, EAST, WEST, NORTHWEST, SOUTHWEST, NORTHEAST, SOUTHEAST, and CENTER. The default value for anchor, and the one exemplified in Figure 11.25, is CENTER. Now we'll make a small modification to the example program to see what happens if we change this anchor value. The modified programs are almost identical to the previous one, except that an additional constraint value is set on the small button to define the anchor. Figures 11.26, 11.27, and 11.28 show anchor values of NORTHWEST, SOUTHEAST, and EAST respectively. The effect of the anchor will be clear from these three examples without showing all the possible values.

FIGURE 11.26 GridBag layout example showing an unfilled component with a NORTHWEST anchor

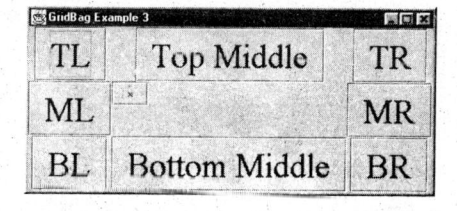

FIGURE 11.27 GridBag layout example showing an unfilled component with a SOUTHEAST anchor

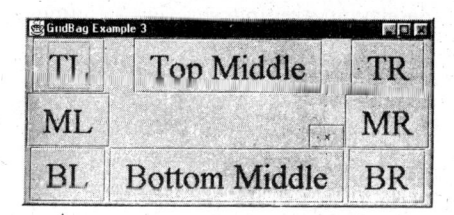

368 Chapter 11 • Layout Managers

FIGURE 11.28 GridBag layout example showing an unfilled component with an EAST anchor

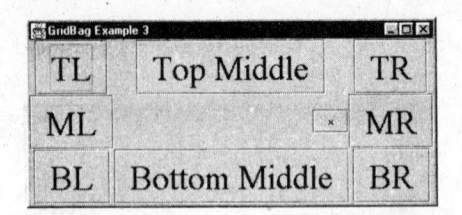

Now let's examine the `fill` feature. We'll start with the same code we used before, but instead of setting `anchor` values for the small button, we will set `fill` values. There are four `fill` values to choose from, and as with `anchor` values, they are defined in the `GridBagConstraints` class. The values are NONE (the default), HORIZONTAL, VERTICAL, and BOTH. In the current example, we can give the button's anchor a default value and its fill a value of `GridBagConstraints.HORIZONTAL` to get the effect shown in Figure 11.29.

FIGURE 11.29 GridBag layout example showing a component with HORIZONTAL fill

Figures 11.30 and 11.31 respectively show what happens if we change the `fill` value to VERTICAL and BOTH.

FIGURE 11.30 GridBag layout example showing a component with VERTICAL fill

FIGURE 11.31 GridBag layout example showing a component with BOTH fill

Layout Policies   369

You can see that the effects of fill somewhat nullify the effects of anchor. That is, if a component is stretched to fill its cell horizontally, then the anchor cannot move it left, right, or center. Similarly, if the component fills its cell vertically, then trying to anchor it to the top, middle, or bottom is meaningless. So, if you have a fill value of HORIZONTAL, then anchor values of WEST, CENTER, and EAST would all produce the same effect. If fill is BOTH, the anchor value has no effect and should most sensibly be left at its default (CENTER).

Controlling the Cell Size for a Component

When you design a GUI using a GridBag layout, you sometimes find that components do not fit neatly into a simple grid, but the layout still presents the general idea of rows and columns. Consider the layout in Figure 11.32.

FIGURE 11.32 GridBag layout example showing components overlapping multiple rows and columns

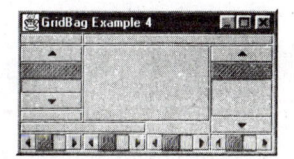

This example has five rows and four columns, although several of the components extend over more than one of each. Figure 11.33 has been modified to show the boundaries of the rows and columns more clearly.

FIGURE 11.33 GridBagLayout example showing boundaries of rows and columns

To achieve this effect of component cells that span multiple rows and/or columns, the GridBagConstraints object provides fields called gridwidth and gridheight. Let's look at the code that produced this example, and you will see these fields in action:

```
1. import java.awt.*;
2. import javax.swing.*;
3.
4.
5. public class CellSize extends JPanel {
6.    public CellSize () {
```

Chapter 11 • Layout Managers

```
7.     setLayout(new GridBagLayout());
8.     GridBagConstraints c = new GridBagConstraints();
9.
10.    // show entire cell region for all components
11.    c.fill = GridBagConstraints.BOTH;
12.    c.gridx = 0; c.gridy = 0;
13.    c.gridwidth = 1;
14.    c.gridheight = 1;
15.    add(new JButton(), c);
16.
17.    c.gridx = 1; c.gridy = 0;
18.    c.gridwidth = 3;
19.    c.gridheight = 1;
20.    add(new JButton(), c);
21.
22.    c.gridx = 0; c.gridy = 1;
23.    c.gridwidth = 1;
24.    c.gridheight = 1;
25.    add(new JScrollBar(JScrollBar.VERTICAL,
26.            0, 10, 0, 100), c);
27.
28.    c.gridx = 1; c.gridy = 1;
29.    c.gridwidth = 2;
30.    c.gridheight = 2;
31.    add(new JButton(), c);
32.
33.    c.gridx = 3; c.gridy = 1;
34.    c.gridwidth = 1;
35.    c.gridheight = 3;
36.    add(new JScrollBar(JScrollBar.VERTICAL,
37.            0, 10, 0, 250), c);
38.
39.    c.gridx = 0; c.gridy = 2;
40.    c.gridwidth = 1;
41.    c.gridheight = 1;
42.    add(new JButton(), c);
43.
44.    c.gridx = 0; c.gridy = 3;
45.    c.gridwidth = 2;
46.    c.gridheight = 1;
```

```
47.        add(new JButton(), c);
48.
49.        c.gridx = 0; c.gridy = 4;
50.        c.gridwidth = 1;
51.        c.gridheight = 1;
52.        add(new JScrollBar(JScrollBar.HORIZONTAL,
53.                0, 10, 0, 100), c);
54.
55.        c.gridx = 1; c.gridy = 4;
56.        c.gridwidth = 1;
57.        c.gridheight = 1;
58.        add(new JScrollBar(JScrollBar.HORIZONTAL,
59.                0, 10, 0, 100), c);
60.
61.        c.gridx = 2; c.gridy = 4;
62.        c.gridwidth = 1;
63.        c.gridheight = 1;
64.        add(new JScrollBar(JScrollBar.HORIZONTAL,
65.                0, 10, 0, 100), c);
66.
67.        c.gridx = 3; c.gridy = 4;
68.        c.gridwidth = 1;
69.        c.gridheight = 1;
70.        add(new JScrollBar(JScrollBar.HORIZONTAL,
71.                0, 10, 0, 100), c);
72.
73.    }
74.
75.    public static void main(String args[]) {
76.        JFrame f = new JFrame("GridBag Example 4");
77.        f.getContentPane().add(new CellSize(),
               BorderLayout.CENTER);
78.        f.pack();
79.        f.setVisible(true);
80.    }
81. }
```

Notice that at line 11 the `fill` value has been set to BOTH and is left at this setting for all uses of the `GridBagConstraints` object. As a result, all components will be stretched to fill their cells; this is the case even if the cell extends over multiple rows or columns. This way, you can see more easily where the boundaries of the cells are.

The next point about this code is that it is considerably longer than it needs to be. For every component that is added, the settings of `gridx`, `gridy`, `gridwidth`, and `gridheight` are explicitly set just before the `add()` method is called. You do so even when a value is not being changed, simply to make it easier to see how each value is set without having to scan up and down too far.

Compare the code with the screen shot in Figure 11.33. You will see the correspondence between `gridwidth` and the number of columns a component spans, and between `gridheight` and the number of rows a component spans. For example, the right button at the top of the layout is created by lines 17–20 of the code. At line 18, `gridwidth` is set to 3, and Figure 11.33 shows that the button extends across three columns.

Similarly, the large central button is set up by lines 28–31. Notice that the `gridwidth` and `gridheight` values are set to 2. Figure 11.33 shows that the button is two columns wide and two rows high.

One aspect warrants further mention. At row 3, column 2, there is a blank space. This is perfectly acceptable, although it is unlikely to happen in a real GUI layout. If you work through all the positions, `gridwidth` values, and `gridheight` values, you will see that no component has been placed in, or overlaps, that region.

That's about it for spanning multiple rows and columns. It's not really difficult, although it may have seemed that way before. Now, let's look at a convenient shorthand mechanism that the GridBag layout offers.

GridBag's Shorthand

You have undoubtedly seen two features used in GridBag layout examples: RELATIVE and REMAINDER. These settings provide a shorthand mechanism designed to reduce typing when you're coding a GridBag layout. They can also simplify maintenance of some types of layout.

If you think back to the earlier examples, you will recall seeing many lines setting values for `gridx` and `gridy`. Very often, the value being set was greater by one than the current value; this is often the case in real layouts, too. If you add your components in an orderly fashion, then you will probably set up the component in row zero, column zero first; then do column one, column two; and so on. You could do so by using code like this:

```
c.gridx++;
```

instead of the explicit numeric assignment used earlier.

In many cases, if you are filling a layout completely, from top-left to bottom-right, one row at a time, then the shorthand mechanism of RELATIVE and REMAINDER will help. Let's look at a simple example:

```
import java.awt.*;
import javax.swing.*;

public class Shorthand extends JPanel {
```

```java
public Shorthand () {
  setLayout(new GridBagLayout());
  GridBagConstraints c = new GridBagConstraints();
  c.fill = GridBagConstraints.BOTH;
  c.weightx = 1;

  add(new JButton("1"), c);
  add(new JButton("2"), c);
  add(new JButton("3"), c);
  add(new JButton("4"), c);
  c.gridwidth = GridBagConstraints.REMAINDER;
  add(new JButton("5"), c);
  c.gridwidth = 1;
  c.weightx = 0;

  add(new JButton("A"), c);
  add(new JButton("B"), c);
  add(new JButton("C"), c);
  c.gridwidth = GridBagConstraints.REMAINDER;
  add(new JButton("D"), c);
  c.gridwidth = 1;

  add(new JButton("a"), c);
  c.gridwidth = GridBagConstraints.RELATIVE;
  add(new JButton("b"), c);
  c.gridwidth = GridBagConstraints.REMAINDER;
  add(new JButton("c"), c);
  c.gridwidth = 1;
}

public static void main(String args[]) {
  JFrame f = new JFrame("GridBag Example 5");
  Shorthand sh = new Shorthand();
  f.getContentPane().add(sh, BorderLayout.CENTER);
  f.pack();
  f.setVisible(true);
 }
}
```

The output of this program is shown in Figure 11.34.

FIGURE 11.34   GridBag layout example using the RELATIVE and REMAINDER shorthands

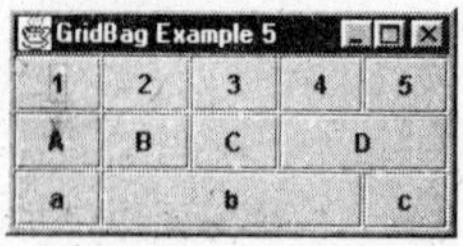

Notice that when the `GridBagConstraints` object is constructed, its values are mostly left constant. Notably, we never set any value for `gridx` or `gridy`; in fact, these values remain at their default—RELATIVE—throughout the program. It's important to realize that the x and y control in this example is done entirely with the `gridwidth` value.

We use the value REMAINDER in the `gridwidth` field to indicate the last component on each line. After each line end, we set `gridwidth` back to 1, because failing to do so would cause every component to be on a line of its own for the rest of the layout.

The button labeled b is interesting, too. You will see that we set a value for `gridwidth` of RELATIVE for this button. As a result, it fills the space from its own starting point to the start of the last column. The documentation describes the component as being the "last but one". This effect can be useful when you are creating a workspace area and want to have a row of buttons either under it or down the right side, as you might for a toolbar.

Clearly, this way of using the GridBag layout can make the code much simpler, although in some layouts it might still be easier to read the code if you explicitly state the x and y coordinate values for each component as you add it. You will have to use your own judgment on this point.

This concludes our discussion of the GridBag layout and of the AWT suite of five layout managers.

Other Layout Options

The five layout managers of the AWT package will support most layout schemes you might want to implement. However, it is useful to know a little about the other options. If you are in a situation where Flow, Grid, Border, Card, and GridBag will not create the layout you need, your choices are

- To find a layout manager from another source
- To create your own layout manager
- To use no layout manager

Finding a third-party layout manager might be simple or hard, depending on the particular behavior you want. Several have been described in books, and more are available as freeware, as shareware, or in commercial graphics libraries for Java.

It is beyond the scope of this book to show you how to concoct your own layout manager, but for simple layout policies it is not especially difficult to do so. The advantage of creating a custom layout manager over setting a container's layout manager to `null` is that you no longer have to write code to detect resizing of the container; you just write code to implement the layout policy, and the system will make the right calls at the right time. Writing your own layout manager class involves implementing the `LayoutManager` interface (or possibly the `LayoutManager2` interface).

You always have the option of using no layout manager at all. To do this, just call

```
myContainer.setLayout(null);
```

If a container has no layout manager, it honors each component's `x`, `y`, `width`, and `height` values. Thus, you can call `setBounds()` on a component, `add()` it to a container that has no layout manager, and have the component end up where you expect it to be. This approach is tempting, but we hope the first part of this chapter has convinced you that layout managers are simple and efficient to work with. Moreover, if your container resides in a larger container (a frame, for example) that gets resized, your layout may need to be redone to save components from being overlaid or clipped away. People who set a container's layout manager to `null` find that they have to write code to detect when the container resizes, and more code to do the right thing when resizing occurs. Doing so ends up being more complicated than creating your own layout manager.

Summary

Layout managers provide a layer of geometrical support that relieves you of having to specify the size and position of each GUI component you create. The tradeoff is that you must be aware of the layout policy implemented by each of the various layout managers. You are forced to think in terms of layout policy, rather than in terms of size and position.

This chapter has discussed the five AWT layout managers: Flow, Grid, Border, Card, and GridBag.

Exam Essentials

The AWT toolkit includes five layout-manager classes. The five layout managers in the AWT are Flow, Grid, Border, Card, and GridBag.

Swing GUIs reside in a `JFrame` or in a `JApplet`. Standalone applications use a `JFrame` and web applets use a `JApplet`.

GridBag is the most powerful layout manager. It can perform the work of the Flow, Grid, and Border layouts if appropriately programmed.

Key Terms

Before you take the exam, be certain you are familiar with the following terms:

column	preferred size
hierarchy	row
justification	weight

Review Questions

1. The layout managers available in the AWT do not include which of the following?
   A. GridBag
   B. Card
   C. SpreadSheet
   D. Flow

2. If you don't specify a layout manager for a component, then the default layout manager will call which of the following functions that will override your selection of component size?
   A. setEnabled()
   B. setSize()
   C. setBounds()
   D. setPosition()

3. The Flow layout manager arranges components in which of the following?
   A. Columns
   B. Rows
   C. Cells
   D. North, South, East, and West

4. Which of the following features is not available using the GridBag layout manager?
   A. Controlling the column width and row height
   B. Placing a component using rectangular coordinates
   C. Defining the size of a cell
   D. Placing a component using polar coordinates

5. When selecting a layout manager to organize and display your GUI components, which of the following are valid options?
   A. Don't use a layout manager
   B. Define your own layout manager
   C. Use multiple layout managers
   D. All of the above are valid options

Answers to Review Questions

1. **C.** GridBag, Card, and Flow are three of the five layout managers available in the AWT.

2. **C.** The layout manager always calls the `setBounds()` method, which will negate any size settings you may have made on a component.

3. **B.** Flow layout uses rows. Grid layout and GridBag layout use cells. Border layout uses North, South, East, and West.

4. **D.** Component location is specified using a row and column (rectangular coordinates), not with radial and angular values (polar coordinates).

5. **D.** You are not required to use a single layout manager for your entire GUI, nor are you required to use a layout manager at all. You can create your own layout manager, or obtain one from a third-party vendor.

Chapter 12

Writing the Network Protocol

The previous two chapters discussed how to write a front-end client GUI using Swing and one or more layout managers. This chapter and the next will discuss how to connect that client to a back-end database.

Whatever method you choose to manage the application, it's always good design to maintain independence between the server that encapsulates the database (or any application it will serve) and the database itself. Ideally, the application and all classes related to its operation should present themselves in as few references as practically attainable within the server code. As the exchange point between all possible clients and the data, the application server already has plenty of functionaries to manage. The initial design goal for it should be to maintain the cleanest possible separation of role-players. One assumption we will maintain in this chapter is that the database has been wrapped in such a manner.

Concurrency, or designing for multithreaded access, is only part of the puzzle. You have to decide early how you are going to institute inter-VM operations. If you want to build incrementally, you can define a network communication protocol, set up a loop to handle incoming requests, and add a scheduling system for the actual jobs. In the world of request-response Internet services, this is solid and well-trod ground. Java's object serialization facility lightens the load a bit, making it possible to send over the network single objects that contain all the details of a given request. There are lots of details to implement and document in this manner, but you can then build in new services one by one, verifying operations along the way. With a little planning, new request types can be written as classes that conform to a general interface contract, making it a simple matter to incorporate new jobs into the client-server scheme.

However, if you want to avoid the details of how services are provided and focus solely on what services to provide, you need another approach. To make one VM's call on another VM's resources appear as a matter of detail—an important concept in distributed computing—you need an API that renders the need for a communications protocol transparent to the programmer. That convenience, of course, exacts its own costs, the first of which is defining client requirements in advance. To take advantage of RMI's services, a de facto network protocol and object transport system, you forego the ability to tinker with and refine services. Redefining a client service with RMI would mean rewriting and recompiling the service objects and the client code, which would become tedious quickly. You have to know what you want in advance so that RMI does what it does best: hides the details of remote resources and expediting requests.

We'll discuss each method in turn in this chapter, weaving in the discussion of threading where appropriate, and saving for last some approaches to job scheduling that would apply equally well to both models.

Client-Server from Scratch

Java makes building the network aspect of a simple client-server application easy. The explosive rise in web server deployment has made communicating over the network, by way of requesting "pages" of data, such a pervasive model that the JDK provides an entire library of tools to adopt it. This rapid change in the way most of us use computers has brought with it some devaluation of the term *client-server*. A client-server system signifies the potential for a persistent connection between two machines; the dividing line between who processes what is somewhat negotiable. Basic web servers are arguably better described as *request-response* information servers. Electronic commerce and other forms of facilitating browser access to a back-end database or other interactive facility are increasingly blurring this distinction, but HTTP servers are so widespread and cheap to implement that people will continue to develop and extend them—and live with their restrictions. Until web servers that can track clients across their individual requests come into wide use, attempts to implement "true" client-server systems will largely remain restricted to individual development efforts.

Server Operation

A server's fundamental job is to run indefinitely, listening for and servicing requests. To reach the server, a client must know the name of the machine the server runs on, the *port* or channel it listens to, and the correct way to state a request. For widely popular service types, these last two elements usually assume the status of convention by way of a standards committee, such as the Internet Engineering Task Force (IETF). The user community relies on such committees to provide consensus or an authoritative message for agreed-upon standards and to make the information available to the public. For example, you usually don't have to find a web server by its port number because a *well-known port* (80) has been agreed on and is even assumed by browsers unless you direct them explicitly to another port.

HTTP servers also use a standardized protocol to which clients adhere in order to receive the services they want. It is common for these types of servers to "speak" across the network in clear text, which makes testing and debugging much easier. The minimum request that a web server honors, once a client connects to it, looks like this:

```
GET /
<A blank line and carriage return signal a completed request.>
...
```

Here the server is instructed to transmit the default or *home* page in its root document directory using version 1 of the HTTP protocol. If you were to telnet into a web server instead of using a browser and submit this request, you'd get a stream of HTML code as a response. The browser simply formats the response according to the HTML tags that are part of the response.

Chapter 12 · Writing the Network Protocol

This paradigm is so widely used that most of the needed behavior is already encapsulated in the java.net classes:

```java
import java.net.*;
import java.io.*;

public class Server implements Runnable {
  public final static int WK_PORT = 2012;
  protected int port;
  protected ServerSocket service;
  private String message = "Hello client!";

  public Server(int portRequested) {
    if (portRequested < 1024 || portRequested> 65535) {
      port = WK_PORT;
    }
    else {
      port = portRequested;
    }
    try {
      service = new ServerSocket(port);
    }
    catch (IOException ioe) {
      System.out.println("Error: Port " + port +
      "was not available.");
    }
    System.out.println("Port " + port +
    " is up and running.");
  }

  public void run() {
    InputStream receiving;
    OutputStream sending;
    while (true) {
      try {
        Socket client = service.accept();
        sending = client.getOutputStream();
        receiving = client.getInputStream();
        // insert code to accept client input
        // return request information, if any
```

```
      sending.write(message.getBytes());
    }
    catch (IOException ioe) {
      System.out.println("Could not accept client " +
      "request or establish streams.");
    }
  }
}

public static void main(String args[]) {
  Server svr = new Server(WK_PORT);
  svr.run ();
}
}
```

After establishing itself as a port listener, the server creates and maintains incoming connections within its own thread of execution. At the same time, it's also possible to run multiple `Server` instances on different ports of the same machine. Our code checks to see whether a legal port number is entered: on Unix systems, ports below 1024 are reserved for the super-user. TCP/IP supports 2^{16} ports, making 65535 the upper limit of the number of ports. We also chose to catch the `IOException` that would be thrown if a `Server` instance attempted to start on a port already in use, in order to clarify the nature of this fault to the user. We could do more, of course, if we did not want the instance to terminate on this error. We also need to think about how to protect the database itself—not a straightforward task to accomplish while also maintaining platform independence.

Within the `run()` method, we've written just enough client-response code to test correct runtime behavior; we've made no attempt to thread client requests yet. Once a request does connect, `ServerSocket` returns an object that encapsulates the client's connection and the means for opening lines of communication between the two. This information is then managed by the `Socket` reference `client`, which invokes input and output streams to facilitate client-server communication. There is of course no need to open an `InputStream` if the socket has no reason to listen to the client.

To test this initial version, you don't need to write any Java. Java's networking library runs over TCP/IP as the transport protocol, which means Java network code can communicate with other TCP/IP-based applications, like Telnet. Telnet is a mainstay tool of Unix systems and is probably available and in your command path. You can then do the following:

```
$ javac Server.java
$ java Server &
$ telnet localhost 2012
Hello client!
```

> **TIP:** On a Windows machine, you must start the Server in its own window, and then telnet to it through another window. Also, be sure a TCP/IP stack has been configured and is currently active among the list of network drivers. You can check this setting in the Control Panel by clicking the Network icon and browsing the Configuration panel's list of drivers.

Connecting Clients to the Server

Our bare-bones server code is not very interesting, but it gives us the first building block we need. As we further define the model for connecting multiple clients and threading the requests they carry, we need to think about mapping out the various tasks and developing a working set of class relationships. One of the first things to consider (because we know we will have to thread client requests) is encapsulating each client connection in its own object running on its own thread. The server code must then provide a way to:

- Remember each client
- Check the state of each client and its request regularly
- Restore resources used by the client when done

Each of these tasks grows more complex or involves more than one basic job, so you should think again about forming classes to divide responsibilities economically. Before we get too deeply engrossed in class design, however, let's establish how the client will call for the services provided by the application.

Communication Protocol

A communication protocol, such as HTTP, defines how the client and server communicate with one another. An HTTP server supports a variety of service-call keywords, like GET and POST, which any client browser can issue. These service calls are transmitted to the HTTP server via the communication protocol, which the server understands. The server recognizes these keywords as signals to invoke the corresponding method call.

If we were to write our own application from the ground up, this is probably where we would begin. By determining what services our application should provide, we can quickly define a communication protocol to implement (however small) that specifies how to service client requests. Other communication protocols might include FTP, Gopher, and DayTime protocols. In a well-disciplined design environment, making such decisions early lets some aspects of client and server development continue in parallel.

Define the Operations

In the project assignment, if you decide to build the client-server interaction from scratch, you will need to document the following:

- The action represented by each service code
- The data, if any, that must follow the code
- The data, if any, that the server should return
- Expected behavior if the data is inconsistent with the request or response
- What to do in "corner cases," or events that result from system operation the request cannot control

This last point is especially important from a maintenance perspective. Anticipating odd but plausible situations early in design helps future maintainers avoid patching problematic situations with exception handling or some other cumbersome workaround, when no one wants to alter an otherwise acceptable design. How will the program behave if a find operation returns a `null` pointer? What if a record you want to delete has already been purged? The more specific and detailed your understanding of system behavior in these cases, the plainer the coding tasks become.

Let's assume for the sake of illustration that our database application wants to make available a minimum complement of services (some of the issues addressed in the previous list are only noted in part here and in the subsequent code example; the assignment documentation should strive to be thorough in this respect):

Add   Given a `String` array that conforms to the record type, this command prompts the database to convert the array into a record and return the unique ID assigned to it. The client is responsible for knowing the record layout and providing appropriate data.

Modify   Given a `String` array that conforms to the record type, this command prompts the database to update a record that is specified by its ID. `Modify` does not protect against multiple concurrent updates—the last change supersedes all previous changes.

Delete   Given a unique ID, this command removes the associated record from the database. Requests to delete a record that has already been purged are ignored.

Find   Given a single `String`, this command returns a list of all records that have matching data in at least one of their fields.

Scheme   This command returns to the requesting client the type and width of all columns used by records in the database.

Implement the Protocol

Interfaces are an ideal repository for static data such as codes that specify the legal calls a client can make to the server. Any class that implements the interface gains access to its list of constants, which in this example are nothing more than named integer values, similar to what you would expect in a C language header file. In the following example, we use integers as placeholder values for each operation we define. These values are sometimes called *magic numbers*, and it's helpful to use hexadecimal notation to express them. Notice how we've used expressions like 0xA0A1, for the simple advantage of making the value more memorable. Such notation could also be useful for debugging, where values extracted from the compiled code are often expressed in hex:

```
/**
 * Services specifies the various operations the client
 * may call on the application to provide.
 *
 * @author Mobile Conferencing IT.
 */
public interface DataServices {

  /**
   * The ADD_RECORD command prompts the database to
   * include the data that follows it as a new record.
   * The client is responsible for the data provided
   * conforms to the record's fields.
   */
  public static final int ADD_RECORD = 0xA0A1;

  /**
   * MODIFY_RECORD must be followed by an existing record
   * ID and the intended modifications.
   */
  public static final int MODIFY_RECORD = 0xB0B1;

  /**
   * DELETE_RECORD must be followed by a record ID. It
   * prompts the database to purge the indicated record,
   * or ignore the request if the record is no longer
   * resident.
   */
  public static final int DELETE_RECORD = 0xD0D1;

  /**
   * FIND_RECORDS is followed by a String representing
   * the match criteria. The database is prompted to find
   * every match among the available records and return a
```

```
 * list of "hits" or a null pointer.
 */
public static final int FIND_RECORDS = 0xF0F1;

/**
 * SCHEME requires no arguments and prompts the
 * database to list the column names and widths that
 * compose each record.
 */
public static final int SCHEME = 0xFFFF;
}
```

Thinking ahead for a second, an additional benefit of the interface is that it gives you a document from which to extrapolate "job" classes, which might operate on a separate thread from the client that initiates the interface. Each type of operation could be contained in a class that implements something like a Job interface, and the job itself could run as a thread in a group, along with other threads that perform the same function. You can look for ways to achieve some economy of threads in one scenario if you bundle certain jobs to run concurrently against the data store (because they don't change anything), whereas others must observe a strict queue. We'll develop this idea further once we have explored both this approach and RMI in full.

The Client Request Structure

As mentioned earlier, the server should keep an account of all current client connections, check their connection status and the progress of their requests, and recoup server resources once a connection terminates. An intuitive first step toward the first objective is to separate out client connections and requests and give them their own classes. Using the Socket reference returned by accept(), you can construct a Client instance and read the service call written by the remote machine to form a Request. Setting up the server to juggle concurrent instances is simple. All the Client class has to do is implement Runnable, construct a thread for itself, call its own start() method, and execute its central processes from that point, thereby keeping the listener loop free of the details and self documenting a map of the object's life.

The Client class can absorb more detail by managing the creation of its associated Request object. A Request should consist of the action the remote client wants to perform, along with the data needed to support it. On its face, it may seem extraneous to form a separate object that uncouples the client's connection from its own request; it certainly isn't essential. But in this case, we are thinking ahead to how we will handle a data request. The request itself is only one part of the client object, so is it necessary to include posting the request within the same thread that governs the client's connection state? One advantage of breaking out the request as a separate object is that the full client object won't have to participate fully in a scheduling model the server might employ to expedite or regulate requests. A Client object could, in one configuration, simply observe its Request and wait for notification of the request thread's termination, indicating it has run its course. The Client then receives any return data by way of the notification update, which is passed back over the stream to the remote client. Figure 12.1 illustrates this relationship.

FIGURE 12.1 The client/request structure

```
                    connection request
                    port address to use r
     Client                                              Server
```

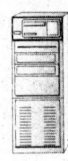

An alternative approach might be to make `Request` an inner class of `Client`, avoiding the overhead of the `Observer` notification model and the burden of negotiating field access between the two. Once data has been sent back to the remote client, the `Client` can close its data streams and flag itself for removal. The request object, focused solely on getting processed and passing back return data, can be scoped and dereferenced by the server during a routine check.

This brings us to our second objective: to have the server support some form of client tracking. A container suffices to store object references, but we also want to query each stored element to determine its current state. The least cumbersome way of accomplishing this goal is to add a `boolean` flag to the contained elements that indicates whether their purpose has been served. `Client` objects will close their own streams, so in normal processing we don't have to worry about connections staying open. If this were a full-fledged application, we would need to check for client connections that fail while their requests are in progress and respond accordingly.

The elements of the `Server` class that derive from our discussion are included in this code fragment:

```
public class Server implements Runnable {
  private Vector connections;
  private Vector jobs;
  private Client clientTmp;
  private Request request;
  private Database dbs;
  private ServerSocket listener;
  ...

  public Server(int port) {
    listener = new ServerSocket(port);
    // Stores client connection
    connections = new Vector();
    // Stores request portion of client
    jobs = new Vector();
    // Loads the database into memory
    dbs = new Database("reservations.ser");
    Thread t = new Thread(this);
```

```
      t.start();
   }

   public void run() {
      while(true) {
         try {
            clientTmp = new Client(listener.accept(), dbs);
            request = clientTmp.getRequest();
            connections.add(clientTmp);
            jobs.add(request);
            clientTmp = null;
            request = null;
         }
         catch(IOException ioe) {
            System.out.println(
            "Listener aborted irregularly");
            ioe.printStackTrace();
         }

         Iterator connectList = connections.iterator();
         Iterator jobList = jobs.iterator();

         while (connectList.hasNext()) {
            clientTmp = (Client)connections.next();
            if (clientTmp.isDone()) {
               connectList.remove();
            }
         }
         while (jobList.hasNext()) {
            request = (Request)jobList.next();
            if (request.isComplete()) {
               jobList.remove();
            }
         }
      }
   }
   ...
}
```

There are more than a few blanks to fill in for this class; they are left as development exercises for those who wish to complete the code. To keep this illustration brief, we have left some things

390   Chapter 12 • Writing the Network Protocol

undone that would make the overall design more elegant. We are currently maintaining `Client` and `Request` objects in separate vectors, but as intimately related as the two objects are, a tighter association between them is a necessity.

The last portion of the `run()` method satisfies our third objective: to provide some form of cleanup for expired connections and jobs. If we wanted to keep the server's loop focused on efficient listening, we could perform vector monitoring through a separate `Cleanup` class and run it on its own thread. Vectors are already internally synchronized, so we wouldn't have to worry about removing elements while the listener is trying to add a new one. But if we wanted to use `wait()` and `notifyAll()` to preempt the cleanup thread when either vector is unavailable, we'd still have to synchronize on them. Neither the compiler nor the runtime allows `wait()` and `notifyAll()`, except within a synchronized block of code; there is no cross-check in the compiler to see whether the object in question really needs it.

The `Client` class that follows is also incomplete, but it illustrates the features we've discussed. It encapsulates the streams connecting the server's machine to the remote client, instantiates its request as a discrete object, and implements an `Observer` for keeping tabs on the request's progress. This is by no means the only choice. Using a Beans-oriented approach, our connection object could implement an event listener to be notified of changes in the `Request` object, thereby taking advantage of Java's built-in event-handling mechanism. In the sense that the request portion of a client represents its model, and the connection portion a type of view, there are a variety of ways to consider capturing the relationship effectively—one of which would be an MVC type of pattern. These techniques have the advantage of being more flexible. The `Observer/Observable` interface/class pair has the advantage of being easy to implement and ideally suited to the immediate problem. The `boolean` flag *done* can be set to `true` once the data returned from the database call (if any) has been written back to the remote machine. With a few basic modifications, however, this class could also support a persistent connection to the server, using its `run()` method as a loop for handling successive service requests:

```java
public class Client implements Runnable, Observer {
    protected Thread runner;
    private InputStream incoming;
    ObjectInputStream objInput = new
        ObjectInputStream(incoming);
    private OutputStream outgoing;
    ObjectOutputStream objOutput = new
        ObjectOutputStream(outgoing);
    private Request req;
    private boolean done = false;
    private Object returnData;
    private Database db;

    public Client(Socket connection, Database db) {
        try {
```

```
      incoming = connection.getInputStream();
      outgoing = connection.getOutputStream();
      req = new Request(this, objInput.readObject(), db);
      runner = new Thread(this);
      runner.start();
    }
    catch(IOException ioe) {
      System.out.println("Couldn't open socket streams");
    }
  }

  public Request getRequest() {
    return req;
  }

  public boolean isDone() {
    return done;
  }

  public void update(Observable request,
  Object retData) {
      returnData = retData;
  }

  protected void finalize() {
    incoming = null;
    outgoing = null;
    runner = null;
  }

  public void run() {
    while (!isDone())
    {
      try {
        objOutput.writeObject(returnData);
        objOutput.flush();
      }
      catch (IOException ioe) {
        System.out.println(
        "Couldn't write return data back to the client");
```

Chapter 12 · Writing the Network Protocol

```
        ioe.printStackTrace();
    }
    done = true;
  }
  ...
}
```

This class implements the `Observer` method `update()`, which is then called by any `Observable` that has added this class to its list of listeners. As design patterns go, it is similar to the way event handlers work and is very useful when one object needs to base its behavior on the state change in another object. Also notice the assumption that the client's request is sent as a single `Request` object, reducing the protocol for client-server communication to a single `readObject()` call. Because this class has no role in dealing with data other than as a middleman, it requires an `Object` reference only to pass it back and forth.

The last class fragment we have roughed out in this preliminary sketch is `Request`. This class extends `Observable` so it can register its owner's interest in knowing when the job has completed. `DataServices` is implemented for access to the service codes. At the end of the thread run, the request notifies its client of any data that may have been returned when the call to the database finished. The `boolean` field `completed` is also set to true to expedite dereferencing the thread used by this object:

```
public class Request extends Observable
implements Runnable, DataServices, Serializable {
  protected int command;
  protected Object data;
  protected boolean completed = false;
  protected transient Thread runJob;
  private Database db;

  public Request(Client owner, Object obj, Database db) {
    Request req = (Request)obj;
    command = req.getCommand();
    this.db = db;
    data = req.getData();
    runJob = new Thread(this);
    addObserver(owner);
    runJob.start();
  }

  public int getCommand() {
```

```
    return command;
  }

  public Object getData() {
    return data;
  }

  protected void setData(Object dbReturn) {
    data = dbReturn;
  }

  public boolean isComplete() {
    return completed;
  }

  public void run(){
    switch(getCommand()) {
      case ADD_RECORD: db.add((String[])getData());
                       break;
      case SCHEME:     Object obj = db.getListScheme();
                       break;
      // remainder of service calls
    }
    setChanged();
    notifyObservers(getData());
    completed = true;
  }
}
```

We have a limited number of data services, so a simple switch on getCommand() will suffice. But if the command list will grow to any size, it makes sense to consider a parent class that all requests can subclass or perhaps an interface they can all implement; see Figure 12.2 for one such arrangement. Another way to maintain uniform communication between client and server, regardless of the service requested, is to encapsulate all the relevant objects into one, perhaps in a Response object. This technique almost trivializes the argument that straight VM-to-VM communication over streams requires the developer to maintain a special protocol. Allowances must be made for threads and other objects that do not serialize—notice that Request implements Serializable but marks its Thread reference transient—but hiding the details of transmitting objects over the wire is worth it.

FIGURE 12.2 A flexible parent class

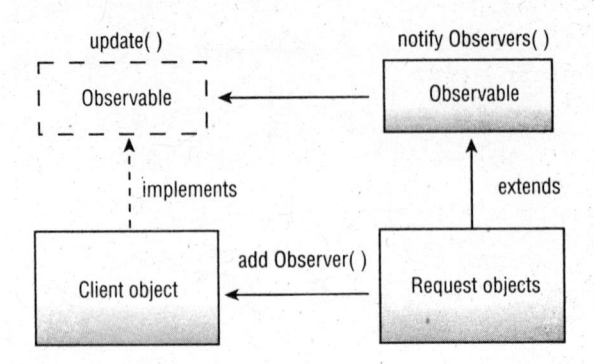

Limitations of the Model

Before object serialization was added to Java, one of the chief complaints about the JDK, regardless of its newcomer status, was its lack of a ready-to-use persistence model. Before the arrival of an object serialization facility, in order to commit an object type to a stream, programmers had to break the object into its constituent parts. Once an object was "unrolled" into integers, floats, byte arrays, and so on, it could be placed on the stream, one `writeUTF()` call at a time. Reading those values back in was, of course, the same call-intensive and order-sensitive process. The methods that were written to handle this process were little more than hand-coded object protocols. The process wasn't ugly just because it was tedious and prone to error; it was ugly because there was no way to ensure that any two people would write the same class to the stream in the same way. Every object mapping was a potential exercise in lengthy, detail-oriented, throwaway code. Most workarounds, such as trying to share object-serial maps in advance of the classes themselves, simply defeated the benefits that a network-aware language was supposed to offer.

Now, object serialization makes the task relatively easy. Where it is possible to abstract the types sent over the network so that as few objects as possible are part of the transmission, the resulting code is straightforward and easy to read. With a small application, such as the one the project assignment will require you to write, building a quick-and-dirty protocol and defining a few object types to communicate may be all you need. But there is a limit to the effectiveness of a state-oriented communication scheme. In general, the constraints of passing objects between autonomous VMs are the constraints of version control and updating.

Once you commit an object to the stream, its state is fixed. It's like sending a letter, in the sense that the information it contains is only current for so long. The more volatile the information, the less useful the letter is, especially if its delivery is slow or the recipient doesn't read it right away. If that object is being sent to a file, your only concern is keeping the stored data current. But if it is going to another VM, keeping both VMs in sync on the object means limiting object communication to state-oriented updates, making sure neither VM would need to change the object while it is in transit, or ensuring the changes aren't material to inter-VM communication.

The usual style of communicating through streams is procedural: the client sends a request, and the server sends a response. If you want to develop an exchange that feels more interactive or reflects several turns the exchange might take, the script might be made more elaborate, but it remains tied to a synchronous model. As the communication becomes more complex, you end up with a new protocol. This has been a predominant objection among developers who see the ease of serializing individual objects but remember the lesson of writing individual objects into serial form by hand. Serialization alone relies on the programmer to maintain the protocol for communicating. Eliminating one layer of tedium—the atomic level of persistence—merely shifts the problem to higher ground. In the absence of a set way to communicate multiple objects between any two machines, you must still distribute the protocols, and the class files that embody them, to cast serialized objects back to their correct type.

Remote Method Invocation (RMI)

The end goal of Java's serialization facility is to simplify the task of persisting objects. Saving objects to a file or to another VM is now a straightforward, standardized, sometimes even trivial process.

Serialization handles the details of writing object-level protocols so you can send objects to a stream without worrying about their elemental structure or ordering. In much the same way, RMI provides a means for distributing objects as services so that a remote service request looks as much like a local one as you can manage. This approach overcomes at least one potential limitation in the approach we just discussed: rather than send an object back and forth between VMs, you station it in one place. The VM responsible for serving the object declares it exportable and puts it where an RMI object server can call on it when a request comes in.

To use the object's services, the remote client must first obtain a reference to it. In order to do that, the client must of course know where to find the object, what it is called, and what method calls it provides. Once that information is acquired, however, RMI takes care of the rest:

- Object serialization
- Object transport, using its own "wire protocol"?
- Exception handling specific to network errors
- Security management

Taking advantage of all these services requires some forethought. You must consider which objects to serve based on the applicability of their services to remote access. Although the risks of distributed computing are similar in nature to straightforward protocol-based communication, trying to make these variances transparent through RMI casts some murkiness over the exception process, possibly making it seem complex. Network connections can be severed physically or logically. The client or server may go down or drop the connection. The occasional extreme latency in network transmissions may cause a timeout just before a request is fulfilled. Any of these can disrupt the expected flow, leaving the server's current state and the client's understanding of it uncertain. The elegance of RMI is a fine thing, but we do not want to inherit a spate of exceptions on every remote call just to achieve it.

A Model RMI Transaction

For a client to be able to call on an object that resides on a remote machine, the client must first have a reference to the object. To retrieve the reference and use it, the client has to know substantially more about the object than we need to know to find a web page. The only concise way to do this is to embed that lookup information in the client code. It is possible to find and determine remote services at runtime, but short of wanting to write an object browser in and of itself, you do not want to explore remotely available services and determine their facilities in runtime before using them. You just want to use them, so advance knowledge of the available method calls is essential. Before changes in the JDK 1.2, RMI facilitated this discovery through a custom pair of classes called *skeletons* and *stubs*. These two classes derived directly from the class file of the remote object and are generated using the `rmic` compiler.

When the remote client calls on an object, it does so by way of a lookup. This lookup is coded into the client, as are the explicit calls to the object's methods. If the lookup succeeds, the RMI server returns the remote object's stub, which acts as a stand-in for the remote object's class and methods. Upon a call to any one of these methods in pre-1.2 code, the stub sends the request to the skeleton reference, which resides on the server side. The skeleton retrieves the operations of the local object that the client is interested in and maintains a `dispatch()` method to coordinate routing the object's response back through the stub. This method of internal communication-by-proxy is still available in the JDK 1.2, but RMI changes in the 1.3 and later releases have brought the skeleton's role into the `RemoteObject` class.

The communication between stub and skeleton (whether discrete or part of `RemoteObject`) takes place over RMI's remote reference layer (the "wire protocol" we referred to earlier), which in turn relies on the transport layer already provided by TCP/IP. But the point of all this layering is to render the mechanics of network communication as transparent as possible, freeing the programmer to focus on the semantics of routine method calls. Figure 12.3 shows a logical view of an RMI-based interaction. In this diagram, the remote object is a `Request`, through which the client can call the same services we provided through the protocol interface shown earlier in the chapter.

FIGURE 12.3 An RMI-based interaction

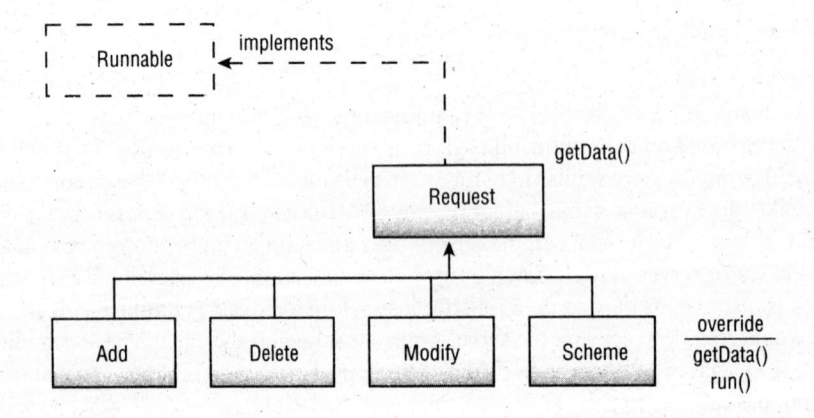

Implementing RMI

Once the questions surrounding proper design have been settled, writing the code for RMI requires several steps, but it is not overly complicated. In this example, we'll redesign the `Request` class as an object our client will access to enter a transaction request. We need to provide both the client and server resources. The `Request` class now assumes the dimensions of a protocol similar to `DataServices` but has the advantage of being self-describing in its implementation:

```
import java.rmi.*;
public interface RemoteRequest extends Remote {
  public void add(String[] newRecord)
    throws RemoteException;
  public void modify(Object id, String[] changes)
    throws RemoteException;
  public void delete(Object id)
    throws RemoteException;
  public String[][] find(String match)
    throws RemoteException;
}
```

`Remote` is a "tagging" interface, like `Serializable`. All it does is identify implementers of this interface to the VM as objects that are eligible for remote access. It's also necessary for each abstract method to declare throwing `RemoteException`, the parent class for all the processes that can go wrong during a remote invocation.

The class that implements `RemoteRequest`, which we will name `Request`, must meet three conditions. First, it needs the semantics that are peculiar to identifying an object in a remote context: its hashcode, `toString()` representation, and so on. Second, it must give the host VM a way to export it to the object server providing its lookup service. The easiest way to satisfy these first two requirements is by extending `UnicastRemoteObject`, which provides an export method the VM can call automatically when binding the object to its object server. This class also inherits its remote identification semantics from its parent, `RemoteObject`. Third, `Request` must explicitly provide a default constructor that throws `RemoteException`:

```
import java.rmi.*;
import java.rmi.server.*;

public class Request extends UnicastRemoteObject
implements RemoteRequest {

  public Request() throws RemoteException {
    super();
  }
```

Chapter 12 · Writing the Network Protocol

```
    public void add(String[] newRecord)
    throws RemoteException {
    // code to add a record to the local database
  }
  ...
}
```

If this class for some reason must extend some other class, `UnicastRemoteObject` also supports a static `export()` method that takes the current object as an argument. This call can be added to the constructor:

`UnicastRemoteObject.export(this);`

Once the remote interface and implementing class are complete, we can generate the skeleton and stub classes that will be used to manage the communication endpoints between client and server. The tool that does this, `rmic`, takes the implementing class (not the `.java` source) as its argument and produces class files using the same name, but with `_Skel.class` and `_Stub.class` suffixes:

```
$ javac RemoteRequest.java Request.java
$ rmic Request
$ ls *.class
RemoteRequest.class
Request.class
Request_Skel.class
Request_Stub.class
```

RMI respectively calls on or distributes each class once a remote request occurs. The only requirement for these classes is that they reside in the same package space as the class they are generated from. To accommodate classes that are part of a package, the `-d` flag for `rmic` works the same as it does for `javac`.

The server code that sponsors the `Request` object is responsible for binding it to an RMI server. This service is launched through a tool bundled with the JDK called `rmiregistry`, which is really just another server like the one built early in this chapter. It sets itself up on an available port and waits for a request from any client, local or remote. It functions as a registry by tracking all remote objects that any local VM binds to it. Because it operates autonomously from any VM on the same system, the VM must be given the port address of the registry. By default, `rmiregistry` attempts to use 1099 as its service port, but an optional port can be provided by passing the appropriate argument.

> **TIP** RMI for Java 2 adds a very interesting feature to its repertoire: the ability to launch the registry of one machine on demand by way of a remote object request. The current registry has to run all the time, potentially taking up resources when it has no work to do. The JDK provides another tool, `rmid`, which behaves similarly to a Unix daemon or NT service, polling for requests to start up the registry when needed. A tutorial on activation is supplied with the JDK documentation. From the root directory for the documentation, locally or online, it is available at `docs/guide/rmi/activation.html`.

To bind a remote object to the registry, the server must first implement security. This step is a precaution against the client trying to pass an argument type with less than honorable intentions through the object server back to the application server. RMI does not mandate the use of a security manager, but it will refuse to load new classes coming from the client without one.

If we wanted the `Request` class to host its own registration code, we could add a `main()` method to implement security and call `Naming.rebind()`. The `rebind()` method takes two arguments, a URL-style `String` representing the remote object's location, and a reference to the remote object itself:

```
public class Request extends UnicastRemoteObject
implements RemoteRequest {
...
  public static void main(String args[]) {
    System.setSecurityManager(new RMISecurityManager());
    try {
      // assume port 1099
      String URL = "rmi://www.objserver.net/DataRequest";
      Naming.rebind(URL, new Request());
    }
    catch(IOException ioe) {
      // the parent exception to both RemoteException
      // and MalformedURLException; rebind() throws both
      ioe.printStackTrace();
    }
  }
}
```

> **TIP** The `Naming` class has a static `bind()` method, but in practice it is not often used. `bind()` throws one more exception than `rebind()` does, called `AlreadyBoundException`, which directly subclasses `Exception`. Both methods are intended for the same purpose, but the `rebind()` method does not complain if its object reference wasn't already bound before being called, so it's provided to refresh either a null or existing object registration. The `rebind()` method requires less exception-handling code than the `bind()` method.

The registration process by no means limits you to a single instance of the remote object type, but each instance does have to be uniquely named and individually registered.

In a system of any complexity, it would make sense to compose a single remote object through which other server resources could then be accessed. This single resource could even be the application server itself, providing a remote public interface to clients while reserving its internal operations—calls to the database, thread scheduling, and other local tasks—behind the scenes. This would certainly reduce name-space confusion when writing the client code. Under less than ideal circumstances, client-side programmers would have to document all the object URLs required or add them and recompile code as they become available; doing so becomes quickly tedious. The server-side developer, with good planning and design, can encapsulate all the required services through one remote reference and avoid that situation.

Any way it's handled, using an incremental approach to adding RMI services means extra work. The new services have to be written and compiled, new stubs and skeletons generated, new registration code added, and client code modified to use them. We're almost back to where we started with creating elaborate protocols! Design before implementing and there will be less to remember and maintain.

All this work on the server side translates to a relatively trivial coding task for the client. The client must be able to cast a remote reference to its class, although it may not use the class reference to instantiate objects of that type; it must instead use the `Naming` class to look up the object via an RMI protocol handler and the correct URL:

```
public class ClientSide {
  Request myRequest;
  String [][] schema;
  ...
  public void issueRequest() {
    try {
      myRequest = (Request)Naming.lookup(
        "rmi://www.objserver.net/DataRequest");
      // port 1099 assumed
      schema = myRequest.listScheme();
    }
    catch(AccessException re) {
```

```
        // A RemoteException subclass - for illustration
        }
        catch(RemoteException ae) {
        // all remote accesses throw this
        }
        catch(NotBoundException nbe){
        // an Exception subclass thrown if the lookup fails
        } .
    ...
    }
    ...
}
```

The client code then calls methods on the `myRequest` reference just as if it were a local object. RMI handles all the subsequent details. Here we've also laid out in detail the exceptions that a call to `lookup()` requires us to catch. Often these are ignored in example code by catching `RemoteException`, the parent class to most exceptions thrown when using RMI. Taking this shortcut also obscures the opportunity to recover from specific faults. On an `AccessException`, for example, a specific message pertaining to what action was denied could be crucial information to debugging. If we just catch the parent class, we can get an exception name and a stack trace if we want them, but no further information that could be provided in an exception-specific `catch` clause.

Limitations of RMI

Glossing over exceptions in complex, distributed code is a mild symptom of one of the more severe limitations of choosing RMI in any project: it can be exceptionally hard to debug a complex distributed application, particularly if the client and server are multithreaded. RMI renders many underlying operations transparent to the application code, which is a great advantage in many ways. It's not RMI's fault that it's easy to defeat proper exception handling by catching parents and super-parents. Nonetheless, the fact that runtime bugs can be obscured by the lack of a robust reporting mechanism may influence the perception that somehow RMI is at fault. However transparent RMI renders remote services at the code level, you must take a deeper responsibility for a proper and thorough implementation of RMI's services. It is not a pop-in replacement for a more straightforward, if less robust, technique for writing proprietary serialization schemes.

Step-tracing through an RMI problem can be a technically overwhelming task without the right tools—assuming anyone has them. A debug walk-through in this environment means being able to walk through the stacks of two (or more) independent VMs, each of which is running simultaneously and quite possibly threading its activities among local and remote tasks. That said, there's no reason RMI programming must be overly complex, but it's easy to slip into bad habits and take a few shortcuts just to get something up and running. If multithreading is added as an afterthought, the application could well be at risk. The protocol-based approach we took earlier in the chapter makes us write more of the ground-level code by hand, but there is always only one VM acting on a serialized object at a time, which is easier to isolate.

> **WARNING** Read Java Software's current FAQ on RMI and object serialization for a rundown on common misunderstandings developers encounter when deploying RMI. The FAQ is available locally or online, relative to the documentation's root directory, at docs/guide/rmi/faq.html.

Another condition any RMI implementation has to look out for is the way remote requests enter the server's local threading scheme. It's possible for Client A to look up Remote Reference B, which calls on Server Object C, on which some other server-local object is synchronizing. Without carefully negotiating the asynchronous requests of remote clients with what the server wants to execute locally, the potential for deadlocking the server and hanging the VM is high. Again, this problem goes back to design and properly accounting for interaction on the server side.

Various newsgroups and mailing lists have discussed RMI's performance extensively. The range of experiences reported in these forums is almost exclusively comparative and seems to vary from much faster than CORBA to a degree or two slower, depending on the design and type of implementation. It's difficult to determine where the true mean in experiences lies—it's far easier to write toy code and benchmark it than it is to invest in a full-fledged example and gauge experience in production.

You can certainly infer that serializing entire objects when only a small part of the data needs to be sent plays a part in reports of sluggish performance, a point that brings us to a major difference between RMI and CORBA. RMI can pass objects by value, whereas CORBA—a model predicated on distributed code among heterogeneous systems—only passes values by reference. You must be aware that passing a 10MB vector is just as easy as passing a 15-character `byte` array, where RMI is concerned. Careful design, again, is imperative to keep track of exactly what kind of information (and how much of it) the completed system will send over the wire.

A full appreciation of RMI starts with understanding the functional differences between a local object and a remote one. With those characteristics fully understood, the benefits of the architecture can be weighed more effectively against its potential costs. At the same time, RMI is not so complex that experimenting with it will take substantially longer than writing straight "object protocol" code, once you've committed the functional steps to memory.

More on Threads

Concurrent programming, and Java threads in particular, are respectively multiple-volume and book-length subjects in their own right. It's not easy to simply survey threading strategies, so in this chapter's final section we will take a look at one thread-pooling strategy that may prove to be a useful complement to building the network server.

Sharing Threads

One complex aspect of writing a multithreaded application server is choosing a way to define how client requests will run. A request to the server implies a temporary need for its resources, which can be restored and allocated to subsequent requests—if you remember to reclaim them. But when that resource is a thread, a notably finite resource on any system, extra caution is warranted. Threads are not intended, by their nature, to be instantiated, run, and dereferenced without some regard for the system-level resources involved in maintaining them. You can demonstrate this by creating a *thread pool*, or a collection of thread references that are continually "re-referenced" as their current tasks run their course, and compare that technique side by side with an application that creates new threads on demand and de-allocates them when their execution tasks complete.

Intuitively, you should expect to conserve a substantial amount of resources. As the need for more threads increases, the cost of object creation and garbage collection should also increase, perhaps rising proportionately with the number of threaded tasks submitted. In a pooled-resource model, your thread-creation costs are incurred up front. After that, you reuse those resources continually, avoiding object creation and destruction in favor of referencing and de-referencing Runnable objects. It also stands to reason that the more efficient the arrangement for managing the thread pool, the more time or system-level resources can be conserved, up to some hard limit.

Another important point to make about threading: Just because an object is Runnable doesn't mean it needs a thread. Runnable is just an interface. It is a contract to implement a run() method, and an agreement into which any class may enter. By itself, the run() method is not especially significant. If a subclass of Applet were to implement Runnable, calling its start() method would not invoke threaded behavior. What makes a Runnable object so potentially powerful is that one of the Thread class's constructors will accept one as an argument. The Thread class itself contains the tools necessary to endow a Runnable with its own line of execution, and only a thread construction ties up system resources.

To demonstrate all these points, and to give you something more to think about in preparation for the project assignment, we've provided the ShareThread class in the following sample code. Discussion follows the code.

```
/**
 * ShareThread is a poolable thread resource capable of
 * repeatedly accepting and executing small * Runnable jobs.
 *
 * @author Sybex Certification Study Guide authors
 */
public class ShareThread extends Thread {
    private Runnable workToDo;

    /**
```

```
 * Sets this "pooled thread" instance as a daemon so
 * the program can exit if this is the only thing left.
 */
public ShareThread() {
  setDaemon(true);
}

/**
 * execute() waits until the internal Runnable
 * reference is null, then assigns it a new job.
 *
 * @param Runnable - an object that requires
 * a thread resource
 */
public void execute(Runnable job) {
  synchronized(this) {
    while(workToDo != null) {
      try {
        wait();
      }
      catch(InterruptedException ie) { }
    }
    workToDo = job;
    notifyAll();
  }
}

/**
 * executeIfAvailable() checks once to see if no job is
 * pending. If not, a job is assigned, the boolean flag
 * set to true, and all waiting threads notified.
 *
 * @param Runnable - an object that needs its run()
 * method called.
 * @returns boolean - indicating whether a job was
 * successfully assigned
 */
public boolean executeIfAvailable(Runnable job) {
  boolean executed = false;
```

```
    synchronized(this) {
      if (workToDo == null) {
        workToDo = job;
        executed = true;
        notifyAll();
      }
    }
    return executed;
}

/**
 * A "snapshot" check whether a job is currently
 * assigned. Not reliable beyond the moment of the test
 *
 * @return boolean - indicates whether a job is
 * assigned.
 */
public boolean available() {
    return (workToDo == null);
}

/**
 * Rejects any thread that is not owned by the current
 * instance. Waits until a Runnable job is assigned,
 * then calls its run() method directly, acting as its
 * surrogate Thread instance. Signals for another job
 * by dereferencing the current one. Terminates when
 * no more user-level jobs are available.
 */
public void run() {
    if (Thread.currentThread() == this) {
      Runnable job = null;
      while (true) {
        synchronized(this) {
          while (workToDo == null) {
            try {
              wait();
            }
```

```
            catch(InterruptedException ie) {}
        }
        job = workToDo;

        notifyAll();
        workToDo = null;
      }
      job.run();
    }
   }
  }
}
```

This is a very simple subclass of `Thread` with just four methods and one constructor. All the constructor does is call `setDaemon()` and set it to true. Daemon threads are a special case; any application that has them can exit if only daemon threads are currently running. Two methods attempt to run a submitted job: `execute()` and `executeIfAvailable()`. Both synchronize on the current `ShareThread` instance. `execute()` waits until `workToDo` loses its current reference, and then assigns it a new one. `executeIfAvailable()`, on the other hand, tests `workToDo` to see whether it is set to `null` during the current synchronized execution. If so, `workToDo` is given a new job. This is a one-shot attempt that makes the method appear clumsy. At the same time, it returns a `boolean` indicating success or failure in assigning a new job, so the responsibility is on the programmer to write a proper loop and test it.

Then `ShareThread`'s `run()` method does an interesting thing. It synchronizes on its own instance, immediately returning if any thread other than the correct instance of `ShareThread` tries to run it. The method then waits until `workToDo` acquires a reference, rather than loses one. When that condition occurs, the new job is immediately reassigned to a temporary variable created within `run()`. Just after calling `notifyAll()`, `workToDo` is de-referenced again so that either execute method can assign a waiting job to it. But outside the synchronized block, the temporary variable calls `run()` directly on the `Runnable` object it now refers to. Because the current instance of `ShareThread` is already a thread, the job does not require a thread of its own.

The call to `job.run()` illustrates that the `run()` method itself has no inherently threaded properties. If a job is called and executed within another threaded instance, it performs the same way as if it had constructed its own threaded instance, minus the costs of object creation. The jobs that are submitted to this class could be any object that implements `Runnable`, such as the `Request` class, minus its thread instantiation code. This class lends itself well to a round-robin approach to satisfying data requests. Round-robin techniques don't scale well, unless more "robins" can be added easily. In this situation, that's precisely the case. The more requests that are expected, the more `ShareThread` objects that could be created to meet demand. Of course, the limiting factor will still lie in the ability of the database to expedite requests.

As a final demonstration, the following code is suitable for `ShareThread`'s `main()` method. It compares the time needed for a given number of `ShareThread` objects to execute a number of joblets against the time needed for the same number of jobs to instance their own threads and run individually. Use this code and experiment with a variety of pooled thread and joblet-count combinations. When you are satisfied that there is a clear difference in performance between the two, consider applying this model to your future project assignment:

```java
public class UseShareThread {

  /**
   * Test facility that compares pooled threading to
   * straight threading of every submitted job. Launch
   * this program with the following syntax:
   * <PRE>java UseShareThread <num_threads> <num_jobs> <num_runnables> <jobs>
   * num_threads is how many threads to pool.
   * num_jobs is total number of Runnable jobs to queue.
   * num_runnables is the number of classes (job types) submitted
   * jobs are classes that implements Runnable</PRE>
   */
  public static void main(String args[])
  throws Exception {

        //timing variables
    long startPool, startThreads, stopPool, stopThreads;

    final int totalJobs = Integer.parseInt(args[1]);
    final int threadPool = Integer.parseInt(args[0]);
    // runnables accounts for mult. job types submitted
    final int runnables =
      Integer.parseInt(args[2]);

    Runnable[] joblets = new
      Runnable[totalJobs * runnables];

    // populates the joblets array with number of jobs
    // requested times the total Runnable types given
    for (int i = 0; i < runnables; i++){
      Class cls= Class.forName(args[i + 3]);
      for (int j = 0; j < totalJobs; j++) {
        joblets[(totalJobs*i)+j] = (Runnable)
        (cls.newInstance());
      }
    }
```

```java
System.out.println("Running " + joblets.length +
  " jobs in " + threadPool + "worker threads.\n");
// begin timer on threadpool
startPool = System.currentTimeMillis();

ShareThread[] workers = new ShareThread[threadPool];
for (int i = 0; i < workers.length; i++) {
  workers[i] = new ShareThread();
  workers[i].start();
}

// simple looping strategy to assign a job to any
// available worker instance
int iLoop = 0;
int jLoop = 0;
while (iLoop < joblets.length) {
  while (!workers[jLoop].executeIfAvailable(
    joblets[iLoop])) {
    jLoop++;
    if (jLoop == workers.length) jLoop = 0;
  }
  Thread.yield();
  jLoop = 0;
  iLoop++;
}

// another simple loop to see if all workers are idle
// if so, we're done
for (iLoop = 0; iLoop < workers.length; iLoop++) {
  while(!workers[iLoop].available()){
    Thread.yield();
  }
}
stopPool = System.currentTimeMillis();
System.out.println("Pooling all joblets took: " +
  (stopPool - startPool) + " milliseconds.\n");


System.out.println(
```

```
    "Now giving each job a thread.\n");


    // Use a threadgroup to monitor all threads
    ThreadGroup group = new
      ThreadGroup("Threaded joblets");
    startThreads = System.currentTimeMillis();

    // Launch a thread for each joblet, and track all
    // joblet completions as a group to stop the clock.
    for (int i = 0; i < joblets.length; i++) {
      Thread thr = new Thread(group, joblets[i]);
      thr.start();
    }
    while(group.activeCount() > 0) {
      ;
    }

    stopThreads = System.currentTimeMillis();
    System.out.println("Threading all joblets took: " +
      (stopThreads - startThreads) + " milliseconds.\n");

  }
}
```

The test class doesn't need to be much, just enough to cause a tick or two. As the number of jobs scales, the threaded test won't have any problem chewing up time. With pooled threads, make sure the sample `Runnable` can burn a few cycles, or you may get a few test runs that report taking no time. Here's an example test:

```
public class Tester implements Runnable {
  public void run() {
    double val = getX() * getY();
  }

  private double getX() {
    return 3;
  }

  private double getY() {
    return 4;
  }
}
```

Summary

Although the choices for network communication are relatively few, they are very different—and each technique has its own range of strengths and limitations. Building a network protocol between client and server is easy, but it is limited to a synchronous exchange of objects between the two VMs and doesn't allow for interaction between them beyond what has already been scripted into the code. Object serialization hides the details of committing objects to a stream but still requires you to handle writing objects over the network in a sequence you have to define; there's no getting away from writing a proprietary protocol.

RMI makes everything very simple from the client perspective. Instead of instantiating objects that exist on a remote server, you simply look them up to start using them. Each object you work with is otherwise transparent in its remoteness. Each object always resides on one machine, virtually eliminating the problem of state inconsistency that could arise with overly complex interactions in which objects themselves are being passed back and forth over the wire in serial form. At the same time, RMI hides so many layers of detail that when something goes wrong, it can be difficult to find. Not the least of the obstacles is determining which VM originated the problem. RMI requires considerable planning and design consideration before implementation. Casual oversights in RMI mean lots of maintenance later on, and lots of class rewrites and recompiles if you try to fix problems wholesale.

Once the choice of network technique has been made, however, you can give more thought to how threading plays a role in the whole scheme. This is admittedly a lot trickier to contend with in an RMI scheme, and multithreading questions should be pursued early in an RMI scheme rather than late.

As a final note, when you're looking for an efficient way to deal with lots of short requests to the application, consider using a thread pool to conserve object creation and destruction.

Exam Essentials

Your application must be implemented using client-server technology. Specifically, the server code must provide a way to remember each client, check the state of each client and its request, and restore resources used by the client when the client request is completed.

RMI provides a means for distributing objects as services so that a remote service request looks like a local one. This approach maintains a single object located on a single server. The VM responsible for serving the object declares it exportable and puts it where an RMI object server can access it.

Key Terms

Before you take the exam, be certain you are familiar with the following terms:

concurrency

magic numbers

port

thread pool

well-known port

Review Questions

1. What is a server's fundamental job?
   A. To run in a finite loop and listen for client requests
   B. To run in an infinite loop and establish connections to clients
   C. To run in an infinite loop and listen for client requests
   D. To run in a finite loop and establish connections to clients

2. Which of the following protocols does Java use for connection-oriented networking?
   A. UDP
   B. ICMP
   C. TCP
   D. RPC

3. RMI does *not* implement which of the following features?
   A. Remote methods
   B. Remote objects
   C. Client-server networking
   D. Concurrency

4. Which statement is true regarding objects that implement the `Runnable` interface?
   A. `Runnable` objects require threads.
   B. `Runnable` objects must have the `run()` method implemented.
   C. `Runnable` objects must have the `start()` method implemented.
   D. Threads require `Runnable` objects.

5. What is the goal of Java's serialization facility?
   A. To provide data protection from concurrent access
   B. To provide data persistence
   C. To provide remote access to data
   D. To improve performance

Answers to Review Questions

1. C. Servers always run in an infinite loop as background daemons and listen for client requests.

2. C. UDP is used for connectionless networking. Neither ICMP nor RPC is used in Java.

3. D. RMI is used to connect clients to servers so that the client can access remote objects and invoke their methods. It is up to the programmer to account for concurrency.

4. B. Even though a thread may be constructed with a Runnable object, threads do not require Runnable objects (nor do Runnable objects require threads). The run() method is the only method that must be implemented for a Runnable object.

5. B. Serialization provides no means of protecting data from concurrent access, nor does it provide for remote access, even though serialization may be used for data that is accessed both remotely and concurrently. Serialization has nothing to do with performance. In fact, serialization consumes system resources so that data may persist.

Chapter 13
Connecting Client and Server

In this chapter, the focus of our discussion turns back to architectural issues. So far, we've covered each piece of the Developer's Exam as a substantial collection of related details. Now that we are looking at ways to connect the two major components—the client and the server—it's time to consider some design-level strategies we can apply to the assignment as a whole.

It's easy, on a first reading, to mistake the exam for a collection of related but separate requirements: write a conversion tool, replace some deprecated methods, write a GUI, add a locking feature, and so on. Certain other requirements, like configuring the server application so that a client can connect locally or remotely, can add to this sense of fragments creating a whole.

We want to introduce the idea of a near-universal solvent for many of these tasks: notification-based objects. The chapter starts with a primer on the subject, so if you are comfortable with the foundation, feel free to skim forward. By chapter's end, we will have covered:

- Event basics
- Using Java Bean conventions
- Java Beans and the MVC design pattern
- Listeners
- Remote notification
- Distributed notification

Also, some of you may be new to the term *design patterns*. A design pattern is an arrangement of classes by their relations and working collaborations. Properly used, design patterns help provide a structure to solve a well-known problem and help reduce programming effort. You do not need to know any patterns to pass the Developer's Exam, but chances are you've seen one and simply didn't know it had a name. If you are in the habit of writing reusable code, you are almost certainly applying a pattern to do it—you just may not know that a formal term describes it.

We will call the family of patterns described in this chapter *event notification* patterns.

Events Basics

Most Swing component types emit events when activated by a user. Examples of such user actions include clicking a mouse button, pressing or releasing a key, and selecting an item in a list. An *event* is an instance of some subclass of `java.util.EventObject`. This superclass provides the `getSource()` method, which returns the component from which the event originated.

Event Naming Conventions

The event model is easy to use because it is based on a few simple naming conventions. The naming conventions tell you the following:

- For almost every event type *XXX*Event, there is an interface called *XXX*Listener. The methods of this interface are all `public void` and take a single argument, of type *XXX*Event. (The naming convention has nothing to say about the names of the methods in the interface.)
- If a component emits events of type *XXX*Event, then that component has a public method called add*XXX*Listener(*XXX*Listener). Any object that implements this interface can be registered with the component as a listener for *XXX* events. When the component is activated in a way that causes it to emit *XXX* events, all registered listeners receive a call to one of the listener interface methods.
- In addition to the add*XXX*Listener(*XXX*Listener) method, a component that emits events of type *XXX*Event also has a public method called remove*XXX*Listener(*XXX*Listener). This method allows listeners that are no longer interested in *XXX* events to be unregistered.

For example, the `JTextField` class emits Key events, which are represented by the `java.awt.KeyEvent` class. The naming convention tells us that there must be a `KeyListener` interface. (It can be found in the `java.awt.event` package.) We also know that `JTextField` must have the methods `addKeyListener(KeyListener)` and `removeKeyListener(KeyListener)`. The naming convention does not predict what listener methods will be called under what circumstances. For that information, you have to refer to the API for each interface. In our example, the `KeyListener` interface defines three methods (`keyPressed()`, `keyReleased()`, and `keyTyped()`); exactly which method gets called depends on the input activity performed by the user.

Event Notification

Notification is a form of object-oriented messaging for which Java programming is a remarkably good fit. Event-driven coding is a staple form of communication among AWT and Swing widgets. The pattern they use is also the foundation of Sun's Java Beans specification, which describes a few fundamental roles that are played out time and time again in different contexts and arrangements. These fundamental roles are

- Event object
- Event handler
- Event source
- Event target

Event objects define and encapsulate an action or state change that took place in some other object, an *event source*. An event source creates event objects and sends them to other objects

418   Chapter 13 • Connecting Client and Server

it tracks as listeners, otherwise known as *event targets*. An object can become a target in one of two ways:

- It acquires a reference to the event source and registers its interest. Java components do this through a source's add*XXX*Listener() method. Targets that implement the same interface the source uses for event-firing receive events through a method call on that interface. Figure 13.1 depicts this interaction.
- It acquires a reference to another object that knows how to register to the source. From the point of view of the target, this intermediary is known as an *event handler* (see Figure 13.2).

How the final target responds once it receives the event object may depend on the event object's content, or the target's function, or both, or neither. In other words, the resulting behavior could be anything within the range of the target's abilities, and that's the point. Any two objects can talk, either directly or through a handler. If the intermediary also happens to translate, filter, or perform some other service, we call it an *event adapter*. Figure 13.3 demonstrates a substantive event adaptation.

FIGURE 13.1   A simple callback relation

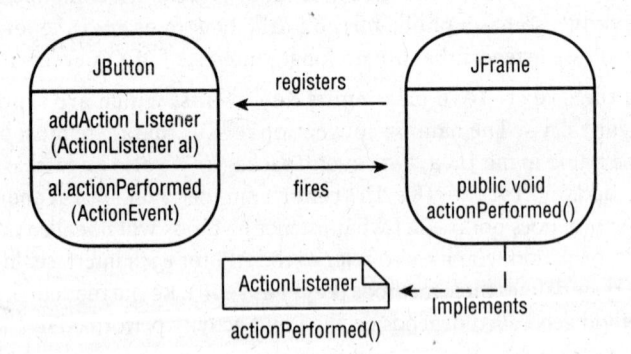

FIGURE 13.2   An indirect callback

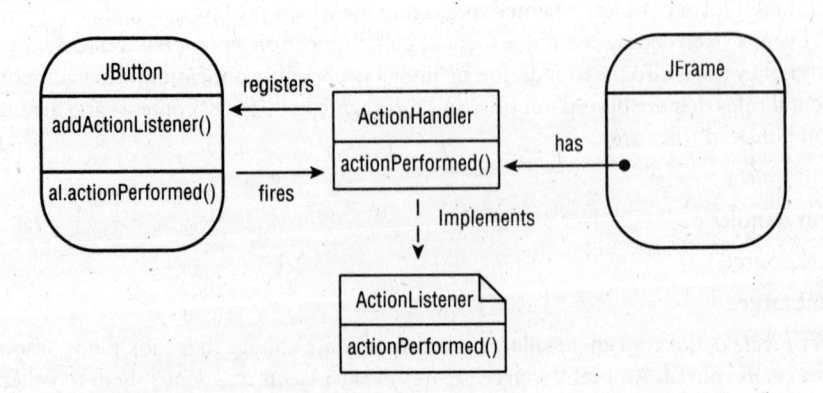

FIGURE 13.3 Adaptive event behavior (multiplexing)

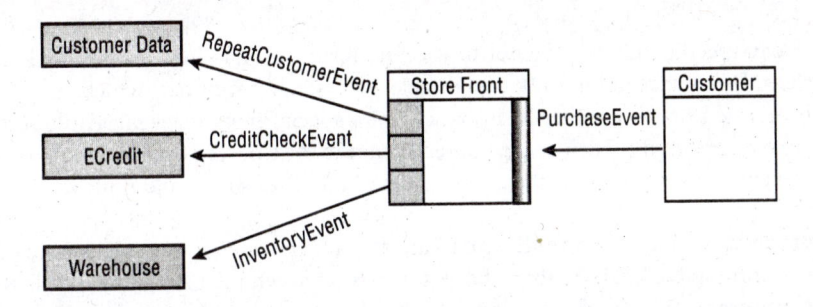

Notification is such a flexible, and therefore powerful, object-oriented strategy that it is modeled in a variety of ways. Some frequently described and widely documented variations of this general construct include:

Model-View-Controller The data, presentation, and data controls are separated from each other.

Observer-Observable A collaboration focusing on the relation of one observable to many observers; a generic notification model.

Publish-Subscribe A source of continuous events, and a set of listeners that use policies or filters to discriminate among the event types.

Callbacks A term coined in Motif/X window programming to describe one widget's interest in another widget's property or state changes.

These models vary based on how they stress (or de-emphasize) two high-level aspects all notification schemes share: *coupling* and *context*. Coupling is an expression of how *tight* or *loose* the objects become when they share a notification scheme. An example of a tight relation is two objects that must maintain mutual references in order to communicate. A context defines an environment in which the objects operate. It can be a containment system (the BeanContext library, an EJB container), a communications framework (Lotus' InfoBus), both (a builder tool), or something as simple as the Virtual Machine (VM) environment itself.

The broader the context is, the more general the notification strategy becomes, and therefore the looser the couplings between objects. The more deterministic the context, the more it defines the available roles. Coupling may get tighter as well, but with the added benefit of sharing more meaningful information.

For more information on these technologies, refer to these sources:

Bean Context Services The java.beans.beancontext package

InfoBus http://java.sun.com/beans/infobus/index.html

Enterprise Java Beans http://java.sun.com/products/ejb

Using Java Bean Conventions

The Java Bean specification is not a notification pattern; it's a naming convention. In a runtime environment, Beans care about only two things: events and *properties*, which can be communicated from one Bean to another Bean by way of a special-purpose event. A property is any value in an object that has been encapsulated by a get/set or is/set method pair. If a Bean is also an event source, it supports a method pair to add listeners to and remove them from its registry.

A JButton will send an ActionEvent to all its listeners when a user clicks it, for example, but there is nothing GUI-driven about how it does so. Shown next is a Monitor class that has no visual appearance but supplies the same event behavior we just described for JButton. It also has an alert property that, when re-set by way of a setAlert() call, fires an ActionEvent:

```java
import java.awt.event.*;
import java.util.*;

/**
 * Monitor maintains a single alert property.
 * When some other object changes the value of alert,
 * it fires an ActionEvent.
 *
 * @author The CJ2CSG Guys
 */
public class Monitor
{
  private Vector listeners = new Vector();
  private String alert;

  /**
   * Registers an action listener to this object.
   * Ignores repeat registrations.
   */
  public void addActionListener(ActionListener acl) {
    if (!listeners.contains(acl)) {
      listeners.add(acl);
    }
  }

  /**
```

Using Java Bean Conventions

```java
 * De-registers an action listener from this object.
 * Ignores repeat de-registrations.
 */
public void removeActionListener(ActionListener acl) {
  if (listeners.contains(acl)) {
    listeners.remove(acl);
  }
}

/**
 * Sets the alert property of this object.
 * Fires an event if the value changes.
 */
public void setAlert(String alert) {
  if (!alert.equals(this.alert)) {
    this.alert = alert;
    notifyListeners();
  }
}

/**
 * Returns the alert property value.
 * @returns java.lang.String
 */
public String getAlert() {
  return alert;
}

private void notifyListeners() {
  ActionEvent ae;
  Vector copy;
  Enumeration enum;

  int evt = ActionEvent.ACTION_PERFORMED;
  ae = new ActionEvent(this, evt, alert);
  copy = (Vector)listeners.clone();
  enum = copy.elements();

  while (enum.hasMoreElements()) {
```

```
      Object obj = enum.nextElement();
      ActionListener al;
      al = (ActionListener)obj;
      al.actionPerformed(ae);
    }
  }
}
```

We used `get/set` and `add/remove` method pairs to adhere to the Java Beans convention. We'd do this if we intended to treat `Monitor` as a Bean; however, there's no other benefit to doing this. If we deployed `Monitor` as a Bean, we could use the `java.beans.Introspector` class to load it, break it down using the Reflection API, and use the reflected data to build `Descriptor` objects. Descriptors provide hooks into event and property types, as well as into the whole Bean. Figure 13.4 illustrates the two-step process of reflecting and introspecting a Java class.

FIGURE 13.4 The Monitor class gets reflected and introspected

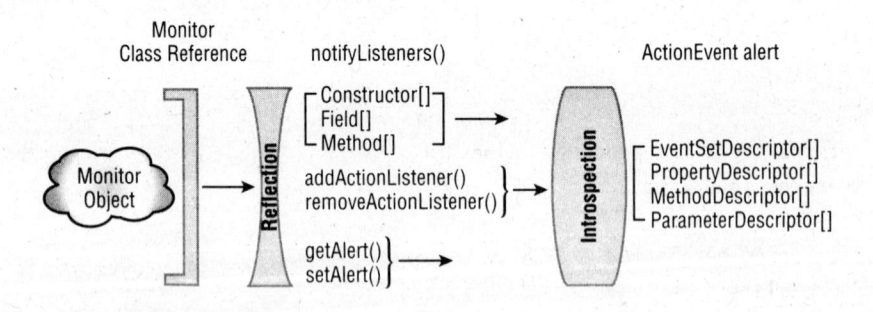

If none of this matters to you, you can use any method names you want. The class behavior would remain the same; it just wouldn't have a Bean-aware public interface.

> **WARNING** The descriptor classes in `java.beans` are designed to support low-level controls in Bean-aware graphical builder tools. Because descriptors rely on reflection data, they can be used to manipulate a Bean's appearance and operate on it at an extra "level of remove." Some programmers use these descriptors in their applications to analyze objects on the fly and to experiment with adaptive behavior. As with any powerful tool, using these techniques in mainstream applications can lead to inadvertent exploits in your own code. They are not recommended tools for routine development.

Java Beans and the MVC Design Pattern

The event model is far more conspicuously intertwined in Swing than in the AWT. To the 13 listener interfaces defined in `java.awt.event`, Swing adds 23 more in `javax.swing.event`, which defines notifications for everything from content changes in a data model to an undo operation. This technique of separating the definition of listening from any one class is the foundation for Swing's implementation of the well-known *Model-View-Controller* (MVC) design pattern.

In that pattern, the data, presentation, and data controls are decoupled from each other. Separating these roles into discrete classes allows the data to provide a generic interface to all possible views so that any number of views can form their data descriptions from a single, centralized source. Each view can then visually describe the model according to the set or subset of data it is most interested in. The term that best describes Swing's view of this arrangement is *model-delegate*. The important concept enforced by this renaming is that Swing employs a two-role version of MVC: the data model and the view controller.

The controller function is already built-in to Java by way of its event-handling facility, but Swing goes a step further by taking full advantage of Java Beans' architecture in its components. For the purposes of our discussion, Beans can be oversimplified a little: they are characterized by a series of properties that are simply a class's existing field members supplied with a pair of formulaic `get`/`set` method signatures. Should you pick up a comprehensive book on Swing, you'll undoubtedly notice numerous references to the properties of each component. Beans are also designed to communicate state changes to their properties, not just that they've been passed over by a mouse or been iconified. Other interested Beans can listen to these fired changes and behave appropriately. For example, if the listening Bean has an identical property, it can match the change. This action might result in a change to the color of one component that would cause a whole group of components to change together. The advantage of this scheme is that changes in one Bean can be bound to changes in another, making it possible for one Bean to act as a *controller* for any component that wants to subscribe to the service.

As a further step, Beans can be configured to veto changes sent to them, rejecting values that exceed a normal range for the target Bean or whatever rule that Bean institutes. Of course, this process has value to the sending Bean only if it can learn whether its target accepts or rejects a change, and then it can respond. The sending Bean may wish to *roll back* to the previous state if the target Bean cannot comply, or, in the case of multiple targets, the sender may attempt to set all target Beans to the last agreed-upon state. See Figure 13.5 for an illustration of each of these Bean-style events.

There's more to the total makeup of Beans, but much of the rest deals with managing them in a builder tool, which you don't have to worry about. The following sections discuss two component types that are particularly important: tables and lists. In keeping with Swing's model-delegate paradigm, we'll examine both aspects of these components: the way they present themselves and the way they hold the data that is used to create the presentation. As for toolkit design, this is a practice of the first quality. Take time to look around the source code for some of these classes and make some notes on how it's been implemented.

FIGURE 13.5 Three Bean event models

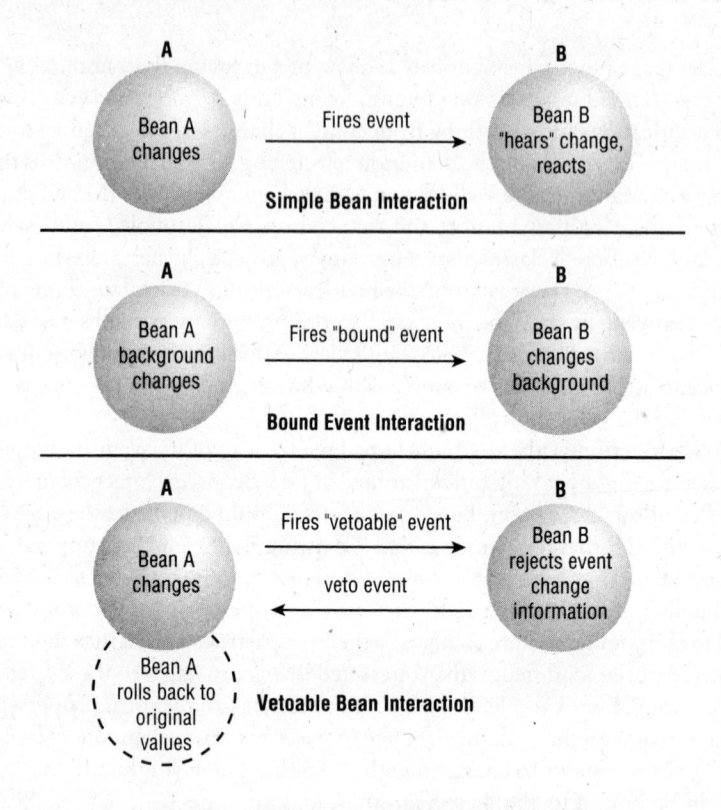

Simple Bean Interaction
- A: Bean A changes
- Fires event →
- B: Bean B "hears" change, reacts

Bound Event Interaction
- A: Bean A background changes
- Fires "bound" event →
- B: Bean B changes background

Vetoable Bean Interaction
- A: Bean A changes
- Fires "vetoable" event →
- ← veto event
- B: Bean B rejects event change information
- Bean A rolls back to original values

The MVC pattern separates and encapsulates these roles from each other, clearly defining the interface of each. Messaging among them then takes place by some form of callback, a technique in which one object has a reference to the other. If access is direct, then one object simply makes method calls on that reference. Indirect access is necessary when the sender and receiver have no prior knowledge of each other. The solution is a common third reference, known as a *listener* (or adapter or delegate) object, which the sender knows about and the receiver contains or implements as part of its own interface. One such MVC implementation that uses callbacks for communication might look like Figure 13.6.

Swing changes the commonly understood roles of MVC by altering the nature of its implementation. Models and views still communicate by way of event-driven messaging, but controls are instead collapsed into the view that uses them. Controls are made accessible as properties—values within an object whose state can be accessed or changed through a method pair. You can change a `JTable`'s view, for example, by changing the underlying model and firing an event to which the table listens. You can change a data cell's mutability, however, only by directly acting on the view itself. Figure 13.7 illustrates that relationship.

FIGURE 13.6 An MVC layout

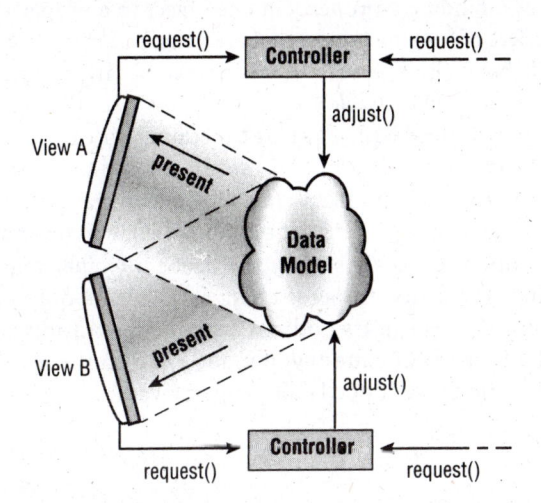

FIGURE 13.7 A JTable data update and controller update

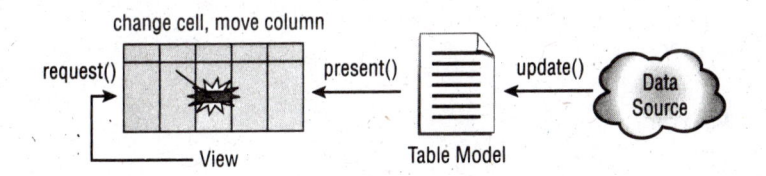

Listeners

There are 36 listeners and listener interfaces defined in `javax.swing.event` and `java.awt.event`. You can also create new events (by subclassing) and event objects (by implementing `java.util.EventListener` and extending `java.util.EventObject`). The only thing that functionally separates data and property management in a complex Swing component, therefore, is a well-defined model for event handling. But there is a support structure for handling property changes as events: it's part of the specification for Java Beans.

The `java.beans` package contains interfaces and classes that form the entire library for passing property-change notifications between two classes:

- `PropertyChangeListener` (interface)
- `PropertyChangeSupport`
- `VetoableChangeListener` (interface)
- `VetoableChangeSupport`

The primary goal of these interfaces and classes is to provide support for bound and constrained property changes. Binding a property in one object to a property of the same type in another object has the effect of keeping those values consistent. A constrained property is usually a bound property as well, but it also knows how to behave if the target property rejects the change issued by a source (hence the term *vetoable*).

Any value that you encapsulate with a `get`/`set` method pair can be treated as a property, according to the Java Beans specification. (An `is`/`set` method pair for `boolean` properties is supported as an alternative.) Communicating a property change between objects is supported by way of a `PropertyChangeListener` object. The `PropertyChangeSupport` and `VetoableChangeSupport` classes supply the needed listener registration methods, so any class that wants to treat its property changes as events only has to include a `PropertyChangeSupport` object in its body, wrap the registration methods in its own add/remove pair, and add a `firePropertyChange()` call to the given property's `set()` method. Here's an example using a `boolean` property value:

```java
import java.beans.*;

/**
 * A demonstration class that knows how to broadcast its
 * active property value.
 *
 * @author The CJ2CSG Guys
 */
public class Monitor
{
  private PropertyChangeSupport pcs;
  private int powerOn = 1;

  public Monitor() {
    pcs = new PropertyChangeSupport(this);
  }

  /**
   * Registers listeners interested in the "active"
   * property of this object by wrapping a
   * PropertyChangeSupport reference.
   *
   * @see java.beans.PropertyChangeSupport
   */
  public void
  addPropertyChangeListener(PropertyChangeListener p) {
```

```java
    pcs.addPropertyChangeListener(p);
}

/**
 * De-registers listeners interested in the "active"
 * property of this object by wrapping a
 * PropertyChangeSupport reference.
 *
 * @see java.beans.PropertyChangeSupport
 */
public void
removePropertyChangeListener(PropertyChangeListener p)
{
    pcs.removePropertyChangeListener(p);
}

/**
 * Returns true if the object is currently active,
 * false if not.
 */
public boolean isActive() {
    if ( powerOn == 0) {
        return false;
    }
    return true;
}

/**
 * Changes the value of the active property. This
 * method ignores calls that do not change the current
 * value, in order to avoid firing property changes
 * unnecessarily.
 *
 * @see java.beans.PropertyChangeSupport
 */
public void setActive(boolean active) {
    if ((active == true) && isActive()) {
        return;
    }
    if ((active == false) && !isActive()) {
```

```
      return;
   }
   pcs.firePropertyChange("active", isActive(), active);
   if (active) {
      powerOn = 1;
   }
   else {
      powerOn = 0;
   }
  }
}
```

Notice that the name of the `active` property derives only from the methods using that word in their identifiers. The property's data type is determined through method signatures as well, hiding the actual implementation in the class. This technique is in accordance with the way Bean properties are analyzed in a builder-tool environment by the `Introspector` class. Property identification relies on correct naming and method declaration. Therefore, you have far more flexibility in representing data to the public interface.

> **NOTE** For details on the required syntax to support properties, including support for `int` and `boolean` primitive parameters, see the Java Beans specification at http://java.sun.com/products/javabeans/docs.

The `firePropertyChange()` method requires that both old and new property values be passed as parameters. There's no real need for a bound property to pass the old value. The listener, however, has the option to validate that parameter if desired. The old value is necessary in a vetoable change, though, because without it, the issuing object wouldn't be able to roll back and maintain the same state as its vetoing target. Also, notice that the object maintains the actual support—the use of the `firePropertyChange()` call defines the property as bound.

> **TIP** Both Support classes now have overloaded registration methods in the Java 2 Software Developer's Kit. Originally, the only parameter was a `PropertyChangeListener`; now a property name, given as a `String`, can be included. The first version is intended for invoking the listener on any property change. The second specifies firing a change only when the named property is affected.

A bound recipient implements the `PropertyChangeListener` interface and gathers property-change information from the `PropertyEvent` object it receives in a call to `propertyChange()`:

```
public class Pager
implements PropertyChangeListener
```

```
...
  public void propertyChange(PropertyChangeEvent pce) {
    Object theOld = pce.getOldValue();
    Object theNew = pce.getNewValue();
    String name = pce.getPropertyName();
    if name.equals("active") {
      if (((Boolean)theNew).booleanValue() == false) {
        issueAlert();
      }
      else {
        issueOK();
      }
    }
  }
  ...
}
```

The versatility of this approach to property changes isn't lost on Swing. `SwingPropertyChangeSupport` is available in the `javax.swing.event` package to assist with binding properties across components. However, Swing makes stringent demands to accommodate the sensitive nature of the single thread used for updating components in a Java GUI. Intense event dispatching can cause contention or blocking on the system thread, creating the same problem with refreshing the screen that occurs if you use event code to call `paint()` directly instead of `repaint()`. Any code that might block on the AWT's thread is risky code, because it can interfere with the GUI's ability to update itself. Therefore, the `SwingPropertyChangeSupport` class is intentionally thread-unsafe. Desynchronizing any code that issues events, of course, has the added benefit of improving performance.

`PropertyChangeSupport` and its Swing subclass provide a readymade tool for sharing data of any kind across multiple components. Sharing controller-oriented values between two tables, for example, so that one data model can update another, is one possibility. Chaining data propagation in this way allows for filtering or other intermediate operations as well. Figure 13.8 illustrates this kind of collaboration.

FIGURE 13.8 Treating a data update as a property-change event

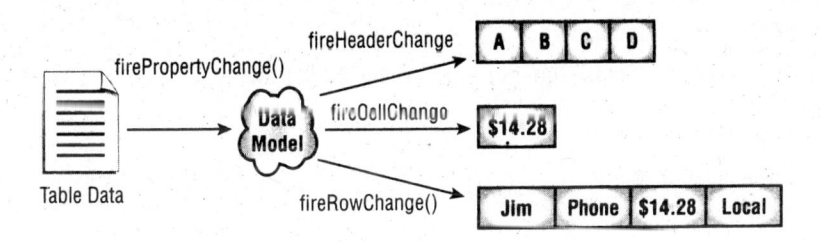

The key benefit to this approach is loose coupling among components that may be related only by their common task. Relating components through neutral event types makes it easier to avoid combining objects together, although it is perhaps not as intuitively compelling as using inner classes.

As an exercise in thinking more about listeners, consider the list of firing methods supported by `DefaultTreeModel` and `AbstractTableModel` and shown in Table 13.1. What form of listener would you write so that each model informs the other of changes to its state?

TABLE 13.1 Firing Methods in Two Data Models

AbstractTableModel	DefaultTreeModel
fireTableCellUpdated()	fireTreeNodesChanged()
fireTableChanged()	fireTreeNodesInserted()
fireTableDataChanged()	fireTreeNodesRemoved()
fireTableRowsDeleted()	fireTreeStructureChanged()
fireTableRowsInserted()	
fireTableRowsUpdated()	
fireTableStructureChanged()	

An easy way to start building a library of listeners is to write a class that implements the listener for a component you want to learn more about. These classes become the functional equivalent of the `Adapter` classes in the `java.awt.event` library, with the exception that your classes will do something. We find it convenient to use `JOptionPane` dialogs for this purpose, especially when working with an unfamiliar component. The following code implements a few tree listeners for experimentation. Note how each event-handler method simply pops a dialog box to acknowledge a successful event-driven operation:

```
import javax.swing.*;
import javax.swing.event.*;

/**
 * A sample listening class--on our way to building an
 * adapter.
 *
 * @author The CJ2CSG Guys
 */
```

Listeners

```java
public class ListeningTree
implements TreeModelListener,
        TreeExpansionListener,
        TreeSelectionListener
{
  // Abbreviation for long identifier
  private int MSG = JOptionPane.INFORMATION_MESSAGE;

  /**
   * Part of TreeExpansionListener
   * Posts the event toString() to a dialog box
   */
  public void treeCollapsed(TreeExpansionEvent tee) {
    JOptionPane.showMessageDialog
      (null, tee.toString(), "Tree Collapsed", MSG);
  }

  /**
   * Part of TreeExpansionListener
   * Posts the event's toString to a dialof box
   */
  public void treeExpanded(TreeExpansionEvent tee) {
    JOptionPane.showMessageDialog
      (null, tee.toString(), "Tree Expanded", MSG);
  }

  /**
   * Part of TreeSelectionListener
   * Posts the image of the tree's new state to the
   * dialog box.  Currently hangs the tree.
   */
  public void valueChanged(TreeSelectionEvent tse) {
    JOptionPane.showMessageDialog
      (null, tse.getSource(), "Value Changed", MSG);
  }

  /**
   * Part of TreeModelListener
   */
  public void treeNodesChanged(TreeModelEvent te) {
    JOptionPane.showMessageDialog
```

```
    (null, te.getSource(), "Nodes Changed", MSG);
}

/**
 * Part of TreeModelListener
 */
public void treeNodesInserted(TreeModelEvent te) {
  JOptionPane.showMessageDialog
    (null, te.getSource(), "Nodes Inserted", MSG);
}

/**
 * Part of TreeModelListener
 */
public void treeNodesRemoved(TreeModelEvent te) {
  JOptionPane.showMessageDialog
    (null, te.getSource(), "Nodes Removed", MSG);
}

/**
 * Part of TreeModelListener
 */
public void treeStructureChanged(TreeModelEvent te) {
  JOptionPane.showMessageDialog
    (null, te.getSource(), "StructureChanged", MSG);
 }
}
```

In experimenting with a `JTree`, we now have a way to see which of our actions on the GUI trigger which method calls on this class. For the purposes of prototyping, a class like this could act as default behavior for a GUI that is being assembled. It might be reasonable to subclass it; throughout the course of development, the dialog boxes could serve as a checklist for all event methods that must be handled before the code is complete.

Remote Notification

Event notification schemes can be created on the local VM with a small amount of effort. RMI's design goals include, among other things, allowing you to ignore most semantic differences between local and remote method calls. Taking those two points in hand, it isn't that hard to put together a callback setup that runs over the network—a notification scheme using RMI.

The easiest way to do it is to build the notification scheme on the server, and then export the object the client is most interested in. The exported class provides a registration model that accepts a listener interface type the client maintains locally. When the exported object happens to fire an event, the client's handler method is called back just as if the source were local.

The bulk of the work is on the server side, obscuring the details of implementation from the client. Figure 13.9 shows the classes needed to develop a remote callback. The heart of the operation is the `DataProxy` class, which is the only object exported from the server side. In this view, we suggest that the `DataProxy` object could be an event target for the `DataSource`. `DataProxy` implements the interface of remotely available calls (`DataInterface`) and extends `UnicastRemoteObject`. The `Client` class represents the outmost encapsulation of the client-side logic: it implements the `ClientListener` interface so it can register interest in the `DataProxy` class.

FIGURE 13.9 Remote notification using RMI

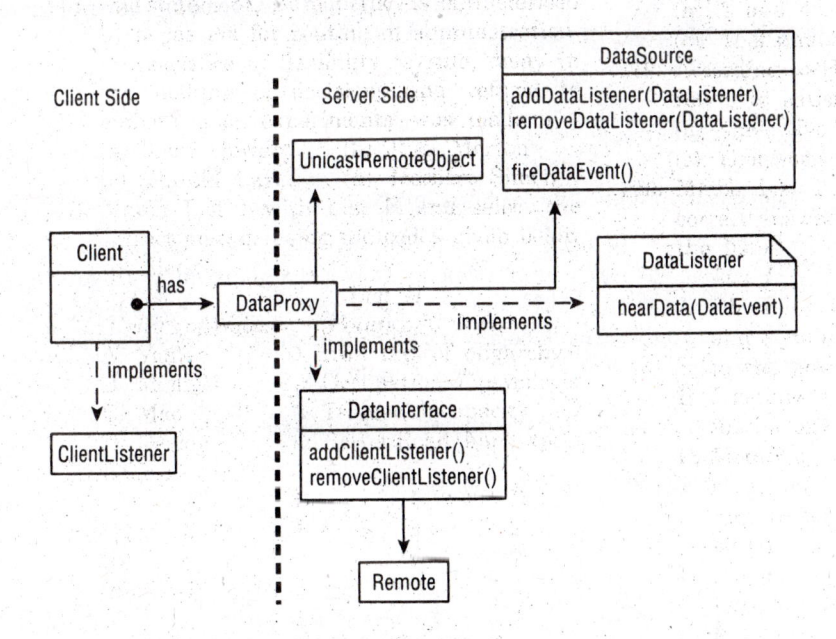

DataProxy must be set up to listen to and receive `DataEvent` objects from `DataSource`. This callback relation is server-local only. `DataProxy` then uses this notification to trigger a call to its listeners, including, of course, the `Client` that has registered interest in his events. The `Client` class could be a client-side event adapter that knows how to rebroadcast the events it receives. Or by the more direct approach, the `Client` class could be replaced by a subclass of `DefaultTableModel`.

Using Distributed Notification

With a bit more work, we could upgrade our remote notification scheme into a *distributed notification* scheme. In remote notification, we simply put the event source and target together on the server but export the target for remote client access and hookups.

In a distributed model, we want notification to work in both directions: from the server to all clients, and from all clients to the server. The class roles don't change that much from the remote approach, but there are better ways to visualize the domain. Publish-Subscribe seems to be the right model, because its structure is designed to push a steady stream of event messages from multiple sources, and then allow each subscriber a view on to the messages board.

This "newsflash" approach to event messages is particularly well suited for keeping clients updated on each other's doings. Any candidate who wants to go above and beyond the call of duty for the Developer's Exam assignment, for example, should feel free to establish server-active record locking; that is, the server notifies all clients which records in the database are locked and reminds them when the records are released. Once you've grasped all the roles that need to be incorporated into this scheme, instituting server-push notification isn't that bad. The difficult part is developing a clear but comprehensive map of all the classes and their relations:

- News (interface)
- Subscriber (Remote interface)
- NewsService (Remote interface)
- Subscriptions (maintained by the NewsService)

Figure 13.10 outlines the top-level relations. The client accesses remote services through the Subscriber interface. The notification scheme can be made more interesting through the Subscription class, for example by using preference objects and news filters ("sports and weather only"). Once you've assembled a working structure of this order, you'll be able to do whatever you please to complete the developer assignment.

FIGURE 13.10 Elements of a distributed notification scheme

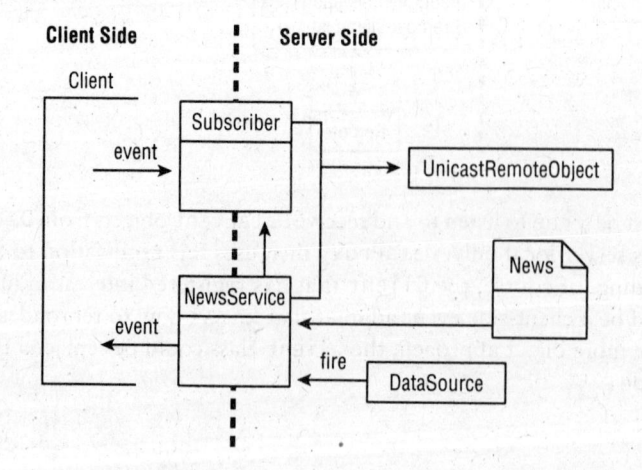

Summary

Events have a naming convention for each event named *XXX*Event. There is an interface named *XXX*Listener. If a component emits an event of type *XXX*Event, then that component has a public method called add*XXX*Listener() and another named remove*XXX*Listener().

The Java Beans specification is a naming convention. Beans communicate events and properties from one Bean to another. A property is any value in an object that has been encapsulated. If a Bean is also an event source, it supports a method pair to add listeners to and remove them from its registry.

Swings employs a two-role version of the MVC design pattern: the data model and the view controller. The only thing that functionally separates data and property management in a Swing component is a well-defined model for handling events. Java Beans can be used to handle property changes as events.

There are 36 listeners and listener interfaces are defined in javax.swing.event and java.awt.event. You can also create new events and event objects. The only thing that functionally separates data and property management in a complex Swing component, therefore, is a well-defined model for event handling.

Notification schemes can be as simple or as complex as you like. Base your design on the needs at hand, but remember that notification schemes are easy to build and provide a lot of flexibility when they are chained together. Remember to write simple adapters to get two unlike classes to collaborate. They can seem tedious to write at times; it's easy to conclude, especially after some long hours of coding, that you're just writing another class that "doesn't really *do* anything." Sooner or later, however, classes have to be brought together.

Exam Essentials

Swing decouples the responsibilities of data presentation and manipulation into two different class groups. As a result, the data model places no real constraints on the potential views of it, and vice versa.

The Java Beans specification defines four roles for events. These roles include the event object, the event handler, the event source, and the event target.

Adapters provide the glue to any event-notification scheme. Their purpose is to make it possible for any two objects to communicate.

Event notification comes in two types—one-way and distributed. One type of event notification is a one-way notification from server to client. Another type of event notification is distributed notification in which clients can notify servers and servers can notify clients.

Key Terms

Before you take the exam, be certain you are familiar with the following terms:

context

controller

coupling

design pattern

distributed notification

event

event adapter

event handler

event notification

event objects

event source

event targets

listener

model-delegate

Model-View-Controller

properties

roll back

vetoable

Review Questions

1. How does an application register itself as an event listener for a Swing component?
   A. By calling the application's add*XXX*Listener() method
   B. By calling the event's add*XXX*Listener() method
   C. By calling the component's add*XXX*Listener() method
   D. By calling the listener's add*XXX*Listener() method

2. Which of the following Java packages support the handling of property changes as events?
   A. java.awt
   B. java.awt.event
   C. javax.swing
   D. java.beans

3. What is the name of the design pattern in which the data, the data presentation, and the data controls are defined separately?
   A. Model-View-Controller
   B. Publish-Subscribe
   C. Observer-Observable
   D. Reader-Writer

4. Which of the following statements best describes the Java Beans specification?
   A. It is a naming convention.
   B. It is a notification pattern.
   C. It is a design pattern.
   D. It is part of the standard java.lang package.

5. Which two of the following interfaces are defined in the java.beans package?
   A. PropertyChangeListener
   B. EventListener
   C. ActionListener
   D. VetoableChangeListener

Answers to Review Questions

1. C. Every component that emits events of type *XXXEvent* have a public add*XXX*Listener() method.

2. D. Java Beans are used to identify changes in an object's properties as events.

3. A. Options B and C describe a notification, not a design pattern. Option D is not a design pattern at all.

4. A. Java Beans is neither a notification nor a design pattern, and it is contained in its own package (javax.swing).

5. A, D. EventListener and ActionListener are interfaces in the java.awt package.

Chapter 14

Enhancing and Extending the Database

In this chapter, we discuss the part of the Developer Exam that requires enhancing the database. We begin by distinguishing the two-tier database scheme—the scheme we will be required to use in our programming assignment—from other types of database schemes. We discuss two different approaches for designing our two-tier database, including the use of interface and the use of abstract classes. Fortunately, the assignment will have an already-defined database scheme, and it will be our task to extend and enhance its functionality. We discuss the choices in the design of and implementation of a database and in extending its features, including exception handling and thread safety. We will review the topic of exceptions and then discuss how to handle them within the context of our databse implementation. We will review the topic of thread safety and then differentiate ways of synchronizing the code, including synchronizing on the entire data structure as oppposed to synchronizing on individual data members within a data structure. In the last part of the chapter, we briefly address adding new features to the database, including the ability to search and replace records and fields, sorting records, and implementing a record lock.

Two-Tier Databases

In this chapter, we do not assume you know a lot about databases or that you have studied the Java Database Connectivity (JDBC) API. We will concentrate on an application structure that adheres to a simple *client-server* architecture. In a client-server structure, the database system is integrated with or running in the same process space as the mechanism that handles client requests and serves data back. The next few paragraphs cover common terms relating to database design and structure; they supply a context to aid our approach to design.

The most widely used database model today is the *relational database*. Relational databases are composed of multiple *tables* of information. A single table comprises any number of *records* of a specific kind. A table stores each record in its own *row*, which consists of ordered *fields* of data. Each field is, in turn, defined by its column, which declares what *type* of data it will store and the maximum space (*width*) available to each field in the column.

Relational design, as the name suggests, makes it possible to declare relations between tables that share columns of the same type. For example, one table of baseball players might be used to show current batting statistics. Each player belongs to a team, of course, but it would be cumbersome to include all the information associated with the player's team in this same table. In a relational design, you might create a second table that is *keyed* on team names. When you look up player data, you will see the team name. The database programmer may then allow you to drill down to team data by using this key to call on the second table.

This arrangement of data has several potential benefits. For example, highly redundant field data can be replaced by lookup references to another table. On a more sophisticated level, you can develop new relations from existing tables to meet a new user requirement. This functionality comes at the price of substantial complexity—certainly enough to justify the vast industry behind relational database management systems (RDBMS) seen on the market today. In fact, the JDBC API merely addresses a vendor-neutral way to incorporate an existing RDBMS package into a Java application.

For the purposes of discussing the project assignment, we will use a "flat" data model in this chapter. The database model offered in the project is *two-tiered* in structure. Simply put, this means that the server and database portions of the project are integrated and running on the same virtual machine (VM). The user (*client*) runs on a separate VM, which might be located on the same machine or on a remote machine accessible via a network. This relation between the two processes is one variation of the client-server computing model.

The explosion of commercial interest in the Internet over the last few years has brought the *three-tier* (alternatively, *n tier*) model into more widespread use, particularly in areas where client interaction is intense and response times are critical. This arrangement logically separates the server component from the database and allows the server component to focus on managing client demands so that the database can be optimized for storage and retrieval performance. The advantages of *n*-tier models extend in several potential directions. A common strategy is to deploy multiple servers between the clients and the back-end application. The server portion may spend more time interpreting or preparing client requests than submitting them. In this case, having multiple servers speaking to one database may be the best solution. If you're concerned that the server application could crash and take the database with it, this separation also achieves some amount of data protection.

A few servers could also be needed to support a wide variety of request types that the servers must then route to the correct data server. You might prefer to build multiple distributed databases but access them through a common server. The server itself would then handle the various incoming requests, making maintenance and updating easier and avoiding any elaborate client-side coding for determining which database to connect to. N-tier architectures provide a wealth of other strategies on top of these more common approaches, including the introduction of architectural concepts such as *application partitioning* (a means for moving application demand loads from one server to another as a form of load-balancing). Many companies interested in adjusting for the volatility of Internet demand look to these schemes as a way of expanding their ability to serve customers without bringing systems down to refit their hardware. As with many strategies for increasing flexibility, the key is advance planning and design.

Designing a Basic Scheme

A *flat data model* simply implies that the scheme for organizing data records is largely, if not completely, self-describing. Relational or other data-indexing schemes can be very powerful, but they impose complexities, not the least of which is a separate language to access the scheme's feature set. A flat file is ideal for small databases that do not require a complete subsystem to facilitate searching and organizing data.

There are only so many meaningful ways to write a scheme that is little more than the data itself. Some of the most common types include the following:

- An ASCII-based file of human-readable information, in which the rules for delimiting or parsing data are often hard-coded in the application logic or self-evident in the layout of the file itself.
- A binary file, written with an encoded definition of its own structure, called a header or *metadata*, followed by data records adhering to that structure.
- Multiple data files indexed by a control file. Schemes of this type (such as a browser's disk cache) often use the file system's directory structure as a readymade structure for facilitating searches.
- A data structure that resides completely in memory but is saved to a file on regular intervals.

Simple text files are, of course, easiest to read and edit directly. Binary files can be read faster and are ideal for random access; they can also obscure the contained information, which may or may not be desirable.

Using Interfaces

Establishing the design by writing interfaces has multiple advantages. One advantage is that writing only the abstractions first helps to determine what actions and class relations are necessary without committing to a specific means of achieving them. Interfaces achieve the broadest sense of polymorphic behavior because they supply the definition of the behavior that is wanted but not the means to implement behavior. They can also provide a bridge for using the same underlying data in several concrete classes that share the same high-level design, in the same way Java 2's Collections framework allows several container types to store one set of data.

One risk in any development effort that begins with concrete coding is the potential for implementation obstacles that cost as much to throw away as they do to solve. Once you're in that regrettable situation of facing a rewrite, there is the further risk of scrapping otherwise useful design elements because the specific code in which they are obscured failed to work. By using an interface design at the start, the possibilities for implementation remain open and some investment is preserved.

The simplest structure we have to create is a field type. A field is a member in a record that contains one type of data. The type and width of the field are defined by a column, which is the representation of one field type across multiple records. To leave open the possibilities of using the column in some meaningful way, we decide to define it abstractly:

```
/**
 * GenericColumn describes the behavior of a general
 * data column.
 *
```

```
 * @author Mobile Conferencing IT
 */
public interface GenericColumn {

  /**
   * getTitle() returns the name of the column.
   *
   * @return String - the name assigned to the column
   */
  public String getTitle();

  /**
   * getWidth() gives the maximum length one column
   * entry can take.
   *
   * @return int - the width allotted to any entry.
   */
  public int getWidth();
}
```

A record consists of an ordered set of fields, each of which is described by a column. Given the simplicity of our scheme, we decide somewhat arbitrarily that we want records to be able to report their own organization; therefore, we need a method to return the list of columns the record contains. A record will also have to have some form of unique identification within the table. The identification type should not be limited to a primitive such as `int`, in case the data container implemented allows a non-numeric ID:

```
/**
 * GenericRecord defines any record that knows its own
 * schema and the unique identifier given to it in a
 * table.
 *
 * @author Mobile Conferencing IT
 */
public interface GenericRecord {

  /**
   * getSchema() returns the list of columns that
   * compose a record.
   *
   * @return GenericColumn[] - the abstract type of a
```

```
 * column that reports its name and width.
 * @see GenericColumn
 */
public GenericColumn[] getSchema();

/**
 * getID() returns the Object representation of the
 * class used to store a record's unique ID.
 *
 * @return java.lang.Object
 */
public Object getID();
}
```

Defining a field—a cell that is part of every record—can be tricky in this scheme. Following simple rules of thumb may not always determine a best choice. We can say every field has a column; the phrase "has a" then signifies that a field object should include a column member in its class definition. On the other hand, a field "is a" kind of column—one with a single row—which suggests that subclassing makes intuitive sense. Rather than commit to a design choice for either one, we'll leave the decision to a subsequent stage of development.

You may also be wondering whether a method like `getData()` should be included in the interface. There are at least two schools of thought on this matter. A minimalist approach suggests the interface should only declare methods that this type must support for the benefit of other classes. Assuming we want to publicly define our records within our framework only by their schema and unique ID, this interface is arguably sufficient for now. We may determine later that `GenericRecord` should enforce `getData()`—if for no other reason than to ensure consistent naming and type return—and simply include it. The need to apply further methods to the interface is therefore compelled by demonstration rather than intuition. If we do include `getData()` now, we will have to decide on (and fix) its return type. The benefit is that we can start drawing on this part of the interface right away, because a record's data could then be returned through its abstract type. The only real question is whether to defer specifying `getData()` until the best implementation presents itself, or to put it in now and worry about any needed changes to its signature later.

Finally, we want to define a `DataBase` interface to specify the real work. As a description of data control, it must account for the following tasks:

- Manipulating records: adding, modifying, deleting
- Counting records
- Finding a record by a field value contained there
- Saving data to a backing store
- Knowing the scheme of the database

The DataBase interface declares that all the methods we want to ensure are employed. By describing them here, we document the methods other programmers may rely on when they write related or dependent classes:

```
/**
 * DataBase outlines the basic services required of any
 * implementing database.
 *
 * @author Mobile Conferencing IT
 */
public interface DataBase {

  /**
   * recordTotal() should return the number of records
   * currently residing in the database.
   *
   * @return long - number of database records
   * currently stored.
   */
  public long recordTotal();

  /**
   * getRecord() returns the Record matching a unique
   * ID. The ID value and type are determined by the
   * implementing class.
   *
   * @param Object - a key or ID value in an object
   * wrapper.
   * @return String[] - the full record matched to
   * the unique ID.
   */
  public String[] getRecord(Object ID);

  /**
   * find() searches through the available records and
   * returns all records that match Column data to the
   * String provided.
   *
   * @param String - a text value that matches data in
   * a Record.
```

```
 * @return String[][] - an array of matching Record
 * objects.
 */
public String[][] find(String matchItem);

/**
 * add() accepts a String array which is assumed to
 * conform to the Record type in use.  Means for
 * handling an improper parameter is left to
 * implementation.  Client validation or
 * exception-handling are possible avenues.
 *
 * @param String[] - Data values conforming to the
 * record scheme.
 */
public void add(String[] newData);

/**
 * modify() allows Record update.
 *
 * @param Object - the key or wrapped ID of the
 * original Record.
 * @param String[] - the original Record with
 * updated values.
 */
public void modify(Object ID, String[] changes);

/**
 * deleteRecord() removes a Record from the
 * database.
 *
 * @param Object - ID of the object to be removed.
 */
public void delete(Object ID);

/**
 * Commit current state of database to file.
 */
public void save();
```

```
/**
 * listScheme() allows caller to see the layout
 * of a Record.
 *
 * @returns GenericColumn[] - Ordered list of column
 * names and widths used in the current scheme.
 */
public GenericColumn[] listScheme();
}
```

Part of the task in reading code that's been given to you, particularly in a test situation, is to read for what's missing as well as what's explicitly troublesome. In the previous case, something is missing—something that is a potential trap to our interface: none of the previous methods throw exceptions. Unlike adding methods to an interface, which is a matter of adding on and then tracing through any existing implementations, adding exceptions later is not a simple option. Consider the following:

```
public interface Commit {
  public void save();
}
public class Persistent implements Commit {
  public void save() throws CommitException { }
}
```

The class will not compile under the rule that an overriding method cannot add to a parent method's declared list of exceptions. Therefore, an interface that provides a series of process-sensitive methods must include the semantics of those exceptions up front. Otherwise, implementing the interface becomes very awkward. An interface's methods are always public, and overriding methods cannot further restrict a method's scope. If we were forced to work under such constraints, it would still be possible to include some kind of precondition within each method that disallowed access to all but the instance itself. Having done that, we could then supply other new public methods that throw the required exceptions, but this would be a seriously compromised and confusing implementation at best. If we want to support exception handling, we must incorporate it at the design level. Backtracking in this regard is not difficult, but it does involve revising all implemented methods, which can be tedious. For further discussion on why the interface should not throw generic exceptions, see the "Issues in Implementation" section later in this chapter.

Using Abstract Classes

In designing and reviewing a set of interfaces over time, it is likely that some new requirements will emerge and others will boil out. The effort to achieve efficient abstractions can also get lost in generalities, with lots of methods taking `Object` parameters and returning `Object` types. In extreme cases, so many options are left completely open that it becomes unclear how to implement the model meaningfully or how to avoid constant casting and type-checking down the line.

By the same token, anticipating a concrete solution can also cause problems in design. Adding methods that point overtly to one implementation may obscure the interface's usefulness to a feasible set of alternatives. Moreover, an interface that tempts developers to null-code methods in order to get at what they want becomes, at best, tedious. Unless the interface methods are specifically designed to be ignored safely (such as the listener classes in `java.awt.event`), the implementing class may be of limited use.

A good way to remain partial to abstractions while nailing down some important details is to write an abstract class. Because abstract classes can include constructors and non-`public` methods and add or defer method implementations as desired, they are an effective means for signaling insights and intended approaches to a given design. An ideal use for an abstract class models the style of abstract implementations shown throughout the JDK. In the bulk of those implementations, the abstract class implements some amount of code that all its subclasses can use. But one or more of those implemented methods then call on the abstract methods in the class, which you must implement in order to complete the subclass for use. The `Component` class is in the AWT stock example of this technique. However, abstract classes needn't be confined to this toolkit-oriented interpretation of their use.

Partial coding gives us a way to address the previously raised question about whether to write a `Field` class that subclasses a column or includes an object of that type. An abstract class lets us have it both ways. The following example leaves out any additional abstract methods that might be useful, such as package-private methods for setting the width or title, to keep the illustration simple. Comment code is also omitted for this and other brief examples:

```java
public abstract class ModelColumn
implements GenericColumn {
  private String title;
  private int width;

  ModelColumn(String name, int width) {
    title = name;
    this.width = width;
  }

  public String getTitle() {
    return title;
  }

  public int getWidth() {
    return width;
```

```
  }
  ...
}
```

With the constructor and methods already written, a concrete version of `Column`, suitable for use in a `Field` class, is trivial:

```
public class Column extends ModelColumn {

  public Column(String name, int width) {
    super(name, width);
  }
}
public class Field implements Serializable {
  private String datum;
  private Column col;

  public Field(String datum) {
    this.datum = datum;
  }
}
```

Or `Field` could simply use a `Column` in one of its constructors and extend the abstract class:

```
public class Field
  extends ModelColumn implements Serialiazable {
  private String datum;

  public Field(Column col, String datum) {
    super(col.getTitle(), col.getWidth());
    this.datum = datum;
  }

  public Field(String column, int width, String datum) {
    super(column, width);
    this.datum = datum;
  }
}
```

Abstract classes are also useful for pointing out implementation strategies that, by definition, an interface cannot convey. Any developer who wants to implement `DataBase`, for example, will write a constructor to read in an existing data file. It may be less obvious to create a second constructor in order to create new data files as needed and self-document the layout data files must conform to:

```java
public abstract class ModelDatabase implements DataBase {

  public ModelDatabase(String datafile) {
    FileInputStream fis = new FileInputStream(datafile);
    // Read metadata or index from datafile
    // Verify file integrity
    // Read in records
  }

  public ModelDatabase(String file, GenericColumn[] newScheme) {
    // Read in newScheme array
    // Use newScheme metrics to determine metadata
    FileOutputStream fos = new FileOutputStream(file);
    // Write metadata to newfile
  }
  ...
  protected String[] getMetadata(){ }
  void close();
}
```

This skeleton code illustrates the most likely implementation of a backing store for a database: reading information to and from files. Just as important, it describes a way to create a new data file and automatically build its metadata. Now the developer does not have to track these details; a short program to generate new data files is reduced to passing a name for a file and the columns it will contain.

These two sections that illustrate interfaces and abstract classes are by no means complete. They are merely intended to suggest that some conceptual work before writing an application can help to clarify common elements. The result may be the development of a more flexible framework that can be applied to other problems or simply recognition that certain well-known patterns have emerged through conceptual realization and can be applied with better understanding now that the application goals have been laid out.

More important, well-designed applications promote more effective maintenance. Programmers assigned to maintain an existing application can read its interfaces first to cleanly separate issues of design from implementation in their own minds. Code reuse, with respect to other projects, is not always a practical objective, particularly for tasks such as this project assignment. Nonetheless, maintenance is not a great factor in this test either, aside from defending your code as maintainable. Where they are practical, worth the effort, and justifiable in the time required to design them, interfaces offer a lot of benefit.

Issues in Implementation

The fact that we had no assignment code in hand gave us a means to introduce the use of design abstractions. We could anticipate what a simple database application might look like simply by considering what elements were required and by avoiding the specifics of implementation other than surveying common tactics. A variety of articles is available on the Web that describe how to implement various types of databases; they address specific techniques in great detail.

The actual code you receive will spell things out soon enough. There are enough variations to make a comprehensive discussion here fairly tedious and not necessarily helpful; the assignment will not necessarily even center on using a low-level database. In that area, you must rely on your general experience to adapt to the assignment specifics as best you can.

Our focus here is the general set of implementation problems the exam will pose, which should revolve around one or more of the following topical areas:

- Exception handling
- Design flaws
- Thread safety
- Supporting new features

Thread safety will almost certainly be a central issue in all assignment variations, and the exam objectives will influence other potential problem areas, such as writing in new features or dealing with deliberate design flaws. We'll handle these topics point by point, referring to the potential impact on thread safety and its server counterpart, concurrent access, as we go.

Exception Handling

Exceptions in Java define the conditions in normal program operation that would otherwise interrupt execution, based on nonroutine circumstances. There are as many as four objectives to pursue when dealing with aberrant but nonfatal processing in a program:

- Determine whether modifying the existing code will eliminate the problem.
- Inform the user.
- Save the data whenever possible.
- Offer the user a choice of subsequent action.

A fundamental exception type might preclude one or more of these objectives being met. Other exceptions may be benign and require no action from the user. If normal operation can be resumed with no threat to data loss, the exception might be noted in a log for someone who maintains the application. However, the user should not be alerted to circumstances beyond their control and that do not affect their work. Beyond these two cases, however, a robust program will provide any user with clear problem reports, data safety, and the courses of action open to them.

The parent class of all these operations is `Throwable`. From `Throwable`, exception classes are defined in three major branches:

- Error
- RuntimeException
- Exception

Descendants of `Error` represent system- or VM-level interruptions (such as `OutOfMemoryError`) in which the question of recovering user access is probably a moot point. It is possible to briefly catch some of these exception types, but the level of service then available may be indeterminate. These classes are therefore intended simply to name the specific error, when possible, and provide a stack trace of execution as an aid to ruling out fundamental bugs in the underlying VM or other low-level resource.

`RuntimeException` subclasses define type violations and other faults that cannot be trapped at compile-time, such as a `NullPointerException`. The VM will use these classes to specify the fault type, so they are not types you should intentionally throw. Although they can be caught, it's a fundamental mistake to conditionally handle problems that originate with faulty code. Consider the following:

```
public class MathWhiz {
   ...
   public long add (String num1, String num2) {
      long n1 = Integer.parseInt(num1);
      long n2 = Integer.parseInt(num2);
      return (n1 + n2);
   }

   public static void main(String args[]) {
      MathWhiz mw = new MathWhiz();
      try {
         mw.add("3","FOOD");
      }
      catch(NumberFormatException nfe) {
         ...
      }
   }
}
```

This is not a subtle example, but it illustrates the burden placed on a `catch` clause that attempts to rectify the situation. This clause could report the error by name, but the VM already provides that service. It could report the specific input values that were used when the exception was thrown, but doing so merely shifts attention from the problem to its symptoms. Finally, the `catch` code could perform the work expected of the original method, but doing so would merely underscore how poorly the original method handles its assigned task. Runtime exception conditions should be traced and solved and treated as program bugs. Any handling in this regard can only be considered a short-term hack that must be applied each time the class is used.

Classes that directly extend Exception lie between system faults and code flaws, usually dealing with events that reflect the necessary risks of the activities they relate to. Dealing with stream or thread operations, as two examples, requires some means for anticipating IOException and InterruptedException objects, respectively. When a method executes a "risky" operation, it has the option of dealing with it by catching the potential exception or deferring its handling to a calling method by throwing (or rethrowing) the exception. The key criterion is the portion of the resulting program that is best able to inform the user, preserve data integrity, and provide alternatives to the intended operation, including repeat attempts.

Every exception object knows three things: its name, the trace of execution leading to the point where it was constructed from the top of its thread, and any data that was passed to its constructor (usually a String). An exception's name is provided by its toString() method, which is useful when a try block only captures a parent exception. It is therefore always a good idea to develop a family of exceptions for any application of substance, much as a list of error codes is compiled for an elaborate C program. Often these exceptions simply add a naming scheme for context. Extending Exception is all that's required. To support message passing, the parent class of an application's exception hierarchy then provides two constructors: one to accept a String message and a default that either requires no message or passes along a generic one:

```java
public class ReservationException extends Exception {

  public static final String generic =
    "General exception fault.";

  public ReservationException() {
    this(generic);
  }

  public ReservationException(String message) {
    super(message);
  }
}
```

Problems in adequate exception handling are typically noted by their absence rather than by poor deployment. Look for meaningful points in process control where adding exception handling makes sense. If the sample code provides an exception class, consider whether extending it would clarify risky operations specific to the application. If it does not, provide at least one for context. Finally, as a general rule, avoid using exceptions to handle data validation, unless the code gives you no other reasonable choice. Exception handling, by definition, is a controlled deviation from the normal flow of control followed by code that runs only in the event of that deviation. Consequently, exception code may run up to an order of magnitude slower than inline code covering the same operations and using expected entry and return points.

Design Impediments

In the application code you receive, you may find one or two methods that, based on the instructions you are given, pose more hindrance to than help in completing the assignment. Obstacles of this sort may be the result of hastily written code, where the central principles of object-oriented programming—data encapsulation, polymorphism, access control, inheritance—were not given adequate forethought, leaving subsequent programmers some form of maintenance headache. The easiest way to approach such problems is to break them down into four steps:

1. Identify the ideal or conventional technique to complete the code.
2. Determine that it cannot be used.
3. Consider the less attractive options.
4. Implement the least of those evils.

Chances are there won't be a right decision but rather a choice between two or more bad solutions that sacrifice different virtues.

Consider a parent class whose public methods make frequent use of a variety of private methods, which are intended to spare any programmer who wants to write a subclass some burdensome details of implementation:

```
public class DoDirtyWork {

  // record key
  private Object key;

  public void addRecord() {
  // private method
    checkDataIntegrity();
  // private method
    handle = getObjectID();
    try {
      // code that changes fields the subclass
      // wants left alone
    }
    catch(Exception ex) {}
  }
}
```

Let's say a subclass of `DoDirtyWork` needs the two private methods at the beginning of `addRecord()`, but wants to override the processing within the `try` block:

```
public class MyWork extends DoDirtyWork {
  public void addRecord() {
    super.addRecord();
    // now what?
    ...
  }
}
```

The desired actions are private and, from the point of view of the subclass, impossible to get at without executing the unwanted code. Assuming that the work of the parent class within the `try` block could be reversed, the subclass has two ugly choices:

- Call the parent's `addRecord()` method to first perform the integrity check and get a copy of the record's key. Then set the values altered by the parent's `try` block back to their original state in the remainder of the overriding method.
- Copy the private methods into the subclass using the parent source code, including any necessary private fields and other dependencies to make the calls work.

Neither of these choices represents inspired object-oriented work. In fact, they may be all the more difficult to realize because they require abusive programming to solve the problem. However, they do pose very different potential problems, and the justification chosen for either approach will depend on which problems are deemed least severe.

In the first approach, the chief danger is exposure to concurrent accesses. Assume for one reason or another that the overriding version of `addRecord()` cannot be synchronized. Thread R calls the overridden method in the parent class, which changes state data and then returns. Before Thread R can revert state back to the original values, it is preempted by Thread W, which accesses those values through a different method and writes them to another record. In this specific case, Thread W's subsequent behavior may be indeterminate. In the best case, it is preempted again by Thread R, which then has a chance to rectify the situation. In the worst case, data gets corrupted in one record or possibly all subsequent records.

The second approach, copying the relevant source from `DoDirtyWork` into `MyWork`, severs the chain of inheritance. The parent class's private methods are modified, possibly to account for the use of a more efficient data structure or to introduce other hidden fields that expand the versatility of the class. Because the changes occur to private members and methods, there is no reason `MyWork` shouldn't compile, and it could be a long time before the disconnect in logic is detected. Any attempt to subclass `MyWork` leads to the same dismal choice as before.

A case like this has no good answer, much less a right one. It is more likely that the solution you choose here will influence the remainder of the project. A problem of this type may well be covered in the follow-up exam; examine the problem carefully and choose from the alternatives you can devise, rather than taking the first work-around that comes to mind.

Thread Safety

Making data *threadsafe* is just one of two considerations in implementing an effective multithreading strategy. Achieving thread safety means guaranteeing serial access to the data on some level. Serial or *synchronized* access to data guarantees that any number of concurrent operations, which share access to the data and may modify it, do not interfere with each other. Another way of saying this is that the object that contains or wraps the data usually assumes a passive or defensive role against concurrent access. In a two-tier database model, the database portion assumes this role. Based on how data is safeguarded, the server code is responsible for managing and applying incoming client requests to data retrieval and storage in a manner that acknowledges such limits.

In practice, the balance between these processes can shift considerably, depending on the design goals of the application. If the database permits only one access at a time of any kind to the entire data structure, then there is no possibility of corrupting the data through conflicts in concurrent requests. Global enforcement of data safety comes at a price, however: a very limited potential for performance, which may become unacceptable as data operations take more time to process. There's no advantage to improving server efficiency if requests are prepared faster than the database can accept and process them, but for small databases supporting very basic requests, serially ordered access to all data is easy to program and maintain and is a viable approach for many situations.

Achieving greater performance requires data access below the level of the entire data structure coupled with a technique for processing requests that corresponds to how deeply the data is exposed. The finer the granularity of the access, the more sophisticated the techniques available to exploit it. Of course, the more complex the strategy, the greater the burden on the developer to ensure it is implemented and maintained correctly. Simply put, a scheme for multithreading that offers optimal performance is not right for all occasions. The cost of such a scheme must be justified by the potential benefits it can return. Some of those schemes are covered here.

Synchronizing on the Data Structure

Synchronizing data access has to occur on some level, but it can take many forms. Some container types guarantee threadsafe access as part of their structure. For other containers, the same result can be achieved within a code block that invokes synchronization on the data object as a precondition to the block's execution:

```
...
public void modifyRecord() {
  synchronized (theData) {
    //modify the record
  }
  ...
}
...
```

This approach is not as stifling to performance as it might first seem. Calls to the `Object` class's `wait()` and `notify()` methods within a synchronized block can be used to defer operation as desired, allowing thread control to change hands based on some conditional state. By using a series of wait/notify conditions with each potential data change, some degree of interleaving is possible, again depending on which threads are subsequently eligible to run. Without the use of `wait()` and `notify()` (and `notifyAll()`), the `synchronized` qualifier confers exclusive access to the executing thread on the lock of any `Object` classes (instead of `Thread` classes) it operates in or declares. If that declared object encapsulates the data, serialized access is achieved for the duration of that block.

You also have the option of synchronizing the methods that access the data structure to achieve the same effect; methods and blocks both acquire the object lock before they operate. Synchronizing on the method may seem to make simpler and "cleaner" code, but there are, as always, trade-offs. A long method that is synchronized may wrap process-intensive code that doesn't need an object lock. In extreme cases, such methods that access several major resources can create a deadlock condition by calling on competing processes, but employing a large number of synchronized blocks can be just as inefficient. Acquiring the lock over several code blocks in the same method is certainly slower than acquiring it once, but the difference may be marginal. The bigger danger is in synchronizing on objects other than the one represented by `this`, which can also create deadlock. However, in choosing to synchronize methods rather than code blocks, you must ensure that nonsynchronized method operations don't rely on data that synchronized methods actively manipulate. Conversely, nonsynchronized methods can't be allowed to change data that synchronized methods are supposed to handle.

Other rules to bear in mind about synchronized methods:

- Calls from one synchronized method to other synchronized methods in the same object do not block.

- Calls to a nonsynchronized method, in the same object or elsewhere, also do not prevent the complete execution of the calling method.

- Synchronization is not inherited, nor does the compiler require the keyword in an overriding method. An abstract class that supports a synchronized abstract method will compile, but the declaration is not meaningful. The abstract synchronized method aside, a `super.method()` call to a synchronized parent can create a block you are not expecting.

Data Structure

Java 2's Collections API, located in `java.util`, offers containers that by default are not threadsafe. Each of these containers is supported by a static method in the `Collections` class that returns serialized control in the form of an interface reference that wraps and "backs" the original container type:

```
public class DataStore {
  private HashMap hm;
  private Map map;
```

458   Chapter 14 · Enhancing and Extending the Database

```
  public DataStore() {
  // "raw" access
    hm = new Hashmap();
  // threadsafe access
    map = Collections.synchronizedMap(hm);
    ...
  }
}
```

The key to ensuring serial access is to eliminate any reference to the "raw" class. Otherwise, the means for accessing the container is open to your determination:

```
public class DataStore2 {
  private Map map;

  public DataStore2() {
    map = Collections.synchronizedMap(new HashMap());
    // threadsafe access only
    ...
  }
}
```

The philosophy behind this support is twofold. If protection against concurrent access is not required, the container form can be used as is; to make it threadsafe, the entire object should be synchronized. In fact, the API documentation goes so far as to insist on using a synchronized reference to the container whenever multithreaded operations will rely on it.

This does *not* mean that synchronizing on a container protects it completely at all times, only that individual operations are guaranteed to be atomic. Most of the time, in practice, you rely on multiple operations to complete a single task, such as reading a record, modifying it, and writing back to the data store. You must still devise a strategy for how records are handled during compound operations: whether the record is locked for the duration or may change asynchronously, whether the user is notified of other current locks or the latest change simply writes over any previous modifications, and so on.

This all-or-nothing rationale behind container synchronization merely rests on the idea that requiring you to design a more granular thread-safety scheme, in the name of optimal performance, is not typically justified by an application's actual requirements. It may be better to achieve performance through other means, such as faster hardware or a more efficient VM. Less complicated programming strategies that do not involve defensive techniques can also aid performance. These include reducing file accesses, partitioning data structures in memory, or perhaps applying a design that would permit read-only threads to run asynchronously (while write-oriented threads are queued and scheduled for execution). But if optimal performance remains a central concern, nothing beyond advice prevents you from writing your own interleaving schemes and applying them to native container types.

Data Elements

Each thread can be required to synchronize on the record objects it wants to write or modify. As a general rule, synchronizing on an object other than the one currently executing can be dangerous. Any code block that synchronizes on one autonomous object and then calls a method that threads its own attempt to synchronize on that same object runs the risk of creating a deadlock condition, hanging the system.

The alternative is to synchronize all the methods in a record object (and maintain complete encapsulation), but again this is only part of the entire scheme needed. You must still guarantee that each new record will receive a unique ID and will get written to a location in the container that is not already in use. Some container types inherently guarantee this based on the record ID as a key, which then maps to its value pair; other structures do not. An ordered container, such as a linked list or a low-level file using a random-access pointer, should be wrapped so that acquiring the record's unique ID and adding the record are atomically executed, ensuring no conflicts with other record inserts. With respect to an actual file, you must then also account for the space left by a deleted record and determine when best to reorganize files that fill up with null records.

Supporting New Features

Any feature you are expected to add to the existing code may imply, through its own requirements, a preferred way to implement threadsafe operations and still provide scalable performance. The considerations for achieving performance in the project assignment are, again, a decision each candidate will have to make based on the solution you feel most comfortable justifying. The following examples are intended to suggest potential threading strategies for the assignment, based on supporting features such as:

- Search and replace
- Sorting
- A record "lock"

Each of these features rests on a means for getting a list of records from the database, ignoring elements that fail to match the search criteria, and modifying those that succeed. In the case of a search-and-replace request, it isn't possible to know ahead of time whether the executing thread will only read (no matches), sometimes write, or always write. To avoid blocking the entire database, you need some way to list through the data and release records once they are no longer needed. An optimal solution for performance would also permit other threads to act on records not yet needed by the current thread but still on the list.

This kind of job has been supported by the `Enumeration` interface, which can be used to list the contents of a `Vector` or another ad hoc container type that implements it. The Collections framework provides an eventual successor to `Enumeration` called `Iterator`, which offers a tighter binding to all the container types in `java.util`. An `Iterator` knows how to remove elements from the container type and updates itself accordingly; an `Enumeration` has no such association with its container. However, an `Iterator` cannot cope with modifications made by another `Iterator` or any other process that modifies the database; the program must ensure that records cannot be added or deleted while a list is running.

Sorting can be even more demanding because elements are required until the sort is complete. One workaround to avoid blocking for the duration of the process is to copy the contents to sort into a temporary container and return the results from there. Using this same technique to hold records pending an update, sometimes called a "dirty buffer," can lead to improved performance. Write processes must be confined to using the dirty buffer, which only offers synchronous access. The original buffer is always readable. A copy of all dirty records remains in the original buffer but is marked "read-only" until the dirty buffer writes it back. Such writes must then take place while client write requests are blocked.

Ultimately, adding some type of state reference to the record object is required to track interested threads, iteration lists, buffer assignments, or even simple locks on a record while it is being added, updated, or deleted. This can take the form of a wrapper around the record that includes, for example, a vector of thread references. The methods of the controlling database must be updated to wait or notify based on record state, including a means to update the set of active references.

Summary

The programming assignment requires each candidate to extend code that is supplied with the project and make it threadsafe. In our example, illustrating the potential development of a simple database, we've shown how some very simple oversights in design can lead to problematic development for future programmers—a context very close in purpose to what the assignment poses. In particular, when multithreaded design is not considered as a factor in initial design, you assume a burden in retrofitting an effective scheme.

Working from a design using interfaces or abstract classes can also be problematic. It's important to note up front any missing elements, such as exception lists, as well as signatures with narrow scope. Without a thoughtful review, any limitations may not surface until implementation is well under way, possibly forcing a hack workaround or, worse, a rewrite.

Achieving thread safety can be as simple as guaranteeing synchronous access to the entire data structure. Providing it in such a way as to optimize concurrent access increases the potential for performance but at the cost of adding considerable complexity to the overall project. There is such a thing as "too much" performance, from the perspective of the cost in time and future maintenance to achieve it.

Exam Essentials

The easiest model to use when designing a database is the flat data model. There are other models you can use for designing a database, such as a relational data model, but the programming assignment will not require that you use that level of complexity.

The programming assignment will require that you implement exception handling, thread safety, and new features. Even though the actual programming assignment will not be known to you until you download it, you're guaranteed that these requirements must be implemented.

Key Terms

Before you take the exam, be certain you are familiar with the following terms:

client-server
fields
flat data model
metadata
n-tier
records

relational database
tables
threadsafe
two-tiered
width

Review Questions

1. Which of the following is not a standard component of a database?
   A. Table
   B. Record
   C. Field
   D. Cell

2. A flat data model is ideal for implementing which of the following types of databases?
   A. A large database
   B. A fully searchable database
   C. A small database
   D. A relational database

3. Every exception object knows which of the following three things?
   A. Its name
   B. The cause for the exception
   C. Its execution trace
   D. Data passed to its constructor

4. A program that is threadsafe provides which of the following?
   A. A guarantee that multiple threads will never attempt to access the same data at the same time
   B. A guarantee that multiple threads accessing the same data at the same time will not corrupt the data
   C. A guarantee that the server is written using a single-threaded programming model
   D. A guarantee that the server is written using an *n*-tier programming model

5. The primary advantage to using an interface to implement your database server is which of the following?
   A. Interfaces provide the highest degree of polymorphism.
   B. Interface methods can always be safely ignored.
   C. Interfaces implement some amount of code that all its subclasses can use.
   D. Interfaces remain partial to abstractions while providing concrete implementations where necessary.

Answers to Review Questions

1. **D.** A database consists of a set of tables. A table consists of a set of records. A record contains one or more fields.

2. **C.** Industry-grade databases are best implemented using a relational database model that is both scalable and fully searchable. Small databases are most easily implemented using a flat data model.

3. **A, C, D.** An exception object has no way of knowing why the programmer's code generated the exception other than the exception was, in fact, thrown.

4. **B.** Multithreaded programs must guarantee that concurrent data access is coordinated in a way that prevents data corruption.

5. **A.** One of the problems inherent when using an interface is that it may be unclear which methods must be implemented and which can be safely ignored. Options C and D are variations of the same fact that interfaces do not provide any behavior.

Chapter 15

Building the Database Server

In the previous chapter, we discussed issues surrounding the design of a database scheme. In this chapter, we will look at implementation details including the use of RMI, exporting objects using a `UnicastRemote` object, and exporting objects using an `Activatable` object. Although the use of RMI is not explicitly required, it is probably the best choice to make to connect the client and server in the programming assignment. RMI makes writing client-server code much easier by hiding many of the low-level networking details, such as managing sockets, from the developer. As such, you can focus your time and energy on developing the front-end GUI and back-end database rather than reinventing the wheel of how to connect them. RMI is introduced in detail in Chapter 12, "Writing the Network Protocol," and is discussed here because it must be addressed in the database server implementation.

One of the requirements of the assignment is to add new features to an already existing database. One of these features may be the implementation of record locking. Solutions for record locking in the Developer's Exam do not need to be elaborate. The principle applied and the operation that expresses it must be sound but not bulletproof against the unknown. Part of the reason is that most programmers do not have a lot of experience in multithreaded environments. The other part of the reason is that you are expected to make less-than-elegant choices in an imperfect situation and then document your awareness of the solution's limits.

The last part of this chapter will discuss strategies for the implementation of record locking.

Database Requirements

In addition to the client-server implementation, two other architectural requirements are written into the Developer's Exam. The first is that the resulting application must allow for either local or networked access to the database; the second is that the client must be able to access all the public methods provided in the exam's database code. The access requirement sounds sticky. The GUI client must connect at startup, based on user choice, to either the local VM or a remote one. One way to interpret this requirement is to launch client and server code from a single bootstrap program, such that the server always has a built-in client; the client can connect to that or to any remote data server, without restriction. By the same token, however, every client would then need to have a server attached to it for this approach to work, which does not sound like great design.

After some thought, we inferred that the real reason for the requirement was to ensure that the developer deals with thread safety in the received database and not just in the RMI code alone. It's an interesting problem; the straightforward solutions are ugly, but the elegant ones are code intensive. Given those options, defending a solution is likely to be far more important in scoring than the solution itself, so pick the method that suits you best.

Database Requirements

The second requirement tells which operations must work in our application. These operations consist of:

- Retrieving the schema
- Getting a total record count
- Retrieving a record based on its key
- Matching a record based on a search string
- Adding a record
- Modifying an existing record
- Deleting a record
- Closing the database

In addition to these operations, three more must be added and made accessible to client control:

- Locking a record based on its key
- Unlocking a record based on its key
- Matching against multiple records based on multiple criteria

You can write a subclass or directly modify the provided code. Either approach will have benefits and drawbacks; it's your job to defend the choice made and demonstrate awareness of those strengths and weaknesses.

Implementing RMI

RMI makes it possible to export to other VMs the interface of a concrete object on the local machine. RMI hides the details of object serialization and network communication and places the bulk of the preparation for remote access on the server side. As a result, client code that calls a local method does not look substantially different from code that makes remote calls. After the client initiates a lookup to the remote objects it is interested in, remote and local calls will, in fact, look the same.

The interactions between an RMI client and the server objects it uses can go a long way to help define the category of network communication they engage in. We call this scheme "client-server" largely because of its long association with centralized database resources and multiple concurrent users. Many contemporary computing models employ similar schemes, but the term would be meaningless if it simply referred to any two machines communicating over a network.

What Exactly Does Client-Server Mean?

The term "client-server" suffers from a fair amount of dilution and misinterpretation—in some contexts, it means any interaction between two machines. We find it helpful to maintain distinctions among the terms *client-server*, *distributed computing*, and a more recent term, *request-response*.

> Client-server interaction most often describes a structure for permitting access to a centralized data store that clients can manipulate in some way: by adding or deleting records, initiating complex queries, and so on. This interaction for the most part is not what is usually meant with static-content services like HTTP, sometimes referred to as *request-response* services. Some people contend that web content is becoming more dynamic, and to the degree that a web server is really a graphical front end to a fully functional database, it's a reasonable contention. At the same time, most HTTP servers distribute one type of content (possibly with multiple views) to all subscribers, until the server side changes that content. Information about the user may shape the data, but the users' range of options for gathering data based on their own input is typically very limited.
>
> Distributed computing is a separate beast altogether: it refers to the process of breaking down a job into parts and garnering the resources of very many or very specialized systems to process the parts and return them. Possibly the largest distributed computing model working today is the Search for Extraterrestrial Intelligence (SETI) Project based in UC Berkeley's Space Sciences Laboratory. At this writing, more than two million subscribers have volunteered computer time to that project.

To give a client access to server resources, we first build an interface that extends the `Remote` interface. `Remote` is a tagging interface, meaning it has no methods of its own we must implement. Much like the `Serializable` interface, which only identifies the objects the VM may convert to a stream of bytes, `Remote` is only used to flag its implementing classes as available for export:

```
import java.rmi.*;

/**
 * Defines database operations available to remote
 * clients.
 *
 * @author The CJ2CSG Guys
 */
public interface DBServer extends Remote
{
  /**
   * Retrieves the column structure of the records in the
   * implementing database.
   *
   * @returns array of Field objects
   */
```

```java
public Field[] getSchema() throws RemoteException;

/**
 * Returns the total number of records currently in the
 * implementing database.
 */
public int getRecordCount() throws RemoteException;

/**
 * Returns the Record associated with the record
 * number.
 */
public Record getRecord(int key)
throws RemoteException;

/**
 * Given a String to match against, returns the first
 * exact match found in the implementing database.
 */
public Record matchOne(String match)
throws RemoteException;

/**
 * Accepts a String array and adds it as a Record to
 * the implementing database.
 */
public void addRecord(String fields[])
throws RemoteException;

/**
 * Modifies the disparate fields in the Record that
 * matches the parameter Record's key value.
 */
public void modifyRecord(Record rec)
throws RemoteException;

/**
 * Deletes the record with the same key value as the
 * one provided by the parameter Record.
 */
```

```java
    public void deleteRecord(Record rec)
        throws RemoteException;

    /**
     * Closes the database.
     */
    public void close() throws RemoteException;

    /**
     * Locks the Record with a matching key, provided it is
     * not locked.
     */
    public void lock(int key) throws RemoteException;

    /**
     * Unlocks the Record with a matching key. This method
     * currently offers no protection against an unlock()
     * attempt that was not preceded by a lock().
     */
    public void unlock(int key) throws RemoteException;

    /**
     * Given a String with multiple matching criteria,
     * returns an array of records that match exactly all
     * the criteria given.
     */
    public Record[] matchAll(String matchList)
        throws RemoteException;

}
```

All methods in a `Remote`-extending interface must declare `RemoteException` in a `throws` clause. `RemoteException` extends `IOException`, appropriately enough, but it is also a useful front for any problems the client has using the method.

We can proceed one of two ways from here. To make our remote object available only while its server process is active, we can implement the preceding interface in a concrete class that also extends `java.rmi.server.UnicastRemoteObject`. To keep the object available over time but only use system resources as needed, we can extend the `java.rmi.server.Activatable` class instead. Objects that are `Activatable` rely on a daemon process (or service) to wake them when a client request is pending. They can also maintain changes to data using the `MarshalledObject` class.

Exporting with *UnicastRemoteObject*

To walk through both approaches in a short amount of space, we'll use an interface with a single method:

```
import java.rmi.*;

/**
 * Describes a remotely available interface for
 * retrieving a count of records.
 *
 * @author The CJ2CSG Guys
 */
public interface RecordCounter extends Remote
{
  /**
   * Returns a total number of records.
   */
  public int getRecordCount() throws RemoteException;
}
```

We take our first pass by extending `UnicastRemoteObject`:

```
import java.rmi.*;
import java.rmi.server.*;

/**
 * RecordCountImpl is a UnicastRemoteObject
 * implementation, so it will only be available while its
 * server process is up and running.
 *
 * @author The CJ2CSG Guys
 */
public class RecordCounterImpl
  extends UnicastRemoteObject implements RecordCounter
{
  private static int requests = 0;
  private int count = 0;

  /**
   * Constructors must throw RemoteException, therefore
```

Chapter 15 · Building the Database Server

```
 * the default constructor must be declared explicitly.
 */
public RecordCounterImpl() throws RemoteException {

}

/**
 * Returns zero; increments the local "request" counter
 */
public int getRecordCount() throws RemoteException {
  requests++;
  return count;
}

/**
 * Returns total count of remote requests made during
 * uptime. Available only to local objects.
 */
public int getRequestCount() {
  return requests;
}
}
```

The only thing that takes us out of our way here is the default constructor, which is required because the parent constructor throws `RemoteException`. This class always returns a count of zero, but it maintains a separate counter for how many times the count value has been requested, and the value is available only to another local object. This simple technique creates the separation that we want to maintain between database and client access.

Now we need a server application that can export this object to the outside world:

```
import java.rmi.*;
import java.rmi.server.*;
import java.net.*;

/**
 * A bootstrap class for launching the RecordCounter
 * service.
 *
 * @author The CJ2CSG Guys
 */
public class BootUnicast
{
```

```java
    public static void main(String args[]) {
      System.setSecurityManager(new RMISecurityManager());
      try {
        RecordCounterImpl rci = new RecordCounterImpl();
        Naming.rebind("RecordCountServer", rci);
      }
      catch(RemoteException re) {
        re.printStackTrace();
        System.err.println
        ("Creation error: RecordCounterImpl");
      }
      catch(MalformedURLException mfe) {
        mfe.printStackTrace();
        System.err.println("Malformed URL: " +
                           mfe.getMessage());
      }
    }
  }
```

Loading classes across the network, either from client to server or vice versa, is not permitted without an appropriate `SecurityManager` installed. If we do not install a `SecurityManager`, class loading is restricted to only what is available on the local CLASSPATH.

From the implementation of the remote interfaces, we can then create the files that act as endpoints between client and server on RMI's transport system. These proxy files, known as *stubs* and *skeletons*, are generated for each concrete type. Once we start the `rmiregistry`, we can run our `UnicastBoot` class and wait for client requests. Here's a throwaway client that indicates a successful remote call by popping a `JOptionPane`:

```java
import java.rmi.*;
import java.awt.event.*;
import javax.swing.*;
import java.awt.BorderLayout;
import java.net.*;

/**
 * A bootstrap client to prove the remote service works.
 *
 * @author The CJ2CSG Guys
 */
public class CountClient
{
  public static void main(String args[]) {
    static RecordCounter rc = null;
```

```
        try {
            rc = (RecordCounter)Naming.lookup
                ("//localhost/RecordCountServer");
        }
        catch(MalformedURLException mue) {
          mue.printStackTrackTrace();
          System.err.println ("//localhost/RecordCountServer : no such URL");
        }
        catch(RemoteException re) {
          re.printStackTrace();
          System.err.println
            ("Error accessing remote object");
        }
        catch (NotBoundException x) {}
        final JFrame jf = new JFrame("Count Client");
        JButton jb = new JButton("Request Count");

        jb.addActionListener(new ActionListener( {
            public void actionPerformed(ActionEvent ae) {
              try {
                rc.getRecordCount();
                JOptionPane.showMessageDialog(jf,
                    "It's still zero", "Count Request",
                    JOptionPane.INFORMATION_MESSAGE);
              }
              catch (RemoteException re) {
                re.printStackTrace();
                System.err.println
                  ("Error getting record count");
              }
            }
        });

        jf.getContentPane().add(jb, BorderLayout.SOUTH);
        jf.setDefaultCloseOperation(JFrame.EXIT_ON_CLOSE);
        jf.pack();
        jf.setVisible(true);
    }
}
```

Notwithstanding a few details—setting the server's `CLASSPATH` properly, making sure the stubs and skeletons aren't in it, and creating a policy file—this model covers a general RMI scheme as supported by `UnicastRemoteObject`.

Exporting an *Activatable* Object

If we want to support on-demand activation of an RMI server resource, we need to subclass `Activatable` instead. Setting an RMI server object to be `Activatable` means that no server resources are committed to making that object available except when it is in use by one or more clients. Requirements for extending `Activatable` start right with its constructors. The daemon or service process that runs on the server (`rmid`) uses the provided constructor to perform an on-demand or lazy instantiation of the `Activatable` object. If the remotely available object stores data that it wants to save to a file between uses, a `MarshalledObject` instance is required to manage that data. Passing an `Object` as a parameter to a `MarshalledObject` constructor has the effect of serializing its state, which can then be retrieved through the object's `get()` method. The tools needed to store state data between remote calls are an `Activatable` object's `restoreState()` and `saveState()` methods, and a stream that points to a backing store, such as the file system. Figure 15.1 illustrates the differences in state action between the two remote types.

FIGURE 15.1 (left) A UnicastRemoteObject state using rmiregistry and (right) an Activatable using rmid

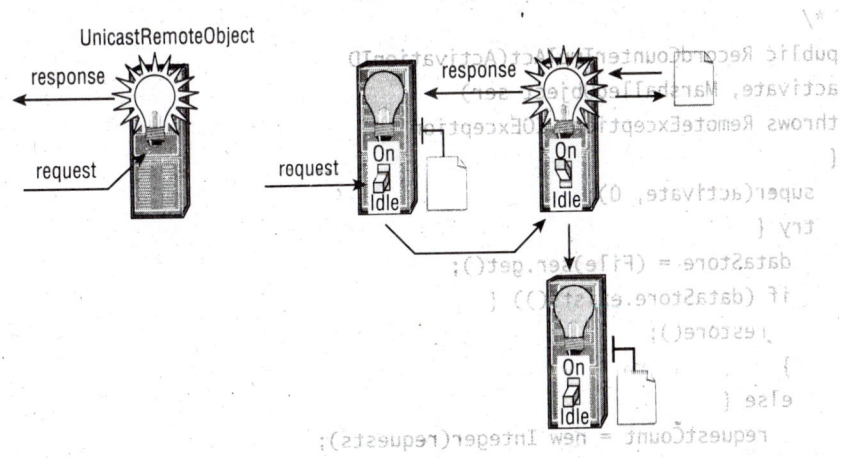

Server implementation of either type is transparent to the client. The server-side implementation is free to choose either model or switch from one to the other with no impact to client code. Here is a sample implementation using `Activatable` in place of `UnicastRemoteObject`:

```
import java.io.*;
import java.rmi.*;
import java.rmi.activation.*;
```

```java
/**
 * This class implements the RecordCounter as an
 * Activatable object. It persists the request counter
 * between uses.
 *
 * @author The CJ2CSG Guys
 */
public class RecordCounterImplAct extends Activatable
implements RecordCounter
{
  private File dataStore;
  private static Integer requestCount;
  private static int requests = 0;
  private int count = 0;

  /**
   * Constructor passes activation ID and integer (0) to
   * the parent class. Persists the request counter to a
   * file between uses.
   *
   * @see java.rmi.activation.ActivationID
   */
  public RecordCounterImplAct(ActivationID
  activate, MarshalledObject ser)
  throws RemoteException, IOException
  {
    super(activate, 0);
    try {
      dataStore = (File)ser.get();
      if (dataStore.exists()) {
        restore();
      }
      else {
        requestCount = new Integer(requests);
      }
    }
    catch (ClassNotFoundException cnfe) {
      cnfe.printStackTrace();
      System.err.println
        ("Error: Trouble finding File class?");
```

    }
}

/**
 * Increments the request counter after each call.
 * Returns zero.
 */
public int getRecordCount() throws RemoteException {
  FileOutputStream fos;
  ObjectOutputStream oos;
  File f = dataStore;
  try {
    fos = new FileOutputStream(f);
    oos = new ObjectOutputStream(fos);
    requests = requestCount.intValue() + 1;
    requestCount = new Integer(count);
    oos.writeObject(requestCount);
    oos.close();
  }
  catch(IOException re) {
    re.printStackTrace();
    System.err.println("Error: Saving requestCount.");
  }
  return count;
}

/**
 * A separate method for restoring the serialized
 * object, to make the constructor more readable.
 * It makes sense to balance the code separation with a
 * save() method.
 */
protected void restore()
throws IOException, ClassNotFoundException {
  File f = dataStore;
  try {
    FileInputStream fis;
    ObjectInputStream ois;
    fis = new FileInputStream(f);
    ois = new ObjectInputStream(fis);
```
```

```
      requestCount = (Integer)ois.readObject();
      ois.close();
    }
    catch (IOException ioe) {
      ioe.printStackTrace();
      System.err.println
        ("Error: Restoring requestCount");
    }
  }
}
```

The majority of this code performs simple serialization and deserialization and the associated housekeeping for exception conditions. The `ActivationID` provides a unique identity for this service once it has been exported. There are several options for retrieving a unique ID; we use `Activatable.register()` in our bootstrap code. The `register()` method returns a `Remote` stub, which is cast back to the implementation type and exported via the `Naming` utility `bind()` or `rebind()`. Also, because we wish to write a file locally, we need to set a policy. Java 2 comes with a binary called `policytool`, which helps you create an access rule without mastering the syntax required, but that's overkill for what we want to show here. A simple wide-open policy will suffice for demonstration (justifying it on the exam might be a stretch!):

```
grant { permission java.security.AllPermission }
```

Finally, the bootstrap code spends most of its effort constructing various activation objects needed to build up to registering our service:

```
import java.io.*;
import java.util.*;
import java.rmi.*;
import java.rmi.activation.*;

public class BootStrapAct
{
  // If this doesn't work, might as well fault and exit.
  public static void main(String args[]) throws
    IOException, ActivationException, RemoteException
    {
    RecordCounter rc;
    ActivationDesc ad;
    ActivationGroupDesc agd;
    ActivationGroupDesc.CommandEnvironment ace = null;
    ActivationGroupID agi;
```

```
    File store = new File("Requests.ser");
    MarshalledObject serData;

    System.setSecurityManager(new RMISecurityManager());
    Properties props = new Properties();
    props.put("java.security.policy", "policy");

    agd = new ActivationGroupDesc(props, ace);
    agi = ActivationGroup.getSystem().registerGroup(agd);

    serData = new MarshalledObject(store);
    ad = new ActivationDesc(agi, "RecordCountServer",
      ".", serData);

    rc = (RecordCounter)Activatable.register(ad);
    Naming.rebind("RecordCountServer", rc);

    // No reason to hang around; rmid is in charge now
    System.exit(0);
    }
}
```

Record Locking

The exam requires you to demonstrate control over overlapping safety mechanisms: the synchronized method calls already in the assignment source and a method that will flag a data element as unavailable if it is in use by a client. A rigorous programmer with a great imagination can easily turn this aspect of the exam into a black hole, so don't read too much into the requirement.

The lock() and unlock() methods are intended as public methods, and so are required to be made available for use by the GUI client. From that perspective, a few different approaches to implementation are possible. Each associated figure shows a possible evolution to the strategy:

Active client Highlighting a row locks the record (see Figure 15.2).

On-demand client Locking is integral to all add/delete/modify operations (see Figure 15.3).

Lazy client Requests are queued; notification occurs on a subsequent thread (see Figure 15.4).

FIGURE 15.2   Record locking for an active client

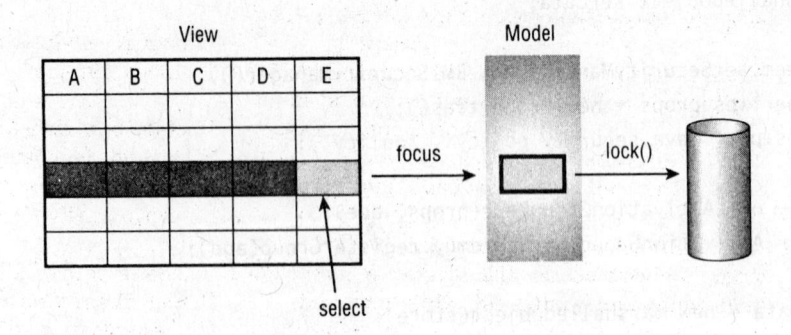

FIGURE 15.3   Record locking for an on-demand client

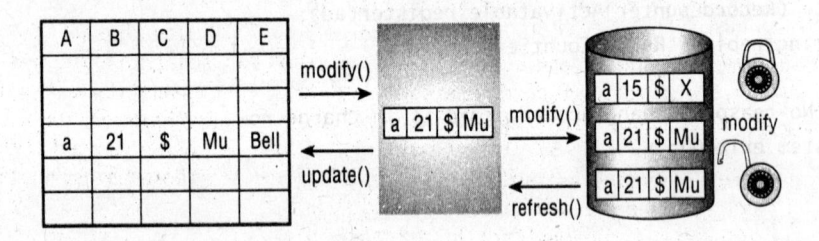

FIGURE 15.4   Record locking for a lazy client

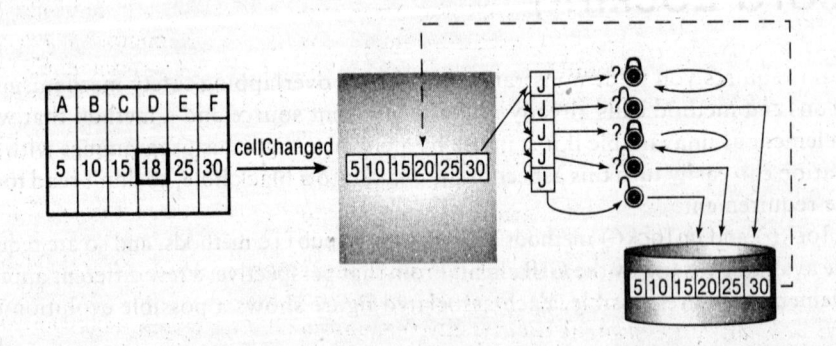

Each model has its advantages and disadvantages. As a general rule, the more active the strategy, the less appropriate it is for large numbers of users. The more passive the strategy, the more available the database seems, at least under moderate use. Passive strategies also typically require more careful designs because each subprocess takes on a thread of its own, and deference is sorted out among competing processes.

For each strategy, some tactic can usually be applied to mitigate drawbacks. An active client can be supported with a timer thread. If the client senses no user activity in the course of a timed loop, the client can release the lock and notify the user through a modal dialog. Or the server can host the timer, possibly polling the client for signs of life as well and reclaiming locks only when the connection client appears to die.

On-demand clients can suffer from lengthy blocks under heavy usage, blocking the GUI application until some action is resolved. Swing prevents this kind of behavior in an RMI server environment by not allowing remote calls to take place on the GUI's event dispatch thread. To work around this limitation, remote calls that need to run on this thread can be encapsulated as `Runnable` objects. `SwingUtilities.invokeAndWait()` and `SwingUtilities.invokeLater()` each accept a `Runnable` parameter, which they can then execute synchronously or asynchronously, respectively, on the AWT event dispatch thread.

Lazy clients are our closest strategy for record locking as it might be modeled in a relational database. Relational database management system (RDBMS) designers have to concern themselves with record locks that can occur during a large join operation, making it computationally expensive to assess which records are in use and which are free. Notification in such environments is usually required to be as quick as possible, separate threading or not. The usual solution: more memory, faster CPUs, and more efficient storage systems. To achieve a similar effect for this assignment, look to build a server algorithm that queues jobs and uses a publish-subscribe or event-delegation model to notify the client.

Summary

As an exam candidate, you will have to support a fundamental list of data-oriented operations in a client-server environment. Most details for server-side storage have been decided in the assignment source code, so it's really up to you to decide what kind of design you can best defend. There are two possibilities for RMI-based networking: export the object using `UnicastRemoteObject` so that it is always up and running, or extend the `Activatable` service class and set up a `MarshalledObject` to persist the data between uses. Remember to follow the documentation guidelines for instituting security and writing a policy file, and refresh your understanding of how the CLASSPATH can interfere with proper RMI behavior.

Record locking ensures that one change operation on a record can't be interrupted by another change to the same record. Without that guarantee of serially ordered (or `synchronized`) operations, the integrity of the data could be lost. It is your job to provide for efficient concurrent access without jeopardizing data. Manipulating records as discrete objects is one way to provide for threadsafe operation. In a client-server arrangement, it's tempting to synchronize the client at the moment it requests access to the remote object, but truly threadsafe code must center on the shared data itself.

Exam Essentials

The programming assignment must allow for either local or networked access to the database. Your application must behave the same regardless of the type of access.

The client must be able to access all the public methods provided in the exam's database code. All the functionality that is provided by the database must be available within the client GUI.

The client-server connectivity must be implemented using RMI. Even though you can implement network connectivity using other tools, such as sockets, you are required to use RMI.

The database server must allow for concurrent access. You must implement some form of record locking in your database so that multiple clients can connect to the database concurrently.

Key Terms

Before you take the exam, be certain you are familiar with the following terms:

distributed computing	skeletons
request-response	stubs

Review Questions

1. To make remote objects available only while their server process is active, you can extend which of the following classes?
   A. java.rmi.server.Activatable
   B. java.rmi.server.UnicastRemoteObject
   C. java.rmi.server.UnicastLocalObject
   D. java.rmi.server.BroadcastRemoteObject

2. Constructors for the class (or subclasses of) UnicastRemoteObject must throw which of the following exceptions?
   A. RemoteException
   B. UnicastException
   C. ArrayOutofBoundsException
   D. IOException

3. The tools needed to store state data between remote calls for an Activatable object's include which two of the following?
   A. restoreState()
   B. setState()
   C. getState()
   D. saveState()

4. Which of the following behavior typifies an on-demand client?
   A. Highlighting a row locks the record.
   B. Locking is integral to all add/delete/modify operations.
   C. Requests are queued and notification occurs on a subsequent thread.
   D. The server is stopped and started for every client request.

5. The programming assignment includes all but which of the following requirements?
   A. Getting a total record count
   B. Matching a record based on a search string
   C. Adding, modifying, and deleting records
   D. Linking database tables

Answers to Review Questions

1. **B.** The `java.rmi.server.Activatable` keeps objects available over time. Options C and D are absurd because they do not exist.

2. **A.** Option B is absurd because the exception class does not exist. Option C defines an exception thrown when using arrays. Option D defines an exception thrown when performing IO.

3. **A, D.** Options B and C include methods that are not defined in the `Activatable` class.

4. **B.** Option A describes the behavior of an active client. Option C describes the behavior of a lazy client. Option D is absurd because the server must always be running in order to accept new client connections.

5. **D.** Linking database tables together is achieved using a relational database model. The programming assignment does not require using such a model.

Practice Exam

1. Given the following code, the default constructor will automatically be provided:

```
public class ConstructorTest {
    public int one() {
        return 1;
    }
    public int two() {
        return 2;
    }
    public static void main(String [] args) {
        ConstructorTest ct = new ConstructorTest();
        System.out.println("One: " + ct.one());
        System.out.println("Two: " + ct.two());
    }
}
```

   A. True
   B. False

2. What statement is needed to request the garbage collector to run?
   A. System.garbage();
   B. System.garbage.collect();
   C. System.gc();
   D. System.garbagecollect();

3. How would you enter 2342 as a long?
   A. 2342
   B. L2342
   C. 2342L
   D. (long)2342

4. Select the correct outcome for -15 % 6.
   A. 2
   B. -2
   C. 3
   D. -3
   E. None of the above

5. What will be printed out when the following application is executed?
   ```
   public class MaxTest {
      public static void main (String [] args) {
         System.out.println("" + Math.max(5, -5));
      }
   }
   ```
   A. 5
   B. -5
   C. 0
   D. Does not compile

6. Which of the following statements does NOT define a String array called str that contains three elements?
   A. `String[] str = new String[3];`
   B. `String [] str = new String[3];`
   C. `String []str = new String[3];`
   D. `String[3] str = new String();`

7. Which of the following flow structures will always guarantee you at least one iteration? (Select all that apply.)
   A. for loop
   B. switch block
   C. do/while loop
   D. while loop
   E. if/else block

8. Select the correct form of creating arrays:
   A. `int [] array;`
      `array[] = new int[15];`
   B. `int array[];`
      `array = new int[15];`
   C. `int [15] array = new int[];`
   D. `int array = new int(15);`
   E. `int [] array = new int[];`
      `array.setLength = 15;`

9. What will be printed out when this for loop is executed?
   ```
   for (int x = 0; x <= 10; ) {
       System.out.println("X = " + x);
   }
   ```
   A. "X = 0", "X = 1" ... "X = 10"
   B. "X = 0" infinitely
   C. Does not compile
   D. Does not run

10. Which of the following are not objects? (Select all that apply.)
    A. A class
    B. A method
    C. A constructor
    D. A Boolean
    E. None of the above

11. Which of the following signatures are valid for the method main? (Select all that apply.)
    A. `public static void main(String []arg) {}`
    B. `public void static main(String args[]) {}`
    C. `public void main(String[] args) {}`
    D. `public static void main() {}`
    E. `static public void main(String args[]) {}`

12. Select all overloaded operators:
    A. -=
    B. *
    C. +
    D. -
    E. +=

13. The keyword `implements` refers to what type of relationship?
    A. "is a"
    B. "has a"
    C. "was a"
    D. "will be a"
    E. None of the above

14. Given the following method, which of the methods that follow are considered to be overloaded? (Select all that apply.)

```
public void close(int apple) {}
```

- **A.** `public int close(int a) {}`
- **B.** `public void close(int a, int b) {}`
- **C.** `public void close(int door) {System.exit(0);}`
- **D.** `public void close(float door) {}`
- **E.** `public void close(double d, boolean b)`

15. The developer can force garbage collection by calling `System.gc()`.
- **A.** True
- **B.** False

16. If a class has two methods that access the class's instance data, synchronizing one of the methods will not protect the data from corruption.
- **A.** A.True
- **B.** B.False

17. Select all classes whose width and height are initially set to zero, regardless of the number of components added.
- **A.** Dialog
- **B.** Frame
- **C.** Panel
- **D.** Applet

18. In Java, threads are always time-sliced.
- **A.** True
- **B.** False

19. The following method call is legal.

```
int a = Math.random();
```

- **A.** True
- **B.** False

20. Which of these are not possible return values from `Math.random()`? (Select all that apply.)
- **A.** 0
- **B.** 1
- **C.** 32
- **D.** -25
- **E.** 0.34

Practice Exam

21. What do you expect the following method call to return?
```
Math.ceil(6.29);
```

  A. 6
  B. 6.0
  C. 6.5
  D. 7
  E. 7.0

22. What will happen when the following application is executed?
```
public class Construct {
    public Construct(int x) {
        System.out.println("" + x);
    }
    public static void main(String [] args) {
        Construct c = new Construct();
        Construct c1 = new Construct(5);
    }
}
```

  A. "5" will be printed out.
  B. A blank line, then "5" will be printed out.
  C. Nothing will be printed out.
  D. Does not compile.

23. Given the following partial statement, which of the following int assignments legally complete it? (Select all that apply.)
```
int i = _____
```

  A. 7;
  B. (short)3;
  C. new Integer(5).intValue();
  D. (int)3.14;
  E. (integer)3.14;

24. A thread that is blocked by a call to wait() will be sent to the same queue as threads that are blocked by a call to sleep(long time).

  A. A.True
  B. B.False

25. Given the following object, which of the statements that follow will successfully change the object's value to "abcdef"?

    ```
    String str = new String("abc");
    ```

    A. `str.concat("def"");`
    B. `str = "abc" + "def";`
    C. `str + "def";`
    D. `str += "def";`
    E. None of the above

26. Which of the following are illegal method calls? (Select all that apply.)

    A. `Math.max(5, 500)`
    B. `Math.max(100000000L, 400000000L)`
    C. `Math.max('A', 'a')`
    D. `Math.max(5F, 6L)`
    E. None of the above

27. Which of the following collections generates a series of elements, one at a time, then uses the nextElement() method to retrieve successive elements of the series? (Select all that apply.)

    A. `Iterator`
    B. `Enumeration`
    C. `ListIterator`
    D. `Collection`
    E. `HashMap`

28. Select all the incorrect return methods:

    A. ```
       public int method() {
           return 4;
       }
       ```
    B. ```
       public double method() {
           return 4;
       }
       ```
    C. ```
       public void method() {
           return;
       }
       ```
    D. ```
       public int method() {
           return 3.14;
       }
       ```
    E. ```
       public Object method() {
           return null;
       }
       ```
       ```

29. How do you declare and initialize a `String` array with two elements in a single line of code?
    A. `String [] strArr = ["element 1", "element 2"];`
    B. `String [] strArr = {"element 1", "element 2"};`
    C. `String [] strArr = ("element 1", "element 2");`
    D. `String [] strArr = new String ["element 1", "element 2"];`
    E. None of the above

30. Labels are allowed to which of the following types? (Select all that apply.)
    A. `if/else` blocks
    B. `static` blocks
    C. `for` loops
    D. `do/while` loops
    E. method blocks

31. Which of the following are true statements?
    A. Classes can throw exceptions.
    B. Attributes can throw exceptions.
    C. Constructors can throw exceptions.
    D. Methods can throw exceptions.
    E. A static code block can throw exceptions.

32. Which of the following are not valid hexadecimal values? (Select all that apply.)
    A. 0x4ABF
    B. 0x0021
    C. 0xHAAC
    D. 0x12A7
    E. 0xeAee

33. Given the following code, which of the statements that follow would successfully call line 3 from another class within this package?

```
1. public class Outer {
2.     class Inner{
3.         public void print() {
4.             System.out.println("Inside");
5.         }
6.     }
7. }
```

    A. `new Inner().print();`
    B. `Outer.this.print();`
    C. `new Outer().print();`
    D. `new Outer().new Inner().print();`
    E. None of the above

34. Which of the following methods will return a value of 8?
    A. `Math.sqrt(16);`
    B. `Math.round(7.89);`
    C. `Math.round(7.89F);`
    D. `Math.abs(-8.3);`

35. Which of these collections contains no duplicate elements? (Select all that apply.)
    A. Set
    B. List
    C. Map
    D. Collection
    E. Vector

36. Select all answers that will correctly create objects from the following classes:

    ```
    public class Animal {}

    public class Horse extends Animal {
        Horse(int age) {}
    }

    public class Pony extends Horse {
        Pony(double weight) {}
    }
    ```

    A. `Animal a2 = new Animal();`
    B. `Horse h1 = new Horse(5);`
    C. `Pony p1 = new Pony();`
    D. `Pony p2 = new Pony(200.5);`
    E. None of the above

37. Given the following code, what will happen?

```
public class Tree {
    private static long noLeaves;
    public void grow() {
        int noLeaves;
        this.noLeaves = noLeaves + 5;
    }
    public static void main(String []arg) {
        new Tree().grow();
    }
}
```

A. The code will not compile because you cannot define a variable of the same name.

B. The code will not compile because the variable noLeaves has not been initialized.

C. The code will compile but will not run.

D. The code will compile and run.

38. Which of the following are valid assignments? (Select all that apply.)

A. boolean yes = 1;

B. int first = 'a';

C. short ha = 0xBAAC;

D. boolean honest = false;

E. short hex = 0xAAC;

39. Given the following code, what results will occur?

```
1.  import java.awt.*;
2.  import java.util.*;
3.  import java.awt.event.*;
4.  public class GUI extends Panel {
5.      public GUI(final ArrayList array1) {
6.          final java.awt.List lst = new java.awt.List();
7.          lst.addItemListener(new ItemListener() {
8.          public void itemStateChanged(ItemEvent e) {
9.              Iterator it = array1.iterator();
10.             while(it.hasNext()) {
11.                 lst.add((String)it.next());
12.             }
13.         }
14.         });
15.     }
16. }
```

A. The code will not compile because of line 5.
B. The code will not compile because of line 6.
C. The code will not compile because of line 7.
D. The code will not compile because of line 9.
E. The code will compile.

40. The following code example will compile and execute.

```
public class MyTest {
    public String oneMethod(int number) {
        return new Integer(number).toString();
    }
    public String oneMethod(String number) {
        return number;
    }
    public static void main(String [] args) {
        MyTest mt = new MyTest();
        System.out.println(mt.oneMethod(1));
        System.out.println(mt.oneMethod("One"));
    }
}
```

A. True
B. False

41. Given the following class, what outcome would you expect?

```
1.  public class Calc {
2.      int a = 3;
3.      int b = 4;
4.      int c = 6;
5.      int d = 8;
6.      public int calc() {
7.          return a + b
8.              + c + d;
9.      }
10.     public static void main(String [] args) {
11.         Calc c = new Calc();
12.         System.out.println(c.calc());
13.     }
14. }
```

A. The code will not compile because of line 6.
B. The code will not compile because of line 7.
C. The code will compile and print out 21.
D. The code will compile and print out 3468.

42. Which of the following Math.min() method calls are illegal? (Select all that apply.)
    A. Math.min(500D, 400F)
    B. Math.min(78, 'c')
    C. Math.min(4321, -3)
    D. None of the above

43. Line 12 refers to which size variable?
    ```
    1. class Parent {
    2.     public int size;
    3.     public int getSize() {
    4.         return this.size;
    5.     }
    6. }
    7. public class Child extends Parent{
    8.     int size;
    9.     class InnerChild {
    10.        int size;
    11.        public void method(int size) {
    12.            Parent.Child.this.size = 5;
    13.        }
    14.    }
    15. }
    ```

    A. Line 2
    B. Line 8
    C. Line 10
    D. Line 11
    E. None of the above; the code does not compile.

44. What will be printed out when the following application is executed? (Select all that apply.)

```
public class SwitchTest {
   public static void run(int x) {
      switch x {
         case 0:
            System.out.println("0");
         case 1:
            System.out.println("1");
         case 2:
            System.out.println("2");
            break;
         default:
            System.out.println("default");
      }
   }
   public static void main(String [] args) {
      new SwitchTest().run(2);
   }
}
```

- **A.** "0"k
- **B.** "1"k
- **C.** "2"k
- **D.** "default"
- **E.** Does not compile

45. Given the following code, what will be the outcome?

```
1. public class Two {
2.    public static void main(String[]arg) {
3.       int value =0;
4.       do {
5.          System.out.print (value);
6.          if (value == 0)
7.             continue;
8.       } while(value < 0);
9.    }
10. }
```

A. The code will compile and print out "00".
B. The code will compile and print out "0".
C. The code will compile and run successfully but it won't print out anything.
D. The code will compile and run but hang.
E. The code will not compile.

46. What will be the outcome when the following application is executed?

```
public class ThreadTest {
    public void newThread() {
        Thread t = new Thread() {
            public void run() {
                System.out.println("Going to sleep");
                try {
                    sleep(5000);
                } catch (InterruptedException e) {}
                System.out.println("Waking up");
            }
        };
        t.start();
        try {
            t.join();
        } catch (InterruptedException e) {}
        System.out.println("All done");
    }
    public static void main(String [] args) {
        new ThreadTest().newThread();
    }
}
```

A. "Going to sleep", then "Waking up", then "All done"
B. "All done", then "Going to sleep", then "Waking up"
C. "All done" only
D. "Going to sleep", then "Waking up"
E. Does not compile

47. To create a thread, you must do which of the following? (Select all that apply.)

   A. Thread t = new Thread();
       t.run();

   B. Thread t = new Thread();
       t.start();

   C. Runnable r = new Runnable();
       r.start();

   D. Runnable r = new Runnable();
       r.run();

   E. Thread t = new Thread(new Runnable());
       t.start();

48. What will the following application print out?
```
public class AbsTest {
   public static void main (String [] args) {
      System.out.println("" + Math.abs(57823498123D));
   }
}
```

   A. 5.7823498123E10
   B. 57823498123
   C. Does not compile

49. Select all of the following statements that are true:

   A. Overridden methods can exist in the same class.
   B. Overloaded methods only exist in the same class.
   C. Overridden methods must have a different number of arguments and types.
   D. Both overloaded and overridden methods require that the name of the methods be the same.
   E. Both overloaded and overridden methods require that the access modifiers be the same.

50. Which of the following operations return a value of 4?

   A. 8 & 3
   B. 12 & 5
   C. 5 & 12
   D. 10 & 4
   E. 4 & 5

Answers to Practice Exam

1. **A.** If no constructor is defined for a given class, the Java Virtual Machine provides a default constructor to instantiate and initialize the object. The default constructor takes in no arguments.

2. **C.** The method call `System.gc()` suggests that the Java Virtual Machine expend effort toward recycling unused objects in order to make the memory they currently occupy available for quick reuse.

3. **C.** To enter a long value, you must place either a lower-case "l" or (preferably) an upper-case "L" at the end of the number.

4. **D.** The modulo operator returns the remainder value –15 divided by 6. Because –15 is negative, the remainder value takes on the signed value.

5. **A.** The `Math.max()` method returns the larger of two given integers.

6. **D.** The `String` array must first be declared by placing brackets either before or after the array reference name. The size of the array must then be defined in the `String` brackets after `new` is called.

7. **C.** The `do/while` block will always run through one iteration and then check the condition.

8. **B.** The first option is incorrect because after you declare an array, the reference does not require brackets during the instantiation. The size of the array is defined in the brackets located after the new, making the third and fifth options incorrect. Finally, the fourth option is incorrect because constructors or parentheses are not used to build arrays.

9. **B.** The construction of the `for` loop takes three arguments—the variable initialization, the variable test, and the variable processing—any of which may be omitted. Because the variable processing piece of the `for` loop is not included, x is initialized as 0 but never incremented, so the value of x remains at 0. Each time the `for` loop executes, the value of x is less than 10, so the loop continues to print out "X = 0".

10. **E.** When a class is loaded into memory, an instance of that class is stored with a reference of a `java.lang.reflect.Class` type. From that class, a `Method` object is created for each method invoked, as well as each constructor, and the class `java.lang.Boolean` allows you to wrap primitives into objects.

11. **A, E.** The `main` method must be static so that the interpreter can gain access to it and because an instance of the class is not created to access this method. There is no return type, and the method must be called `main`. Regardless of whether arguments are passed in at runtime, you must still include the array option in the parameters of the method. The brackets for an array type may exist either before or after the actual reference name. While the last option may seem a bit odd, it is still legal because the access modifiers precede the return type and method name.

12. **C, E.** Overloading operators is not allowed in the Java language. The designers however, have overloaded the + sign to allow the concatenation of strings.

Answers to Practice Exam 501

13. E. There is no document relationship for the `implements` keyword. "Is a" is reserved for classes that use `extends`. The "has a" relationship is implemented by providing the class with member variables. "Was a" and "will be a" are fictitious and therefore not options.

14. B, D, E. An overloaded method is a method that has the same name but different argument types. The return type can be different, but that difference is secondary to the requirement of having different argument types.

15. B. Garbage collection cannot be forced by the developer. The call to `System.gc()` schedules garbage collection in the thread queue, but it is up to the Java Virtual Machine to allow the garbage collection to run.

16. A. When you synchronize a method, you are requiring a thread to obtain a lock before invoking the method. If, however, you have another method that is not synchronized, multiple threads can access that method or other nonsynchronized methods and corrupt the data. You must synchronize all methods that alter sensitive data to prevent corruption.

17. A, B. Both `Dialog` and `Frame` require a call to `setSize(int width, int height)` or `pack()` to allow added components to be visible.

18. B. In Java, whether a thread is time-sliced or preemptive depends on the design of the JVM.

19. B. The `Math.random()` method returns a `double` greater than or equal to 0.0 and less than 1.0. Because an int is smaller than a `double`, no automatic casting is performed, and an explicit cast is required.

20. B, C, D. The `Math.random()` method returns a `double` greater than or equal to 0.0 and less than 1.0. Because A and E are greater than or equal to 0.0 and less than 1.0, they are valid returns. B, C and D are equal to or greater than 1.0, so they are not valid returns.

21. E. The `ceil` method returns the smallest (closest to negative infinity) double value that is not less than the argument and is equal to a mathematical integer.

22. D. Because there is a constructor defined, the default constructor provided by the Java Virtual Machine is never defined. In order to construct a new `Construct` object without passing any parameters in, you must first define the method `public Construct()`.

23. A, B, C, D. The second option is legal because the `short` will automatically promote to an int; consequently, `int = int`. The `new` option is also correct because after creating an integer object, you then unwrap it back into a primitive, which can be correctly assigned. The final option is an incorrect cast, versus the right way to cast an int as shown in the fourth option.

24. B. When `wait()` is called on an object, the accessing thread will be sent to a waiting pool for that object. This is a different state than if `sleep(long time)` is called on that thread. A call to `sleep(long time)` will cause that thread to go into a blocked state until it times out. A thread in the waiting pool will remain there until the object makes a call to `notify()` or `notifyAll()`.

25. E. Strings are immutable, so no matter what method or operator you call on the original string object, you are not changing that string. Rather, you are creating a new object with a different address location or position within the string literal pool.

26. E. The (5, 500) option accepts two integers, which is a valid method signature. The next option accepts two longs, which is also a valid signature. The third option, ('A', 'a'), accepts two chars, which are promoted to integers, therefore accepting two integers, which is a valid signature. The fourth option accepts both a float and a long, which is legal because both values are automatically promoted to a double. In this situation, data corruption is possible.

27. B. Both Iterators and Enumerations generate a series of elements. Only Enumerations use the nextElement() method.

28. D. The 3.14 option is incorrect because you cannot return a double when the method expects an int. The first option is correct because 4 is an int and an appropriate return type. The second option is also correct, because int 4 is promoted to a double via automatic promotion. It is acceptable to have a return statement without a handle as long as the return for the method is a void, so the third option is also correct. It is perfectly legal to return a null value as an object, and therefore the last option is also legal.

29. B. Curly braces are used to hold all objects for the array.

30. A, C, D. static blocks cannot be identified via a label, and neither can methods. Labels are not an attempt to replace the infamous "goto." Instead, labels are a way to control certain nested blocks and looping structures.

31. C, D. Only methods are allowed to throw exceptions in Java, but because constructors are considered methods to the class, they too can throw exceptions.

32. C. Hexadecimal values range from 0 to F. Case is irrelevant, so 0xeAee is valid. The value 0xHAAC fails because H is outside of the scope.

33. D. To access a (non-static) inner class method, you first need an instance to the outer class. From that outer class instance, you can obtain an inner class instance, which you can use to access the desired method.

34. B, C. The Math class offers two overloaded methods for rounding. One round method takes in a double and the other takes in a float. The first option is incorrect because the square root of 16 is 4. Finally, the absolute value of −8.3 is 8.3, not 8.

35. A. A List, which includes Vectors, allows duplicates because each element is accessed by an index value, defining its location. Maps also allow duplicate objects to be added, as long as the key values are unique. A Collection is the root collection, which is simply defined as a group of elements. No limitations are set.

36. A, B. The first option is correct because you are provided a default constructor if you do not include any constructors that take in arguments. The second option is also correct because the constructor that takes in an int will be called for Horse, which will first invoke the default constructor for Object, then the default constructor for Animal, and then nondefault constructor for Horse. The third option is incorrect because you no longer have a default constructor or constructor with no arguments if the class provides one with arguments. Finally, the last option is incorrect because Horse does not have a default constructor.

37. **B.** Local or automatic variables must be initialized because the constructor only initializes variables defined under the class name.

38. **B, D, E.** The first assignment is incorrect because the only valid values for a `boolean` are true and false. The second assignment is correct because the char 'a' is automatically converted to an integer. The first `short` option is incorrect because the hex is too large to fit in a short, but the last short option, hex, is acceptable because it is the appropriate size. The `honest` option is correct because the assignment is one of the valid values for `boolean`.

39. **E.** All local variables are declared `final`, so the inner class has no access problems.

40. **A.** The compiler and interpreter will know which `oneMethod` to call based on the arguments passed into the method's parameters.

41. **C.** Java allows whitespace and usually ignores it. When the `calc()` method is called, the interpreter will add the values of *a*, *b*, *c*, and *d* to return the value 21. Because there is no terminator at the end of line 7, the interpreter will look to the next line for the concluding portion.

42. **D.** In the first option, the float is cast to a double, which is legal. In the second option, the char is cast to an integer, which is legal. The third option contains two integers as parameters, which is legal.

43. **E.** There is no way to reference a super class's variable from an inner class method if the outer class overrides that same variable.

44. **E.** The signature for a switch statement is as follows:

    ```
    switch (int) {
       case int:
          ...
       default:
    }
    ```

    Because the integer to be switched on is not enclosed in parentheses, indicating it is a parameter, the switch block is illegal and unknown and therefore will not compile.

45. **B.** The `continue` keyword causes the `while` to be checked before the block is reentered. The code compiles fine and when invoked will cause "0" to be printed once. After the `continue` statement, line 8 will be executed. The print stream will then flush when the main thread dies.

46. **A.** With the call to `join()` after the new thread is created and started, the main thread will wait for the new thread to finish its execution before continuing any processing after the call to `join()`.

47. **B.** Calling the `run` method of a thread does not spawn off a new thread, it only tells the current thread to execute that method. Consequently, the first option is incorrect. The `Runnable` interface is used to define the body or `run()` method of a thread; however, it cannot be instantiated directly, which cancels out both of the `Runnable r` statements. The last option uses the nondefault constructor to build a thread; however, it does not provide a `run()` method for the `Runnable` object, so it will not compile either. The second option creates a thread and spawns off the thread by calling its default `run()` method.

48. A. The call to Math.abs(double) returns a double value. The two numeric answers are exactly the same value, but the first is in scientific notation. After 99999999D, or eight values on the right of a decimal, the system will display in scientific notation to improve readability. When the value on the right of the decimal increases, the system will round when it reaches a high level of precision.

49. D. Overridden methods must exist in different classes, otherwise the compiler will complain about creating a duplicate method. Consequently, the first option is false. The second option is also false because you can create a method with the same name and different arguments in a child class and overload the method defined in a parent. Most commonly overloaded methods are in the same class, but that is not a requirement. The third statement is incorrect because overridden methods require the argument types match. Finally, the last option fails because overridden methods have a rule stating that you cannot define an overridden method with an access modifier more private than that of its parent.

50. B, C, E. The single ampersand works on Boolean values as well as bits. The binary result for 12 & 5 is the same as the binary result of 5 & 12. Order makes no difference.

Glossary

A

abstract modifier The abstract modifier can be applied to classes and methods. A class that is abstract may not be instantiated (that is, you may not call its constructor). Abstract classes provide a way to defer implementation to subclasses.

access modifier Access modifiers dictate which classes are allowed to use a feature.

anonymous class A class without a name is called an anonymous class. Anonymous classes can be declared to extend another class or to implement a single interface. The syntax does not allow you to do both at the same time, nor to implement more than one interface explicitly.

arithmetic operators Arithmetic operators are symbols that represent mathematical operations, such as addition, subtraction, multiplication, and division.

arithmetic-promotion conversion The system performs type conversion to ensure that operands can be meaningfully incremented, multiplied, divided, and compared. These conversions are all widening conversions. Thus they are known as arithmetic-promotion conversions because values are promoted to wider types.

array A Java array is an ordered collection of primitives, object references, or other arrays.

assertion Assertions provide a convenient mechanism for verifying that a class's methods are called correctly. This mechanism can be enabled or disabled at runtime. The intention is that assertions will typically be enabled during development and disabled in the field.

assignment conversion Object reference assignment conversion happens when you assign an object reference value to a variable of a different type.

assignment operators Assignment operators are symbols that set the value of a variable or expression to a new value.

automatic variable An automatic variable of a method is created on entry to the method and exists only during execution of the method, and therefore is accessible only during the execution of that method.

B

bitwise inversion Bitwise inversion works by inverting all the 1 bits in a binary value to 0s and all the 0 bits to 1s.

bitwise operators The bitwise operators provide bitwise inversion, AND, XOR, and OR operations. They are applicable to integral types.

blocking Many methods that perform input or output have to wait for some occurrence in the outside world before they can proceed. This behavior is known as blocking.

branch node A node in a tree that can have children is called a branch node.

C

callback A callback is a form of messaging in which one object has a reference to the other. If access is direct, then one object simply makes method calls on that reference. Indirect access is necessary when the sender and receiver have no prior knowledge of each other.

cascading style sheet A cascading style sheet is a helper file that the `javadoc` tool generates to provide default values for all fonts and colors used in the generated HTML documentation.

casting Casting is explicitly telling Java to make a conversion. A casting operation may widen or narrow its argument. To cast, just precede a value with the parenthesized name of the desired type.

catch block A `catch` block is a block of code to deal with an exception that might arise during execution of the `try` block. If multiple exception classes might arise in the `try` block, then several `catch` blocks are allowed to handle them.

checked exception Checked exceptions describe problems that can arise in a correct program—typically, difficulties with the environment such as user mistakes or I/O problems.

child node Any node in a tree that has a parent branch node is called a child node.

class invariant A class invariant is a constraint on a class's state that must be met before and after execution of any nonprivate method of a class. (Private methods might be used to restore the required state after execution of a nonprivate method.)

class variable A class variable is created when the class is loaded and is destroyed when the class is unloaded. There is only one copy of a class variable, and it exists regardless of the number of instances of the class, even if the class is never instantiated.

client-server In a client-server program, there is system that is running a background process (known as the server) that is waiting for incoming connections from remote or other local processes (known as clients).

column A column is an integer that represents the vertical position of a Swing component within a Swing container when using the Grid or GridBag layout manager. A column is also referred to as a field in a row of a database.

comparison operators Comparison operators perform a mathematical relation between two operands that returns a `boolean` result.

compilation units Three top-level elements known as compilation units may appear in a file. None of these elements is required. If they are present, then they must appear in the following order: package declaration, import statements, class definitions.

concatenation Concatenation is the joining together of string objects.

concurrency Concurrency describes access to the same piece of data by multiple, independent threads at the same time.

condition A condition is a `boolean` expression.

conditional operator The conditional operator takes three operands and provides a way to code simple conditions into a single expression.

container components Container components are Swing components that can contain other components (including other containers).

context A context defines an environment and a set of rules in which objects operate.

controller A controller is a Java Bean to which other Java Beans can be bound.

conversion Conversion occurs when the compiler implicitly changes the type of an object.

coupling Coupling is an expression of how tight or loose the objects become when they share a notification scheme.

D

deadlock The term deadlock describes a class of situations that might prevent a thread from executing. If a thread blocks because it is waiting for a condition, and something else in the program makes it impossible for that condition to arise, then the thread is said to be deadlocked.

default access Default is the name of the access of classes, variables, and methods if you don't specify an access modifier. A class's data and methods may be default, as well as the class itself. A class's default features are accessible to any class in the same package as the class in question.

default constructor If you do not explicitly code any constructors for a class, the compiler automatically creates a default constructor that does nothing except invoke the superclass's default constructor. This "freebie" constructor is called the default constructor. It has public access if the class is public; otherwise its access mode is default.

default package If you do not explicitly create a package to contain your Java classes, then the current working directory in which your classes are contained constitutes an unnamed default package.

design pattern A design pattern is an arrangement of classes by their relations and working collaborations. Properly used, design patterns help provide a structure to solve a well-known problem and help reduce programming effort.

distributed computing Distributed computing refers to the process of breaking down a job into parts, and garnering the resources of very many or very specialized systems to process the parts and return them.

distributed notification In a distributed notification model, notification should go from the server to all clients, and from all clients to the server.

E

encapsulation Encapsulation is the aggregation of data and behavior.

equality comparison Equality comparisons test whether two values are the same and may be applied to values of non-numeric types.

error Errors generally describe problems that are sufficiently unusual and sufficiently difficult to recover from that you are not required to handle them. They might reflect a program bug, but more commonly they reflect environmental problems, such as running out of memory. As with runtime exceptions, Java does not require that you state how these are to be handled. Although errors behave just like exceptions, they typically should not be caught, because it is impossible to recover from them.

event An event is an instance of some subclass of `java.util.EventObject`.

event adapter See *listener*.

event handler See *listener*.

event notification Objects that emit events communicate the event to established listeners using an event notification scheme.

event object Event objects define and encapsulate an action or state change that took place in some other object.

event source An event source creates event objects and sends them to other objects it tracks as listeners.

event target See *listener*.

exception Exception conditions in Java are circumstances, such as trying to access a file with an invalid filename or trying to access illegal memory (for example, referring to an element beyond the end of an array); they are represented using objects. A subtree of the class hierarchy starting with the class `java.lang.Throwable` is dedicated to describing them.

expression The expression (short for "iteration expression") portion of a `for()` loop structure is executed immediately after the body of the loop, just before the test is performed again. Commonly, it is used to increment a loop counter.

F

feature A feature is a class, a method, or a variable.

field See *column*.

final modifier The final modifier applies to classes, methods, and variables. The meaning of final varies from context to context, but the essential idea is the same: final features may not be changed.

flat data model A flat data model is one in which the scheme for organizing data records is largely, if not completely, self-describing. A flat file is ideal for small databases that do not require a complete subsystem to facilitate searching and organizing data.

floating-point literal A floating-point literal expresses a number that contains one of the following: a decimal point; the letter E or e, indicating scientific notation; the suffix F or f, indicating a `float` literal; or the suffix D or d, indicating a `double` literal.

framework A framework is a collection of classes that have been designed with a common abstraction of data container behavior in mind, ensuring uniform semantics wherever possible. At the same time, each implemented type is free to optimize its own operations.

friendly If a feature has no access modifier, its access defaults to a mode that has no standardized name. The default access mode is known variously as package, friendly, or default.

G

garbage collector The system keeps track of the memory that is allocated and is able to determine whether that memory is still useable by a low-priority thread that is referred to as the garbage collector. When the garbage collector finds memory that is no longer accessible from any live, it takes steps to release it back to the heap for re-use.

H

hash table A hash table is a data structure that stores and retrieves data that requires some unique identifying key to be associated with each data item, which in turn provides efficient searching.

hierarchy When discussing classes, hierarchy refers to the structure of inheritance from superclass to subclass. When discussing GUIs, hierarchy can refer to the containment structure of GUI components, such as applets, frames, panels, buttons, and so on.

I

identifier An identifier is a word used by a programmer to name a variable, method, class, or label. Keywords and reserved words may not be used as identifiers. An identifier must begin with a letter, a dollar sign ($), or an underscore (_); subsequent characters may be letters, dollar signs, underscores, or digits.

inheritance Inheritance describes how all the data and methods in a superclass implicitly belong to all its subclasses.

inner class An inner class is declared inside (that is, between the opening and closing curly braces of) some other class. You can declare nested classes in any block, including blocks that are part of a method.

instance method Instance methods have an implicit variable named `this`, which is a reference to the object executing the method.

iterator An iterator is an object that returns the elements of a collection one by one.

J

justification The justification of a Swing component is its vertical or horizontal alignment within its containing Swing component.

L

late binding Late binding refers to a delay in the decision to bind a method call to a set of machine-level instructions.

leaf node A node in a tree that cannot have children is called a leaf node.

linked list A linked list is a data structure that stores and retrieves data such that elements can be added or removed at any location; it allows the size of the collection to grow arbitrarily.

list An ordered collection of data is known as a list.

listener A listener is an object that listens for notifications that a particular event has occurred.

literal A literal is a value specified in the program source, as opposed to one determined at runtime. Literals can represent primitive or string variables and may appear on the right side of assignments or in method calls. You cannot assign values into literals, so they cannot appear on the left side of assignments.

local variable Local variables are not initialized by the system; every automatic variable must be explicitly initialized before being used.

lock A lock is part of an object and is controlled by, at most, one single thread. A thread that wants to execute an object's synchronized code must first attempt to acquire that object's lock. If the lock is available—that is, if it is not already controlled by another thread—then the thread may execute. If the lock is under another thread's control, then the attempting thread will wait and becomes ready only when the lock becomes available. When a thread that owns a lock passes out of the synchronized code, the thread automatically gives up the lock.

M

magic number Magic numbers are numeric values that describe the data (or file) with which it is associated.

manifest The manifest specification is a key selling point for the JAR format. By providing certain tags in the manifest, you can signal a particular kind of usage or delivery

map A map is a data structure that uses a set of key values to look up, or index, the stored data.

member class Classes that are defined directly in the scope of a class are called member classes.

member variable A member variable of a class is created when an instance is created, and it is destroyed when the object is destroyed. Subject to accessibility rules and the need for a reference to the object, member variables are accessible as long as the enclosing object exists.

menu components Menu components allow the programmer to organize Swing components in menus instead of placing all the components in the user's view.

metadata Metadata is a type of data that describes other data.

method-call conversion A method-call conversion happens when you pass a value of one type as an argument to a method that expects a different type.

method-local A method-local is created on entry to the method and exists only during execution of the method; therefore, it is accessible only during the execution of that method.

model-delegate Model-delegate is a design pattern in which each view can visually describe the model according to the set or subset of data it is most interested in.

Model-View-Controller MVC is a design pattern in which the data, its presentation, and its controls are separated into the role of model, view, and controller respectively.

modifiers Modifiers are Java keywords that give the compiler information about the nature of code, data, or classes. Modifiers specify, for example, that a particular feature is static, final, or transient.

modulo operator The modulo operator gives a value that is related to the remainder of a division. It is generally applied to two integers, although it can be applied to floating-point numbers, too.

monitor A monitor is any object that has some synchronized code.

multithreaded A multithreaded program has a first entry point (the `main()` method), followed by multiple entry and exit points for other methods that may be scheduled to run concurrently with the `main()` method.

N

narrowing conversion   Narrowing conversions change a value to a type that accommodates a more narrow range of values than the original type can accommodate. In most cases, the new type has fewer bits than the original and can be visualized as being "narrower" than the original.

native modifier   The native modifier can refer only to methods. Like the `abstract` keyword, `native` indicates that the body of a method is to be found elsewhere. In the case of abstract methods, the body is in a subclass; with native methods, the body lies entirely outside the Java Virtual Machine (JVM), in a library.

***n*-tier**   N-tier is a model for architecting a service in such a way that there may be several (n) tiers of servers that must be contacted to satisfy client requests.

O

object comparison   Object comparisons compare the data of two objects.

object reference   An object reference in Java is an address that accesses the data and methods in that object.

object-type comparison   Object-type comparisons determine whether the runtime type of an object is of a particular type or a subclass of that particular type.

ordinal comparison   Ordinal comparisons test the relative value of numeric operands.

ordinary components   Ordinary components are Swing components in which the user or programmer directly inputs data.

overloading   Reusing the same method name with different arguments and perhaps a different return type is known as overloading.

overriding   Using the same method name with identical arguments and return type is known as overriding.

P

package access   If a feature has no access modifier, its access defaults to a mode that has no standardized name. The default access mode is known variously as friendly, package, or default.

package sealing   Another aspect of the JAR format, package sealing causes JAR itself to mandate that all associated classes working with the JAR be contained in it as a control against class-spoofing.

port A port is a channel of communication through which clients and servers may exchange data.

postcondition A postcondition is a constraint that must be met on return from a method. If a method's postconditions are not met, the method should not be allowed to return. A method's postconditions are typically functions of its return value and the state of its object. In a general sense, if a precondition fails, the problem lies in the method's caller, whereas if a postcondition fails, the problem lies in the method itself.

post-decrement The post-decrement operator is positioned after an expression and reduces the value of the expression by 1.

post-increment The post-increment operator is positioned after an expression and increases the value of the expression by 1.

precondition A precondition is a constraint that must be met on entry of a method. If a method's preconditions are not met, the method should terminate at once before it can do any damage. A method's preconditions are typically functions of its arguments and the state of its object. Argument range checking at the start of a method is a common form of precondition testing.

pre-decrement The pre-decrement operator is positioned before an expression and reduces the value of the expression by 1.

preemptive scheduling Preemptive scheduling is a method of scheduling threads to execute in such a way that threads with higher priority can run in the place of a lower priority thread.

preferred size The preferred size expresses how big the component would like to be, barring conflict with a layout manager. Preferred size is generally the smallest size necessary to render the component in a visually meaningful way.

pre-increment The pre-increment operator is positioned before an expression and increases the value of the expression by 1.

priority Every thread has a priority, which is an integer from 1 to 10; threads with higher priority should get preference over threads with lower priority. The priority is considered by the thread scheduler when it decides which ready thread should execute. The scheduler generally chooses the highest-priority waiting thread. If more than one thread is waiting, the scheduler chooses one of them. There is no guarantee that the thread chosen will be the one that has been waiting the longest.

private access The least generous access modifier is private. Top-level (that is, not inner) classes may not be declared private. A private variable or method may only be used by an instance of the class that declares the variable or method.

properties Java Beans are characterized by a series of properties that are simply a class's existing field members supplied with a pair of formulaic `get`/`is`/`set` method signatures.

protected access   Only variables and methods may be declared protected. A protected feature of a class is available to all classes in the same package, just like a default feature. Moreover, a protected feature of a class is available to all subclasses of the class that owns the protected feature. This access is provided even to subclasses that reside in a different package from the class that owns the protected feature.

public access   The most generous access modifier is public. A public class, variable, or method may be used in any Java program without restriction.

R

raised   When an exception "appears" either from the immediate cause of the trouble, or because a method call is abandoned and passes the exception up to its caller, the exception is said to have been raised.

record   A record is a row in a database. It consists of fields of data.

reference   Java programs do not deal directly with objects. When an object is constructed, the constructor returns a value—a bit pattern—that uniquely identifies the object. This value is known as a reference to the object.

reference comparisons   Reference comparisons compare the memory locations of two objects.

relational database   Relational databases are composed of multiple tables of information. A relational database, as the name suggests, makes it possible to declare relations between tables that share columns of the same type.

request-response   Request-response refers to a manner of providing a service in such a way that it is managed by a single, central server (which only makes responses to queries when requested).

roll back   A Java Bean is said to roll back when it changes the value of a property to a previous value.

root node   A node in a tree from which all other nodes extend is called the root node. There is only one root node in a tree.

round-robin scheduling   In round-robin scheduling, a thread is allowed to execute only for a limited amount of time. It insures against the possibility of a single high-priority thread infinitely running or otherwise starving all other threads from doing their jobs.

row   A row is an integer that represents the horizontal position of a Swing component within a Swing container when using the Grid or GridBag layout manager. In the context of databases, a row is an entry in the table and contains one or more columns.

runtime exception Runtime exceptions typically describe program bugs. You could use a runtime exception as deliberate flow control, but it would be an odd way to design code and rather poor style. Runtime exceptions generally arise from things like out-of-bounds array accesses, and normally a correctly coded program would avoid them. Because runtime exceptions should never arise in a correct program, you are not required to handle them.

S

sequence See *list*.

set A set is a collection of data that imposes the specific condition that it cannot contain the same value more than once.

shift operator Shifting is taking the binary representation of a number and moving the bit pattern left or right. The shift operators may be applied to arguments of integral types only.

single-threaded A single-threaded Java program has one entry point (the `main()` method) and one exit point. All instructions are run serially, from start to finish.

skeleton A skeleton is a block of proxy code that is generated for the server side of an RMI connection.

sleeping thread A sleeping thread passes time without doing anything and without using the CPU. A call to the `sleep()` method requests the currently executing thread to cease executing for (approximately) a specified amount of time.

statement The statement portion of a `for()` loop is executed immediately before the loop itself is started. It is often used to set up starting conditions and can also contain variable declarations.

static initializer Static initializer code is executed exactly once, at the time the class is loaded. At class-load time, all static initialization and all free-floating static is executed in order of appearance within the class definition.

static modifier The static modifier can be applied to variables, methods, and even a strange kind of code that is not part of a method. You can think of static features as belonging to a class, rather than being associated with an individual instance of the class.

static variable See *class variable*.

string context A string context is an expression that includes nonstring literals but that is still evaluated as a string.

string literal A string literal is a sequence of characters enclosed in double quotes.

stub A stub is a block of proxy code that is generated for the client side of an RMI connection.

suspending Suspending a thread is a mechanism that allows any arbitrary thread to make another thread unready for an indefinite period of time. The suspended thread becomes ready when some other thread resumes it.

synchronized code The `synchronized` keyword controls access to critical code (code in which shared data is accessed by multiple threads concurrently) in multithreaded programs.

T

table A table is a part of a database that comprises any number of records of a specific kind.

ternary operator A ternary operator is an operator that takes three operands.

thread pool A thread pool is a collection of thread references that are continually "re-referenced" as their current tasks run their course.

threadsafe A class or group of classes is considered threadsafe if any thread can call any method of any instance at any time.

thread scheduler The thread scheduler is the part of the JVM that determines which thread is running on each available CPU at any given time.

throw The process of an exception "appearing" either from the immediate cause of the trouble, or because a method call is abandoned and passes the exception up to its caller, is called throwing an exception in Java.

time-sliced scheduling See *round-robin scheduling*.

transient modifier The transient modifier applies only to variables. A transient variable is not stored as part of its object's persistent state.

tree A tree is a data structure that stores its data in a hierarchical fashion, starting with a root node and extending to branch and leaf nodes.

try block Lines of code that are part of the normal processing sequence but that might throw an exception are placed in a `try` block.

two-tiered A two-tiered database is a type of database in which the database server and the database itself are both running on the same machine.

U

unary operator A unary operator is an operator that takes one operand.

V

vetoable In the context of Java Beans, a vetoable property is a constrained property that knows how to behave if the target property rejects the change issued by a source.

volatile modifier The volatile modifier indicates that such variables might be modified asynchronously, so the compiler takes special precautions. Volatile variables are of interest in multiprocessor environments.

W

waiting state The waiting state of a thread starts when the threads `wait()` method is invoked. The waiting state of a thread ends when either the `notify()` or `notifyAll()` method is invoked. During the time that the thread is waiting, it cannot execute.

weight The weight of a Swing component is an integer that defines the amount that the component can be stretched or shrunk when the containing Swing component is resized in the GUI.

well-known port A well-known port is a special port whose number is registered with and reserved by the IETF for a particular service.

widening conversion Widening conversions change a value to a type that accommodates a wider range of values than the original type can accommodate. In most cases, the new type has more bits than the original and can be visualized as being "wider" than the original.

width The width of a field in row of a database table defines the maximum size of a value that may be stored in that field.

wrapper class A wrapper class is a class that encapsulates a single, immutable value. Each Java primitive data type has a corresponding wrapper class.

Y

yielding A thread can offer to move out of the virtual CPU by yielding. A call to the `yield()` method causes the currently executing thread to move to the Ready state if the scheduler is willing to run any other thread in place of the yielding thread.

Index

Note to reader: **Bolded** page numbers refer to definitions and to main discussions of a topic. *Italicized* page numbers refer to illustrations.

Symbols

-- (decrement operator), **32**, *32*
& (AND) operator
    bitwise operations, 51–53, *52*
    boolean operations, 54–56, *55*
    Q & A, 499, 504
    short-circuit logical operations, 56–58
! (boolean complement operator), 33–34
!= (inequality comparison operator), 50–51
$ (dollar sign), 5, **174**
* (asterisk), import keyword and, 4–5
* (multiplication operator), 35–36
/ (division operator), 35–36
; (semicolon), 4–5
?: (conditional operators), 58–59, 63
[ ] (square brackets), 11
^ (XOR) operator
    bitwise operations, 51–54, *52*
    boolean operations, 54–56, *55*
_ (underscore), 5
{ } (curly brackets), 125, 207
+ (addition operator)
    appending strings, 240
    arithmetic operator, 37–39
    unary plus operator, 32–33
++ (increment operator), **32**, *32*
< (less than) operator, 47–48
<< (left-shift) operator, 42–45
<= (less than or equal to) operator, 47–48
> (greater than) operator, 47–48
>= (greater than or equal to) operator, 47–48

A

abstract classes, 289–290, 447–450
abstract modifiers
    defined, 506

features of, *88*
overview, 80–82, *81*
Q & A, 90, 95
AbstractTableModel, 319–322, *322*
access modifiers, 72–79
    default, 75–76, *76*
    defined, **506**
    marking member classes with, **177**
    of overloaded methods, 166
    overview, 72–73
    private, 73–75
    protected, 76–78
    public, 73
    Q & A, 92, 95
    subclasses and method privacy, *78*, 78–79
accessibility, method overriding, 168, 170
Accessible interface
    building JTable, 316–317, *317*
    building JTree, 323
Action events
    JButton, 307–308
    JCheckBox, 308–309
    JComboBox, 313–314
    JMenu, 327–329, *329*
    JRadioButton, 310
actionPerformed( ) method, 308
Activatable object
    exporting, *475*, 475–479
    Q & A, 483–484
active clients, 479–481, *480*
add( ) method, 359
add(abstractButton) method, 309
add/remove( ) method pairs, 420–422, 426
addition operator (+)
    appending strings, 240
    arithmetic operator, 37–39
    unary plus operator, 32–33
addXXXListener(XXXListener) method, 417

Adjustment events, JScrollBars, 311
alignment (justification), 344–345, 511
anchors, 365–368, 367–368
AND (&) operator
   bitwise operations, 51–53, 52
   boolean operations, 54–56, 55
   short-circuit logical operations, 56–58
anonymous classes
   construction/initialization of, 180–181
   defined, 506
   example, 182–183
   overview, 179–180
APIs, 269–270
append( ) method, 240
applets
   adding components to, 338
   Flow layout manager for, 343–345, 344–345
application partitioning, 441
args array, 14
arguments
   overriding vs. overloading, 166
   passing, 16–18, 18, 181
arithmetic error conditions, 40–41
arithmetic operators, 35–41
   arithmetic-promotion conversions, 104, 104
   defined, 506
   error conditions, 40–41
   summary, 61
   types
      addition and subtraction, 37–39
      modulo, 36–37
      multiplication and division, 35–36
arithmetic-promotion conversions
   defined, 506
   of operands, 46–47, 47
   overview, 103–104, 104
arrays
   Collections API storage, 243
   data structures, 284
   defined, 506
   instanceof operator and, 49–50
   limitations, 241–242
   non-rectangular, 13
   object reference conversion, 109, 109–110

order of, 11–13, 12
Q & A, 24, 27, 487, 500
assertion
   defined, 506
   overview, 143–146
   Q & A, 155, 157
assignment conversion
   defined, 506
   literal values and, 102
   object reference, 108–109, 108–110
   primitive, 99–102, 100–101
   Q & A, 118, 121, 494, 503
assignment operators, 59–60, 506
assignment, Developer's Exam. see Developer's Exam
asterisk (*), import keyword and, 4–5
automatic variables
   defined, 14, 506
   initialization, 15

B

bag, 242
Beans. see Java Beans
bind( ) method, 400
binding, late, 169
bit size, 7–8, 26–27
bitwise inversion, 506
bitwise operators
   bitwise inversion operator, 33
   boolean operations, 54–56
   defined, 506
   overview, 51–54
Blocked state. see blocking
blocking
   Blocked state, 197–198, 198
   defined, 506
   overview of, 202–203, 203
   Q & A, 490, 501
boolean complement operator (!), 33–34
boolean literals, 9
boolean operations
   overview, 54–56, 55
   short-circuit logical operations, 56–58
booleanValue( ) method, 233

Border layout manager
    choosing, **286–287**
    overview, **347–354**, *348*, *350–352*, *354*
boundary conditions, **161**
brackets, curly ({ }), **125**, **207**
brackets, square ([ ]), **11**
branch nodes, **323**, **506**
break statements, **124**, **130**

C

callbacks, **286**, **419**, **507**
capacity, StringBuffer class, **238–239**
Card layout manager, **286**, **354–359**
cascading style sheets, **279**, **507**
case labels, **132**
case sensitivity, **275**
cast operator, **34–35**
casting
    defined, **507**
    exam essentials, **115–116**
    key terms, **116**
    legal and illegal, **106–107**
    object reference casting, **111–115**, *112–113*
    overview, **98**
    primitive casting, **105–107**, *106*
    Q & A, **119–121**
catch blocks
    catching multiple exceptions, **136–137**
    checking checked exceptions, **140–141**
    defined, **507**
    flow control in exceptions, **133–135**, *135*
    Q & A, **151–153**, *157*
CellEditorEvent object, **316**
char literals, **9–10**
characters
    Developer's Exam coding tips, **275–276**
    identifier, **5**
    package name, **4**
charValue( ) method, **233**
check boxes
    adding to menu item, **316–318**
    JCheckBox, **308–309**, *309*

checked exceptions
    checking, **140–141**
    defined, **507**
    method overriding and, **168**
    overview, **138–140**, *139*
child nodes, **323**, **507**
class definitions, **4–5**
class invariants, **145**, **507**
class locks, **213**
class variables
    defined, **14**, **507**
    initialization, **15**, **16**
classes, **162–192**
    constructors and subclassing
        overloading constructors, **172–173**
        overview of, **170–171**
    exam essentials, **183–184**
    exam objectives, **159**
    inner, **173–183**
        constructing, **175–176**
        defined inside methods, **177–183**
        member classes, **176–177**
        overview of, **173–175**
    key terms, **184–185**
    locks, **213**
    main( ) method, **14**
    needs of subclasses defining, **143**
    object reference conversion rules, **109–110**
    overloading methods
        invoking, **165–166**
        method names, **164**
        overview of, **163**
        usefulness of, **164–165**
    overriding methods
        invoking, **169**, **170**
        late binding, **169**
        method, **166**
        overview of, **163**
        usefulness of, **166–168**
    relationships, **162–163**
    review Q & A, **185–191**
    variables and initialization, **14–16**
CLASSPATH, **279**, **473–475**
client request structure, **387–394**

client-server, 381–395
  client request structure, 387–394, *388*, *394*
  communication protocol, 384–397
  defined, 507
  Developer's Exam, 274–275, *275*
  limitations, 394–395
  overview, 467–468
  Q & A, 412–413
  server operation, 381–384
  two-tiered database architecture, 440
client-server connections, 415–438
  distributed notification, *434*, 434
  events
    naming conventions, 417
    notification, 417–419, *418–419*
  exam essentials, 435
  Java Beans
    conventions, 420–422, *422*
    MVC design pattern and, 423–425, *424–425*
  key terms, 436
  listeners, 425–432, *429–430*
  overview, 416
  remote notification, 432–433, *433*
  review Q & A, 437–438
  summary, 435
code
  Developer's Exam, 269–270, 275–277
  maintenance, 247–253
  re-use of, 162
  synchronized. *see* synchronized code
Collections API, 241–253
  code maintenance, 247–253
  data structures, 284, 457–458
  defined, 242
  equality and sorting, 244
  hashCode( ) method, 245–246
  implementation classes, 246–247
  overview, 241–242
  summary, 254
  types, 242–444
columns
  database design, 442–444

defined, 440, 507
Grid layout, 345–347, *346–347*
GridBag layout, 359–365, *361–364*
combo boxes, 313–314, *314*
comma separators, 128
communication protocols
  defining operations, 385
  implementing, 385–387
  overview, 384
  Q & A, 412–413
compareTo( ) method, 244
comparison operators
  defined, 507
  equality, 50–51
  ordinal, 47–50
compilation units
  assertions and, 144
  defined, 507
  overview of, 4–5
components, 339
  GUI requirements, 297
  managing. *see* layout managers
  Q & A, 334–335
  types
    container, 302–305
    menu, 314–316
    ordinary, 305–314
compound assignment operators, 59–60
concat( ) method, 240
concatenation
  defined, 507
  overloading + operator for, 38
  overview, 240–241
concurrency, 380, 507
conditional operators (?:), 58–59, 508
conditions
  defined, 508
  for( ) loop, 127–128
connections. *see* client-server connections
constructors
  building JTable, 316–318, *318*
  constructing String with, 236
  Q & A, 186–188, 190–191, 486, 490, 500–501

String, 236
subclassing and, 170–173
container components
  defined, 508
  JFrame, 303–304, *303–304*
  JPanel, 304–305, *305*
  layout managers and, 338–341
  overview, 302
  synchronizing on, 457–458
content panes, JFrame
  Border layout manager, 347–354, *348–354*
  JOptionPane, 331–332, *332*
  JSplitPane, 330–331, *331*
  using, 303–304
contexts, 419, 508
continue statement
  defined, 124
  Q & A, 149, 156
  using in loops, 129–130
controllers
  defined, 508
  MVC design pattern, 423–424
conversion. *see also* casting
  assignment conversion, 102
  defined, 508
  exam essentials, 115–116
  explicit and implicit type changes, 98–99
  key terms, 116
  object reference conversion, 107–111
  overview, 98
  primitive conversion
    arithmetic promotion, 103–104, *104*
    assignment, 99–102, *100 101*
    method-call, 103
    overview of, 99
  review Q & A, 117–121
  summary, 115
CORBA, 402
corner cases, 385
CounterThread, 195
coupling, 419, 508
curly brackets ({ }), 125, 207

D

data structures, 284, 458
data types
  primitive, 6–9, *7–8*
  Q & A, 24, 27
  signed integral, 7
database servers, 465–484
  developing, 273–274, *274*
  exam essentials, 482
  key terms, 482
  record locking, 479–481, *480*
  requirements
    exporting Activatable object, *475*, 475–479
    exporting with UnicastRemoteObject, 471–475
    implementing RMI, 467–470
    overview of, 466–467
  review Q & A, 483–484
databases, 439–464
  designing basic scheme
    overview of, 441–442
    using abstract classes, 447–450
    using interfaces, 442–447
  exam essentials, 460–461
  implementation issues
    design impediments, 454–455
    exception handling, 451–454
    supporting new features, 459–460
    thread safety, 456–459
  key terms, 461
  review Q & A, 462–463
  two-tiered, 440–441
DataProxy class, 433
Dead state, 197–198
deadlock, 215–217, 508
debugging
  limitations of RMI, 401
  print statements, 240
  with toString( ) method, 229
declarations
  anonymous inner classes, 180–181
  array creation, 11–12
decrement operators (--), 32, *32*

default access mode
  defined, 73, 508
  features, *88*
  overriding, 78
  overview, 75–76, *76*
  summary, 79
default constructors, 170, 508
default packages, 279, 508
descriptors, **422**
design patterns
  defined, 508
  follow-up exam, 287
  MVC. *see* MVC (Model-View-Controller)
  using standard, 276
Developer's Exam, 264–294
  assignment
    structure, 268–270
    topics, 267–268
  assignment example
    client-server logic, 274–275
    database/server development, 273–274
    GUI development, 272–273
    overview of, 270–272
  coding tips
    adhering to supplied naming, 275
    stress readability, 275–276
    using standard design patterns, 276
  downloading assignment, 266–267
  exam essentials, 291
  follow-up exam, 267
  follow-up exam preparation
    abstract classes, 289–290
    data structure, 284
    design patterns, 287
    exceptions, 285
    layout managers, 286–287
    listeners, 285–286
    Thread class vs. Runnable interface, 284–285
    using protected and default scope, 287–289
  grading, 268
  key terms, 291
  readiness for, 264–265
  review Q & A, 292–293
  submission requirements
    file structure, **279–280**, *280*
    javadoc options, *278–279*, **278–279**
    overview of, **276–278**
    using JAR tool, **282–283**
    writing README file, **281–282**
dirty buffer, **460**
distributed computing, 467–468, 508
distributed notification, *434*, **434**, 508
division operator (/), **35–36**
do loops, **126**
documentation
  coding tips, 275–276
  Developer's Exam, 278
doit( ) method, 217
dollar sign ($), 5, **174**
double indirection, **17**
DownCounter class, 196
downloading, Developer's Exam, 266–267

E

else block, 131–132
empty for( ) loops, **128**
encapsulation
  defined, 509
  overview, 160–161
  preserving, 288
  reuse and, **162**
EnclosingClassName, 180
Enumeration interface, **459**
equality comparison, 47, 50–51, 509
equals( ) method
  constructing wrappers, 232
  defining, **51**
  equality comparison operators, 50
  hashCode( ) method, 245–246
  Object class and, 228–229
  String class, 235–236, *236*
  StringBuffer class, 240
errors
  arithmetic, 40–41

exception handling, 452
    as exceptions, 138–139
    overview, 509
evaluation order, 31
event adapters, 418
event handlers. *see* listeners
event notification
    defined, 509
    distributed, *434*, 434
    order of, 212–213
    overview, 417–419
    remote, 432–433, *433*
event object, 417, 509
event source, 417, 509
event target. *see* listeners
events
    defined, 509
    JButtons, 307
    JCheckBox, 308
    JFrames, 304
    JRadioButtons, 310
    JScrollBars, 311
    JTable, 316–317
    JTree, 323
    naming conventions, 417, 420–422
    overview, 416–417
exams, Developer's Exam. *see*
    Developer's Exam
exams, practice, 485–504
excecute( ) method, 406
excecuteIfAvailable( ) method, 406
exceptions, 133–143
    catching multiple, 136–137
    categories, 138–139
    defined, 509
    follow-up exam, 285
    handling, 451–454
    method overriding and, 166
    overview, 133
    Q & A, 151, 154–155, 157, 462–463,
        492, 502
    throwing
        checked exceptions, 138–141
        overriding and, 141–143
        throw statement, 137
        throws statement, 137–138
    try/catch/finally, 133–135, *135*

execution, thread, 195–197
export( ) method, 398
exporting
    Activatable object, 475–479
    with UnicastRemoteObject, 471–475
expressions
    defined, 509
    for( ) loop, 127–128
    for( ) loop and comma separator, 128
    Q & A, 151, 156
extends clause, 163
extends keyword, 228

F

factory, 287
features
    database, 459–460
    defined, 72, 509
    modifiers and, 72–73, 87–88
fields. *see* columns
file structures, 279–280, *280*
fill feature
    controlling component cell size, 371
    GridBag layout, 368–369, *368–369*
final modifier
    defined, 509
    features of, *88*
    Math class and, 229
    overriding method and, 168
    overview, 79–80
    Q & A, 90, 95
finalize( ) method, 19
finally block
    catching multiple exceptions, 136–137
    flow of control in exceptions, 133–135
    overview, 135
    Q & A, 151–153, 157
firePropertyChange( ) method, 426–428
fireTableChange( ) method, 319, 321
flat data models
    defined, 441, 510
    designing basic scheme, 441–442
    Q & A, 462–463
floating-point literals
    arithmetic error conditions, 40

defined, *8*, 8, 510
overview, 10
flow control, 123–158
   assertions, 143–146
   exam essentials, 147–148
   exceptions
      catch, 136–137
      finally, 135
      overview of, 133
      throwing, 137–143
      try, 133–135, *135*
   key terms, 148
   loop constructs, 124–130
      break statement, 130
      continue statement, 129–130
      do loop, 126
      empty for( ) loops, 128
      for( ) loop, 126–128
      for( ) loop and comma separator, 128
      while( ) loop, 124–126
   overview, 124
   review Q & A, 149–157
   selection statements
      if/else construct, 131–132
      switch( ) construct, 132–133
Flow layout manager, 286, 343–345, *344–345*
follow-up exam
   defined, 266
   grading, 268
   preparing for
      abstract classes, 289–290
      data structure, 284
      design patterns, 287
      exceptions, 285
      layout managers, 286–287
      listeners, 285–286
      Thread class vs. Runnable interface, 284–285
      using protected and default scope, 287–289
   Q & A, 292–293
   taking, 267
for( ) loops
   comma separators and, 128
   empty, 128
   overview, 126–128
   Q & A, 488, 500

frames
   adding components to, 338–339
   JFrames, *303–304*, 303–304
   JPanels, 304–305, *305*
frameworks
   Collections API, 242
   defined, 510
free-floating initializer code, 85
friendly access mode. *see* default access mode

G

garbage collector
   causing memory leaks, 20
   defined, 510
   overview, 19–20
   Q & A, 26–27, 486, 489, 500–501
gc( ) method, 19
GeneralException, 137
get/set ( ) method pair, 420–422, 426
getCommand( ) method, 393
getContentPane( ) method, 303–304
getData( ) method, 444
getLocation( ) method, 301
getPriority( ) method, 199
getSize( ) method, 301
getXXX( ) methods, 234
goto statement, 124
grading, Developer's Exam
   ease of use, 278
   overview of, 268
   subjective process of, 266
graphical user interfaces. *see* GUIs (graphical user interfaces)
greater than (>) operator, 47–48
greater than or equal to (>=) operator, 47–48
Grid layout manager
   defined, 286
   JPanels, 305
   overview, 345–347, *346–347*
GridBag layout manager, 359–374
   component cell size, 369, *369–372*
   component position/stretch, 365–369, *367–368*
   defined, 286–287

layout design without, 359
overview, 359
rows and columns, **359–365**, *361–362, 364*
shorthand, **372–374**, *374*
GridBagConstraints class, 359
gridheight
    component cell size, *369*, **369–372**
    RELATIVE and REMAINDER setting, **372–374**, *374*
gridwidth
    component cell size, *369*, **369–372**
    RELATIVE and REMAINDER setting, **372–374**, *374*
GUIs (graphical user interfaces), 295–336
    Developer's Exam
        client-server logic, **274–275**, *275*
        overview of, **272–273**, *273*
    exam essentials, 333
    JMenus and actions, **327–329**, *329*
    JTable
        AbstractTableModel, **319–322**, *322*
        overview of, **316–319**, *317–318*
    JTree, **323**, *323*–**327**, *327*
    key terms, 333
    overview, 296
    panes, **329–332**, *331–332*
    requirements, **297–300**
        identifying components, **297**
        isolating regions of behavior, **299–300**
        layout managers, **300**
        sketching, **298–299**
    review Q & A, 334–335
    Swing components, **302–316**
        container components, **302–305**
        menu components, **314–316**
        ordinary components, **305–314**
    Swing methods, **300–302**

H

"has a" relationships, 162–163
hash tables, 244, 510
hashCode( ) method, 245–246

HashMap class, 246, **284**
HashSet, 246
Hashtable class, 246
height, grid, *369*, **369–374**, *374*
hierarchy, 339, 510
HTTP servers, 381, **384–387**

I

identifiers
    defined, 510
    overview, **6**
    Q & A, 24, 27
IETF (Internet Engineering Task Force), 381
if statements, 125, 129–130
if/else statements
    boolean complement operator and, **33–34**
    conditional operator and, 59
    overview, **131–132**
implementation classes, 246–247
import statements, 4–5
increment operators (++), *32*, **32**
inequality comparison operator (!=), **50–51**
inheritance, 162, 510
initialization
    anonymous inner classes, **181**
    arrays and, *12*, **12–13**
    Q & A, 494, 503
    static, 85
    variables and, **14–16**, *15*
inner class, 173–183
    constructing, 175–176
    defined, 511
    defined inside methods, 177–183
    member classes, 176–177
    overview, 173–175
    Q & A, 492–493, 502
innerMethod( ), 176
instance method, 83, 511
instanceof operator, **48–50**, 169
integral data types, 7, 8, 40
integral literals, 10, 101
interfaces
    abstract classes vs., **289–290**

database design, 442–447
declaring method calls, 289
JTable, *317*, 317
JTree, 323
listener. *see* listeners
maintenance benefit of, 450
object reference conversion, 109–110
Q & A, 462–463
intern( ) method, String class, 236–237
Internet Engineering Task Force
   (IETF), 381
interrupt latency, 46
interrupt( ) method, 197
"is a" relationships, 162–163
is/set ( ) method pair, 426
isArray( ) method, 50
Item events
   JCheckBox, 308
   JRadioButtons, 310
iteration expression, 127–128
iterator, 250, 511
Iterator interface, 459

J

JAR tool
   command options, *282*
   file structure, 280
   submitting Developer's Exam, 277
   using, 282–283
Java Beans
   conventions, 420–422, *422*
   listeners, 425–432, *429–430*
   MVC design pattern and, 423–425, *424–425*
.java extension, 4
Java Programming Language Workshop, 265
java.lang package, 227–260
   Collections API
      code maintenance, 247–253
      collection types, 242–444
      equality and sorting, 244
      hashCode( ) method, 245–246
      implementation classes, 246–247
      overview of, 241–242
      summary, 254
   exam essentials, 254
   exam objectives, 227
   key terms, 255
   Math class, 229–230, *230*
   Object class, 228–229
   review Q & A, 256–259
   strings
      concatenation, 240–241
      String class, 235–238, *236*, *238*
      StringBuffer class, 238–240, *239*
   wrapper classes, *231*, 231–234
java.util package. *see also* Collections API
   data structure choices, 284
   java.util.Collection, 242
   java.util.List, 243
   java.util.Set, 243
javadoc, 277–279, *278–279*
javax.swing package, 302
JButton component, 304, 306–308, *308*
JCheckBox component, 308–309, *309*
JCheckBoxMenuItem class, 316–317
JComboBox component, 313–314, *314*
JFileChooser, 329–332
JFrame component
   adding components, 338
   closing behavior, 318
   inserting JMenuBar into, 316–318
   overview, *303–304*, 303–304
JIT (just-in-time) compiler, 289
JLabel component, 306, *306*
JMenuBar component, 314–316, *316*
JMenuItem, 316–318
JMenus, 327–329, *329*
JOptionPane, 331–332, *332*, 430–432
JPanel component, 304–305, *305*
JRadioButton component, 309–310, *310*
JRadioButtonMenuItem class, 316–317
JScrollBar component, 310–311, *311*
JSplitPane, 330–331, *331*
JTable
   AbstractTableModel, 319–322, *322*

building, **316–319**, *317–318*
   Q & A, **334–335**
JTableHeader, **322**
JTextArea component, **311–313**, *313*
JTextComponent, **311–313**
JTextField component, **311–313**, *313*
JTree, **323**, **323–327**, *327*
justification (alignment), **344–345**, **511**
just-in-time (JIT) compiler, **289**

K

KeyStroke objects, **327–328**
keywords, *5*, **5–6**

L

labels, **130**, **492**, **502**
language fundamentals
   argument passing, **16–18**, *18*
   arrays, **11–13**, *12*
   classes, **13–16**, *15*
   exam essentials, **22–23**
   exam objectives, **3**
   garbage collection, **19–20**, *20*
   key terms, **23**
   keywords and identifiers, *5*, **5–6**
   literals, **9–11**
   primitive data types, **6–9**
      floating-point, *8*
      integral, **7–8**
      mathematical operations, **8–9**
      overview of, *7*
   review Q & A, **24–27**
   source files, **4–5**
late binding, **169**, **511**
layout managers, **337–378**
   choosing for GUIs, **300**
   component size and position, **341–343**, *342*
   exam essentials, **375**
   key terms, **376**
   other layout options, **374–375**
   overview, **286**

policies. *see* layout policies
   review Q & A, **377–378**
   theory, **338–341**, *339*
layout policies. *see also* GridBag layout manager
   Border layout manager, **347–354**, *348*, *350–352*, *354*
   Card layout manager, **354–359**
   defined, **343**
   Flow layout manager, **343–345**, *344–345*
   Grid layout manager, **345–347**, *346–347*
lazy clients, **479–481**, *480*
leaf node, **323**, **511**
left-shift (<<) operator, **42–45**
less than (<) operator, **47–48**
less than or equal to (<=) operator, **47–48**
linked lists
   Collections API, **246**
   defined, **243–244**, **511**
listeners
   defined, **511**
   MVC design pattern, **424**
   overview, **425–432**, *429–430*
   setting up relationships, **285–286**
lists
   Collections API, **242–243**
   defined, **511**
ListSelectionEvent object, **316**
literals
   assignment conversion, **102**
   defined, **511**
   overview, **9–11**
local variable, **511**
lock( ) method, **479–481**, *480*
locks
   class, **213**
   defined, **511**
   record, **479–481**, *480*
   synchronization with object, *207*, **207–208**
loop constructs, **124–130**
   break statement, **129–130**
   continue statement, **129–130**
   do loop, **126**

empty for( ) loops, 128
for( ) loop, 126–128
for( ) loop and comma separator, 128
while( ) loop, 124–126

M

magic numbers, 386, 512
main( ) method
   creating inner class from, 176
   declaring methods as static, 83–84
   overview, 14
   Q & A, 488, 500
   sharing threads, 406–408
manifest specification, 283, 283, 512
maps, 243, 512
MarshalledObject instance, 475
Math class
   overview, 229–230, *230*
   Q & A, 256–257, 259
MAX_PRIORITY constant, 199
member classes
   access modifiers, 177
   defined, 173, 512
   Q & A, 188, 191
   static inner classes, 177
member variables
   defined, 14, 512
   initialization values, 15
memory, 19–20
menu bars, 297–299
menu components, 314–316, *316*, 512
menu items, 316–318
metadata, 442, 512
method declarations, 11, 83
method-call conversion
   defined, 512
   object, 110–111
   overview, 103
   Q & A, 118, 121
method-local, 14, 512
methods
   class definitions
      anonymous classes, 179–183
      variables, 178–179

Math class, 229–230
native modifier and, 85–86
overloading
   invoking, 165–166
   names, 164
   overview of, 163
   usefulness of, 164–165
overriding
   invoking, 169–170
   late binding, 169
   method, 166
   overview of, 163
   usefulness of, 166–168
String class, 237–238
StringBuffer class, 239
subclasses and privacy, *78*, 78–79
Swing, 300–302
synchronizing data access, 457
MIN_PRIORITY constant, 199
minus operator. *see* subtraction
   operator (-)
mixedUpMethod( ), 214
model transaction, 396
model-delegate, 423, 512
models, GUI, 273
Model-View-Controller. *see* MVC
   (Model-View-Controller)
modifiers, 71–96
   defined, 72, 512
   exam essentials, 89
   exam objectives, 71
   features and, 87–88
   key terms, 89
   overview, 72
   review Q & A, 90–95
   static initializers, 85
   summary, 88–89
   types
      abstract, 80–82, *81*
      access, 72–79
      final, 79–80
      native, 85–86
      static, 82–85
      synchronized, 87
      transient, 86–87
      volatile, 87

modulo operator
  defined, 512
  overview, 36–37
  Q & A, 486, 500
monitors, 205–218
  beyond the pure model, 213–215
  class lock, 213
  deadlock, 215–217
  defined, 205, 512
  defining, 197–198, *198*
  monitor states, *204*, 204
  object lock and synchronization, 207–208
  overview, 205–206
  synchronizing code another way, 217–218
  wait( ) and notify( ), 208–213, *209*
multiplication operator (*), 35–36
multiset, 242
multithreaded programs, 194, 512
MVC (Model-View-Controller)
  defined, 419, 512
  Java Beans and, 423–425, *424–425*
  Swing and, 296

N

Naming class, 400
naming conventions
  events, 417
  inner class, 174
  Java Bean, 420–422, *422*
  overloading, 164
  overriding, 166–168
  tips for, 275
  using Card layout manager, 354
NaN (Not a Number)
  floating-point calculations, 40–41
  primitive data types, 8
narrowing conversions
  casting requirements, 105–106, *106*
  defined, 513
  overview, 102
  Q & A, 117, 121
native modifier
  defined, 513

java.lang
  features, *88*
  overview, 85–86
negative numbers, shifting, 42–45
nested classes. *see* inner classes
network protocols, 380–414
  client-server systems, 381–395
    client request structure, 387–394, *388*, *394*
    communication protocol, 384–387
    connecting clients to server, 384
    limitations, 394–395
    server operation, 381–384
  exam essentials, 410
  key terms, 411
  overview, 380
  review Q & A, 412–413
  RMI, 395–402
    implementing, 397–401
    limitations, 401–402
    model transaction, *396*, 396
    overview of, 395
  sharing threads, 402–409
  summary, 410
no-args (no-arguments) constructors, 170
nodes, 323
non-rectangular arrays, 13
NORM_PRIORITY constant, 199
normalized exam questions, 264
Not a Number (NAN)
  floating-point calculations, 40–41
  primitive data types, 8
notification, event. *see* event notification
notify( ) method
  lack of precision in, 213–214
  monitor states, 204
  Object class, 228
  overview, 208–213, *209*
  synchronizing data access, 457
notifyAll( ) method
  client request structure, 390
  monitor states, 204
  Object class, 228
  order of notification, 213–214
  synchronizing data access, 457
n-tier (three-tier) database model, 441, 513
NumberFormatException, 232, 234

O

Object class, 228–229
object comparisons, 50, 513
object locks, 207–208
object reference
    casting, 34–35, 111–115, *112–113*
    conversion, 107–111
    defined, 513
    initialization values for, 15
    overview, 17
object serialization. *see* serialization
object-oriented. *see* OO
    (object-oriented)
object-type comparisons, 47, 513
Observable interface, 286
Observer interface, 286
observer-observable, 419
on-demand clients, 479–481, *480*,
    483–484
OO (object-oriented). *see also* classes
    benefits
        encapsulation, 160–161
        inheritance, 162
        relationships, 162–163
    exam essentials, 183–184
    exam objectives, 159
    key terms, 184–185
    review Q & A, 185–191
operations, 385
operators, 29–70
    arithmetic
        addition and subtraction, 40
        arithmetic error conditions, 40–41
        modulo, 36–37
        multiplication and division, 35–36
    assignment, 59–60
    bitwise
        boolean operations, 54–56, *55*
        overview of, 51–54
    comparison
        equality, 50–51
        ordinal, 47–50
    conditional, 58–59
    evaluation order, 31

exam essentials, 63
key terms, 64
overloading, 165
precedence order, *30*
review Q & A, 65–69
shift
    arithmetic promotion of operands,
        46–47, *47*
    fundamentals of, 41–42
    negative numbers, 42–45
    reduction of right operand, 45–46
short-circuit logical, 56–58
summary, 61–63
unary
    bitwise inversion, 31–34
    boolean complement, 33–34
    cast, 34–35
    increment and decrement, *32, 32*
    plus and minus, 32–33
OR operators
    bitwise operations, 51–54, *52*
    boolean operations, 54–56, *55*
    short-circuit logical operations, 56–58
ordinal comparisons, 47–50, 513
ordinary components, 305–314
    defined, 513
    JButton, 306–308, *308*
    JCheckBox, 308–309, *309*
    JComboBox, 313–314, *314*
    JLabel, 306, *306*
    JRadioButton, 309–310, *310*
    JScrollBar, 310–311, *311*
    JTextField and JTextArea,
        311–313, *313*
overflow conditions, 35
overloading
    addition operator, 38
    constructors, 172–173
    defined, 163, 513
    methods
        invoking, 165–166
        method names, 164
        overview of, 163
        Q & A, 185, 190
        usefulness of, 164–165
    Q & A, 488–489, 499, 500–501, 504

overriding – pushbuttons 533

overriding
    defined, **163, 513**
    exceptions, **141–143**
    final modifier, **80**
    methods
        invoking, **169–170**
        late binding, **169**
        method, **166**
        overview of, **163**
        Q & A, **185, 190**
        usefulness of, **166–168**
    Q & A, **92, 95, 499, 504**
    static modifier, **84**
    subclasses, **78**

P

pack( ) method, **303**
package access mode. *see* default
    access mode
packages
    declaring, **4–5**
    Developer's Exam, **270**
    sealing, **283, 513**
panels, **338–341, 343–345**, *344–345*
panes
    JOptionPane, **331–332**, *332*
    JSplitPane, **330–331**, *331*
parseXXX( ) methods, **233–234**
plus operator (+). *see* addition operator (+)
ports, **381–383, 514**
postconditions, **144–145, 514**
post decrement operator, **32**, *32*, **514**
post-increment operator, **32**, *32*, **514**
practice exam, **485–504**
precedence order, *30*, **31**
preconditions, **144, 144–146, 514**
pre-decrement operator, **32**, *32*, **514**
preemptive scheduling, **200, 514**
preferred size, **343, 514**
pre-increment operator, **32**, *32*, **514**
primitive casting, **105–107**
primitive conversion
    arithmetic promotion, **103–104**, *104*
    assignment, **99–102**

method-call, **103**
overview of, **99**
primitive data types
    overview, **6–9**, *7–8*
    primitive conversion
        arithmetic promotion, **103–104**, *104*
        assignment, **99–102**
        method-call, **103**
        overview of, **99**
    wrapper classes, *231*, **231–234**
primitive values
    casting, **34**
    creating reference to, *18*
priority, **198–199, 514**
privacy, **78, 78–79**
private access modifier
    defined, **514**
    features, **88**
    overview, **73–75**
    rules for overriding, **78**
    summary, **79**
programming by contract, **140**
properties
    changes, **426–430**
    defined, **514**
    Java Bean naming conventions, **420–422**
    syntax supporting, **428**
PropertyChangeEvent, **428–430**
PropertyChangeListener, **426–428**
PropertyChangeSupport class, **426–430**
protected access
    defined, **515**
    features, **88**
    overview, **76–78**
    rules for overriding, **78**
    summary, **79**
protected identifiers, **287–288**
public access modifier
    defined, **515**
    features, **88**
    overview, **73**
    rules for overriding, **78**
    summary, **79**
public classes, **4**
publish-subscribe, **419**
pushbuttons, **306–307**, *307*

Q

Q & A
  casting, 117–121
  classes and objects, 185–191
  client-server connections, 437–438
  conversion, 117–121
  database servers, 483–484
  databases, 462–463
  Developer's Exam, 292–293
  flow control, 149–157
  java.lang package, 256–259
  java.util package, 256–259
  language fundamentals, 24–27
  modifiers, 90–95
  network protocols, 412–413
  operators, 65–69
  practice exam, 485–504
  threads, 221–225
  user interface, 334–335

R

radio buttons
  adding to menu item, 316–318
  JRadioButtons, 309–310, *310*
raised exceptions, 515
range. *see* bit size
ray-tracing threads, 200–201
RDMS (relational database management systems), 441
read( ) call, 203
README files
  Developer's Exam, 277–278
  writing, 281–282
Ready state
  Blocked state transitions, 202–203, *203*
  defining, 197–198, *198*
  Monitor state transitions, 204, *204*
  monitor states, *204*
  Sleeping state to, 201–202, *202*
  yielding to, 199–201, *200*
rebind( ) method, 399–400

records
  defined, 440, 515
  designing with interface, 443
  locking, 479–481, *480*
reduction, 45–46
redundance brackets, 31
reference
  argument passing by, **16–18**
  comparisons, 50, 515
  conversion, 107–111
  defined, 515
registrys, RMI and, 398–399
relational database, 440, 515
relational database management systems (RDMS), 441
relationships, **162–163**
RELATIVE setting, 372–374, *374*
REMAINDER setting, 372–374, *374*
Remote interface, 468–470
Remote Method Invocation. *see* RMI (Remote Method Invocation)
remote notification, **432–433**, *433*
RemoteException, 397–398
RemoteObject, 397–398
removeXXXListener(KeyListener) method, 417
request-response services, **381**, **467–468**, 515
requests
  client request structure, **387–394**, *388*, *394*
  implementing RMI, **396–410**
  setting, 205
reserved words, 5
resume( ) method, 201
retrieveMessage( ) method, 209–211
return types
  overloaded method, 165
  overriding method, 166, 168
re-use, code, **162**
right-shift (>>) operator
  arithmetic promotion of operands, 46–47
  reduction of, 45–46
  shifting negative numbers, 42–45

RMI (Remote Method Invocation), 395–402
    database server development, 273–274, 274, 467–470
    implementing, 397–401
    limitations, 401–402
    model transaction, 396, *396*
    overview, 380, 395
    Q & A, 412–413
    remote notification with, 433, *433*
rmid tool, 399
rmiregistry
    defined, 398
    UnicastRemoteObject using, 475
roll back, 423, 428, 515
root nodes, 323, 515
rotate operation, 42
round-robin scheduling, 200–201, 515
rows
    defined, 515
    layout
        Flow layout manager, 343–345, *344–345*
        Grid layout manager, 345–347, *346–347*
        GridBag layout, 359–365, *361–364*
    relational database, 440
run( ) method
    client request structure, 390–392
    follow-up exam, 284–285
    Q & A, 499, 503
    sharing threads, 403–409
    testing runtime behavior, 383
    thread execution, 195–197
    thread states at, 197
Runnable interface
    follow-up exam, 284–285
    Q & A, 412–413
    sharing threads, 403–409
Running state
    Blocked state transitions, 202–203, *203*
    defining, 197–198, *198*
    Monitor state transitions, *204*, 204
    Sleeping state transitions, 201–202, *202*
    yielding from, 199–201, *200*

runtime exceptions
    assertions, 143
    defined, 516
    exception handling, 452–453
    overview, 138–139

S

scheduling. *see* thread schedulers
scopes, 287–288
scroll bars, 310–311, *311*
Scrollable interface, 323
SecurityManager, 473
Seeking Lock state, 207, *207*
selection statements, 131–133
semicolon (;), 4–5
serialization
    FAQs, 402
    goal of, 395
    object, 394–395
    Q & A, 412–413
servers
    client-server. *see* client-server
    connections. *see* client-server connections
    database. *see* database servers
    Developer's Exam, 273–274, *274*
set, 516
setBackground( ) method, 301
setBounds( ) method, 342–343
setDaemon( ) method, 406
setEnabled( ) method, 301–302
setFont( ) method, 301
setForeground( ) method, 301
SETI (Search for Extraterrestrial Intelligence) project, 468
setLocation( ) method, 301
setPriority( ) method, 199
setSize( ) method, 301, 342
setVisible(false) method, 303
ShareThread class, 403–409
shift operators, 41–47
    arithmetic promotion of operands, 46–47, *47*

with bitwise inversion operator, 33
defined, 516
fundamentals, *41*, 41–42
negative numbers, 42–45
reduction of right operand, 45–46
scenario, 43
short-circuit logical operators, 56–58
simple assignment operators, 59–60
single-threaded, **194**, **516**
size, component
controlling, *369*, 369–372
overview, 341–343, *342*
preferred, **343**
skeletons
defined, **516**
RMI transactions, **396**, **473**
sleep( ) method, 201–202, *202*
sleeping threads
defined, **516**
monitor states and, *204*, **204**
overview, 201–202, *202*
Sleeping state, 197–198, *198*
sorting collections
code maintenance, 251
overview, 244–245
sortStringArray( ) method, 250, 252
source files
overview, 4–5
Q & A, 24, 27
SpecificException, 137
square brackets ([ ]), **11**
Stack class, 246
start( ) method, 195–197
statements. *see also* by type
defined, **516**
using labels on, **130**
states, thread
overview, 197–198
thread control and, 199
static initializers, 85, **516**
static inner classes, **177**
static methods, 176, 233–234
static modifier
defined, **516**

features, *88*
overview, 82–85
Q & A, 91–95
static variable. *see* class variables
stop( ) method, **197**
storage
Collections API, 243–244, 254
Q & A, 258–259
storeMessage( ) method, 210–211
stretching, components, 365–369
String class
overview, 235–238, *236*, *238*
Q & A, 258–259
string context, 241, **516**
string literals, 10–11, **516**
StringBuffer class
overview, 238–240, *239*
Q & A, 257–259
strings
concatenation, 240–241
constructing wrappers from, 232–233
converting operands to, 38–39
Q & A, 256, 259, 491–492, 502
String class, **235–238**, *236*, *238*
StringBuffer class, **238–240**, *239*
stubs
database requirements, 473
defined, **396**, **516**
subclasses
constructors and, **170–173**
defined, 163
defining classes, 143
method privacy and, 78, 78–79
thread execution and, 196
subtraction operator (-)
arithmetic, 40
unary, 32–33
super( ) reference
constructors, 171
overloading constructors, **172–173**
Q & A, 187–188, 191
suspend( ) method, 201
suspending
defined, **517**

overview, 201
Suspended state, 197–198, *198*
Swing
  common methods, 300–302
  components, 302–316
    container components, 302–305
    menu components, 314–316
    ordinary components, 305–314
  JMenus and actions, 327–329, *329*
  JTable
    overview of, 316–319, *317–318*
    using AbstractTableModel, 319–322, *322*
  listeners, 425
  Model-View-Controller design pattern, 423–425, *424–425*
  overview, 296
  panes
    JOptionPane, 331–332, *332*
    JSplitPane, 330–331, *331*
switch( ) construct, 132–133
Sylvan Prometric centers, 267
synchronized code
  another way, 217–218
  client request structure, 390
  defined, 517
  object lock and, *207*, 207–208
  Q & A, 489, 501
  thread safety, 456–459
synchronized modifier, 87, *88*

T

TableColumnModeEvent objects, 316
TableModelEvent constructors, 316
tables, 440–441, 517
tags, JAR format, 283
targets, event, 418
telnet, 383–384
ternary operator (?:), 58–59, 517
this( ) reference
  creating inner classes, 176
  overloading constructors, 172–173
  Q & A, 187–188, 191

thread pool, 403, 517
thread schedulers
  defined, 195, 517
  determining priority, 198–199
  implementing, 204–205
threads, 193–226
  controlling
    blocking, 202–203, *203*
    monitor states, 204
    scheduling implementations, 204–205
    sleeping, 201–202, *202*
    suspending, 201
    yielding, 199–201, *200*
  exam essentials, 219
  follow-up exam, 284–285
  fundamentals
    execution, 195–197
    priority, 198–199
    states, 197–198
    when execution ends, 197
  key terms, 220
  monitors
    beyond pure model, 213–215
    class lock, 213
    deadlock, 215–217
    object lock and synchronization, *207*, 207–208
    overview of, 205–206
    synchronizing code, 217–218
    wait( ) and notify( ) methods, 208–213, *209*
  Q & A, 498–499, 503
  review Q & A, 221–225
  sharing, 402–409
  summary, 218–219
threadsafe
  defined, 242, 517
  overview, 456
  Q & A, 462–463
three-tier (n-tier) database model, 441, 513
throw statement
  overview, 137
  Q & A, 492, 502
Throwable class, 452

throwing exceptions, 137–143
   checked exceptions
      checking, 140–141
      overview of, 138–140, *139*
   defined, 517
   overriding and, 141–143
   throw statement, 137
   throws statement, 137–138
throws statement
   checking checked exceptions, 140–141
   overview, 137–138
time-sliced scheduling
   overview, 200–201
   Q & A, 489, 501
toString( ) method
   converting operands to strings, 38–39
   exception handling with, 453
   string concatenation, 229, 240–242
   wrapper classes providing, 234
traceRays( ) method, 200–201
transient modifier
   defined, 517
   features, *88*
   overview, 86–87
   Q & A, 91–92, 95
TreeMap class, 246, 251–252
trees
   building JTree, 323–327
   Collections API storage, 244
   defined, 517
TreeSet class, 246
try block
   catching multiple exceptions, 136–137
   checking checked exceptions, 140–141
   defined, 517
   flow of control in exceptions, 133–135, *135*
   Q & A, 151–153, 157

try/catch/finally construction, 133–135, *135*
two-tiered databases, 440–441, 517

U

unary operators
   arithmetic-promotion conversions, 104, *104*
   bitwise inversion operator, 33
   boolean complement operator, 33–34
   cast, 34–35
   defined, 517
   increment and decrement operators, 32, *32*
   overview, 31–32
   plus and minus operators, 32–33
   summary, 61
underflow condition, 36
underscore (_), 5
UnicastRemoteObject, 471–475, 483–484
UnkownException, 137
unlock( ) method, 479–481, *480*
uploading, Developer's Exam, 277
user interfaces. *see* GUIs (graphical user interfaces)

V

values
   argument passing, 16–18
   assignment operators, 60
   Q & A, 486, 500
vectors
   adding object to, 233
   choosing for data structures, 284
   Collections API, 246
vetoable, 426, 518

VetoableChangeSupport class, 426–428
volatile modifier
   defined, 518
   features, *88*
   overview, 87

W

wait( ) method
   client request structure, 390
   monitor states, 204
   Object class, 228
   overview, 208–213, *209*
   synchronizing data access, 457
waiting state, 198, 204, 518
Web site information
   Developer's Exam for Java 2, 267
   event notification, 419
   Java 3 registry service, 399
   Java Programming Language Workshop, 265
   RMI implementation, 402
   syntax supporting properties, 428
   uploading assignment, 277
weight
   defined, 518
   GridBag layout manager, 360, 363–365
well-known port, 381, 518
while( ) loop
   comparing to do loop, 125
   comparing to for( ) loop, 127–128
   overview, **124–126**

whitespace
   Q & A, 495–496, 503
   in source files, 5
widening conversions
   casting and, 106
   defined, 518
   overview, **100–101**
   Q & A, 117, 121
width
   defined, 518
   grid, *369*, **369–372**, *374*
   Q & A, 489, 501
Window events, 304
windowClosing( ) method, 304
wrapper class, *231*, **231–234**, 518

X

XOR (eXclusive-OR) operators (^)
   bitwise operations, **51–54**, *52*
   boolean operations, **54–56**, *55*
XXXValue( ) methods, 234

Y

yield( ) method, **199–201**, *200*
yielding
   defined, 518
   overview, **199–201**, *200*

The Complete Java™ 2 Certification Solution

Complete Java 2 Certification Study Guide, 4th Edition
Philip Heller, Simon Roberts·

Written for candidates preparing for the Java Programmer and Java Developer exams, 310-035 and 310-027, this is a revised and enhanced edition of the market-leading Java 2 certification book.

- Contains in-depth coverage of the latest versions of the programmer and developer exams
- Real-World Scenarios offer perspectives and insights from seasoned professionals
- The companion CD is packed with additional study tools—hundreds of challenging review questions to reinforce key topics

Java 2 Web Developer Certification Study Guide
Natalie Levi·
Completely Revised and Updated!

Here's the book you need to prepare for Exam 310-080, Sun Certified Web Component Developer for J2EE Platform. This Study Guide for experienced Java programmers covers all enterprise-level topics and exam objectives including:

- The servlet model
- The structure and deployment of modern servlet web applications
- The servlet container model
- Designing and developing servlets
- Designing and developing secure web applications
- Designing and developing thread-safe servlets
- The JavaServer Pages (JSP) technology model
- Designing and developing reusable web components
- Designing and developing a custom tag library

The companion CD is packed with vital preparation tools and materials, including a custom testing engine for the Java web developer exam. Loaded with hundreds of practice questions, it lets you test yourself chapter by chapter. You'll also find three bonus exams that will help you prepare for the test and a fully searchable electronic version of the book.